SOLDIERS AS POLICE

Soldiers as Police

The French and Prussian Armies
and the Policing of Popular Protest, 1889–1914

ANJA JOHANSEN
University of Dundee

ASHGATE

© Anja Johansen 2005

All rights reserved. No part of this publication may be reproduced, stored in a retrieval system, or transmitted in any form or by any means, electronic, mechanical, photocopying, recording, or otherwise without the prior permission of the publisher.

Anja Johansen has asserted her moral right under the Copyright, Designs and Patents Act, 1988, to be identified as the author of this work.

Published by
Ashgate Publishing Limited
Gower House
Croft Road
Aldershot
Hants GU11 3HR
England

Ashgate Publishing Company
Suite 420
101 Cherry Street
Burlington, VT 05401-4405
USA

Ashgate website: http://www.ashgate.com

British Library Cataloguing in Publication Data
Johansen, Anja
  Soldiers as police : the French and Prussian armies and the policing of popular protest, 1889–1914
  1.Civil–military relations – Germany – History – 19th century 2.Civil–military relations – Germany – History – 20th century 3.Civil–military relations – France – History – 19th century 4.Civil–military relations – France – History – 20th century 5.Armed Forces – Germany – Political activity – History – 19th century 6.Armed Forces – Germany – Political activity – History – 20th century 7.Armed Forces – France – Political activity – History – 19th century 8.Armed Forces – France – Political activity – History – 20th century 9.Germany – Politics and government – 1871–1918 10.France – Politics and government – 1870–1940 I.Title
  943'.083

Library of Congress Cataloging-in-Publication Data
Johansen, Anja, 1965–
  Soldiers as police : the French and Prussian Armies and the policing of popular protest, 1889–1914 / Anja Johansen.
    p. cm.
  Includes bibliographical references and index.
    ISBN 0-7546-3376-4 (alk. paper)
  1. Demonstrations – France–History. 2. Riot control – France – History. 3. Protest movements – France – History. 4. France. Armie. 5. Demonstrations – Germany – History. 6. Riot control – Germany – History. 7. Protest movements – Germany – History. 8. Germany. Heer – History. 9. Prussia (Kingdom). Armee – History. I. Title.

HV6485.F8J64 2004
363.32–dc22

2004008258

ISBN 0 7546 3376 4

Printed in Great Britain by Antony Rowe Ltd, Chippenham, Wiltshire

Contents

List of Tables	*vii*
Acknowledgements	*viii*

Introduction: The Demilitarisation of Protest Policing as a Historical Problem   1

PART I: DOMESTIC MILITARY INTERVENTION IN ITS POLITICAL CONTEXT

1	The French and Prussian Armies in State and Society	33
2	New Problems, New Priorities: Conflicting Policies in Berlin	60
3	The Controversial Issue of Republican Order and Stability	84

PART II: POPULAR PROTEST AND RIOT POLICING

4	Violent Encounters and Challenges to the Public Order	113
5	The Extension of Police and *Gendarmerie* Forces	140
6	Patterns of Military Involvement in the Policing of Protest	153

PART III: BUREAUCRATS, GENERALS AND ELITES IN WESTPHALIA AND NORD-PAS-DE-CALAIS

7	Local Influences on the Requisition of Troops	175
8	Civilian and Military Elites: Social Backgrounds and Interactions	198
9	Civil-Military Cooperation in Nord-Pas-de-Calais	220
10	Mutual Exclusion and Non-Cooperation in Westphalia	249
11	Conclusions: Demilitarisation and 'Modern' Policing	275

Appendix 1	*283*
Appendix 2	*286*
Bibliography	*293*
Index	*325*

List of Tables

4.1	Population of Westphalia and Nord-Pas-de-Calais	115
4.2	Miners in Westphalia and in Nord-Pas-de-Calais	115
4.3	Levels of Trade Unionism	120
5.1	Ratio of inhabitants per police officer in major cities	144
5.2	Ratio of inhabitants for every police officer in the main towns of Westphalia and in Nord-Pas-de-Calais	145
6.1	Major conflicts occurring in Nord-Pas-de-Calais	162
6.2	Protesters and forces mobilised during main conflicts in Westphalia	165

Acknowledgements

In the process of researching and writing this book, thanks are due to many people and institutions. The research grew out of my Ph.D. thesis from the European University Institute, Florence, and was funded by the Danish Ministry of Research. The development of the thesis into this book was made possible by the generous support by the Carlsberg Foundation who funded two years of post-doctoral studies at Clare Hall, Cambridge.

I would like to thank the staff of the many archives consulted in Germany and France: the *Geheimes Staatsarchiv* in Berlin, the Central Archive in Potsdam, the *Hauptstaatsarchiv* in Münster, and the German Military Archive in Freiburg. Similar thanks go to the French National Archives in Paris and the Departmental Archives in Lille and Arras. I am particularly grateful to Colonel Bondinier and his staff at the French Military Archive in Vincennes, who were very helpful and flexible at all times.

Over the years of researching and writing this book, I have received many useful comments and invaluable encouragements from professors, fellows and students at the European University Institute, at Nuffield College, Oxford, and at Clare Hall, Cambridge. I would also like to express my thanks for many patient replies to my countless inquiries about the finer details of the English language.

Thanks are also due to Professor Wilhelm Deist, to Professor Gerd Krumeich, and to Professor Jean-Jacques Becker, whose interest and helpful comments in the early stages of the research gave me the confidence to move into a field that was so scarcely described in the secondary literature. Professor Heinz Reif from the Technical University of Berlin and Professor Christophe Charle, from *L'École Normale Supérieure*, both took the time to engage in constructive discussions about functional elites and elite cooperation in Westphalia and France respectively.

I am most greatly indebted to Professor Raffaele Romanelli and to Professor Michael Müller, my supervisors at the EUI, as well as to the late Dr. Vincent Wright, Nuffield College, who was my external supervisor and who supported the project from its earliest stages. In the process of turning the thesis into this book, Professor Clive Emsley and Professor Roger Morgan have provided invaluable support, while Professor Richard Evans most generously offered me much practical advice on how to transform the thesis into a publishable monograph.

Acknowledgements

I am infinitely grateful to my family who several times drove me together with my papers from one end of Europe to another, to Miranda and Shantanu who read and corrected the manuscript, and to friends in London, Paris, Berlin and Münster who opened their homes to me and made the periods of archival research more enjoyable. My warmest thanks are due to Mark, who first talked me into undertaking this project and who remained an indispensable friend throughout the process.

Introduction:
The Demilitarisation of Protest Policing as a Historical Problem

From military to civilian policing

Until the mid-19th century, military involvement in the policing of disorderly public gatherings was the norm in most parts of Europe. By the end of the First World War, civilian police forces had taken over the responsibility for maintaining public order in the majority of European countries. This book takes its starting point from the observation that during the 1890s, the French Third Republic and the German Empire developed opposite practices in terms of relying on the army for the policing of protest.

Up to the late 1880s, the use of troops in France and Germany followed a similar pattern. Throughout the first half of the 19th century the authorities in both countries mobilised military troops as a general practice whenever popular unrest or riots exceeded the capacity of the local *gendarmerie*, night watch or citizen militia. After the repression of the 1848 Revolutions, and subsequent incidents of popular unrest during the years 1848 to 1851, the role of the army in maintaining public order was in decline in both countries, with the bloody repression of the Paris *Commune* in 1871 standing as a notorious exception.

It was during the 1890s that the use of troops took diverging trajectories in the two countries. This happened at a time when authorities in both countries were increasingly challenged by organised mass protests. Yet after major military involvement in the great miners' strike of 1889, the authorities of the German Empire increasingly refrained from using troops against civilians; by the turn of the 20th century, the role of the Prussian-German army in the policing of strikes and demonstrations had become a rather unusual event.

During the same year, the French army became increasingly busy in policing social conflicts and political protest. The frequency of military interventions in France rose sharply after the turn of the 20th century, and it was not until 1921 with the establishment of the *gendarmerie mobile* that the French army was finally discharged from most of its policing duties.

The dissimilar approaches to the use of soldiers for the policing of popular protest appear paradoxical: after the unification of Germany under Prussian hegemony, civilian society, politics and popular cultures became heavily influenced by military values, and the authorities' approach to social disorder and political opposition maintained many features of authoritarianism throughout the Imperial era. In comparison, the French Republic styled itself as liberal and democratic; the extremely frequent and extended use of troops by successive French governments is remarkable: even if the Republican regime was occasionally challenged by social unrest and political extremism, the vast majority of instances where troops became involved in protest policing could not by any stretch of the imagination be described as threatening the stability of the existing social and political order. The divergent developments in France and Germany therefore call for a closer look at the factors that shaped the decisions by French and German authorities to involve or not involve the army in the policing of popular protest.

Historians have pointed to four main factors to explain the overall decline in the policing functions of national armies in the majority of European countries from the early half of the 19th century to the end of the First World War. Demilitarisation of policing in France and Germany – as in many other European countries – partly coincided with the emergence of modern professional police forces. As police forces took charge of most tasks of crime fighting, law enforcement and order maintenance, increasingly clear limits were drawn around the involvement of the regular army in the management of civilian society.[1]

Yet, the establishment of civilian police forces was only a precondition for gradual military disengagement from the maintenance of public order. The dynamics behind the demilitarisation process arose from the particular problems created by the use of soldiers for policing tasks. One major incentive for governments around Europe to look for alternatives to military involvement was the prospect of alienating important social groups, together with fears of swelling opposition and provoking popular revolt.[2] The French Revolution, the 1848 Revolutions and the Paris *Commune* had given serious warnings about the potential for political and social unrest erupting amongst disaffected workers and the urban poor. In addition, political stability and sustained industrial growth increasingly came to depend on workers not rejecting the existing social, political and economic order. There were little grounds for complacency amongst European ruling elites and only few imagined that popular discontent could be contained with military force in the long term.

These problems became all the more serious for regimes whose national army was based on universal conscription, as was the case for both Imperial Germany and the French Third Republic. This raised concerns about the reliability of soldiers and fostered fears that conscripts might change sides and join a popular rebellion.

In addition to these problems, historians generally link the demilitarisation of protest policing to an emerging democratic culture in many parts of Europe; law enforcement agencies were increasingly expected to act with moderation in their use of force; pressure grew for military actions against civilians to be subjected to strict legal regulations; and governments and their bureaucrats felt increasingly compelled to justify their use of military assistance in terms of necessity and proportionality.[3] In political debates, critics readily linked extended use of troops to low levels of government accountability, while moderation in the application of physical force by law enforcement agencies towards the civilian population became widely perceived as a central aspect of good governance. The issue of military involvement in the policing of civilian society was therefore often linked to demands for constitutionalism and for submission of the use of troops to parliamentary accountability and control. According to the same line of thinking, historians have sometimes pointed to military involvement in the policing of protest as an indicator of authoritarian and repressive governance.[4]

Within the context of individual countries a connection may indeed be established between long-term decline in the military involvement in protest policing, on the one hand, and, on the other, democratisation – including increasing concerns for public opinion – and fears of alienating important sections of the population. However, when comparing countries, we are confronted with a much more ambiguous picture showing many twists and turns in the transition towards demilitarisation of protest policing. In many respects, the process away from military involvement in policing remained incomplete: militarily organised *gendarmerie* corps continued to play a central role in civilian policing in many European countries including France,[5] whilst involvement of the regular army in the handling of situations of high alert – such as terrorist threat or natural catastrophe – remains a persistent and even increasing feature of policing in many European countries to the present day.

Of course, the nature of the regime, the extent to which popular revolt was an imminent concern of the political elites, and the degree to which governments needed to reach an understanding with industrial workers were all important factors in shaping policing policies. Yet, the policing strategies developed to handle social and political unrest did not necessarily lead to consistent reductions in the military involvement.

Nor was effective governmental accountability to an elected parliament, or legal restrictions around the actions of soldiers against the civilian population incompatible with continued frequent military interventions. In Britain, where parliamentary control and legal restrictions around military intervention had been in place since the early 18th century,[6] there were numerous incidents of military intervention throughout the 18th and 19th centuries.[7] In France of the Third Republic as well as in Italy of the *Risorgimento* and the Netherlands, public authorities very frequently involved the army in protest policing right until the end of the First World War.[8] By contrast, the extent of military intervention was in sharp decline in the German Empire,[9] and even in the Austro-Hungarian Empire a gradual decline in military involvement took place in many parts of the Empire, despite major internal problems of national conflicts and riots in the 1890s.[10] Only Imperial Russia presents a straightforward example where autocratic rule was combined with extensive use of the army against civilians.[11]

It is also worth noting that there was increasing unhappiness amongst army officers – at the senior as well as the junior ranks – with the army's traditional role in the policing of social and political protest. The military's opposition to its involvement in policing was largely unrelated to political considerations but focused on the pernicious effects that policing duties had on the morale of troops and the prestige of the army in the wider population. Voices of concern appeared from the German and French military establishments as well as in Italy[12] and Imperial Russia.[13]

The study of the use of troops in Republican France and Imperial Germany from the 1890s to the outbreak of the First World War shows the demilitarisation of protest policing as a multi-dimensional process with strong forces pulling in opposite directions. In both countries, governments were keen on maintaining economic growth and preventing industrial production and trade from being disturbed by social and political unrest. On the other hand, in both countries there were increased concerns for public opinion, with French and German government authorities feeling compelled politically to justify their policing policies when confronted with public criticism of heavy-handed interventions. In both countries, the national army was based on universal conscription, which led to serious concerns about the political wisdom of deploying troops against civilians. All these concerns, for and against the use of troops in the maintenance of public order, appeared in the French as well as in the Prussian debate.

Yet, although French governments were far more vulnerable to public criticism than the Prussian ministers, the Prussian Interior Ministry proved far more willing than its French counterpart to develop policing strategies that depended less on military involvement. If, as historians on German policing argue, concerns for politically legitimising military involvement in protest policing and fears of escalating social unrest convinced the Prussian Interior Ministry about the necessity of radically changing its approach to protest policing,[14] why were these problems not sufficiently compelling for the French authorities to do likewise? Perhaps we need to look for additional forces and interests that pushed the German authorities towards demilitarisation. Similarly we need to identify the dynamics behind the policies and bureaucratic practices surrounding large-scale policing operations in France.

Military involvement in protest policing goes right to the heart of our understanding of the nature of the French Third Republic and the German Empire. The demilitarisation in Germany highlights some of the ambiguity of the German-Prussian 'Police-State tradition' and presents an unusual aspect of the otherwise heavily militarised state and society of the German Empire. A comparison with the frequent use of troops in France opens new perspectives on the intentions behind military involvement. This has implications for our understanding of the nature of policing in both countries and ultimately reflects on the interpretation of each of the two regimes.

The historical literature and its lacunae

That the authorities of Republican France called upon military assistance to civilian police far more frequently than did their German counterparts was already pointed out by contemporary observers, most notably by Karl Liebknecht in his influential pamphlet on *Militarism and Anti-militarism*.[15] To Liebknecht as to many left-wingers it was particularly reprehensible that a Republican regime used the army against its civilian population. At the same time, he pointed out that the less frequent involvement of the Prussian army in the policing of protest did not in any way indicate that German public authorities and police were less heavy-handed than their French counterparts in their handling of popular opposition.[16]

Somewhat surprisingly, the dissimilar military involvement in French and German policing during the late 19th and early 20th centuries has not attracted much attention amongst historians.[17] This may partly be due to the fact that very little comparative research has been undertaken into the policing of 19th century France and Germany. Amongst the exceptions to this rule is an article by Heinz-Gerhard Haupt on the impact of policing on the constitution of the German and French working classes.[18] In addition, two broad comparative works look at France and Germany amongst several other countries, namely Hsi-Huey Liang's study on the rise of political police in European states[19] and Clive Emsley's book on *gendarmerie* forces in Europe.[20] Recently Wolfgang Knöbl has made an important contribution by comparing the development of Prussian policing during the 18th and 19th centuries to the rise of modern police in England and the United States.[21]

The scant attention paid by historians to the dissimilar degree of military involvement in policing in the German Empire and the French Third Republic may partly be explained by the fact that 'policing' is still a relatively new field of study. Whilst studies of the topic emerged amongst British and American scholars in the 1970s and 1980s,[22] French and German scholars initially seemed reluctant to make 'policing' an object of study in its own right. Accordingly, whilst much research was conducted into the forms of popular protest and the organisation, ideology and strategies of the French and German left-wing opposition,[23] the police forces and military troops involved in the policing of popular protest were regarded as merely the instrument of government policies and industrial pressure groups.

This changed in the 1980s and 1990s when ground-breaking studies appeared on policing in 19th century France[24] and Germany.[25] Many of these studies sought to move beyond the political and institutional history of policing by focusing on everyday interactions between the police and the public in its social and cultural context; yet policies of public order maintenance were always amongst the key concerns in studies on 19th and 20th century policing.

Scholars working on 19th and 20th century France have focused on how politicians and bureaucrats of the Third Republic sought to adapt policing policies and tactics to a changing social and political reality, with increasing demands for political accountability and proportionality in the application of force. Some of the studies on French policing are particularly directed at forms of large-scale policing operations to handle popular protest, whether labour conflicts, political demonstrations, social protest or riots.[26]

Historians working on policing within the German area have been more concerned with the everyday control of the public space as an aspect of the wider system of power relations between the elites and ordinary Germans.[27] Apart from legal-institutional changes in policing such as the transition away from military involvement or specific incidents where the army became involved, the strategies behind the policing of mass protest in Germany is generally described simply as everyday policing on a larger scale, involving a variety of public, semi-public and private agencies.

Interpreting the role of the French army in 19th century policing

French scholars' particular interest in the changing strategies of maintenance of public order may be explained by their difficulty in squaring heavy-handed and sometimes brutal interventions by public forces with the proclaimed liberalism of the Third Republic.[28] Within French historiography, the increasing frequency of domestic military intervention – particularly during the first decade of the 20th century – is well-known. It is mentioned both in the general literature on the French Third Republic,[29] in books on the French army,[30] in studies of policing and the maintenance of public order,[31] as well as in works on French labour movements.[32]

Nevertheless, the role of the army in order maintenance has been treated as a marginal aspect of policing by the majority of scholars. The works on French policing are primarily concerned with municipal forces, including the Paris police, and with the militarily organised *gendarmerie* forces.[33] The pioneering study by Georges Carrot includes troops as well as police and *gendarmerie*, but focuses mainly on legal-institutional aspects and covers the entire period from 1789 to 1968.[34] Jean-Marc Berlière's broad and ground-breaking research on French policing of the early Third Republic in its political, social and cultural context is concerned primarily with municipal police forces.[35] His detailed description of the changes in policing strategies in Paris was invaluable for this study in identifying the changing features in the strategic approach to the policing of strikes and demonstrations, and the way in which this differed from German approaches to policing. The studies of Patrick Bruneteaux take up many of the points from Carrot and Berlière, but his aim is to explain the development of French approaches to protest policing and riot control from the early Third Republic to the present day.[36]

The most important exceptions to the marginal interest in the role of the army in protest policing are a rather dated article by Dianne Cooper-Richet[37] and more recent studies by Odille Roynette-Gland. Like the present study, Roynette-Gland's research looks specifically at the military involvement in the policing of protest in Nord-Pas-de-Calais between 1871 and 1914, but focuses primarily on the experience and conditions of soldiers and officers.[38]

In addition, Jean-Jacques Jauffret's article of 1983 is still the most important work on the French debate over the establishment of a police or *gendarmerie* unit specialised in protest policing. Jauffret describes the political and parliamentary context of the on-going debate about approaches to the policing of protest and provides an important contribution to our understanding of the policing politics of the early Third Republic.[39]

Finally, a few studies on the French army devote some attention to its role in protest policing;[40] however the majority of interpretations of the French army are remarkably silent when it comes to the involvement of military troops in protest policing. Most significantly, the five-volume work on French military history edited by Guy Pedroncini devotes merely seven pages out of 474 to the role of the French army in policing activities between 1871 and 1914.[41]

The very scant attention of historians to the role of the French army in policing and the gaps in the existing research has led to important misconceptions about its extent and implications. Whilst the number of military interventions is generally thought to be 'high', there has been no attempt to provide any quantitative indication of frequency, except Perrot's estimations of military interventions in labour conflicts during the years 1870–1890.[42] Instead historians often cite the list of incidents where protesters were killed in confrontations with troops. This, unfortunately, gives the impression that these were the main incidents of military involvement, whilst in reality military participation was far more frequent. This has occasionally led to the misconception that violent clashes and casualties were the norm whenever troops were involved.[43]

The Republican dilemma: Republican ideals and the failings of the French Third Republic

Whilst important basic facts about the role of the French army in protest policing have not been properly established through detailed research, interpretations of the phenomenon have often been highly normative and politicised. The frequent military involvement in protest policing fits awkwardly into the image of the French Third Republic as a liberal regime. At the same time, much of the historical debates and analyses of the early Third Republic revolve around ideological definitions of the true nature of French Republicanism. Comparison with the experience of other European countries is rarely considered in these debates; instead historians tend to compare the political and social reality of the Third Republic against some 'ideal' Republic to show how the regime failed to live up to its self-proclaimed ideals.[44]

Introduction

The frequent mobilisation of military troops against civilian protesters during the early Third Republic constitutes a fault-line in this debate. For some historians, the frequent use of troops results from a series of missed opportunities, where politicians failed to 'do the right thing' and instead continued with a traditional approach for the sake of short-term political gain.[45] From a more radical perspective, some historians formulate a fundamental critique in which the frequent military involvement in protest policing is presented as a clear example of the essentially repressive nature of the 'Bourgeois Republic'.[46] Other interpretations see the use of troops from the perspective of the army. Military historians tend to criticise the frequent use of troops because this practice caused major problems for any effective preparation for warfare and training of recruits.[47]

Conversely, interpretations based on a fundamentally positive attitude towards the Third Republic tend to support the decisions of political leaders, and sometimes justify the use of troops as the regrettable – yet necessary – defence of the Republican institutions against challenges from far-right, as well as far-left, extremism.[48] This is also where most non-French scholars appear, who without being apologetic about the intentions of politicians and not-so-idealistic interests at stake, seek to understand the action of French politicians in terms of *Realpolitik*.[49]

Scholars working specifically on French policing tend to describe the frequent military involvement as the result of a structural problem: during the late 1880s, social and political unrest increased in scale and intensity to an extent that largely exceeded the capacity of poorly trained and understaffed municipal police forces. This structural problem could not be effectively addressed, due to the lack of political will in seeking alternatives, especially the failure to gain political backing for any of the numerous projects to organise a special riot unit within the *gendarmerie*.[50]

By identifying a structural problem of insufficient police and *gendarmerie* forces as the key explanation, historians on French policing avoid getting into a wider critique of the Third Republic. Despite continued military involvement, there is general agreement amongst police historians that the character of French protest policing changed fundamentally between 1890 and 1914, when attempts to introduce modern strategies for protest policing existed side by side with traditional military approaches. Serman and Roynette-Gland go as far as arguing that protest policing – even when the army became involved – was a matter of managing volatile and potentially violent protests through policing tactics, rather than simple 'repression' of popular discontent.[51]

The insights provided by studies on French policing have allowed interpretations of military involvement to move beyond debates about the failures of the Republic to be truly 'republican' and liberal. Of course, there is no denying that protesters were victims of violent confrontations with police, *gendarmeries* and troops acting on behalf of successive Republican governments.[52] However the normative and politicised approach does not constitute a useful framework for understanding the complexities behind government policies of the Third Republic; moreover, this approach is particularly unhelpful in explaining the paradoxes appearing when comparing policing policies in France with the use of troops in Imperial Germany.

Transformations in late 19th century German policing: interpreting the demilitarisation process

The role of the Prussian army in the policing of protest during the Imperial era has been even less studied than the role of the French army. The scant attention given to the role of the army is of course linked to the fact that military involvement became relatively unusual during the Imperial era. Yet, the lack of interest is surprising in the light of the keen attention generally displayed by German historians to any military aspect of the policing of the civilian population.[53]

The only study devoted exclusively to the role of the army in 19th century German policing is an article by Harald Klückmann, published more than a quarter of a century ago.[54] The groundbreaking study by Alf Lüdkte on policing in Prussian garrison towns pays extensive attention to the role of the army, but looks only at the first half of the 19th century. Elaine Glovka Spencer, although devoting some attention specifically to the role of the army,[55] is mainly interested in civilian policing. Similarly the studies of German policing of the second half of the 19th century by Albrecht Funk and Ralph Jessen, and more recently by Wolfgang Knöbl, all focus primarily on civilian policing, while the continued role of the army is of marginal concern. The main themes in these works revolve around policing as part of a wider system of power, the emergence of the *Rechtsstaat* (i.e. the process of establishing legal and bureaucratic restrictions around Prussian policing), and the attempts by the Prussian state to gain control over municipal police forces.[56]

The demilitarisation of German policing during the 19th century is generally explained with reference to overall processes modernisation, such as increased concerns for public opinion and fears of alienating the growing number of industrial workers. Thus, historians tend to faithfully render the arguments put forward by Prussian bureaucrats and successive Interior Ministers in order to justify their opposition to military involvement, namely the serious disadvantages linked to the use of conscript soldiers for maintenance of public order: that infantry and cavalry units could only operate in inflexible military formations; that the mere presence of military troops at a scene of conflict contributed to the escalation of violent confrontations; and that young conscript soldiers were unfit for the policing of sensitive conflicts because they lacked personal authority, were inexperienced and prone to shoot in panic.[57]

The references to the Prussian Interior Ministry's 'rational' justifications for demilitarising protest policing make the interpretations of the process appear rather unproblematic. The fact that the Prussian civilian administration had a problematic relationship with the civilian authorities is mentioned, but rarely mentioned as a key factor in the process.[58]

Yet, even if the demilitarisation was in accordance with overall processes towards modernisation of policing, the ease with which this transition happened begs for more substantial factors to be identified than simply fears that military presence might escalate confrontations with protesters. As in France, the political wisdom of avoiding military involvement clashed with consistent demands from a wealthy bourgeoisie and industrial pressure groups who demanded effective protection of their private property and industrial interests.

Moreover, Lüdtke's study of Prussian policing and administration of civilian society during the first half of the 19th century amply testifies to the significance of direct military interference in numerous aspects of civilian life.[59] Throughout the Wilhelmine era the military establishment consistently threatened to interfere directly both against existing democratic institutions, notably the *Reichstag*, and against the Social Democratic opposition. The fact that, in reality, the Prussian army retired without further ado from its traditional involvement in the policing of civilian society might raise a question or two about the interests of the military organisation in the late 19th century and the dynamics behind the gradual retreat from involvement in policing. Similarly while Funk's study on the rise of the German *Rechtsstaat* shows how the actions of police forces were gradually limited through legislation, he also highlights the absence of effective legal boundaries around the actions of military troops involved in policing.[60]

The limited research on the role of the Prussian army in protest policing in the Wilhelmine era has resulted in some rather conflicting accounts of military involvement in labour conflicts. Interpretations have been based on analyses of isolated conflict where the army became involved, or on analyses of government policies with little attention paid to the extent to which these policies were implemented. This has led to a series of strictly misleading estimates of the importance of military involvement in labour conflicts, particularly as part of general interpretations that strongly emphasise the authoritarian and militaristic aspects of the Imperial German system. Martin Kitchen vastly overestimates the frequency and importance of military involvement in internal conflicts, claiming that calls for military troops to put down strikes happened 'quite often',[61] whilst Manfred Messerschmidt describes the requisitioning of military assistance as a measure that was almost automatically implemented in the case of labour conflicts.[62]

Similarly, in his influential work on the German Empire, Hans-Ulrich Wehler described the Prussian army as 'an instrument for the use in the struggles of internal politics' (*Kampfinstrument nach Innen*);[63] Volker Berghahn too insists on describing the Prussian army as the instrument of violence against the working class.[64]

The idea that the Prussian army fulfilled the role as the iron fist against the Social Democratic Party and industrial workers fits nicely into an overall argument about the repressive nature of the regime and the continued rule of the 'traditional elites' in the Prussian government, the civil service, and the army. However, twenty-two years after the first publication of Wehler's influential synthesis on the German Empire, he concedes that military commanders of the Wilhelmine era generally maintained a pragmatic wait-and-see attitude towards popular protest, which often resulted in non-intervention.[65]

The use of troops and the interpretation of the German Empire as a regime

Wehler's original claim that the Prussian army played an important role in the policing of protest during the Imperial era seemed to be established by inference from the observation that the military establishment exercised significant influence on many other aspects of society and politics of the Empire.

All interpretations of the Prussian army stress the particular powers of the military establishment: the Prussian army was not subjected to the Imperial Constitution and was free from parliamentary accountability; in foreign policy the military establishment upheld a parallel diplomatic system of military attachés in numerous foreign capitals; and in domestic politics, the Prussian officers corps constituted a permanent threat to existing democratic institutions.[66]

The position of the army in state and society is a defining feature in almost any interpretation of the nature of the German Empire; it has earned the regime labels such as 'authoritarian', 'semi-constitutional', 'militaristic' or even a 'military state'.[67] While the German-Prussian system was similarly characterised by its strong bureaucratic tradition and ubiquitous police,[68] it was the military element that distinguished Germany from the French system which also had a tradition for highly interventionist bureaucratic rule and well-developed police organisations. Compared to other European societies, the German Empire was also to a greater extent characterised by a culture of widespread enthusiasm and unqualified reverence for anything military.

Since the reunification of Germany, the interpretations of the long-term developments in German history from the 18th to the 21st century are still trying to find a balance between stressing German 'exceptionalism' and attempts to place the German experience within its wider European context. In this respect, the debate over the German 'special path' (*Sonderweg*) is still alive and well.[69] However, the role of the Prussian army in the policing of protest does not follow the fault-lines over which debates about the nature of the German Empire are generally conducted. Debates over German 'exceptionalism' revolve around the extent to which the development of political institutions and social structures lagged behind or were dissimilar from those of more 'advanced' European democracies, notably France and Britain.[70] However, with respect to the role of the Prussian army in the policing of protest, the German Empire did not seem to take a 'special path'. Quite the contrary: the decline in the military involvement in German policing follows the general trend towards modern policing, whilst the development in Republican France was at odds with this, throughout the period 1889–1914.

The comparison with France opens up a series of aspects for discussion. In the light of widening approaches to Wilhelmine Germany in all its fractured and conflict-ridden complexity, and along with a new interest amongst historians for pockets of liberalism,[71] one might wonder whether the low degree of military involvement in German protest policing indicates a more liberal and permissive approach to protesters compared to France. Or do we need to interpret the use of troops along different lines?

The comparison also raises the issue of the efficient functioning of the German-Prussian system. Military officers, as well as the civil servants in the ministries and the provincial administration, liked to see themselves as the pillars of the German-Prussian State, serving the throne with unparalleled efficiency and dedication to pursue the best interests of the Prussian Kingdom and the German Empire. Yet historians have long been aware of the dysfunctions within the German-Prussian system, with different sections of the state organisation pulling in opposite directions in pursuit of the narrow interests of their particular branch of the state apparatus.[72] Similarly, historians working on policing have questioned the extent to which Prussian authorities were actually able to control and discipline an increasingly volatile German population, which was experiencing rapid changes in its social and economic conditions.[73] The comparison with France adds a new dimension to the debate about elite cooperation in the German Empire by allowing the levels of practical cooperation between senior military commanders and civil servants in the provincial administration to be compared with that of their French counterparts.[74]

Finally, the demilitarisation of protest policing also seems to be at odds with the militarisation of numerous other aspects of German society and political life. Research into German militarism has added new perspectives to our understanding of the political and social role of the Prussian army by focusing more broadly on the military spirit in the wider population and on the self-perception of young men called up for military service.[75] At the same time, studies by David Schoebaum and Nicholas Stargardt have revealed a counter-culture of German popular opposition to the prevailing militarism.[76]

Of course, widespread enthusiasm for anything military, coupled with a popular culture of aggressive nationalism, was by no means limited to the German Empire in the late 19th century. Studies on French attitudes towards the military show both the extent of enthusiasm for the army, whilst also displaying important levels of anti-militarism amongst socialists and anarchists as well as within the French liberal tradition.

In recent years, two studies have been published on the nature and extent of militarism and anti-militarism in the French Third Republic.[77] The comparative analyses by Markus Ingenlath and by Jakob Vogel on German and French militarism clearly show that militarism in France was weaker than in Germany and qualified by various forms of anti-militarism.[78] This adds yet another element to the paradox that it was the French authorities who continued to rely on the assistance of thousands of conscript soldiers for the policing of popular protest.[79] Conversely, in Germany despite widespread militarism and deep involvement of the Prussian military establishment in the shaping of many aspects of German politics, this did not lead to significant military involvement in the handling of social and political protest.

'Historical institutionalism': the importance of bureaucratic practice

In order to understand the dissimilar paths taken by the French Third Republic and the German Empire, we need to search for the factors that shaped the decisions to request military assistance or to rely on the police and *gendarmerie*. The French and German systems display two major differences. One is linked to the emergence in France of new strategic approaches to protest policing. This study therefore focuses on the political processes behind the dissimilar recommendations from the Interior Ministries in Paris and Berlin. This involves an analysis of the options and constraints linked to the two approaches adopted by French and Prussian authorities.

The second important difference lies in the dissimilar ability of French and Prussian civilian and military authorities to engage in practical cooperation. The dynamics in the relationship between civilian and military authorities are particularly important in order to understand why the recommendations from Paris and Berlin were so consistently implemented by senior administrators and military commanders at *départemental* and provincial levels. Much has been written over the years about how powerful and independent French and Prussian civil servants in the provincial administration shaped the social and political development of both countries. Yet, studies tend to focus on the relationship between the provincial administration and local influential groups and individuals as well as on their relationship with the central powers in Berlin or Paris.[80] In contrast, the connections between the provincial administration and the military units based in the regions have not attracted much attention.

This study on the use of troops in the industrial areas of Nord-Pas-de-Calais and Westphalia indicates that the civil-military cooperation in France was characterised by high levels of formalisation, extensive exchange of information, coordination and joint decision-making across institutional boundaries. While some French military historians have stressed the importance of civil-military negotiations and detailed planning for the rebuilding the French army after 1871,[81] these features are not generally recognised as highly significant in shaping the policies of large-scale protest policing. The Prussian example, on the other hand, provides important clues to the problems arising from low levels of inter-institutional exchange of information and coordination between civilian and military authorities.

Observing these differences in the inter-institutional cooperation in the two countries led to integrating an institutionalist perspective in the analysis. Political scientists have shown how institutions tend to build up organisational structures and procedures over long periods of time. These subsequently tend to shape government policies and bureaucratic responses to complex problems. The historical institutionalist perspective offers a framework of interpretation that is particularly useful for understanding the dynamics within the French and Prussian-German systems. Yet the relationship between civilian and military authorities was crucial in shaping the preference for one particular type of approach to the policing of popular protest. The institutionalist perspective focuses on the connections between organisational imperatives of large-scale policing and how these facilitated or impeded military participation.[82]

Historical institutional theorists have identified three features which are of particular relevance to this study.[83] The first is the so-called 'path dependency', i.e. the dynamics of self-reinforcing processes within a political system: through the repeated implementation of one type of solution to a specific problem, key bureaucratic procedures are gradually adapted to fit the logistical and organisational needs of this particular approach. As this solution becomes entrenched in the bureaucratic procedures, it becomes increasingly complicated to adopt a different response because this would require a complete rethink of existing strategies and preparations.

Another crucial element in the smooth functioning of large-scale policing operations is the gradual establishment of the 'rules of the game' or 'standard operation procedures', which are known and accepted by all parties involved. Such 'rules of the game' are particularly important when policing requires civilian administrators and military commanders to cooperate across institutional boundaries.

Finally, institutional learning and accumulation of knowledge is crucial for the smooth functioning of inter-institutional cooperation. In large-scale policing in French and Prussian industrial areas, the accumulation of knowledge and experience made any deviation from previous strategies unattractive because bureaucrats and other involved parties would be forced to operate outside established rules, with limited knowledge and experience. Accordingly bureaucratic logic presented strong reasons for repeatedly implementing strategies and procedures that had been tried before.

This is not to argue that French and Prussian civilian authorities were not in a position to take a different approach. French and Prussian government authorities and bureaucrats still had room for acting contrary to established practices, and in some cases they did. However, the general preference within each system was clear and consistent. It is worth noting that in the early 1890s, both Republican France and Imperial Germany might just as well have developed completely different patterns of military involvement in protest policing. However, once the bureaucratic practices were set up for one particular approach to large-scale policing operations it became increasingly complicated to change the course.

Westphalia and Nord-Pas-de-Calais: comparing two industrial areas

A study on the use of troops for the whole of France and Germany would be a daunting task, particularly in the case of France. This study therefore concentrates on the development of government policies in Paris and Berlin and their implementation in two particularly turbulent areas: the Prussian province of Westphalia and the French region of Nord-Pas-de-Calais.

The French 1st Military Region covering the two *départements* 'Nord' and 'Pas-de-Calais' was one of the most turbulent industrial areas outside Paris. It is also one of the best documented areas from the side of the military because, unlike other French military regions, a very substantial collection of documents from the army corps commander's office in Lille have been retained in the French Military Archive.

The Prussian province of Westphalia also comprised a major industrial area. The general commander in Münster was responsible not only for the three Westphalian districts but also the district of Düsseldorf, although the civilian administration of this district was part of the neighbouring Rhine Province. The 7th Military Region thus covered the entire Ruhr District, which was the centre for the German coal mining and steel industries. Within the federal structure of the German Empire, Westphalia was a province within the Kingdom of Prussia. Accordingly, the Westphalian provincial administration was part of the centralised Prussian state organisation and the military units present in Westphalia belonged to the Royal Prussian Army. References will therefore be made to Prussia rather than to the German Empire as a whole.

Comparing France with Prussia, rather than with the entire German Empire, has a number of advantages in terms of establishing comparable entities. In the first place, France and Prussia were similar in size (38–39 million inhabitants in the France, 40 million in Prussia by the beginning of the 20th century). This facilitates the comparison of global figures for the number of industrial workers within different sectors; the number of trade union members; the number of strikes; and the size of the police and *gendarmerie* forces. In addition, the institutions most involved in the decision-making and implementation of large-scale policing operations (the provincial or *départemental* administration as well as the French and the

Prussian armies) were organised along similar lines: highly centralised structures with provinces and *départements* being administered by government appointed officials and military commanders in charge of the territorial army corps.

The investigation begins in 1889; in both countries, this year opened an era of large-scale labour conflicts and mass demonstrations. The 1890s is also the decade when the Prussian Interior Ministry began to embark on its policy of demilitarising the policing of protest, while French authorities began to make increasing use of military troops to handle popular protest. The study ends by the outbreak of the First World War when the institutional relationship between civilian and military authorities was fundamentally changed as a result of the war.

Contributions, advantages and limits of the comparative approach

Many of the factors that shaped the policies in each country will be familiar to readers already acquainted with the history of the early French Third Republic or with Wilhelmine Germany. It is the comparison of the two that is surprising. This study draws particular attention to certain factors which have not previously been identified as crucial for the development of the policies and practices of large-scale policing. These factors may appear unproblematic or marginal when observed within the national context, yet when presented in a comparative context, they undermine established explanatory models. It is the discovery of how much more frequently the French army was called out than the Prussian and how much closer the French civilian and military authorities worked together than their Prussian counterparts that is surprising. It is the observation that the Prussian police and *gendarmerie* were no better equipped than their French counterparts to take over the full responsibility for maintenance of order that demands further analysis, as does the fact that French soldiers were mobilised in far greater numbers even for smaller incidents of potential conflict.

The comparison also provides a contextualisation that allows analysis of military involvement in protest policing to be analysed beyond a normative framework of interpretation. It is difficult to assess what constitutes 'frequent' military involvement: is it six times over twenty-five years, or is it once every second year? Similarly, which military interventions could be described as 'appropriate' or even 'necessary' and which instances should be described as 'excessive'? Both France and German politicians and regional administrators claimed that the decision to call upon military assistance was an *ulitma ratio* solution, but *ultima ratio* clearly did not mean the same thing in the two countries.

Introduction

Comparison also allows explanations of policies and practices to move beyond the focus on differences in the institutional arrangements, the political profile of governments, or the social structures of the ruling elites. In fact, the policies of military participation in protest policing in the German Empire and the French Third Republic appear counter-intuitive to the social and political structures within each of the two countries. Comparison thereby relegates these factors to a secondary level of importance.

The French and Prussian case studies reveal many common features both in terms of the interests at stake over the maintenance of public order, the problems raised by military involvement, and some of the solutions proposed. Comparison of the two countries makes it possible to distinguish between the features that were particular to each of the two cases and problems which were intrinsically linked to the management of large crowds.

This study concentrates on the aspects that are relevant for explaining the comparative problem. Accordingly, other interesting aspects of military involvement in protest policing may not be given full attention. These include the experiences of protesters, conscript soldiers or officers; the strategies adopted by the French opposition to undermine the legitimacy of the Republican regime by criticising the use of troops; or the question of whether protest actions involving the French far right were treated more leniently in terms of policing than strikes and demonstrations organised by the socialist opposition.

In focusing on the dissimilarities between the two units, generalisations had to be made which may not always have done justice to the complexities within each country. What this study highlights are general trends in policies and practices. It is hoped that subsequent studies will be able to pick up the divergences from the main trends that are not given sufficient attention here.

Factors to be compared and aims of the study

The use of troops in France and Prussia calls for comparison in four key areas: we will look at the political factors which are generally accepted as determining for the demilitarisation process of protest policing in Prussia. This includes analyses of the policies developed in Berlin and Paris: how and why did successive Prussian and French Interior Ministers come to adopt such dissimilar approaches to protest policing during the 1890s?

The comparative perspective also allows for contextualising the argument that frequent military involvement in France was due to structural problems of insufficient numbers of policemen and *gendarmes*. A comparison will be made between the strength of local police and *gendarmerie* forces in Nord-Pas-de-Calais and Westphalia, including the number of policemen and *gendarmes* who could be mobilised from other areas in case of major unrest. It also involves an evaluation of the challenges to internal stability posed by the incidents of protest that occurred in these two industrial areas.

In addition, an assessment will be made of the comparative significance of the pressures coming from local elites and industrial interest groups for the decision to call upon military assistance: were the local 'notables' in Nord-Pas-de-Calais so much more successful than their Westphalian counterparts in influencing civilian and military authorities that it can account for the much more frequent involvement of military troops? Finally, we will analyse the nature of coordination, exchange of information and practical cooperation between the regional administration and the military authorities in Nord-Pas-de-Calais and Westphalia.

The arguments put forward in this book may inadvertently sound apologetic about the use of troops against civilians, or appear overly enthusiastic about the effectiveness of civil-military cooperation in Nord-Pas-de-Calais. This is an unintended consequence of my attempt to revise the interpretation of military involvement in policing on a number of counts.

Firstly the comparison highlights the need to distinguish between the long-term factors behind the gradual disengagement of regular military troops from protest policing on the one hand, and, on the other, the short-term factors behind the upsurge in the involvement of the French army during the late 19th and early 20th centuries. In order to fully understand the preference for military involvement shown by successive French Interior Ministers and prefects, we need to recognise that prevention and containment of violence were at the heart of the French policing strategies, even when the army became involved.

In addition to the factors that are generally understood to have driven the process towards demilitarisation of protest policing in Prussia, we need to recognise the importance of the dynamics between the provincial administration and the military authorities. This study seeks to deepen our understanding of the constraints and options around the policing of protest and the way in which these options became increasingly narrow after the turn of the 20th century.

All this leads to a reconsideration of the implications of military involvement in the French Third Republic and the German Empire. The presence of military troops at strikes and demonstrations did not have the same connotations and political implications in the two countries. Reconsideration of these aspects opens up new interpretations of how military involvement in protest policing reflects on the general nature of policing in each country and ultimately reflects on the two political regimes, their provincial administration and military organisations.

The book seeks to present the main aspects of the comparative paradox. The analysis of military involvement in the policing of protest in France and Germany between 1890 and 1914 is therefore is organised around key themes. The reader will find that sometimes the German case is presented first, sometimes the French; the order of presentation entirely depends on which of the two cases best illustrates the other.

The first part of the book looks at the role of the Prussian and French armies in state and society. It indicates that Prussia had good reasons for demilitarising, but that the French Republican authorities had even more urgent reasons for refraining from involving the army in protest policing. Looking at policies and ministerial initiatives debates in Berlin and Paris, the study analyses why and how the Prussian and French Interior Ministry came to recommend distinctly dissimilar approaches to the policing of protest.

Part II looks at the nature of violence and protest in Nord-Pas-de-Calais and Westphalia and compares the strength of police and *gendarmerie* forces in the provinces, as well as the police force that could be called to these regions. This is set against a detailed analysis of the patterns of military involvement in protest policing in the two regions.

Part III analyses the connections between the actors potentially involved in or influencing decisions to mobilise troops; it also analyses the implementation of large-scale policing operations in Nord-Pas-de-Calais and Westphalia, with particular focus on the relationship between the civil and military elites in Berlin and Paris and at the regional levels. Thus, the dissimilar approaches to the policing of protest not only reflect the nature of policing within the two countries but lay open important aspects of the internal functioning of the French Third Republic and the German Empire.

Notes

[1] Alf Lüdtke, *"Gemeinwohl", Polizei und "Festungspraxis". Staatliche Gewaltsamkeit und innere Verwaltung in Preußen, 1815–1850*, Göttingen: Vandenhoeck & Ruprecht, 1982, p. 251; Clive Emsley, *Policing in its context, 1750-1870*, London: Macmillan, 1983, pp. 143–145; Ralph Jessen, *Polizei im*

Industrierevier, Göttingen: Vandenhoeck & Ruprecht, 1991, pp. 24–25; Jean-Marc Berlière, *Le Préfet Lépine: Vers la naissance de la police moderne*, Paris: Denoël, 1993 (1), p. 170. Ronald van der Wal, *Of geweld zal worden gebruikt! Militaire bijstand bij de handhaving en het herstel van de openbare orde 1840–1920*, Hilversum: Verloren, 2003, pp. 12–20.

[2] Abrecht Funk, *Polizei und Rechtsstaat: Die Entstehung des Staatsrechtlichen Gewaltmonopols in Preußen, 1848–1918*, Frankfurt an Main: Campus, 1986, pp. 155–156; Hansjoachim Henning, 'Staatsmacht und Arbeitskampf: Die Haltung der preußischen Innenverwaltung zum Militäreinsatz während der Bergausstände 1889–1912', in Hansjoachim Henning (ed.), *Wirtschafts- und sozialgeschichtliche Forschung und Probleme – Festschrift für Karl Erich Born*, Frankfurt: Campus, 1987, pp. 167–168; Jessen (1991) pp. 127–137; Jean-Marc Berlière, *Le monde des polices en France*, Paris: Éditions Complexe, 1996, p. 118; Patrick Bruneteaux, *Maintenir l'ordre*, Paris: Presses de Sciences Po, 1996, p. 21; Wal (2003) pp. 17–18.

[3] For Great Britain see Anthony Babington, *Military intervention in Britain: from the Gordon riots to the Gibraltar incident*, London: Routledge, 1990; For France see Berlière (1996) p. 115; Bruneteaux (1996) pp. 34–44. For Germany see Funk (1986) pp. 37–40, 157–176; Jessen (1991) pp. 25, 108.

[4] A typical example of this appears in Eric Hobsbawm's *Age of Empire*, London: Abacus, 1997, p. 305.

[5] Clive Emsley, *Gendarmes and the State in Nineteenth-Century Europe*, Oxford: Oxford University Press, 1999.

[6] The King's use of troops was made accountable to Parliament already by the Bill of Rights of 1688 and the Riot Act of 1715 placed some legal restrictions around military actions in the policing of civilian society.

[7] Roger Geary, *Policing Industrial Disputes: 1893 to 1985*, Cambridge: Cambridge University Press, 1985, pp. 15–17; Babington (1990) pp. 117–121; Emsley (1983) p. 143; idem., *The English Police: a political and social history*, Harlow: Longman, 1996, pp. 54–55. Troops were mobilised in the UK at ten separate occasions between the 'Bloody Sunday' incidents at Trafalgar Square in 1887 and the outbreak of the First World War.

[8] In Nord-Pas-de-Calais alone there were at least sixty-eight separate incidents of military intervention between 1889 and 1914 (for details, see Chapter 6). For Italy see Charles Tilly, Louise Tilly and Richard Tilly, *The Rebellious Century, 1830-1930*, Cambridge MA: Harvard University Press, 1975, pp. 148–164; John A. Davis, *Conflict and Control: Law and Order in Nineteenth Century Italy*, London: Macmillan, 1988; John Gooch, *Army, State and Society in Italy, 1870–1915*, London: Macmillan, 1989, p. 17; Similarly, Ronald van der Wal identifies no less than 189 incidents of military intervention in the Netherlands between 1890 and the outbreak of the First World War, while another thirty-eight incidents took place between 1914 and 1918. (Wal, 2003, pp. 343–348).

[9] Less than thirty incidents for the entire German Empire between 1889 and 1914. (For details see Chapter 6.)

[10] István Deák, *Beyond Nationalism: a Social and Political History of the Habsburg Officer Corps, 1848–1918*, Oxford: Oxford University Press, 1992, pp. 46, 66–68; Gunther E. Rothenberg, *The Army of Francis Joseph*, West Lafayette: Purdue University Press, 1998, pp.121–122, 128–130.

[11] N. J. Westwood, *Endurance and Endeavour*, Oxford: Oxford University Press, 1993, pp. 180–188; David Christian, *Imperial and Soviet Russia: Power, Privilege and the Challenge of Modernity*, London: Macmillan, 1997, p. 133.

[12] On the domestic role of the army of unified Italy see John Whittam, *The Politics of the Italian Army, 1861–1918*, London: Macmillan, 1977; Davis (1988) pp. 347–351.

[13] On the Russian army see John Bushnell, *Mutiny amid Repression: Russian Soldiers in the Revolution of 1905–1906*, Bloomington: Indiana University Press, 1985, pp. 24–27; Christian (1997) p. 143.

[14] Funk (1986) pp. 155–156; Henning (1987) p. 167; Jessen (1991) pp. 25, 77–79; (idem.), 'Unternehmerherrschaft und staatliches Gewaltmonopol: Hüttenpolizisten und Zechenwehren im Ruhrgebiet 1870–1914', in Alf Lüdtke (ed.), *Sicherheit und Wohlfart: Polizei, Gesellschaft und Herrschaft im 19. und 20. Jahrhundert*, Frankfurt: Suhrkamp, 1992, pp. 176–177.

[15] Karl Liebknecht, *Militarism and Antimilitarism*, Cambridge: River Press, 1973, (first published in 1907), pp. 59–61.

[16] Liebknecht (1973) pp. 65–66.

[17] Lüdtke draws parallels with France and England, but only for the first half of the 19th century. Lüdtke (1982) pp. 345–346.

[18] Heinz-Gerhard Haupt, 'Staatliche Bürokratie und Arbeiterbewegung: Zum Einfluss der Polizei auf die Konstituierung von Arbeiterbewegung und Arbeiterklasse in Deutschland und Frankreich zwischen 1848 und 1880', in Heinz-Gerhard Haupt (ed.), *Arbeiter und Bürger im 19. Jahrhundert. Varianten ihres Verhältnisses im europäischen Vergleich*, Munich: Beck, 1986.

[19] Hsi-Huey Liang, *The Rise of Modern Police and the European State System from Metternich to the Second World War*, Cambridge: Cambridge University Press, 1992.

[20] Emsley (1999). Similarly an edited volume by Jean-Noël Luc, *Gendarmerie, État et société au XIXe siècle*, Paris: Publications de la Sorbonne, 2002.

[21] Wolfgang Knöbl, *Polizei und Herrschaft im Modernisierungsprozeß: Staatsbildung und innere Sicherheit in Preußen, England und Amerika 1700–1914*, Frankfurt am Main: Campus, 1998.

[22] Tom A. Critchley, *A History of Police in England and Wales, 1900–1966*, London: Constable, 1967; Wilbur R. Miller, *Cops and Bobbies: Police Authority in New York and London, 1830–1870*, Chicago: University of Chicago Press, 1973; Robert D. Storch, 'The Plague of the Blue Locust. Police Reform and Popular Resistance in Northern England, 1840–1857', *International Review of Social History*, vol. 20, 1975; idem., 'The Policeman as Domestic Missionary: Urban Discipline and Popular Culture in Northern England, 1850–1880', *Journal of Social History*, vol. 9, 1975–1976; Eric Monkkonen, *Police in Urban America,*

1860–1920, Cambridge: Cambridge University Press, 1981; Emsley (1983); idem. (1996).

[23] Tilly, Tilly, and Tilly (1975); Charles Tilly, *The Contentious French*, Cambridge, Mass.: Harvard University Press, 1986; Charles Tilly and Edward Shorter, *Strikes in France 1830–1968*, Cambridge: Cambridge University Press, 1974; Gerhard A. Ritter and Klaus Tenfelde, *Arbeiter im deutschen Kaiserreich, 1871/1875–1914*, Bonn: Verlag Dietz, 1992; Klaus Tenfelde, Heinrich Volkmann and Gerd Hohorst (eds), *Streik. Zur Geschichte des Arbeitskampfes in Deutschland während der Industrialisierung*, Munich: Beck, 1981; Jacques Julliard, *Clemenceau, briseur des grèves: l'affaire de Draveil-Villeneuve-Saint-George*, Paris: Julliard, 1965; Michelle Perrot, *Les ouvriers en grève. France 1870–1890*, Paris: Mouton, 1974 (In the following references will be made to the French edition because the English translation of this book is a highly abbreviated version of the French original); Rolande Trempé, *La France ouvrière*, Part II: 1871–1914, Paris: Les Éditions de l'Atelier, 1995; Friedhelm Böll, *Arbeitskämpfe und Gewerkschaften in Deutschland, England und Frankreich*, Bonn: Dietz, 1992; Dieter Groh, 'Intensification of Work and Industrial Conflict in Germany, 1896–1914', *Politics and Society*, vol. 8, 1978, pp. 349–397; Klaus Saul, 'Zwischen Repression und Integration', in Tenfelde, Volkmann and Hohorst (eds), *Streik: Zur Geschichte des Arbeitskampfes in Deutschland während der Industrialisierung*, Munich: Beck, 1981; Dick Geary, *European labour protest, 1848–1939*, London: Croom Helm, 1980; Stephen Hickney, *Workers in Imperial Germany: Miners of the Ruhr*, Oxford: Clarendon, 1985.

[24] George Carrot, *Maintien de l'ordre, depuis la fin de l'Ancien Régime jusqu'à 1968*, (unpublished thèse d'État), University of Nice, 1984; idem., *Le maintien de l'ordre en France au XXe siècle*, Paris: Veyrier, 1990; Jean-Marc Berlière, *Institution policière en France sous la Troisième République, 1875–1914*, (unpublished thèse d'État), University of Bourgogne, Dijon, 1991; idem. (1993, 1); idem., 'Du maintien de l'ordre républicain au maintien républicain de l'ordre?', *Genèses*, vol. 12, 1993 (2), pp. 6–29; idem., 'Aux origines d'une conception "moderne" du maintien de l'ordre', in Madeleine Rebérioux (ed.), *Fourmies et les Premier Mai*, Paris: Éditions de l'Atelier, 1994; idem. (1996); Patrick Bruneteaux, 'Le déordre de la répression en France, 1871–1921: des conscripts aux gendarmes mobiles', *Genèses*, vol. 12, 1993, pp. 30–46; idem. (1996); Odile Roynette-Gland, 'L'armée dans la bataille sociale: maintien de l'ordre et grèves ouvrières dans le Nord de la France (1871–1906)', *Le Mouvement Social*, vol. 179, 1997, pp. 33–58.

[25] Lüdtke (1982); idem. (ed.), *Herrschaft als soziale Praxis: historische und sozialanthropologische Studien*, Göttingen: Vandenhoeck & Ruprecht, 1991; Herbert Reinke (ed.), *"Nur für die Sicherheit da?..." Zur Geschichte der Polizei im 19. und 20. Jahrhundert*, Frankfurt am Main: Suhrkamp, 1993; Funk (1986); Jessen (1991); idem. (1992); Elaine Glovka Spencer, *Management and Labor in Imperial Germany: Ruhr Industrialists as Employers, 1896–1914*, New Braunswick, NJ: Rutgers University Press, 1984; idem., 'Police–Military Relations in Prussia, 1848–1914', *Journal of Social History*, vol. 19, 1985, pp. 305–317; idem., *Police and the Social Order in German Cities: the Düsseldorf District, 1848–1914*,

DeKalb: Northern Illinois University Press, 1992; Thomas Lindenberger, 'Politique de rue et action de classe à Berlin avant la première guerre mondiale', *Génèses*, vol. 12, 1993, pp. 47–68; idem., *Straßenpolitik. Zur Sozialgeschichte der öffentlishen Ordnung in Berlin*, Bonn: Dietz, 1995.

[26] Diane Cooper-Richet, 'Le Plan general de protection à l'épreuve de la grève des mineurs du Nord-Pas-de-Calais (September–November 1902)', in Philippe Vigier (ed.), *Maintien de l'ordre et polices en France et en Europe au XIXe siècle*, Paris: Créaphis, 1987; Berlière (1994) pp. 185–197; Bruneteaux (1993); idem. (1996); Royenette-Gland (1997) pp. 34–37.

[27] Lüdtke (1982); Wolfram Sieman, *Deutschlands Ruhr Sicherheit und Ordnung: Anfänge der politischen Polizei, 1806–1866*, Tübingen: Niemeyer, 1985; Funk (1986); Jessen (1991); Reinke (1993); Lindenberger (1993); idem. (1995); Knöbl (1998).

[28] Jean-Pierre Machelon, *La République contre les libertés*, Paris: Fondation Nationale des Sciences Politiques, 1976, pp. 7–8.

[29] Madeleine Rebérioux and Jean-Marie Mayeur, *The Third Republic from its Origins to the Great War, 1871–1914*, Cambridge: Cambridge University Press, 1989, pp. 190–191; Maurice Agulhon, *The French Republic 1879–1992*, Oxford: Blackwell, 1993, p. 55; Michel Winock, *La France Politique, XIXe–XXe siècle*, Paris: Seuil, 1999, p. 248.

[30] Raoul Girardet, *La société militaire dans la France contemporaine 1815–1939*, Paris: Plon, 1953, p. 262; David B. Ralston, *The Army of the Republic*, Cambridge: Cambridge University Press, 1967, p. 281, William Serman, *Les officiers français dans la nation, 1848–1914*, Paris: Aubier, 1982, pp. 59–60.

[31] Carrot (1984) p. 647; Bruneteaux (1996) pp. 46–47; Belière (1996) p. 118.

[32] Rebérioux (1989) pp. 190–191, 264; Perrot (1974) pp. 83, 192; Trempé (1995) pp. 322–335.

[33] Emsley (1999), Eric Alary, *L'histoire de la gendarmerie de la renaissance au troisième millenaire*, Paris: Calman-Lévy, 2000; Similarly the recent book on the French *gendarmerie* edited by Jean-Noël Luc (2002).

[34] Carrot (1984).

[35] Berlière (1991); idem. (1996).

[36] Bruneteaux, (1993); idem. (1996).

[37] Dianne Cooper-Richet (1987).

[38] Roynette-Gland (1997).

[39] Jean-Charles Jauffret, 'Armée et Pouvoir Politique: la question des troupes specialisées chargées du maintien de l'ordre en France de 1871 à 1914', *Revue Historique*, vol. 270, 1983, pp. 97–144.

[40] J. Monteilhet, *Les institutions militaries de la France (1814–1924)*, Paris: Félix Alcan, 1926; Girardet (1953) pp. 233–234, 262–263; Paul-Marie de la Gorce, *The French Army: a Military-Political History*, Weidenfeld & Nicholson, 1963, p. 61; Serman (1982) pp. 45–63.

[41] Guy Pedroncini (ed.), *Histoire Militaire de la France de 1871 à 1940*, Paris: Presses Universitaires de France, 1992.

[42] Perrot's quantitative estimations only comprise military involvement in the policing of labour conflict for the period 1870–1890. At the same time her figures involves both the instances where regular troops were mobilised and instances where only the *gendarmerie* intervened. Perrot (1974) p. 195.

[43] Madeleine Rebérioux goes as far as claiming that it was rare that military presence at strikes and demonstrations did not end in bloody confrontations with protesters being killed. Rebérioux (1989) p. 264. Similarly Berlière describes military presence being as "always extremely bloody.", Berlière (1993, 2) p. 9.

[44] Agulhon very accurately expresses these conflicting interpretations of the Third Republic as the 'good' or the 'bad' republic. Maurice Agulhon, *Coup d'État et République*, Paris: Presses de Sciences Po, 1997, pp. 81–82.

[45] Jean-Pierre Azéma and Michel Winock, *La Troisième République: 1870–1914*, Paris: Hachette, 1970, pp. 125–157; Rebérioux (1989) pp. 204–206; Agulhon (1993) pp. 48, 52–55; idem. (1997) pp. 81–82; Winock (1999) pp. 88–89.

[46] Jean-Jacques Becker, *Le Carnet B: les pouvoirs publics et l'antimilitarisme avant la guerre de 1914*, Paris: Editions Klincksieck, 1973; Rebérioux (1994) pp. 11–17; Trempé (1995) pp. 320–335.

[47] Girardet (1953) pp. 262–264; Serman (1982) pp. 45–63; Jauffret (1983) pp. 138–143.

[48] Pierre Miquel, *Clemenceau: la guerre et la paix*, Paris: Tallandier, 1996, pp. 42–45; René Rémond, *La République souveraine: La vie politique en France, 1879–1939*, Paris: Fayard, 2002, pp. 228–232. Similarly Machelon focuses on the necessity of maintaining order within the fragile Republican system. Machelon (1976) pp. 20–21.

[49] Robert Gildea, *The Past in French History*, New Haven: Yale University Press, 1994, pp. 36–42; Robert Tombs, *France 1814–1914*, London: Longman, 1996; Roger Magraw, *Workers and the Bourgeois Republic*, Oxford: Blackwell, 1992, p. 50; idem., *France 1800–1914: A Social History*. London: Longman, 2002, p. 113.

[50] Carrot (1984) p. 665; Berlière (1991) pp. 498–510; idem. (1996) p. 118; Bruneteaux (1993) p. 31. Similarly Agulhon describes the use of troops as due to the 'institutional backwardness' of the system of order maintenance. Agulhon (1993) p. 55.

[51] Serman (1982) pp. 47–48; Roynette-Gland (1997) p. 34.

[52] Rebérioux (1989) pp. 264; Trempé (1995) pp. 325–335; Magraw (2002) p. 103.

[53] Lüdtke (1982) pp. 53–54, 326–338; Funk (1986) pp. 287–311; Jessen (1991) pp. 159–162, 179–185.

[54] Harald Klückmann, 'Requisition und Einsatz bewaffneter Macht in der deutschen Verfassungs- und Militärgeschichte', *Militärgeschichtliche Mitteilungen*, vol. 1, 1978, pp. 7–43.

[55] Spencer, 1984, pp. 305–317.

[56] Funk (1986); Jessen (1991); Knöbl (1998).

[57] Funk (1986) pp. 155–156; Jessen (1991) pp. 17, 40–43, Spencer (1992) pp. 86–87.

[58] Henning raises the issue, but does not go into details on the aspect. Henning (1987) p. 140.

[59] Lüdkte (1982) pp. 238–282, 291–300.
[60] Funk (1986) pp. 307–311.
[61] Kitchen (1968) p. 163.
[62] Messerschmidt (1980) p. 68.
[63] Hans-Ulrich Wehler, *The German Empire, 1871–1918*, Oxford: Berg, 1985, p. 157.
[64] Berghahn (1994) pp. 257–258.
[65] Hans-Ulrich Wehler, *Deutsche Gesellschaftsgeschichte, 1849–1914*, Munich: Beck, 1995, p. 1123.
[66] Gerhard Ritter, *The Sword and the Sceptre: The problem of Militarism in Germany*, London: Penguin, 1972 (first published in 1954), vol. 2, pp. 125–136; Gordon A. Craig, *The Politics of the Prussian Army, 1640–1945*, Oxford: Oxford University Press, 1955, pp. 255–266; Karl Demeter, *The German Officer Corps in Society and State 1650–1945*, London: Weidenfeld & Nicolson, 1965 (first published in 1930); Manfred Messerschmidt (with E. von Matuschka and Wolfgang Petters), *Militärgeschichte im 19. Jahrhundert, 1814–1890*, Munich: Beck, 1979; Volker R. Berghahn, *Germany and the Approach of War in 1914*, Basingstoke: Macmillan, 1993, pp. 19–37.
[67] Hans-Ulrich Wehler, 'Symbol des halb-absolutistischen Herrschaftssytems' in Hans-Ulrich Wehler (ed.), *Krisenherde des Kaiserreichs, 1871–1918*, Göttingen: Vandenhoeck & Ruprecht, 1970; idem. (1985) p. 21. In his great synthesis of German Social History of the 19th century, Wehler prefers the term 'Iron State' to describe the militarised character of the Constitution and institutional arrangements of the German Empire (Wehler (1995) p. 874); Thomas Nipperdey describes the German Empire as a 'military state' (Nipperdey, *Deutsche Geschichte 1866–1918: Machtstaat vor der Demokratie*, Munich: Beck, 1992, p. 201).
[68] Ullmann talks about the long Police State tradition in Germany (Hans-Peter Ullmann, *Das deutsche Kaiserreich*, Frankfurt: Suhrkamp, 1995, p. 173); while Ritter and Tenfelde (1992) p. 683 think that despite the system of police supervision developed to watch over the Social Democrats, the German Empire could not adequately be described as a police state.
[69] Wehler (1995) pp. 1284–1295; Wilfried Loth, *Das Kaiserreich: Obrigkeitstaat und politische Mobilisierung*, Munich: dtv, 1996; Ullmann (1995); Heinrich August Winkler, *Der lange Weg nach Westen*, Munich: Beck, 2000. Hartwin Spenkuch, 'Vergleichsweise besonders? Politische System und Strukturen Preußens als Kern des "deutschen Sonderwegs"', *Geschichte und Gesellschaft*, vol. 29 /2, 2003, pp. 262–293.
[70] The literature on the German *Sonderweg* debate is vast. For a brief introduction in English see David Blackbourn and Geoff Eley, *The peculiarities of German history: Bourgeois society and politics in 19th century Germany*, Oxford: Oxford University Press, 1984; R. G. Moeller, 'The Kaiserreich Recast?', *Journal of Social History*, vol. 17, 1984; Richard J. Evans, *Rethinking German History: Nineteenth-Century Germany and the Origins of the Third Reich*, London: HarperCollins, 1987; idem., *Rereading German History, 1800–1996: From Unification to Reunification*, London: Routledge, 1997.

[71] Alastar P. Thompson, *Left Liberals, the State and Popular Politics in Wilhelmine Germany*, Oxford University Press, 2000; Kevin Repp, *Reformers, Critics, and the Path of German Modernity: Anti-Politics and the Search for Alternatives, 1890–1914*, Cambridge, Massachusetts: Harvard University Press, 2000.

[72] Wehler (1985) pp. 62–65; Wehler (1995) pp. 1000–1168; Wolfgang Mommsen, *Imperial Germany 1867–1918: Politics, Culture and Society in an Authoritarian State*, London: Arnold, 1995, pp. 278–299; Berghahn (1994) pp. 195–196.

[73] Spencer (1985) pp. 305–317; Spencer (1992) pp. 163–164; Evans (1987) pp. 171–174; idem. (1997) p. 73.

[74] Christophe Charle, *Les Hauts Fonctionaires en France au 19e siècle*, Paris: Gallimard, 1980; idem., *Les elites de la République (1880-1900)*, Paris: Gallimard, 1987; Walter S. Barge, *The Generals of the Republic: the corporate personality of high military rank in France 1889–1914* (unpublished Ph.D. thesis) University of North Carolina, 1982; Guy Chaussinand-Nogaret, *Histoire des élites en France au XIXe et XXe siècles*, Paris: Hachette, 1991; René Bargeton, *Dictionnaire Biographique des Préfets, 1870–1982*, Paris: Archives Nationales, 1994. For the German bureaucratic elites see the studies of Nikolaus von Preradovich, *Die Führungsschichten in Österreich und Preußen (1808–1918)*, Wiesbaden: Steiner, 1955; Friedrich Wilhelm Euler, 'Die deutsche Generalität und Admiralität bis 1918', in Hanns Hubert Hofmann (ed.), *Das deutsche Offizierkorps 1860–1960*, Boppard am Rhein: Boldt, 1980; Bernhard vom Brocke, 'Die preußischen Oberpräsidenten 1815 bis 1945', in Klaus Schwabe (ed.), *Die preußischen Oberpräsidenten, 1815–1945*, Boppard am Rhein: Boldt, 1981; Daniel Hughes, *The King's Finest: a Social and Bureaucratic Profile of Prussia's General Officers 1871–1914*, New York: Atheneum, 1987.

[75] Stig Förster, *Die doppelte Militarismus: der deutsche Heeresrüstungspolitik zwichen Status-quo-Sicherung und Aggression, 1890–1913*, Stuttgart: Franz Steiner, 1985; Thomas Rohkrämer, *Der Militarismus der "kleinen Leute": Die Kriegervereine in deutschen Kaiserreich, 1871–1914*, Munich: Oldenburg, 1990; Jeffrey Verhey, *The Spirit of 1914: militarism, myth and mobilisation in Germany*, Cambridge: Cambridge University Press, 2000.

[76] David Schoenbaum, *Zabern 1913: Consensus politics in Imperial Germany*, London: Allen & Unwin, 1982; Nicholas Stargardt, *The German Idea of Militarism: Radical and Socialist Critics, 1866–1914*, Cambridge: Cambridge University Press, 1994.

[77] Hendrick L. Wesseling, *Soldiers and Warriors: French attitudes towards the army at the era of the First World War*, Westpoint, Conn.: Greenwood Press, 2000; Paul Miller, *From Revolutionaries to Citizens: Antimilitarism in France 1870–1914*, Durham, NJ: Duke University Press, 2002.

[78] Markus Ingenlath, *Mentale Aufrüstung: Militarisierungstendenzen in Frankreich und Deutschland vor dem Ersten Weltkrieg*, Frankfurt am Main: Campus, 1994; Jakob Vogel, *Nationen im Gleichschnitt: der Kult der "Nation im Waffen" in Deutschland und Frankreich, 1871–1914*, Göttingen: Vandenhoeck & Ruprecht, 1997; idem., '"Folklorenmilitarismus" in Deutschland und Frankreich', in

Wolfram Wette (ed.), *Militarismus in Deutschland 1871 bis 1945*, Hamburg: LIT, 1999.

[79] See Chapter 1.

[80] Karl-Erich Born, *Staat und Sozialpolitik seit Bismarcks Sturtz*, Wiesbaden: Steiner, 1957; idem., *Wirtschafts- und Sozialgeschichte des deutschen Kaiserreich, 1867/71–1914*, Wiesbaden: Steiner, 1985; Hansjoachim Henning, *Die deutsche Beamtenschaft im 19. Jahrhundert*, Stuttgart: Steiner, 1984; idem. (1987). On French prefects and mayors, see Brian Chapman, *The Prefects and Provincial France*, London: Allen & Unwin, 1955; Jeanne Siwek-Pouydesseau, *Le corps préfectoral sous la Troisième et la Quatrième République*, Paris: Armand Colin, 1969; Vincent Wright and Bernard Le Clère, *Les prefects du Second Empire*, Paris: Armand Colin; Vincent Wright, 'The History of French Mayors: Lessons and Problems', in *Jahrbuch Europäischer Verwaltung*, vol. 2, 1990, pp. 268–280; idem., 'La reserve du corps préfectoral', in Pierre Birnbaum (ed.), *La France de l'Affaire Dreyfus*, Paris: Gallimard, 1994.

[81] Monteilhet (1926); de la Gorce (1963); Ralston (1967).

[82] The historical perspective as central to the understanding of the dynamics in the functioning of institutions was first described theoretically by James March and Johan Olsen, *Rediscovering Institutions: The Organisational Basis of Politics*, New York: The Free Press, 1989, pp. 7–8, 21–26. For a recent assessment of this approach see Theda Skocpol and Paul Pierson, 'Historical Institutionalism in Contemporary Political Science', in Ira Katznelson and Helen Milner (eds.), *Political Science: the State of the Discipline*, New York: Norton, 2002, pp. 693–721.

[83] March and Olsen (1989) pp. 58–63; Skocpol and Pierson (2002) pp. 694–695.

PART I

DOMESTIC MILITARY INTERVENTION IN ITS POLITICAL CONTEXT

Chapter 1

The French and Prussian Armies in State and Society

The army and the nation: a military dilemma

With the recurrence of mass-protest from the late 1880s onwards, French and Prussian government authorities came under growing pressure to justify politically the involvement of military troops in the policing of industrial disputes and other forms of popular protest. With increasing sensitivity in the wider public towards military involvement, heavy-handed intervention in a protest movement might easily arouse widespread sympathy and turn public opinion against the authorities. Above all, an ill-conducted military intervention – particularly if it led to casualties – could be used by a political opposition to undermine the legitimacy of the government, or – more dangerously – challenge the ideological foundations of the regime.

Political justification of military response to popular protest was particularly contentious in France where the Republican regime built its legitimacy on a popular mandate. In comparison, the political legitimacy of the Prussian King and German *Kaiser* and his appointed ministers was less vulnerable to public outcry due to limitations on democratic participation and parliamentary accountability of Prussian ministers. However, with its legitimacy resting upon the concept of the *Rechtsstaat*, the government needed to be seen as acting within the boundaries of the law.[1]

In both countries, legal-constitutional descriptions of the domestic role of military troops were kept vague and open ended in order to allow maximum discretion in the use of military force. In using these discretionary powers, political decision-makers had to reckon with increasingly polarised public opinion. Incompatible demands were voiced by those who called for effective military protection of property and economic interests and those who sought to reduce military involvement in the policing of protest and leave domestic peacekeeping to the police and *gendarmerie*.

The French and Prussian military establishments had their own interests and agendas. Prussian commanders, in particular, contemplated using the army as an instrument in domestic politics, while French military leaders were keen on maintaining the public image of a strictly apolitical army. Yet, in both countries, senior commanders were keen on maintaining extensive institutional independence and exercising significant influence on all issues that concerned the army. On the question of maintenance of public order, both French and Prussian military authorities were keen on distancing themselves from attempts by political and industrial elites to make them the instruments of particular interests.[2] Accordingly, French and Prussian officers were increasingly reluctant to see their troops perform the function of riot police and become involved in the messy affair of handling popular protest.

The conditions under which the French and Prussian military leaders had access to shape the domestic role of the army differed significantly within the two systems; this was both in terms of the degree of institutional autonomy given to the military organisations, the political influence they were allowed to exercise, and the prestige the army enjoyed in wider society.[3] Yet the extent of military influence on policies and strategies for large-scale protest policing was determined not only by the legal and constitutional framework, but also by social context and the power balance between civilian political institutions and the army.

Two questions arise concerning the dissimilar engagement of the French and Prussian armies in the policing of protest. One concerns the dangers involved in using conscript soldiers against civilians and the fears that the use of soldiers for policing would undermine the discipline and loyalty amongst the conscripts as well as the prestige of the army in wider society. Did the French authorities have less reason than their Prussian counterparts to be concerned about these risks?

Secondly, to what extent could the domestic role the French and Prussian armies be linked to the formal powers of French and Prussian military commanders, and the dissimilar legal-constitutional position of the military organisation within the German Empire and the French Third Republic? Undoubtedly, the political position and institutional framework of the Prussian military authorities allowed them better opportunities than their French counterparts in shaping the army's role in maintaining order; yet there were divergent opinions amongst Prussian military leaders about what this role should be.

Soldiers' loyalty and the ideological justification for mobilising the army against civilians

In both the French Third Republic and the German Empire the army constituted one of the main institutions for national integration. Together with compulsory school education, military service was supposed to imbue young men with a sense of patriotism and loyalty towards the political regime. But the fact that soldiers were recruited from the civilian population created particular problems in relation to the functioning of the army in the policing of protest.

One issue that worried government and military authorities alike was the question of loyalty and discipline amongst the conscripts.[4] The fear of mutiny amongst recruits was particularly strong in France, where declining birth rates, the military need for increasing numbers of soldiers, together with Republican notions of equality of all, meant that more than eighty per cent of able-bodied men were called up for military service.[5] The introduction of the three-year conscription law of 1889 abolished the dispensations that previously existed for students, teachers, priests, seminarians and the eldest sons of widows;[6] but it was the influx of an increasing number of industrial workers which caused most concern regarding loyalty.

When the Third Republic introduced universal conscription in 1872, French soldiers were supposed to serve far from their native region in an attempt to promote national integration. This measure was also intended to avoid situations where young conscripts mobilised for policing purposes found themselves face-to-face with friends and family. Over the years, however, exemptions from this rule became so frequent that military commanders had to reckon with a substantial number of locals amongst their soldiers.[7] Despite precautions taken against sending soldiers to conflicts near their home towns there were still serious concerns about discipline and loyalty amongst soldiers from other industrial communities when mobilised for sensitive labour disputes.[8]

In Prussia the military authorities were similarly aware of the problems of discipline and loyalty arising from a largely conscripted military organisation. However, the Prussian army needed to enrol only fifty to sixty per cent of all draftees to fill its ranks.[9] It could therefore select young men from rural areas, who were supposedly less influenced by Social Democratic ideas than young men from the great industrial centres. Even when the Prussian army increased the number of conscript soldiers from 400,000 to 800,000, and it became necessary to recruit some soldiers from the industrialised areas, the military authorities carefully hand-picked their soldiers and dismissed individuals on the slightest suspicion of dubious political affiliations or even sympathies. By 1910, when more than twenty-one per cent of Prussians lived in cities with more than 100,000 inhabitants, only six per cent of soldiers were recruited from these areas.[10] These selective recruitment policies allowed the Prussian military authorities to be more confident than their French counterparts of the discipline and loyalty of their soldiers, and fraternisation between German conscript soldiers and protesters remained less of a threat.

The French Republican regime also faced major problems of ideological justification when using the army against the civilian population. The French Republican army was not only a national army, it was the French Nation, as a collective entity, armed and trained for the defence of national borders and of French interests abroad. The army's representation of the entire nation had its origins in the *levée en masse* during the French Revolutionary Wars and the conscript army of the Napoleonic era. During most of the 19th century, the Nation-in-Arms model for military organisation remained intimately associated with the Revolution and Republicanism,[11] and successive regimes from the *Restoration* to the Second Empire preferred small and largely professional armies.

It was only with the humiliating defeat of 1870–1871 that the founders of the Third Republic acknowledged the military advantages of a well-drilled mass-army like that of Prussia. Yet, when the Nation-in-Arms model was reintroduced by the Third Republic,[12] several conservative and liberal politicians, including Prime Minister Thiers, were strongly opposed, preferring a smaller and entirely professional army. Many had qualms about the ideological implications of an army of conscripts whose loyalty might be undermined by populist movements or might fall apart under the impact of conflicting political influences. Moreover many within the political establishment feared an armed revolt and felt uncomfortable about training peasants and workers in the use of weapons and military operations.[13] Revolts and popular uprising amongst the Parisian population were still a risk to be reckoned with. Indeed, in the wake of the Paris *Commune*, the new Republican regime dissolved the citizen militia, the National Guard, for the very same reasons.

From the opposite side of the political spectrum, the Nation-in-Arms model was by left-wing Republicans as a way of achieving popular control over the armed forces. Socialists and many radicals regarded the abolition of the professional army as the only way to prevent the ruling elites from using it against 'the People'.[14] This was also the position of Jaurès by the eve of the First World War, when he sought to define a socialist framework for a truly democratic army. It goes almost without saying that the army organisation proposed by Jaurès had, as its sole task, the defence of the national territory against external aggression. Accordingly this army could not be used as a force of internal order.[15]

The ideological justification for military action was the defence of the French Nation by the French Nation in the name of the French Nation. Military involvement in policing created an insoluble problem, for how could the Army of the Nation be mobilised against groups within the Nation, and in the name of whom?[16] Of course, the army was defending the Republican regime and its institutions, but if this required turning the army against 'the People' the question was which groups within the Nation did the government actually represent and from whom did it draw its authority? Moreover, even if isolated incidents of popular protest could be defined as rebellion, there was still a serious risk that soldiers might refuse to obey orders. In a Republican system, military intervention against civilians was difficult to justify ideologically, and politically it made governments vulnerable to accusations of using the Republican institutions to protect the interests of the ruling elites.

The Prussian army had been based on universal conscription since its reorganisation in 1807–1815 after the old Prussian army's collapse before Napoleon's mass-army. Throughout the 19th century universal conscription was used – together with compulsory school education and the influence of the Lutheran Church – to maintain highly conservative and hierarchical social and political structures in Prussia and later in the German Empire.

Whereas in France universal military conscription was associated with Republicanism and some degree of popular influence and control over the armed forces, the Prussian notion of the People-in-Arms (*das Volk im Waffen*) fitted into an altogether different ideological complex. Most importantly, in ideological terms, the use of the Prussian army against civilians did not require major justification: the 'Volk' enrolled as soldiers in the Prussian army were 'subjects' who were under a duty to obey orders from the monarch in his capacity of Supreme Warlord.[17] According to the Imperial Constitution, the *Kaiser* held full authority to conduct war; accountable to no one for whatever orders he issued, and any opposition from the soldiers could be treated as a straightforward rebellion.[18] Thus, in the German Imperial system universal conscription did not bring about problems of ideological justifications similar to those arising in Republican France.

The prestige of the Prussian army amongst conscripts and in wider society

In addition to the particular issues arising from the universal military conscription, military leaders in both Prussia and France increasingly regarded the involvement of troops in the policing of civilian society as damaging to the prestige and respect for the national army amongst conscript soldiers as well as in the wider population.[19] Here too the French army was more vulnerable than the Prussian.

Within the German Empire, the Prussian army constituted the backbone of the German Imperial regime together with the Emperor, government and bureaucracy. After three victorious wars of unification, the prestige and authority of the military establishment was almost impossible to challenge. Military officers enjoyed immense prestige within civilian society, with the lowest ranking officer holding higher official rank than even the most senior civil servant. Collectively the officer corps was above criticism, impenetrable and virtually impossible to hold to account.

In the atmosphere of prevailing nationalism, the army was widely regarded as the pride of the nation, with many hopes for future expansion and German domination in Europe associated with it. The extension of military strength and influence in foreign and domestic politics was matched by the aggressive promotion of enthusiasm for military values through the compulsory school education, military service and veterans' clubs as well as popular celebrations of the army.[20] German culture and social life were also increasingly dominated by military attitudes and values, while membership of associations based on military activities or supporting military interests and organisations were often essential for social acceptance. During the Wilhelmine era up to five million Germans directly participated in a vast number of military associations, veterans' clubs, support groups for local military units and the immensely popular Navy League. Those not involved in voluntary organisations would be expected to participate in military-related activities and rallies in compulsory school education as well as in many sports clubs. There were strong pressures for middle-class men to become reserve officers; in many cases this was a precondition for obtaining posts in public administration, in law, or in academia. These military or semi-military activities and affiliations were underpinned by a strong social expectation of patriotic commitment, which made it very difficult to raise a voice of criticism against the Prussian army.

Of course, the Prussian army was also the object of some criticism and ridicule. The army and the officer corps were the pet targets of the satirical magazine *Simplicissimus* and the left-wing publication *Der wahre Jakob*.

Much amusement was drawn from a particularly embarrassing incident in 1906 when a petty criminal in a captain's uniform created havoc in the town of Köpenick, by ordering soldiers to occupy the town hall and arrest the mayor. As Stargardt rightly points out,[21] the level of amusement and undisguised *Schadenfreude* over the grotesque incident spoke volumes about the ambiguous attitude amongst Germans between enthusiasm and exasperation towards military arrogance and pretentiousness. Yet this did not in any way outweigh the widespread prestige of the Prussian army amongst the German population, and the criticism never acquired notable political significance or threatened to seriously undermine the prestige of the army.

Nor was the prestige of the army seriously damaged by the notorious brutality of life in barracks. The suicide rate amongst German conscripts was appallingly high: with 220–240 suicides every year it was fourteen times the rate of the general population.[22] Moreover, each year the military courts handled, on average, 800 cases where officers stood accused of having caused grievous bodily harm – not infrequently followed by death – to conscript soldiers. Penalties for brutality against soldiers were derisory, mostly a few days of house arrest, and even persistent offenders continued their military careers unaffected. Yet a widespread enthusiasm for the military still prevailed.

Opposition to the prevailing militarism came from three different corners. Liberal critics of the Prussian army like Eugen Richter or Ludwig Quidde[23] opposed militarism from the point of view of citizens' rights and individual freedoms and called for the Prussian army to be subjected to parliamentary scrutiny and control. Richter and Quidde's challenge to the military establishment found some sympathisers amongst those German liberals whose enthusiasm for the military glory of the German Nation did not blind them to the abuses taking place within the army and to the arrogance of the officer corps.[24] German Pacifists, by contrast, had a difficult case to make in the face of the prevailing nationalism, and unlike the peace movements in France, the UK and the US, had no political tradition to build on and no German references for their ideology.[25] As a result, the German Peace Movement remained politically marginal. Even within the Social Democratic Party there were few true pacifists, with Karl Liebknecht as the only declared pacifist amongst the party leaders.

Yet, it was the Social Democrats who provided the most vigorous antimilitarist challenge, with their fierce critique of the army in its present form and with their denunciation of militarism as the by-product of capitalism.[26] Rosa Luxemburg was even given a prison sentence for appealing to German soldiers to refuse to shoot at French soldiers. As part of his criticism of the aristocratic military establishment, August Bebel pleaded for the creation of a 'People's Militia' (*Volkswehr*) that could not be mobilised against German civilians.[27] The Social Democratic Party also made great efforts to create a counter-balance to the prevailing militarism through their youth organisations and their publications.

On the other hand, the Social Democratic critique had to be carefully presented in order not to be counter-productive. Those who expressed antimilitary sentiments were all too easily branded as national enemies (*Reichsfeinde*) and their criticism written off as 'unpatriotic'. Social Democratic leaders, therefore, also encouraged those supporters called up for military service to be disciplined and loyal soldiers. Thus, despite the conflicts between the Prussian army and the Social Democratic Party, despite the campaigns of the Peace Movement, despite the satirical targeting of military officers, and despite widespread brutality against conscript soldiers, prestige and loyalty towards the army remained largely unchallenged.

The highs and lows of the French army: prestige and criticism

The position of the French army and its prestige, both amongst recruits and the wider population, was far more fragile than in Germany. The French were deeply divided in their support for the armed forces – roughly along the lines that marked support for or rejection of the Republican regime. Amongst many traditionalist Frenchmen the army enjoyed enormous prestige not unlike the glorification of the Prussian army. The scale and intensity of this support for the French army was most clearly displayed in connection with the Dreyfus Affair. It was often linked to opposition to the Republican regime and not infrequently paired with strongly anti-democratic attitudes and strong attachments to the Catholic Church. In the eyes of many traditional conservatives the army was identified with honour, discipline and integrity – in short everything that the democratic institutions were reproached for lacking. Due to the notorious instability of French cabinets, the democratic institutions were all too easily regarded as incompetent, weak and even corrupted by power and money. Beyond these strongly pro-military groups, the army was regarded as the organisation that would one day restore national pride, after the humiliating defeat in the Franco-Prussian War, and win back the lost territories of Alsace-Lorraine. There was also in France a culture of 'popular militarism' including enthusiasm for military parades and symbols which was not unlike that in Germany.[28]

Officially the attitude of the Republican regime towards the national army was respectful, verging on deferential. For many conservative politicians this positive attitude was undoubtedly genuinely felt; for others the display of respect for the army was a way of appeasing anti-Republican forces and maintaining the 'Holy Alliance' (*Arche Sainte*) between the French army and the Republican regime. Successive governments therefore endorsed and promoted pro-military sentiments through the educational system and in public statements. The image of the army projected in schoolbooks, public ceremonies and to army recruits was that of the expression of the power and the glory of the French Nation.

The forced cordial relations between the Republican regime and its army were strained in the extreme during the reign of the centre-left governments that came to power in the wake of the Dreyfus Affair. The administrations of Waldeck-Rousseau (1899–1902), Combes (1902–1905) and Clemenceau (1906–1909) consistently sought to republicanise the army, break the power and institutional independence of the military establishment and subject the military establishment to effective civilian control. Yet these governments also greatly depended on the loyalty and effectiveness of the army. Anti-military government policies therefore had to be carefully balanced by attempts to generate respect and military enthusiasm amongst young men during their military service.

The frequent involvement of military troops in the policing of contentious labour conflicts left both the government and the army particularly vulnerable to challenges from antimilitarist groups.[29] Antimilitarism in the form of pacifism had a long history amongst French intellectuals, but had been muted during the first two decades of the Republican era.[30] A new form of anti-militarism that targeted the French army in its new role as 'School of the Nation' emerged in the late 1880s with a number of highly critical novels and pamphlets. The challenge came primarily from middle-class authors whose descriptions of military life were largely inspired by personal experiences of military service.[31] Contrasting with the official image, caserns were depicted as places where young innocent men were kept for years in dirty, unhealthy conditions, brutalised by superiors and gradually corrupted by idleness, alcohol and prostitution. These critical views were, to some extent, supported by pamphlets written by socially conscious career officers who condemned the role that soldiers and officers had to play during labour conflicts.[32]

However, most worryingly for the Republican governments, the antimilitarist stance was taken up by the left-wing opposition during the 1890s. Antimilitarism amongst French socialists had its roots in opposition to the Second Empire. Although in principle supportive of an army based on general conscription, socialists of all shades – from Guèsde to Jaurès – saw the 'Nation in Arms' in the form of a citizen militia.[33] On the other hand, the military repression of the Paris *Commune* and the reconciliation of the Third Republic with the French officer corps, with its large proportion of nobles and 'unreconstructed' supporters of previous regimes, became obvious symbols of everything that was wrong with the Republican compromise.

Like their German counterparts, French socialists saw militarism and nationalism as a by-product of capitalism, and incompatible with the internationalist aspirations of the socialist movement. Such abstract connections were perhaps difficult to communicate to workers who had only recently made the transition from traditional rural areas and who had no previous involvement in political battles, or any personal experience of the repression of the *Commune*. Yet the shooting of fourteen striking workers at Fourmies on May Day 1891 gave political credibility to socialist claims that the new Republic was not *their* Republic and that workers were ordered to sacrifice their lives for the interests of great capital. This view was only strengthened by the continuous military involvement in the policing of labour disputes. It was therefore easy for socialists to target young workers and soldiers with their anti-militarist pamphlets and publications.[34]

In 1902 the communist trade union *Confédération générale du travail* (C.G.T.) issued a booklet by Georges Yvetot entitled 'The New Soldier's Manual', which was widely distributed amongst young men. By 1908, the manual was already in its sixteenth edition and more than half a million copies had been printed.[35] In addition to arguments about the immorality of war and the negative effects that military life had on the morality and health of young men, Yvetot argued that the Republic had no right to demand young conscripts to sacrifice their lives for the defence of the Fatherland since 'proletarians have no fatherland' and as proletarians they had nothing to defend. Most damaging for discipline amongst young conscripts, Yvetot encouraged soldiers to refuse to shoot at striking workers, and to 'go on strike' (i.e. refuse to obey orders) if asked to shoot at fellow workers.[36]

The effect of this anti-militarist agitation is difficult to measure. However, it most probably increased the longstanding and widespread aversion amongst French youths against enrolling in the army which Eugen Weber observed.[37] In 1911, War Minister Messimy presented statistics of desertion amongst conscripts which horrified the members of the National Assembly: during the decade 1890–1900, there were roughly 1,900 registered incidents of desertion amongst French conscripts, while between 1909 and 1911 there were 2,600 registered military deserters. During the same years 80,000 young men were wanted by the authorities for failing to turn up for military service.[38]

Thus the use of troops for the policing of protest was politically far more damaging and dangerous for the French Republic than for the German Empire. It seriously risked jeopardising the fragile political compromise upon which the Republican regime rested and exacerbated the potential for alienation amongst industrial workers towards the army and towards the Republican institutions it served. Politically, the links between the Republican government and the French army were weak and controversial; much political capital could be made, both from the left-wing opposition and from pro-military groups, by playing on the potential conflicts between the regime and its army. Military participation in the maintenance of public order was therefore politically more sensitive than in the German Empire, where the government and the Prussian army formed a solid coalition in the face of any public criticism.

French civilian and military authorities: constitutional position and institutional framework

When the French Third Republic was established as the only viable compromise in a deeply divided nation, the new Republic needed an army that was loyal to the extent that the government could count upon its assistance when requested. The French officer corps had served six consecutive regimes in eighty years, and its members were overwhelmingly unsympathetic to the Republic. The new regime needed to submit the armed forces to close political control in order to prevent the military establishment becoming an entity that pursued its own policies and interfered in domestic politics. With the coups of Napoleon in 1799 and of Louis Napoleon in 1851 in mind, there was a perceived need for distributing authority over the armed forces between several political authorities, so that no particular office-holder could single-handedly use the army for his own political purposes.

The constitutional position of the French army and the organisation of civilian and military authorities reflect these dilemmas. The distribution of powers between the armed forces and the political and administrative institutions had to be a compromise between groups who favoured civilian supremacy and others who wanted to maintain a high degree of independence for the military institutions. Due to the fragile political basis of the Republican regime, the relationship with the army was based on a series of compromises. One of these was that French officers were not made to swear an oath of allegiance to the Republican Constitution. Unlike the controversies triggered in Germany over the issue of officers swearing allegiance to the Imperial Constitution,[39] the question did not generate much political debate in France because there was already a series of legal provisions for holding military officers to account.

According to the Constitution of the Third Republic, the President was only nominally the chief of the army. It was the war minister who was supreme commander and accountable to the National Assembly.[40] The French war minister could not act without the consent of the National Assembly, and senior commanders had no authority to act without an explicit order from a civilian authority. Unlike Prussian officers, the French officers were subject to ordinary criminal law, which overruled orders from a superior. Moreover, commanders and officers could be prosecuted for refusing to deliver assistance when requested by a civilian authority.[41]

French officers in active service were not entitled to vote and were barred from active participation in politics.[42] Nevertheless, during the first decades of the Republic, with conservative and sometimes reluctant Republicans in power, retired military commanders played a significant role in politics as ministers, senators, ambassadors and, in the case of General Macmahon, as President of the Republic. Over the following three decades, as Republican institutions were strengthened, the influence of the military establishment on civilian affairs was significantly weakened. With the Dreyfus Affair, and the subsequent rise to power in 1899 of centre-left Radical Republicans, the military establishment became increasingly defensive, struggling to maintain what remained of their institutional independence, official status, and authority of command.

The French military establishment did not constitute a State within the State with a degree of independence coming anywhere near the position of the military establishment in Prussia. Nevertheless, despite the restrictive legal boundaries around the French army, the army still could still put formidable pressure on a regime that could not operate without a working relationship with the military forces. Within the restricted boundaries of the French system, it was therefore the power balance and cooperation between the military establishment and the government in place – as much as the formal legislation – that shaped the domestic role of the French army.

The organisation of French civilian and military authorities at the regional and local levels

French civilian administration was organised according to the highly centralised Napoleonic model where most important matters at regional level were handled by government-appointed civil servants, accountable only to the Interior Minister. French territory was divided into eighty-nine *départements* each administered by a prefect. Each *département* was then subdivided into between four and six *arrondissements* each headed by a sub-prefect.

Parallel to the civilian administration, the army was also organised to cover the entire national territory. This was the Prussian model, adopted by the French after the defeat by the Prussians in 1870–1871. The French territory was divided into eighteen military regions each covering between two and four *départements*. Each military region hosted an 'army corps', under the command of a senior general holding the post as army corps commander.[43]

The 1st Military Region covered the two *départements* 'Nord' and 'Pas-de-Calais' with headquarters in the main garrison of Lille. This town was also the centre for the civilian administration of the *département* 'Nord' whilst the prefect of 'Pas-de-Calais' was based in Arras.

Formally the relationship between civilian and military authorities at the *départemental* and local levels was based on two principles. The main one was the supremacy of the civilian authorities and the strict prohibition of military commanders to intervene in civilian affairs unless explicitly requested by a civilian authority. The position of the prefect, as the representative of the Interior Minister, also allowed him to determine in detail the relationship military officers could have with local civilian society.[44] Prefects held ultimate authority to request troops – because they could cancel any requisition issued by an inferior civilian authority. In addition they had authority to send back troops whenever they thought it appropriate – even if the military authorities might have wished to withdraw at a different moment.[45] Together with the legal obligation of French military commanders to act upon requisitions from a civilian authority, the prefect was in a favourable position to remain in control even when military troops were involved in public order maintenance.

The other principle was the strict separation of the military organisation from civilian influence in internal military matters. This also meant that military commanders formally had full authority to determine all means and measures whenever troops were mobilised, whether for foreign defence or when requested for maintaining and restoring public order. Thus, according to the legislation, the prefects determined whether and when the troops were to be present, the military commander determined how the troops were to operate. In reality the decisions within both areas were intertwined, even if army corps commanders occasionally insisted that the troops were not 'at the disposition of the civilian authorities'.[46]

French legislation on maintenance of public order

The basic French laws on maintenance of order dated from 1791, detailing the distribution of powers and stating the obligations of civilian and military authorities after the collapse of the Old Regime. Since the late 18th century, the French legislation clearly stated that military commanders could only act when formally requested by a civilian authority,[47] but was very non-specific about which civilian authorities could legally request the army. This was only specified by a series of decrees and instructions dating from the 1890s and early 20th century. These defined the civilian authorities who were formally entitled to issue requests for military assistance, notably prefects and sub-prefects, but included mayors, deputy mayors, local magistrates and police authorities as well.[48] In practice, it was the prefects and sub-prefects who carried the main responsibility for military involvement.[49]

The 18th century legislation allowed for military involvement in the apprehension of criminals as well as in the maintenance of public order.[50] The decrees dating from the Third Republic, by contrast, limited its scope to the maintenance of order, including the protection of persons or property (the phrase used for the justification of a military presence at labour conflicts) and to military participation in the implementation of the government's policies.[51]

Another set of legislation, dating from the immediate aftermath of the popular rebellion of May–June 1848, gave the authorities discretionary powers to declare as illegal any activity taking place in a public space, and to break it up with force, if necessary. This meant that police, *gendarmerie* or military troops could legally intervene with armed force against civilians for simply holding a public gathering.[52] While the 1848 law restricted the right of public gatherings, it also extended the procedures to be followed before forceful intervention: force could only be used after clear warnings had been issued and peaceful bystanders should be given sufficient time to get away.[53]

During the Third Republic the legal provisions allowing the authorities to determine the right to public gatherings became central in the struggle over public space. The right to demonstrate in public was not recognised by French legislation until 1935,[54] but marches and gatherings were increasingly tolerated. Nevertheless throughout the period 1890–1914, the 1848 law, as well as various traffic regulations, were still used extensively to justify breaking up marches and demonstrations.

Most of the legislation on military participation in the maintenance of public order was already in place by the establishment of the Third

Republic. However the particularly frequent use of troops during the late 19th and early 20th centuries put civil-military cooperation on policing issues in a different context from under previous regimes. In 1903, when new legislation was introduced on the requisition of additional *gendarmerie* forces,[55] it was followed by two sets of instructions of 1903 and 1907 on military participation in the maintenance of public order.[56] Rather than establishing a new basis for military involvement, those instructions updated and specified already existing rules. In the legislation from the early 20th century, priority was given to the provisions concerning cooperation between civilian and military authorities, rather than stressing the strict distribution of powers. This is important because the civil-military relationship by the early 20th century was increasingly characterised by inter-institutional cooperation that developed between 1890 and 1914.[57]

The constitutional position of the Prussian army

Whilst the relationship between the French Republic and its army rested on a fragile compromise, the Prussian army and the Imperial regime formed a solid coalition against attempts to upset the existing social and political order. In historical debates on the nature of the German Empire there is general consensus in describing it as a militarised state system. Thus both Nipperdey and Wehler, whose monumental interpretations of the German Empire mark opposite poles in the historiography of the 1990s, describe the German Empire as a militarised state.[58] No matter whether the position of the Prussian army outside the constitution is viewed as merely a starting point from which the system might have gradually evolved, or whether it was a fundamental flaw that kept political structures fatally out of step with social and economic structures, the relationship between military and civilian authorities was a central problem in the transition of the German state away from absolutism, and the question dominated the political agenda throughout the Imperial era.

With the establishment of the German Empire under Prussian hegemony, the formal distribution of powers between civilian and military authorities was clearly to the advantage of the latter. Due to the federal character of the German Empire, there were some differences in the distribution of powers between civilian and military authorities in each of the German states. However, in the states where previously independent army organisations were incorporated in the Prussian army – notably Saxony, Württemberg and Baden – it was the Prussian rules for civil-military relations that prevailed. It was only in Bavaria, where the army remained independent of the Prussian military organisation, that the officers were subjected to the Bavarian Constitution, including submission to a politically accountable war minister.

Until the first Prussian Constitution of 1850, the civilian and military representatives at regional level had been two branches of the same monarchical authority. In the Prussian Constitution the civilian administration was detached from direct monarchical control and placed under an interior minister who was politically accountable to the Prussian Diet. The military commanders, however, remained accountable only to the monarch. With the establishment of the German Empire under Prussian hegemony, the *Kaiser*'s unrestricted authority of command remained as a legacy from the absolutist era. It was a constitutional compromise that crucially shaped the Imperial system. Any attempt to put constitutional restrictions on the military organisation or place it under any form of civilian control was obstructed by Wilhelm I, who was fiercely opposed to renouncing any part of his authority over the armed forces.

According to the Imperial Constitution, the army was under full command of the *Kaiser* in war as in peace and all troops were under an obligation to carry out any order coming from the *Kaiser*; he was empowered to declare and conduct war and to intervene with military troops against civilians without counter-signature from any minister.[59] Only if Prussian troops were deployed in non-Prussian areas was a counter-signature required from the responsible minister of the federal state. The *Kaiser* was also empowered to declare a state of siege in any part of the Empire, whereby the civil rights granted by the Constitution would be invalidated and civilian society would come under direct military rule.[60]

Historians have paid much attention to the extra-constitutional position of the officer corps and the right of army corps commanders to declare a provisional military state of siege.[61] These constitutional peculiarities became of significance during the Wilhelmine period, when the most serious challenge to the Constitution came from Wilhelm II and his military entourage persistently threatening to close the *Reichstag* with help from the army in order to establish Wilhelm's 'Personal Rule'. This was all the more serious since Prussian officers were not subject to ordinary criminal law. Their only obligation was to obey orders coming from the military hierarchy, and they could not be prosecuted if they acted against the Constitution on the order of the *Kaiser*.

The only Prussian officer who was under a formal obligation to respect the Imperial Constitution was the war minister. However, his position both in relation to the *Reichstag* and to the military organisation was such that his personal obligation to respect the Constitution had no implications for the rest of the army. Technically the war minister in Berlin was minister only for the Prussian army. Accordingly, he was politically accountable to the Prussian Diet, but not to the Imperial *Reichstag*. The Prussian war minister would appear before the *Reichstag* to give information on military administrative issues, but he was under no obligation to answer questions. Accordingly the *Reichstag* had no other control or influence over matters concerning the army than through the voting of the military budget every seven years.

In relation to the military organisation, the powers of the war minister were limited since the Ministry dealt primarily with administrative matters. The politically influential sections of the army, such as the Military Cabinet, the General Staff and the commanders of the military regions were outside the control of the War Ministry. Nor did the war minister hold any authority of command. This was a matter entirely in the hands of the *Kaiser* and the powerful army corps commanders. On questions concerning military involvement in the policing of protest, these senior generals enjoyed immediate access to the monarch: they reported directly to him and acted in his name only. The war minister could issue recommendations, but the general commanders were under no obligation to follow these recommendations; similarly the war minister had no direct influence on the use of troops.

The Prussian military organisation and legal framework for the requisition of military assistance

Despite the dissimilarities between the German-Prussian system and the distribution of powers between civilian and military authorities within the French Republic, there were many parallels, both in terms of the organisation of civilian and military authorities at the provincial level and in terms of the legislation that defined when and how troops could be requested for policing purposes.

Since the reorganisation of the Prussian State in the early 19th century, the Prussian provincial administration was organised on the basis of the centralised Napoleonic model. Within each of the twelve Prussian provinces the civilian administration and the army constituted two parallel bodies. The civilian administration of each province was headed by a Province Governor (*Oberpräsident*), who was the civilian counterpart to the general commanding the army corps of the province. The civilian administration at the provincial level was divided into thirty-four districts – three or four within each province – each administered by a District Governor (*Regierungspräsident*). At the local level, Prussia's 491 *Kreise* were administered by Local Governors (*Landräte*) who constituted the authority immediately above the locally elected municipal authorities. All the civil servants in charge of the provincial administration were appointed by, and were accountable to, the Prussian interior minister.

As in France, the early Prussian legislation on military participation in the maintenance of public order dated from the late 18th century. The regulations of 1798 on military intervention against riots and gatherings were issued as a specification of some general provision in the Prussian General Code (*Allgemeines Landrecht*) of 1794.[62] Almost the entire body of laws and decrees concerning military involvement in internal peacekeeping and military states of siege dated from the period prior to 1871, with the Imperial Constitution as the latest contribution.[63]

The fundamental principles for requisitioning troops in Prussia shared many features with French legislation in terms of the legal justification for mobilising troops for the policing of protest. The justification for calling for military assistance to maintain the public order was as vague as the French legislation, and like their French counterparts, Prussian authorities held important discretionary powers. Troops could legally be requested for almost any conceivable situation, including brawls, riots and internal unrest (*Tumulte, Excesse, innerer Unruhen*), as well as simple gatherings in public (*Aufläufe*).[64] Troops could also be requested to help civilian authorities in cases of natural catastrophe.[65]

The Prussian legislation also shared many basic features with French legislation in terms of the authorities that could legally request military assistance. While the 1798 regulations were very unspecific in defining the authorities entitled to request military assistance, subsequent cabinet orders stipulated that contacts with military authorities were to pass through the 'civilian administration'.[66] By the 1820s and 1830, it was established practice that contacts with military authorities were to be made by the provincial administration, i.e. the Local Governor, the District Governor, or the Province Governor.[67] That troops could only intervene when formally requested by a 'civilian administration' was confirmed by the Prussian Constitution of 1850 and the 1851 service regulations concerning military use of weapons.[68] However, whether 'the civilian administration' could also include municipal authorities and local police authorities was not entirely clear. As late as 1904, the Province Governors of Westphalia and the Rhine Province discussed with the Prussian Interior Ministry whether city mayors and police authorities could also issue a requisition for military assistance in case of extreme urgency.[69] The following year, during the great miners' strike of 1905, pressure for military intervention from the municipal authorities and local police chiefs was seen as a risk to effective implementation of the policing measures. In the aftermath of the strike, the exclusion of local authorities from access to military requisition was therefore confirmed.[70]

As in France, organisation at the regional level of the Prussian civilian administration and the army was based on strict separation of the military organisation from civilian influence. Although the civilian and military authorities were encouraged to cooperate, the conditions and nature of the cooperation was not formally stated. Within the legal framework there was plenty of room for close cooperation on a wide range of issues, but the legislation left the civilian and military authorities to determine between themselves the extent and conditions of that cooperation.

At the same time, Prussian legislation on military participation in the policing of civilian society was less detailed than the French, and important areas of the law were left open to interpretation. Sometimes old provisions, which had never been formally abolished, offered instructions and regulations which could be used to overrule or counteract more recent legislation. Most famously, the Prussian service regulations on military use of weapons, issued by the War Ministry in 1899, included a Cabinet Order that was no longer recognised as valid by the civilian administration[71] – as became obvious during the Zabern Affair of 1913.[72]

The relationship between the provincial administration and the military authorities was characterised by a vast grey zone within which any practical detail had to be negotiated between the senior civil servants and military commanders. Over the years, civil-military cooperation became gradually confined by established bureaucratic practice and shaped by the personal inclination of those who were at the time army corps commander or province and district governor.

The powers of French and Prussian general commanders

While there were many similarities in the French and Prussian legislation on military participation, there were quite significant differences in the powers attributed to the French and Prussian military commanders. It is important to note, however, that the bureaucratic practices that developed between 1890 and 1914 in military involvement, to some extent limited the practical implications of some of the most significant differences between the powers of French and Prussian military commanders.

The powers granted to Prussian commanders were far more extensive than those of French commanders. When involved in policing tasks, French military authorities were only in command of the military troops. Their Prussian counterparts, by contrast, were in charge of all policing measures concerning the military troops as well as those concerning police and *gendarmerie* forces, who all came under direct military command from the moment a requisition was issued. Thus, when Prussian civilian authorities decided to call for military assistance they lost all influence over the means and measures by which they handled the situation, including even the use of police and *gendarmerie*.

As important for the power balance between civilian and military authorities over the maintenance of public order was the fact that the Prussian commanders were under no obligation to act upon a request from the civilian authorities for military assistance. Unlike the French commanders, who were under legal obligation to carry out any requisition issued by a civilian authority, without discussing the appropriateness of intervening with military troops, the Prussian military commanders might refuse to deliver troops, if they considered that the situation was not sufficiently serious for military involvement.

In practice, the Prussian commanders' right to refuse to deliver troops when requested was rarely used. The military authorities tended to follow the requisitions issued by the civilian administration, sometimes grudgingly, often not to the extent that the civilian authorities wished, but no incident has been found where a request from a district or province governor was flatly rejected. However, it was undoubtedly a strong reason for seeking ways of policing protest that reduced to a minimum their dependency on military assistance.

Another notable difference between the position of French and Prussian commanders was the right of Prussian commanders to declare a provisional military stage of siege in situations of emergency.[73] Under a state of siege all civilian authorities would immediately be transferred to the military commander.[74] In 1874, Bismarck sought unsuccessfully to integrate these provisions from the Prussian legislation into the Imperial military legislation.[75] The army corps commanders' right to declare a state of siege was not a precondition for a *coup*, given that the German constitution already entitled the *Kaiser* to declare a military state of siege and to mobilise the army without the consent of the *Reichstag*. Yet, in the political climate of the early Wilhelmine era, the army corps commanders' right to declare a state of siege without the consent of the civilian authorities certainly added to the impression that existing democratic institutions were undermined by the powerful position of the army.

It is important to note that the military commanders' right to declare a state of siege was never used in practice without the consent of the civilian administration.[76] During the Imperial era there were only two incidents of a declaration of state of siege: in Königshütte in 1871 and in Bielefeld in

1885. On both occasions, the declaration was made by the local military authorities on the explicit request of the provincial administration.[77] Indirectly, however, the legal position of the military commanders shaped civil-military relations because civilian authorities were painfully aware of their inability to control or limit the actions and measures that a military commander might find appropriate. That military commanders preferred not to be restricted by legal niceties when they intervened against civilians was declared often enough by senior generals and by the *Kaiser*; similarly, all known military instructions for large-scale military intervention in case of popular revolt are based on the assumption that a military state of siege had been declared.[78]

In addition, Prussian military commanders were empowered – or at least believed they were – to intervene against civilian unrest even without being formally requested by a civilian authority. The right to intervene on their own initiative was granted by a Cabinet Order of 1820 and was maintained in the Military Service Regulations issued by the War Ministry in 1899. However, throughout most of the 19th century, right up until the eve of the First World War, the provision was never used.[79]

In November 1913, when a local military commander in the Alsacian town of Zabern allowed his soldiers to attack a local demonstration without being formally requested by the civilian authorities, he justified this step by referring to the Military Service Regulations. It came as a complete surprise to the public, to the *Reichstag* and to the civilian authorities that military commanders were apparently entitled to bypass the civilian authorities and intervene against civilians on their own initiative.[80] The legality of this clause was subsequently challenged by legal experts, who argued that the provisions from the cabinet order of 1820 were overruled by Article 36 in the Prussian constitution of 1851, and in any case a Prussian cabinet order from 1820 was in no circumstances valid in Alsace-Lorraine.

The Zabern Affair developed into the one of the most serious public attacks on the military establishment during the Imperial era and resulted in the removal of the infamous paragraph from the military service regulations. Historians have disagreed about whether the Zabern Affair showed that the Prussian army by 1913 was still beyond civilian control and entitled to define its rules of engagement without any consideration of constitutional provisions for civil rights,[81] or whether the incident demonstrated the limits of what the Prussian army could get away with.[82] As for the Prussian military commander's right to intervene against civilians on his own initiative, it seems that by 1913 this only existed as long as it was not implemented. The moment a commander tried to make use of it, it had to be abolished in the face of public outcry.

The legal, institutional and political context of military involvement in protest policing

When comparing the use of troops in Imperial Germany with Republican France it is important to make a clear distinction between the formal legislation and practice. The French and Prussian legislations were based on similar principles: both operated with numerous restrictions around activities that were allowed to take place in public, and granted extended discretionary powers to public authorities to intervene against any form of gathering in public.

The French and Prussian legislation both granted the right to call for military assistance to municipal authorities as well as to the civilian administrators appointed by the Interior Ministry; in practice however, any contact to the military authorities increasingly went through the civil servants of the provincial and *départemental* administration. Within the Prussian system the mobilisation of troops also depended on the consent of the individual military commander.

The extended powers granted to Prussian commanders, as well as their institutional independence in relation to the provincial administration, constituted the most significant difference from the French system. In practice, however, the Prussian commanders' extended powers had only limited implications because they were so rarely used.

In France there were many formal restrictions around the military commanders; yet, some French commanders – particularly those who served in the very turbulent areas – acquired significant influence over the development and implementation of policing measures through cooperation with their civilian counterparts.

In both countries, there were concerns for the detrimental effects that frequent military involvement in protest policing might have in terms of alienating the working class, and undermining the morale and loyalty of conscript soldiers. However, the French Republic and its army were far more vulnerable than their Prussian counterparts to the risk of undermining the political legitimacy of the regime as well as the prestige and effective functioning of the national army. From a political point of view, it was therefore the French authorities – civilian and military – who had the most pressing reasons for limiting the use of troops against civilians.

Notes

[1] Funk (1986) has amply shown the correlation between the strengthening of the notion of the *Rechtsstaat* and the gradual marginalisation from everyday policing.

[2] See details Chapter 7.

[3] All authoritative studies on the Prussian army of the Imperial era demonstrate the particularly extended degree of institutional independence of the various branches of the military organisation. (Gerhard Ritter (1972) vol. 1, pp. 161–185; Craig (1955) pp. 219–232; Demeter (1965) pp. 157–160; Messerschmidt (1979) pp. 287–347. In contrast, the French army of the Third Republic is often seen as particularly constrained by constitutional restrictions, even if opinions differ between those who stress the limitations around the military establishment of the Third Republic and the political attempts to break the institutional independence of the army (Girardet (1953) pp. 257–266; Serman (1982)) and those who focus on the possibilities for political influence and areas of some degree of institutional self-determination of the French army (Ralston (1967); Carrot (1990) p. 60).

[4] In 1892, War Minister General von Gossler and the newly appointed Chief of the General Staff von Waldersee issued a secret memorandum suggesting the formation of a small professional army that could ensure the internal order. The concerns about the possible influence of Social Democratic ideas amongst the army recruits only increased as the army had to give up relying solely on recruits from rural areas. (Wehler (1985) pp. 157–158; Berghahn (1993) pp. 28–29). For France, see Chapter 3.

[5] Alfred Vagts, *A History of Militarism*, London: Hollis & Carter, 1959, p. 217.

[6] Law of 15–17 July 1889 establishing the three-year conscription.

[7] Serman (1982) p. 60.

[8] In June 1907, after a number of incidents of subordination amongst conscript soldiers during major protests amongst wine growers in the south of France, two senior generals mentioned the regional conscription as the real cause of such incidents rather than influence of antimilitarism. (Interview with General Donop, *La France Militaire*, 13 June 1907; similarly a front page article by General Proudhomme 'Les incidents du 100e' *La France Militaire*, 15 June 1907.)

[9] Vagts (1959) p. 217.

[10] Wehler (1995) p. 1123.

[11] Girardet (1953) pp. 54–55; Richard D. Challener, *The French Theory of the Nation in Arms, 1866–1939*, New York, 1955, p. 24.

[12] Law of 27 July 1872 on the recruitment of officers and soldiers; Law of 6 August 1873 on the organisation of the army.

[13] This was also the main objection from Thiers during the debate about the reorganisation of the French army 1871–1873. Jauffret (1983) pp. 100–101; Gerd Krumeich, 'Zur Problematik des Konzepts der "nation armée" in Frankreich', *Militärgeschichtliche Mitteilungen*, vol. 2, 1980, pp. 37–39; idem. 'Zur Entwicklung des "nation armée" in Frankreich bis zum Ersten Weltkrieg', in R. G. Foerster (ed.), *Die Wehrpflicht: Entstehung, Erscheinungsformen und politisch-militärische Wirkung*, Munich: Oldenburg, 1994, p. 141.

[14] Krumeich (1994) pp. 142–143.

[15] Jean Jaurès, *L'Armée nouvelle: Œuvres de Jean Jaurès, tome IV*, Paris: Rieder, 1932, (first published 1911), p. 460, Article 16 of his proposition for a new army organisation.

[16] Jauffret (1983) p. 100; Bruneteaux (1996) p. 32.

[17] Colmar von der Goltz, *Das Volk im Waffen. Ein Buch über das Heerwesen*, Berlin: Mittler, 1890, (first published 1883).

[18] Imperial Constitution of 1871 Article 64. In 1891, Wilhelm II famously declared in front of a group of recruits that he might one day order them to shoot on their parents and brothers, but even then they were expected to follow orders blindly. (cit. Klückmann (1978) p. 21.)

[19] A similar view was expressed by General von Waldersee during a major strike amongst dock workers in Hamburg 1896–1897 (*Denkwürdigkeiten des General-Feldmarschalls Alfred von Waldersee*, Berlin: Mittler, 1922, entry of 2 December 1896). See also pp. 73–75.

[20] In addition to many studies on popular militarism in the German Empire by Förster (1985); Rohkrämer (1990); Verhey (2000), Jacob Vogel's recent comparison of popular militarism in the German Empire and the French Third Republic confirms the particularly pervasive nature of militarism amongst 'ordinary' Germans (Vogel (1997) p. 289).

[21] Stargardt (1994) p. 3.

[22] Kitchen (1968) p. 184; Blackburn (1997) p. 378.

[23] Ludwig Quidde, *Der Militarismus im heutigen deutschen Reich*, Stuttgart, 1893; Ludwig Quidde, *Caligula: Schriften über Militarismus und Pazifismus*, Frankfurt am Main: Campus, 1977, (first published 1894).

[24] Stargardt (1994) p. 3; Roger Chickering, *Imperial Germany and a World without War*, Princeton: Princeton University Press, 1975, pp. 245–253.

[25] Chickering (1975) pp. 384–385.

[26] Liebknecht (1907); Rosa Luxemburg, 'Miliz und Militarismus', in *Leipziger Volkszeitung*, 25 February 1899; idem., *Die Akkumulation des Kapitals*, Berlin, 1913.

[27] August Bebel, *Nicht stehendes Heer sondern Volkswehr!*, London, New York: Garland, 1972, (first published 1898).

[28] Vogel (1997) p. 280ff.

[29] Paul Miller, *From Revolutionaries to Citizens: Antimilitarism in France, 1870-1914*, Durham, NJ.: Duke University Press, 2002.

[30] Wesseling (2000) pp. 11–16.

[31] Paul Bonnerain, *Autour de la caserne*, Paris, 1885; Abel Hermant, *Le Cavalier Miserey, 21e Chasseurs. Moeurs militaires contemporaines*, Paris: G. Charpentier, 1887; Henry Fèvre, *Au Port d'armes*, Paris, 1887; Lucien Descaves, *Les Sous-Offs, roman militaire*, Paris: Tresse & Stock, 1889; Georges Darrien, *Biribi*, Paris, 1890; A. Dumont, *Les Offs, roman de moeurs militaries*, Paris, 1891.

[32] Le Lieutenant Z., *L'armée aux grèves: grève générale des mineurs, oct.–nov. 1902*, Paris: Société nouvelle de librairie, 1904; Capitaine E. Laurent, *Impressions de grève*, Paris: Charles-Lavauzelle, 1904.

[33] Jaurès (1911); Michel Winock, 'Socialisme et Patriotisme en France (1891–1894)', *Revue d'histoire moderne et contemporaine*, vol. 20, 1973 pp. 376–379.

[34] Urbain Gohier, *L'armée contre la nation*, Paris: Revue Blanche, 1898; Gustave Hervé, (numerous articles in *La Guerre Sociale*); Raoul Verfeuil, *Pourquoi nous*

sommes anti-militaristes, Villeneuve-Saint-Georges, 1913. Similarly frequent articles in socialist publications such as *Les temps nouveaux, La guerre sociale* or *Le sou du soldat* that specifically addressed itself to conscript soldiers.

[35] Becker (1973) p. 67.

[36] Georges Yvetot, *Nouveau mauel du soldat. Patrie, l'Armée, la Guerre*, Paris, 1902.

[37] Eugen Weber, *Peasants into Frenchmen*, Stanford: Stanford University Press, 1976, pp. 292–302.

[38] Becker (1973) p. 37.

[39] Craig (1955) pp. 122–125; Manfred Messerschmidt, 'Die Armee in Staat und Gesellschaft – Die Bismarckzeit', in Michael Sturmer (ed.), *Das kaiserliche Deutschland*, Düsseldorf: Droste, 1970, p. 89.

[40] Constitutional law of 25 February 1875, Articles 3 & 6.

[41] French Penal Code, Article 234.

[42] Article 7 of the Law of 27 July 1872 on military recruitment prohibited French officers in active service from voting in elections; the Law of 30 November 1875 barred them from being deputies to the National Assembly; finally a law of 22 April 1884 took away their previous access to be members of the French Senate.

[43] Law of 24 July 1873, Article 8.

[44] See Chapter 8.

[45] Law of 27 July–3 August 1791; Decree of 4 October 1891, Articles 17–18.

[46] M[ilitary] A[rchive], Vincennes, 1st A.C. /2.I.2: Confidential letter of 25 June 1885, from General Billot, army corps commander in Lille to the Commander of the Second Division. See also MA, Vincennes, 1st A.C. /2.I.330: *Instruction en cas de grèves ou de troubles* (15 February 1893) issued by General de France.

[47] Law of 27 July–3 August 1791 on requisition of public forces, Article 20.

[48] Decree of 4 October 1891 on rules for military presence in garrison towns and in non-garrison towns, Article 64; Instructions of 24 June 1903 on the requisition of the armed forces, Article 3; Instructions of 20–31 August 1907 on the participation of the army in the maintenance of public order, Article 2.

[49] See Chapter 7.

[50] Law of 27 July–3 August 1791 on requisition of public forces, Articles 1 & 2.

[51] Decree of 4 October 1891 on rules for military presence in garrison towns and in non-garrison towns, Article 63; Instructions of 24 June 1903 on the requisition of the armed forces, Article 4; Instructions of 20–31 August 1907 on the participation of the army in the maintenance of public order, Article 7.

[52] Law of 7 June 1848 on crowds and gathering in public.

[53] Law of 7 June 1848 on crowds and gathering in public, Article 3.

[54] Law decree of 23 October 1935 abolishing the Article 6 of the 'Naquet Law'.

[55] Decree of 20 May 1903 on the requisition of the *gendarmerie*.

[56] Instructions of 24 June 1903 on military participation in the maintenance of public order; Instructions of 20 August and of 18 October 1907 on military participation in the maintenance of public order.

[57] See further analysis Chapter 9.

[58] Nipperdey (1992) p. 201; Wehler (1995), pp. 873–874.

58   Soldiers as Police

[59] Imperial Constitution of 1871, Articles 63 & 64.
[60] Imperial Constitution of 1871, Articles 66 & 68.
[61] Demeter (1965) pp. 160–161; Ritter (1972) vol. 1, pp. 176–185 & Vol. 2, pp. 124–128; Craig (1955) pp. 122–125, 241–251; Klückmann (1978) pp. 13–15, 31–35; Messerschmidt (1979) pp. 290–295, 307–308; Wilhelm Deist, 'Kaiser Wilhelm II. als Oberster Kriegsherr', in Wilhelm Deist (ed.), *Militär, Staat, und Gesellschaft, 1890–1945*, Freiburg: Militärgeschichtliches Forschungsamt, 1991 (3), p. 4; Wehler (1995) pp. 874, 1016–1020.
[62] Decree of 30 December 1798 on military intervention against riots and gatherings on the requisition of the civilian authorities.
[63] Cabinet Order of 17 October 1820 on military participation in the restoration of order when public tranquillity is being disturbed by riots; Law of 20 March 1837 on the military use of weapons. Specifically on the state of siege, see the Prussian Constitution of 31 January 1851, Article 111; the Law of 4 June 1851 on the state of siege; and the Imperial Constitution of 16 April 1871, Article 68.
[64] Decree of 30 December 1798, Article 1; the Prussian Constitution of 31 January 1850, Article 36.
[65] H[aupt]S[taats]A[rchiv], Münster, OP 6095 (documents 9-11): Regulations of March 1888 on the military assistance to civilian authorities in case of natural catastrophe.
[66] Decree from the Interior Ministry of 4 August 1822 and the Instructions of 31 December 1825 on administrative procedures.
[67] Lüdtke (1982) pp. 60–61; Jessen (1991) p. 41.
[68] The Prussian Constitution of 31 January 1850, Article 36; Similarly 'Instructions on the military use of weapon and on the participation of the army in the repression of unrest' of 1851.
[69] HSA, Münster, Regierung Münster, VII – 57, vol. 1 (document 197): Letter of 31 August 1904 from Interior Minister von Hammerstein to the District Governor in Münster.
[70] HSA, Münster, OP 6095 (document 78): Letter of 28 September 1906 from Interior Minister Bethmann-Hollweg to Province Governor von der Recke in Münster.
[71] Cabinet Order of 17 October 1820 on the participation of the military authorities in the restoration of order, when public tranquillity is being disturbed by riots; Decree of 17 August 1835 on the maintenance of public order.
[72] See below p. 53.
[73] Law of 4 June 1851 on Military State of Siege, Article 2.
[74] Law of 4 June 1851 on Military State of Siege, Article 4.
[75] Klückmann (1978) pp. 13–14.
[76] Ernst R. Huber, *Deutsche Verfassungsgeschichte seit 1789*, vol. III, 'Bismarck und das Reich', Stuttgart: Kohlhammer, 1963, p. 1043.
[77] Klückmann (1978) p. 31.
[78] See Chapter 10.
[79] Ernst R. Huber, *Deutsche Verfassungsgeschichte seit 1789*, Vol. IV, 'Struktur und Krisen des Kaiserreichs', Stuttgart: Kohlhammer, 1969, pp. 596–597.

[80] Schoenbaum (1982) p. 107.
[81] On this point, Nipperdey (1992), pp. 204, 234–235 and Blackburn (1997) p. 418 tend to agree with Wehler (1970) pp. 79–82; idem. (1995) p. 1129.
[82] Schoenbaum (1982) pp. 180–184.

Chapter 2

New Problems, New Priorities: Conflicting Policies in Berlin

The Prussian Interior Ministry and its policing policies: a problem of historical interpretation

In the 1870s and 1880s, the resistance to military involvement in the policing of protest in Germany came almost exclusively from the political opposition. The Social Democrats were naturally unsympathetic to soldiers being used against workers struggling to improve their humble conditions; similarly the Catholic Centre Party consistently complained about the requisition of soldiers to police religious processions and simple gatherings in public during the *Kulturkampf* of the 1870s. At the same time, ethnic minorities like the Poles in the eastern provinces, the French in Alsace-Lorraine and the Danes in Schleswig-Holstein, resented the bullying and discrimination they were subjected to by the military present in their areas. It was only in the 1890s that the domestic role of the army became a live political issue among governmental authorities, bureaucrats and army officers.

The military intervention in the first nationwide miners' strike of May 1889, together with the legalisation of the Social Democratic Party in the spring of 1890, triggered serious rethinking of existing practices for the policing of public protest. The Prussian Interior Ministry therefore began to encourage local authorities to significantly strengthen existing police and *gendarmerie* forces, particularly in the new industrial areas. The Prussian Interior Ministry — although far from liberal in its policies — also increasingly recognised the political and practical problems of military involvement in the policing of social and political protest. From the early 1890s, the Interior Ministry therefore began to recommend to the provincial administration that requisition of soldiers be limited only to situations of absolute emergency.

Historical interpretations of the demilitarisation process in Germany tend to focus very narrowly on the new policies of the Interior Ministry in explaining why military involvement in Germany decreased markedly during the Wilhelmine era. According to the main interpretations the marginalisation of the army from protest policing is described primarily as the result of the Interior Ministry's recommendation to avoid military requisition and its attempts to increase existing police and *gendarmerie* forces.[1] Accordingly, the few incidents where military troops were called upon between 1890 and 1914 are described either as failures of the demilitarisation policy or as demonstrating how far it was possible to avoid military involvement in the policing of protest.[2]

Because of the apparently unproblematic transition from military to civilian forms of maintaining public order, little attention has been paid to the question of how such an important change of practice came about. Indeed, Funk notes with some amazement that they happened within a remarkably short period of time.[3] Looking at Germany, with the development in other countries in mind, at least three aspects appear remarkable. In the first place it is notable to what extent provincial administrators actually followed recommendations from the Prussian Interior Ministry and changed well-established practices for calling upon the army. Given that protest policing was an extremely difficult area to regulate politically, with many particular interests at stake, one would expect great discrepancies between the Interior Ministry's guidelines and the measures which were actually implemented. Therefore, the very fact that the ministerial recommendations were largely followed by administrators at the provincial level calls for further explanation.

Another remarkable feature is the high level of consistency in the restraint in calling upon military assistance. The Prussian Interior Ministry adopted its demilitarisation policy in a period when social and political protest was rife and on the increase. The number of policemen and *gendarmes* increased significantly in the decades following the great miners' strike of 1889. Yet the authorities in charge of public order could never keep pace with the constant growth in the urban population. By 1914, the police and *gendarmerie* were still hopelessly inadequate, particularly in industrial areas where the population of workers had risen sharply.[4] If the Interior Ministry and the provincial administration generally refrained from calling upon the army, this was not out of their comfortable trust in the ability of the police and *gendarmerie* forces to control riots and popular unrest. One might therefore expect some discrepancy between the overall aim of avoiding military involvement and the immediate need for staying in control during highly sensitive conflicts. Nevertheless, among senior administrators at the provincial level, there was a high degree of consistency in avoiding military involvement in the policing of protest and popular unrest. Over two and a half decades, recourse to the use of the military happened on remarkably few occasions, considering the seriousness of the conflicts that took place and the limited number of policemen and *gendarmes* that were used for large-scale protests.

Finally, it is worth noting that the policy of the Interior Ministry was paralleled by initiatives from powerful forces within central government, and among the advisers close to the *Kaiser*, who worked in a different direction. Some forces within the War Ministry, many local authorities as well as great industrialists and their organisations, all pursued their particular agenda for increased military involvement in the policing of protest. The War Ministry in particular challenged the policy of demilitarisation with several initiatives that aimed to give the army a more active role in the fight against the Social Democrats. Historical research has amply shown how the central military institutions – the War Ministry and the General Staff – sought confrontation at many different levels towards anything that smacked of Social Democratism, trade unionism, or other types of organised labour activities.[5] Such heavy-handed initiatives from sections of the military establishment would almost certainly be supported by Wilhelm II, whose attitude towards social and political protest increasingly moved towards 'flog them and hang them'. The pressure for military interventionism in domestic politics became significantly less active after the turn of the 20th century when the *Kaiser* and his entourage had given up attempting to establish his 'Personal Rule'. Nevertheless the War Ministry's instructions and circulars, as well as initiatives from individual generals, continued to defend the right of the military authorities to intervene against internal enemies, and never gave up the idea of armed confrontations with the Social Democrats.

In order to understand the dynamics behind the demilitarisation of protest policing we need to look at the different positions of three key actors involved in the mobilisation of troops for policing purposes. These include the forces close to central government and the *Kaiser*, who favoured a more military approach to social and political unrest; we also need to look at those forces within the Interior Ministry and the provincial administration who sought to minimise the dependency on military assistance for the maintenance of public order. Finally we need to consider the position of the generals commanding the provincial army corps who were increasingly reluctant to become involved in the policing of protest and the surveillance of the activities of the Social Democratic Party. This lack of enthusiasm from senior military commanders at the provincial level to deliver troops for the policing of protest was crucial to the change of practice. It pushed the provincial administrators further towards relying primarily on their own forces. The policy of demilitarising the maintenance of public order was successfully implemented not least because the senior military authorities at the provincial level tended to work towards the same goal as the Interior Ministry, although for completely different reasons.

The forces favouring a military solution to maintenance of order

During the early 1890s, when the Interior Ministry began re-conceptualising the forms of protest policing away from military involvement, strong forces within the military establishment in Berlin worked in a different direction. The idea of conducting civil war against the political left was, as Wehler puts it, part of the most deeply engrained habitual thinking among the Prussian military leaders.[6] A similar line was taken by Bismarck who saw the fight against the social democratic movement not only as a matter of legislation, but of warfare.[7] This line of thought was followed by the young *Kaiser*, whose initial conciliatory stance towards the striking Westphalian miners in May 1889 was soon replaced by implacable hostility once it became clear that Bismarck's social policy did not prevent mass rallying of industrial workers around the Social Democratic Party. From the early 1890s onwards, those in favour of a confrontational line towards the Social Democrats could therefore be confident of gaining support from Wilhelm II for almost any initiative that proposed heavy measures against any form of social or political protest.

The division within the Prussian government on the broad principles for military involvement in internal security is clearly illustrated by the projects which were developed in the War Ministry between 1890 and the First World War. In the aftermath of the nationwide miners' strike of May 1889, and immediately after the abolition of the anti-Socialist legislation in March 1890, War Minister, Verdy du Vernois, issued a decree to the generals commanding the provincial army corps.[8] The decree contained a series of instructions detailing how the general commanders should keep themselves informed about Social Democratic activities within their province and prepare for military repression of open revolt.

In his decree, Verdy du Vernois made explicit that in future the general commanders bore the burdensome responsibility of the maintenance of domestic order. His recommendations comprised five main points: First, the army corps commander should keep himself informed about the organisation, publications, activities and leaders of the Social Democratic party in his province and report back to the King. Secondly, the army corps commander, having the legal authority to declare a military state of siege independently of the civilian administration, was invited to make use of this power, if he considered it appropriate in a situation of popular unrest. The declaration of a state of siege would mean that the provisions in the Prussian Constitution concerning fundamental civil rights were suspended, as well as the limitations on the authority of the military commander. It was understood that the military commanders were supposed to use this freedom to launch a crack-down on suspect persons and organisations. This becomes obvious in the light of the third key element of the decree. The decree recommended that, in case of internal unrest, all Social Democratic leaders be arrested, including members of the *Reichstag* with no regard to their parliamentary immunity. It also advised the military authorities to confiscate and close down dangerous publications. Fourth, the general commanders were supposed to prepare their troops for this type of action, and to make sure that any revolt would be stopped whilst still in its embryonic stages through a convincing display of force. Finally, Verdy du Vernois informed the Interior Minister that each general commander was held responsible for ensuring that Social Democrats did not enter the army as reservists or conscript soldiers.[9] As Deist rightly points out, this was an attempt to prepare the army for repressive actions internally, for which loyal recruits were an absolute necessity.[10]

The determination of the War Ministry to use the army in the fight against the Social Democratic party also emerges in the 'Service Regulation concerning the Military Use of Weapons', issued by the War Ministry nine years later. The first chapter of the 1899 Service Regulations describes how soldiers and officers had the absolute duty to intervene and restore order, with no consideration as to whether or not they had been formally requested to do so by a civilian authority. These provisions could easily be applied to strikes and demonstrations, where stone-throwing and even armed attacks were not uncommon. The second chapter of the Military Service Regulations establishes the conditions under which military troops could be requested, stipulating that military troops should only be mobilised in situations when public order could no longer be maintained by the police and *gendarmerie*. However, since it was left to the army corps commanders to define whether a situation was sufficiently serious for troops to be mobilised, the military authorities maintained the right to refuse in assisting the civilian authorities. The third and longest chapter concerned the conditions under which a military state of siege could be declared. In comparison with previous summaries of the existing rules, which were mainly a description of the limitations surrounding the use of weapons,[11] the 1899 Service Regulations placed emphasis on two particular elements; one was the duty of the soldier to intervene with weapons when being attacked by armed civilians; the second key element was the attention paid to the rights of the military commander to take supreme authority, even without consulting the civil authorities. Together with the Verdy du Vernois decree of 1890, the 1899 Service Regulations on the military use of weapons constituted the basis of the official policy of the War Ministry, and was constantly referred to in recommendations from the War Ministry right up until the eve of the First World War.[12]

In addition to the decrees and service regulations emanating directly from the War Ministry, three studies were recommended by the War Ministry as examples to be followed. A General Staff study from 1907 entitled 'Fighting in Insurgent Towns' provided the guiding principles of how to repress armed revolts in urban areas. The study was sent to all the province commanders. During the following years, the suggestions of the General Staff study were taken up and developed by two province commanders. One was a set of instructions from General von Bissing, army corps commander in Westphalia, issued to his subordinate commanders, entitled 'Conduct in case of internal unrest'.[13] Similarly, General von Hindenburg, army corps commander in Magdeburg, developed a series of instructions in 1908 which were implemented in practice during a major miners' strike in Mansfeld in October 1909.[14] The recommendation by the War Ministry of the General Staff Study, of the Bissing instructions and the Hindenburg instructions leaves little doubt about the continuous attempts by successive ministers to provide the army with a more active role in the repression of social unrest and political opposition.

The Bissing instructions, in particular, operated with measures that went a great deal beyond what was otherwise standard practice for domestic military interventions. These included demolishing workers' houses and using machine-guns against popular disorder. It created major public consternation and great embarrassment for the War Ministry when the Bissing instructions were leaked to the press in November 1910, and War Minister von Heeringen subsequently dissociated himself from this particular set of instructions.[15] However, the other studies and instructions remained the basis of the War Ministry's policy. A belief in the army as a key actor in the fight against the Social Democracy remained a part of War Ministry's initiatives throughout the period, which is clear from War Ministry's regulations and instructions as late as 1912.[16] Less than one month before the last great Westphalian miners' strike in March 1912, War Minister von Heeringen issued a decree to the army corps commanders which again referred to the 1907 General Staff Study and to Hindenburg's instructions as examples to be followed.[17] With direct reference to the Verdy du Vernois decree of 1890, von Heeringen yet again advised the general commanders to prepare themselves for internal military intervention. Senior commanders were again urged to inform themselves about the growth of the working population in the industrial areas and to keep an eye on the Social Democratic activities in the area.[18]

The confrontational tone and authoritarian spirit of the initiatives from successive war ministers were perfectly in tune with the political line of Wilhelm II. Any heavy-handed military action against social and political protest was almost certain to win his support. Throughout his reign, Wilhelm II was known for his dramatic rhetoric, not least when declaring his readiness to repress any social or political unrest with unrestricted military force. The incidents were many: for example in 1891, when he famously declared to a group of recruits that he might ask them to shoot their parents and brothers.[19] In 1903, the *Kaiser* began to talk about the forceful repression of the Social Democrats in terms of a 'revenge' for the Revolution of 1848.[20] Similarly, General von Waldersee reports several strong declarations of Wilhelm II, for example in 1896, when the King told Waldersee to intervene with military troops in a strike among Hamburg dock workers, even without a request from the Hamburg Senate.[21] In 1899 he declared to Eulenburg, his personal friend and adviser, that 'matters will not improve until the troops drag the Social Democratic leaders out of the *Reichstag* and gun them down'.[22] Similarly, in 1905, Wilhelm shocked the Reich Chancellor von Bülow by declaring: 'First shoot, behead and get rid of the Social Democrats, by a bloodbath if need be, and then fight a war outside...'.[23] The degree to which Wilhelm intended to carry these declarations into action has been the object of much debate, since there were often great discrepancies between his forceful statements and his actual support of heavy-handed measures. Nevertheless, the orders coming from Wilhelm during major strikes were unequivocally in favour of forceful military repression.

Rethinking maintenance of order: the policies and priorities of the Prussian Interior Ministry

This was the position from the War Ministry and the *Kaiser* that the Prussian Interior Ministry was up against when it embarked on a new approach to public order policing in the early 1890s. Initially, even among the civil servants in the Interior Ministry and the provincial administration, there was a widespread preference for effective military intervention against disturbers of the public order. The attempts to avoid military involvement in policing of labour conflicts and popular unrest began during a short period of liberalism towards industrial workers, when new forms of protest policing were part and parcel of attempts to extend Bismarck's social welfare programme of the 1880s.[24] Over the following decades the demilitarisation policy was maintained by Interior Ministers who had no sympathy for workers' grievances and who took a rather confrontational stance towards public unrest. The marginalisation of the army from maintenance of order was no longer a matter of liberalism, it was a question of the balance of power between the different branches of the Prussian State and its relationship with local authorities.

The close linkage of social welfare programmes and attempts to gain better control over the working population was nothing new in German politics. Bismarck's progressive social laws from the 1880s, that met some of the basic needs of workers, were introduced in an attempt to prevent the labouring poor from gathering around the more radical demands of Social Democrats. In May 1889, when the Prussian authorities were confronted with the first nationwide miners' strike, some of the more perceptive minds within the provincial administration and among government ministers saw the urgent need to make further concessions in order to reach a *modus vivendi* with the ever-increasing group of industrial workers. Moreover, in the early days of the strike, a certain degree of sympathy for the miners' demands could be found among political leaders in Berlin. The young Wilhelm II even agreed to receive a delegation of strikers, provided that in no way did they represent the Social Democrats nor any other workers' organisation.

One of the most progressive civil servants was Freiherr von Berlepsch, district governor in Düsseldorf. He belonged to what Kevin Repp describes as the 1890 generation, whose early career was characterised by the hopes and expectations they placed in the young *Kaiser* as the initiator of radical social reforms.[25] During the miners' strike of 1889, von Berlepsch came to play a central role in the negotiations between employers and employees, and argued that labour conflicts could no longer be dealt with through criminalisation and forceful repression.[26] In his own district, where 7,000 coal miners went on strike, he preferred to handle the situation with municipal police forces and *gendarmerie*, without requisitioning military assistance. Von Berlepsch and his colleague in Aachen were the only district governors who did not request military troops during the 1889 miners' strike.[27] Both kept postponing the moment for calling upon the army so that the crisis eventually passed without further steps becoming necessary. It emerges from his correspondence with the Interior Ministry, both during the crisis and afterwards, that he was very proud of his own manoeuvres. Similarly, von Berlepsch was fiercely opposed to the idea of declaring a state of siege.[28] Contrary to the Westphalian province governor, von Hagenmeister, who called for more troops to be sent and for a military state of siege to be declared, von Berlepsch became the most important advocate for meeting the workers' demands through negotiation and for handling the policing without involving military troops. In the immediate aftermath of the crisis, it seemed that the governmental authorities in Berlin appreciated von Berlepsch's dexterity. Whereas Hagenmeister was sacked in the middle of the crisis, von Berlepsch was first promoted to province governor of the Rhineland and was then called to Berlin less than six months later to become the head of the newly established Prussian Ministry for Trade and Industry.

The end of liberal government policies, but not of the demilitarisation policy

During the first two years as Minister for Trade and Industry, von Berlepsch introduced some important reforms in the conditions of industrial workers.[29] However, he was soon to discover that those within the Prussian government who tried to address social unrest through legislation and negotiation with workers faced stiff opposition from forces within government as well as from influential industrial pressure groups, who sought confrontation with the Social Democrats.[30] Between 1894 and 1899, the Prussian government adopted an increasingly confrontational line, with a series of initiatives aimed at fighting the Social Democratic movement through tough legislation. Moreover, believing that the existing criminal laws and the legislation on high treason were not sufficiently efficient to break the backbone of the Social Democratic Party, they wanted to provide the army with legal means to undertake searches, confiscations and imprisonments in the case of a general revolt. Conflicts increased within the Prussian government, between von Berlepsch's social policy programme and the hard-line Interior Ministers von Koeller (1894–1895) and von der Recke von der Horst (1895–1899). When von Berlepsch was gradually marginalised and finally left the government in 1896, most of his social welfare programme was abandoned.

Despite these overall changes in government policy, the Interior Ministers von Köller and von der Recke continued their attempts to demilitarise the policing of protest. The key element in the new approach to popular protest was to strengthen municipal police and *gendarmerie* forces to an extent that would allow the local or provincial administration to manage most incidents of conflict and unrest with their own forces.[31] At the same time, the Interior Ministry asked the provincial administration to cooperate with local governors and municipal police authorities in order to coordinate their forces. The aim was to improve the efficiency of the civil forces by elaborating detailed plans for municipal police forces to be transferred from calm areas to the points of conflict and for the way in which *gendarmes* should be distributed in case of major labour conflicts.[32] This type of cooperation, initiated immediately after the events of 1889, resulted in nationwide designation lists which were regularly updated throughout the later period.

There could be several reasons why hard-line Interior Ministers like von Köller and von der Recke preferred to maintain the policy of avoiding military involvement in the policing of protest. Funk dismisses the argument that the use of troops was abandoned simply because it was incompatible with military honour; however he maintains that the primary reason for the Interior Ministry's new approach was that the military solution might be dangerous for the regime.[33] Whilst this was undoubtedly an important factor, it was just as important for the Interior Ministry to disengage the provincial administration from its traditional dependence on the military authorities.

The military organisation was an awkward partner. At ministerial level, any cooperation between the Interior and the War Ministry on policing issues was problematic because the War Ministry did not have any authority over the powerful general commanders at provincial level. Moreover, the Interior Ministry and the provincial administration tended to be suspicious of the military authorities who could not be checked or prevented from acting independently of the civilian authorities.[34] On the other hand, the Interior Ministry never considered giving up the right of provincial administrators to call for military assistance as an *ultima ratio* solution. Indeed, the possibility of military intervention or a military state of siege remained ever-present in the minds of the civil servants in the Prussian Interior Ministry and the provincial administration.[35] However, the military authorities being unpredictable and uncontrollable, even hard-line Interior Ministers saw the advantages of keeping military involvement in the maintenance of order to a minimum.

Another attractive feature about demilitarising the maintenance of order was that it would strengthen the provincial administrators' control of the law-and-order measures implemented by local authorities. In policing matters, there was – as Jessen observes – a precarious balance to be struck between the self-regulation of local communities and the right of the central government to take over responsibility.[36] Although the province governors directly controlled the state police forces and the *gendarmerie*, more than fifty per cent of all policemen in Prussia belonged to municipal police forces, and for financial reasons there was no wish on the part of the Interior Ministry to take over these forces. However, where major conflicts extended over several municipalities, districts or even provinces, the province governor and his subordinate district governors would be in charge of the overall policing measures. Even if the representatives of the Interior Ministry in the provinces could not entirely control the use of municipal policemen, they were in the crucial position of coordinating the various police and *gendarmerie* units. If local authorities called upon the army, all forces, military as well as civilian, would come under the authority of the commanding general. The powers of the provincial administration in policing matters could therefore be undermined if local authorities used their right to request military assistance. The Interior Ministry could not entirely prevent local authorities from contacting the local garrison for military assistance. However, by extending the police and *gendarmerie* forces and urging the local authorities not to call upon the army except in case of extreme urgency, the Interior Ministry tried to change the practice of local authorities and gradually to reduce the military involvement in the policing of protest.

In the 1890s on a certain number of occasions the military authorities were solicited for policing purposes; however their number decreased thereafter. After 1905 there are only seven recorded incidents throughout the entire Empire where military authorities were contacted to provide assistance for the maintenance of public order.[37] Confidence in the demilitarisation policy was significantly strengthened during the second great Westphalian miners' strike of 1905. Although close to 200,000 miners went on strike, there were only minor incidents of trouble and order was ensured without any military involvement. Similarly, in January 1906, when the Social Democrats announced nationwide demonstrations calling for reform of the electoral system to the Prussian Diet, the government stressed that troops were not to be mobilised except in the case of extreme urgency.[38] In all larger towns, the troops were kept in their garrisons ready to intervene,[39] but despite great tensions and clashes between the local police and demonstrators in many towns, troops were not requested to intervene anywhere.

The Interior Ministry and the provincial administration thereby saw its belief confirmed that even situations of large-scale protest with mass gatherings could be managed without military assistance. However, during the great miners' strike of March 1912, the Westphalian mining areas were again occupied by military troops. This conflict indicated the limits of how far the Prussian authorities thought they could go before calling in the army,[40] and even critical historical accounts admit that the military intervention of March 1912 was a reasonable response to a conflict with a high potential for violence.[41]

The implications of the demilitarisation policy

Whilst the Interior Ministry had important reasons for preferring not to involve military troops in the policing of protest, this decision also placed serious limitations on its sphere of action. Policemen and *gendarmes* were not capable of providing the same level of protection of private property as military troops. Of course, those who had influence and money could normally obtain better protection than ordinary citizens or themselves pay out for a couple of *gendarmes* or private security guards.[42] Thus, wealthy citizens and industrialists got the level of protection that they were prepared to pay for. Increasingly, however, labour conflicts were not simply a local matter between individual factory, or mine, owners and their employees. Strikes and protest movements often extended over several municipalities, districts or even provinces, and thereby also became the responsibility of the provincial administration.

During major conflicts, the province and district governors in charge of coordinating the policing measures were forced to operate with a rather narrow set of policing aims, due to the scarcity of forces. Priority was given to the protection of a few sensitive points which would be covered by the permanent presence of police or *gendarmerie*. In the wider areas, they would only appear on random patrols, or when something extraordinary happened. Yet forces were stretched and the police or *gendarmerie* often arrived too late to provide any protection. At the same time, police intervened against crowds rather than against the individuals who committed violence or vandalism, because targeted policing required much more manpower.[43] Similarly, due to the scarcity of forces during labour disputes, there was little or no protection for strike-breakers outside the plant or factory. Whereas the protection of strike-breakers entering a factory or a mine remained a high priority, the personal safety of strike-breakers outside the workplace was not.

In terms of maintaining 'public order', the Interior Ministry's decision to handle chaotic and volatile situations with very limited numbers of men implied a significant risk of situations becoming out of control and degenerating into violence and riots. Even during the relatively peaceful miners' strike of January 1905, a good number of the local governors, together with mayors and the local police authorities, claimed that their forces were insufficient to ensure 'public order'.[44] The problem was that once small-scale unrest went out of control, the authorities could only restore order through repressive military means, since there was no intermediate stage between hopelessly stretched police and *gendarmerie* presence and full-scale military intervention.

The correspondence from the Prussian civil administrators shows that the leaders of the provincial administration were painfully aware of the risks connected with the policing of mass protest by forces that were obviously inadequate to handle a situation developing into riots and violence.[45] However, they accepted this risk and managed conflict after conflict as well as they could with the police and *gendarmerie* available. At the same time they reserved the option for using military action if a situation went out of control. When assessing the demilitarisation policy it is worth bearing in mind that the Interior Ministry and the heads of the provincial administration considered the very likely prospect of full-scale military repression of unrest. This was a risk that they were prepared to take in order to keep the military authorities away except for situations of extreme urgency.

The Interior Ministry's demilitarisation policy also seriously limited the ability of the central government to support industrial interests against disruption by striking workers. Strikes and disruption in the mining industry and heavy industry were damaging not only for the particular interests of industrial magnates but for the government itself, since a substantial number of mines in the Ruhr area and Saarland were state owned. Any long-lasting miners' strike also placed national security at serious risk, due to the strong dependence of foreign defence on coal and steel production. By demilitarising the maintenance of internal order, the Prussian Interior Ministry thus opted for a form of policing that was not only against the interests of its traditional supporters, but also in certain cases against the financial and military interests of the Prussian State.

Military attempts to limit the use of troops against civilians

If the handling of public protest underwent significant transformation during the 1890s, the gradual demilitarisation of policing was only partly due to the recommendations from the Interior Ministry and their implementation by the provincial administration. Just as important was the fact that the generals commanding the provincial army corps became increasingly reluctant to pursue their traditional task of ensuring internal order.

Officially, military leaders kept affirming their readiness to intervene with military force against those who disturbed public order. In 1911, War Minister von Heeringen declared that the army would regard it as its duty to wage internal war, if Social Democratic activities made such a step necessary.[46] As late as 1914, in the wake of the Zabern Affair, the War

Minister, General von Falkenheyn, declared in the *Reichstag* that the role of the army was 'the secure defence of peace at home and abroad.'[47]

On the other hand, however, successive war ministers publicly described the involvement in protest policing as a disagreeable duty. In 1898 during a debate in the *Reichstag*, the Social Democratic leader August Bebel sharply criticised the Verdy du Vernois decree which had been leaked to the press;[48] the War Minister, Bronsart von Schellendorff, immediately replied that the army would prefer to leave the burdensome task of fighting with workers in the street to the police.[49] Similarly in 1910, when General von Bissing's highly controversial instructions concerning domestic military intervention were leaked to the press and triggered serious protests in the *Reichstag*, the War Minister von Heeringen claimed that the army had no taste for domestic intervention.[50] Two years later he expressed his support for the attempts of the Interior Ministry to call upon the army only as a solution of last resort.[51]

Whilst the position of the War Ministry and military leaders in Berlin remained ambiguous over the question of domestic military involvement, the generals in charge of the provincial army corps were increasingly reluctant to using their troops for policing purposes. Significant discrepancies therefore often existed between the initiatives developed by the War Ministry and the General Staff on the one hand, and, on the other, the willingness of the general commanders at the provincial level to become involved in the fight against Social Democratic activities.

Most surprisingly, among military leaders, opposing views were expressed, often by the same person, depending on the context. In their private letters and published works general commanders expressed their strong commitment to defending the existing social and political order against a 'social revolution'; on the other hand, in actual situations of major conflict, the army corps commanders were often reluctant to become involved and preferred to leave responsibility for maintaining and restoring order to the police and *gendarmerie*.

Even generals who displayed highly interventionist attitudes when occupying leading positions in Berlin tended to become far more prudent once they became commanders of a military region: they quickly accommodated to the policy pursued by the provincial administration of not involving the army if it could be avoided.

General commanders and labour unrest in the industrial centres

The discrepancy between rhetoric and reality in military readiness to become involved in the maintenance of public order can be seen in the decisions of five prominent commanders, three of whom served in Westphalia. General von Albedyll, who commanded the army corps of the Westphalian province from 1889 to 1893, was a commander of the old school who had no professional or ethical qualms about domestic military intervention. Nevertheless, he was the first commander to point out, during the great Westphalian strike of 1889, that it was not in the interest of the army to settle conflicts between employers and employees. From the very beginning of the military intervention in the miners' strike, General von Albedyll complained about the requisitions from the civil authorities demanding protection from important contingents of soldiers. This brought him into opposition, not only with the civilian administration, but also with the War Ministry and to Wilhelm II.[52] Although he described the reaction of the Interior Ministry and the provincial administration as wildly exaggerated,[53] he did not object to the initial requisition for military assistance in early May 1889. His main objection was that the mobilisation of 10,000 soldiers was a waste of military time and resources, and declared that he could ensure public order with many fewer men, if only he had his hands free to repress the disturbance with traditional military means.[54]

After the end of the strike, in his account to Wilhelm II, von Albedyll expressed his deepest concern about the prospect of frequent military assistance to the civil forces in the future. Fearing that an ever-increasing frequency of mass-strikes would lead to the army spending most of its time and resources on the policing of labour disputes and small-scale social unrest, he became a strong supporter of the idea of increasing the police and *gendarmerie* to an extent that would enable these forces to handle most policing tasks without military assistance.[55] Von Albedyll was not opposed to the idea of domestic military intervention as such, but if soldiers were to be used in a conflict with the populace, it should in his view be the military authorities, not the provincial administration or the Social Democrats, who decided the time and the place.

During the 1890s more generals came to express similar views. In 1890, General Loë, general commander in the Rhine Province, declared to his friend and colleague, von Waldersee, that he had tried to discourage civilian authorities from calling for military assistance on the occasion of May Day.[56] The views of General von Bissing, general commander in Westphalia between 1901 and 1907 were similar, although his orders to the soldiers and officers of the Westphalian army corps show no sign of mercy towards an unruly population. In his correspondence with the provincial administration, he repeatedly opposed any arrangement that gave the army a more active role in the maintenance of order in the unruly Westphalian province.[57]

General von Waldersee, the former chief of the General Staff and a notorious supporter of the idea of a military *coup* against the *Reichstag*, made no secret of his readiness to launch a violent crackdown on anything that smacked of Social Democratism. In 1891, when taking over the command in the Hamburg area, which was one of the strongholds of the Social Democratic party, Waldersee had clear intentions of conducting his own crusade against the Social Democrats, whether or not he was being requested to do so by the Hamburg civilian authorities.[58]

However, after a few years in office, even General von Waldersee seemed to lose his appetite for heavy-handed military interventions. In the winter of 1896–1897, a major strike broke out among the Hamburg dock workers. When urged by Wilhelm II to do something about it without asking the Hamburg Senate for permission, Waldersee gracefully declined by referring to the illegality of such a step.[59]

In a later account of the Hamburg dockers' strike, Waldersee wrote to the *Kaiser* that it was best to postpone the military repression of the workers' movements. Interfering in a major strike would be a way of letting the Social Democrats decide the time and place of the big battle. Instead it was better to take action against the Social Democrats when the workers were not already mobilised for a strike.[60] Waldersee had not abandoned his plans for waging war against the Social Democrats; however his idea of a battle against 'the rioting masses' bore little resemblance to the labour disputes which actually occurred. The messy reality of poor people, including women and children, throwing stones and shouting abuse was too unheroic for the glorious Prussian army to become involved in.

A similar conversion was undergone by General von Einem. As War Minister between 1903 and 1909, General von Einem gained a reputation as a hardliner due to his recommendation of the General Staff study entitled 'Fighting in Insurgent Towns' and of General von Hindenburg's instructions for domestic military intervention. In his memoirs he also insists on the right and duty of military commanders to repress popular unrest, as well as to impose whatever means they considered appropriate.[61]

Nevertheless, when General von Einem held the post as army corps commander in Westphalia between 1909 and 1913, he showed little interest in preparing for military intervention to restore public order. When he was called upon to deliver troops on the occasion of the Westphalian miners' strike of March 1912, he did his best to limit the extent of the military display of force. From his correspondence with the district governors in Münster and Arnsberg it appears that during the intervention in March 1912, General von Einem was not only cooperative and attentive to the wishes of the civil authorities, but implemented only the measures that the civil authorities explicitly asked him to pursue.[62]

It is remarkable how von Einem, as had Albedyll, Loë, Bissing and Waldersee before him, lost his appetite for active military intervention once he occupied the post of army corps commander. As general commanders in Münster, Einem, Bissing and Albedyll all showed themselves to be rather prudent when it came to sending troops to ordinary labour conflicts, and in the cases where troops were in fact mobilised, they were very careful to follow the wishes of the civil authorities, about when to send troops, where and how many. It was not that the Prussian generals ever refrained from the idea of intervening with military might to maintain and restore public order. However, the type of conflict they imagined was open revolt or civil war. Despite the military rhetoric of zero tolerance towards Social Democratic activities, in practice they found most incidents of mass strikes or political protest not sufficiently serious for the army to become involved.

The reluctance of general commanders to become involved in the maintenance of order in their region indirectly supported the demilitarisation policy of the Interior Ministry and the provincial administration. General commanders almost never used their powers to bypass the civilian administration. Moreover, the reluctance of the generals at the provincial level undermined any attempt, by the War Ministry or by Wilhelm II, to give the army a more active role in domestic politics. At the same time, the army corps commanders also tightly controlled the use of troops by their subordinate commanders, thus effectively hindering alliances at the local level between local authorities and garrison commanders.[63]

The marginalisation of the Kaiser

General commanders increasingly sought to avoid involvement in the policing of social and political protest, which was an important factor to counter-balance the wills and whims of Wilhelm II who repeatedly issued orders to launch a crackdown on the Social Democrats. The *Kaiser*'s dramatic declarations gave the German public the impression that Wilhelm was personally in charge and at the centre of decision-making whenever the army was mobilised for the purpose of maintaining and restoring public order. However, as has been observed in other areas of German politics of the Wilhelmine era,[64] the actual influence of the Monarch on decision-making was limited. Already by the mid-1890s there was a gap between Wilhelm's wishful absolutist rhetoric and his actual influence, as Chris Clark rightly points out.[65]

This characterised not only his relationship with members of the Prussian and Imperial government, but also his relationship with senior members of the military establishment. Wilhelm could easily be influenced and tended to shift his position depending on the advice he received. The army corps commanders with their direct access to the *Kaiser* were in a particularly strong position to assert influence over him, even against the war minister. Any mobilisation of troops or military intervention in the non-Prussian parts of the Empire formally required an order from the *Kaiser*. However, the army corps commanders who operated within the Prussian territory were empowered to mobilise troops without formal consent from the monarch.

It is nevertheless worth noting that in none of the cases when troops were mobilised in Westphalia, did the original initiative for the intervention come from Berlin. Instead, questions concerning whether, when and how, to use troops were determined at the provincial level by the province governor and by the army corps commander. The *Kaiser* was informed, but his approval was *post hoc*.

During the military intervention in Westphalia in May 1889, General von Albedyll only informed Wilhelm by telegram on 6 May that he had already given the order to mobilise troops the day before.[66]

In June 1899 during riots by young Polish miners, it was the army corps commander, General von Mikusch-Buckberg, who in the early hours of 28 June, informed the *Kaiser* by telegram about the riots in Herne. The General explained that, on the request of the Province Governor, he had already sent one battalion of infantry to the town.[67] It was only after having received the news that troops had already been sent to Herne, that Wilhelm replied by an order in his usual dramatic style by which he made the commanding general personally responsible for the reestablishment of order.[68]

During the great miners' strike of March 1912, civil servants at all levels declared for several days that they would do their best to manage without military assistance.[69] Only after a week did they begin seriously to discuss the possibility of military intervention. When the military authorities were contacted, the procedure was the same as in 1889 and 1899: in the evening of 13 March, the Province Governor requested military assistance directly from General von Einem, who immediately gave the order to mobilise troops. At 11 p.m. he sent a telegram to inform Wilhelm about the intervention, but it was only the following morning that General von Einem received the formal 'order' from His Majesty.[70]

Not only did army corps commanders mobilise troops before receiving the formal green light from Berlin, they also disregarded explicit orders from Wilhelm II. In 1889 during the great Westphalian miners' strike, General von Albedyll informed the *Kaiser* on 5 May that he had already sent troops to Gelsenkirchen.[71] In his reply, the King ordered von Albedyll to use all troops available.[72] The *Kaiser*'s instructions were not followed, since General von Albedyll never mobilised the full potential manpower and, moreover, tried to limit the number of forces. However, at no moment did Wilhelm intervene to enforce his initial order, and the final decision about the size of the military intervention was therefore left to von Albedyll's discretion.

A similar procedure can be observed in 1896 during the Hamburg dock workers' strike, when General von Waldersee refrained from military intervention against explicit orders from Wilhelm. General von Waldersee replied to the *Kaiser* that a military intervention was not possible since no unrest had taken place. When in March 1912 General von Einem had informed Wilhelm about the mobilisation of troops to the Westphalian mining areas, he received an order from the Monarch to mercilessly repress any resistance with the use of machine guns and artillery.[73] As was the case with von Waldersee in 1896, General von Einem later openly dissociated himself from the measures proposed by Wilhelm in a hand-written note on the reverse side of the telegram:

> This telegram is the reply to a message that I sent to the *Kaiser* on 13. 3. 1912 at 11 p.m. informing that I had given the order to mobilise troops to the strike area. The senior telegraph official who brought me the telegram was shocked, but assured me that only the clerk who had received the wire had any knowledge of what it contained. I did not send His Majesty any reply.[74]

Insofar as this note from the hand of von Einem, which presumably was written much later after the fall of the Empire, gives an accurate account of the immediate reaction to the *Kaiser*'s order, it illustrates how Wilhelm's strongly-worded orders were received by the most senior commanders at the provincial level. Due to the particularly independent and powerful position of Prussian army corps commanders, generals could – and often did – ignore the orders they got from the Supreme Commander. Contrary to the order he received, General von Einem did his best, as earlier had von Albedyll, von Waldersee and von Mikusch-Buckberg, to avoid bloody repression of unrest, and implemented only the measures he considered strictly necessary. In his later account of the 1912 strike von Einem declares with pride that no violent confrontation took place between the troops and the striking miners.[75]

The alliance of forces for the demilitarisation of protest policing

The adoption in the early 1890s of demilitarisation policy by the Prussian Interior Ministry was undoubtedly in line with overall processes of modernisation. However, its consistent implementation by the Prussian Interior Ministry and provincial administration was due not simply to concerns for social peace and public opinion.

Senior civil servants within the Interior Ministry and in the provincial administration favoured policies that would limit their dependency on the military authorities and strengthen their control over the policing policies implemented by local authorities. At the same time, the increasing reluctance of general commanders to deliver military assistance compelled the civilian authorities to restructure their forces and reconceptualise their strategies in a way that made them less dependent on military assistance. While both the civilian administration and the military authorities expected a major confrontation with the working population to break out, the civilian administration increasingly managed to deal with minor conflicts, and to delay the moment when a military intervention became necessary. During each incident of great tension, senior administrators at the provincial level, and their military counterparts, closely observed the development of the crisis, whilst trying to appease the forces in Berlin and in the local communities who called for heavy-handed military intervention.

The military authorities never gave up the idea of ultimately launching a forceful crackdown on the Social Democrats. However, whilst the military authorities elaborated wild plans for a military coup or civil war, they were unprepared for the type of conflicts which actually occurred. As Sauer and Deist both point out,[76] there was a vast grey zone between a situation of great strike and a civil war. As long as a conflict could not clearly be defined as a revolt, the military commanders preferred to leave the responsibility for dealing with it to the civil authorities. The Interior Ministry's policy of demilitarising the policing of labour conflicts and popular protest was consistently implemented because, at the provincial level, both province and district governors and individual military commanders worked persistently – though not jointly – in the same direction towards limiting military involvement.

Notes

[1] Henning (1987) p. 140; Funk (1986) pp. 155–156, 233–234; Spencer (1992) pp. 87–88.
[2] Henning (1987) p. 158; Jessen (1991) p. 132.

[3] Funk (1986) p. 233.
[4] See Chapter 4.
[5] Demeter (1965) pp. 166–173; Höhn (1969); Saul (1981) pp. 209–232; Wehler (1995) pp. 1121–1125.
[6] Wehler (1995) p. 1122. See also Funk (1986) pp. 153–156.
[7] Höhn (1969) p. 66.
[8] C[entral] A[rchive], Potsdam III, R 43, film signature 12425–12426 or M[ilitary] A[rchive], Freiburg, PH2 /466: Decree of 20 March 1890 from War Minister Verdy du Vernois to the army corps commanders.
[9] Decree of 31 March 1890 from Interior Minister Herrfurth to the province governors. Ref. Deist (1991, 1) p. 34.
[10] Deist (1991, 1) p. 25.
[11] CA, Potsdam III, R 43, film signature 12403–12404, 'Erläuterung der Bestimmungen über das Einschreiten und den Waffengebrauch der Wachtposten', (1886); 'Zusammenfassung der im Reich und in den Bundesstaaten geltenden Bestimmungen über den Waffengebrauch der Wachtposten', (1892).
[12] MA, Freiburg, K 02–5/2: Decree of 17 November 1910 from the War Ministry; HSA, Münster, OP 6095, (documents 206–215): Instructions of 8 February 1912 from War Minister von Heeringen to the army corps commanders.
[13] CA, Potsdam III, R 43, film signature 12425–12426: Order by General von Bissing of 30 April 1907 'Verhalten bei inneren Unruhen'.
[14] B[ayersiche] H[auptstaatsarchiv] IV, Munich, MKR 2497: Order by General von Hindenburg of 4 February 1908 'Bestimmungen über die Verwendung von Truppen zur Unterdrückung innerer Unruhen'.
[15] MA, Freiburg, K 02–5/2: Decree of 17 November 1910 from War Minister von Heeringen to the army corps commanders.
[16] HSA, Münster, OP 6095 (documents 206–215): Instructions of 8 February 1912 from War Minister von Heeringen to the army corps commanders. Similarly, BH IV, Munich, MKR 2497: Decree of 9 November 1908.
[17] HSA, Münster, OP 6095 (documents 206–215). Instructions of 8 February 1912 from War Minister von Heeringen to the army corps commanders.
[18] HSA, Münster, OP 6095 (documents 206–215). Instructions of 8 February 1912 from War Minister von Heeringen to the army corps commanders.
[19] Cit. Funk. (1986) p. 351.
[20] Berghahn (1994) p. 255.
[21] Waldersee (1922) Diary entry of 29 November 1896.
[22] Cit. John Röhl, *The Kaiser and his Court: Wilhelm II and the Government of Germany*, Cambridge: Cambridge University Press, 1996, p. 14.
[23] Bernhard von Bülow, *Denkwürdigkeiten*, Berlin: Ullstein, 1930, vol. II, p. 198.
[24] Saul (1981) p. 219; Jessen (1991) p. 128.
[25] Repp (2000) pp. 23–25.
[26] Hans Freiherr von Berlepsch, *Sozialpolitische Erfahrungen und Erinnerungen*, Mönchen-Gladbach: Volksvereinsverlag, 1925, p. 24.
[27] Spencer (1992) pp. 86–87.

New Problems, New Priorities 81

[28] CA, Potsdam III, R 43, film signature 11971–11972 (documents 71–90): Minutes from a meeting in Dortmund of 10 May 1889 between Interior Minister von Herrfurt and the province and district governors concerned with the miners' strike of May 1889.

[29] The *Lex Berlepsch* of 1891 extended the legislation on working conditions and introduced maximum number of working hours.

[30] Hans-Jörg von Berlepsch, *"Neue Kurs im Kaiserreich"? Die Arbeiterpolitik des Freiherrn von Berlepsch, 1890 bis 1896*, Bonn: Neue Gesellschaft, 1987, p. 34.

[31] Funk (1986) pp. 203; Henning (1987) pp. 139–141.

[32] Hauptstaatsarchiv, Düsseldorf, Regierung Düsseldorf 15 904: Circular letter of 11 April 1890 from Interior Minister Herrfurth. Cit. Henning (1987) p. 168.

[33] Funk (1986) p.156.

[34] Henning (1987) pp. 172–174.

[35] HSA, Münster, Regierung Münster VII–57 vol.1, 1890–1905 (document 197): Letter of 31 August 1904 from Interior Minister von Hammerstein to Province Governor von der Recke of Westphalia. Similarly the debate between the Interior Ministry and the province governors of Westphalia and the Rhine Province about establishing protection plans in cooperation with the military authorities, see HSA, Münster, OP 6095 (documents 37; 41–49); HSA, Münster, OP 6889 (document 46): Letter of 12 March 1912 from Interior Minister Dallwitz to the district governors in Düsseldorf, Münster and Arnsberg. See also Funk (1986) p. 351.

[36] Jessen (1991) p. 16.

[37] Worms, Brandenburg (June 1909); Karlsruhe, Baden (August 1909); Mansfelder coal area near Magdeburg (October–November 1909); Neumünster (February 1910); Schwerts near Danzig and Mariewerder (January 1912); Westphalia (March 1912); Zabern, Alcase (November 1913).

[38] Minutes from a meeting in the Prussian State Ministry on the 8 January 1906. Cit. Henning (1987) p. 171.

[39] MA, Freiburg, N 87 /43, Papers from General Otto von Below: Unpublished memoirs, pp. 507–508.

[40] Henning (1987) pp. 139–141.

[41] Henning (1987) pp. 139–141; Jessen (1991) p. 137.

[42] Jessen (1991) pp. 121–125.

[43] Henning (1987) p. 150.

[44] HSA, Münster, OP 6681 (documents 131–132): Letter of 9 November 1909 from the district governor in Arnsberg to Province Governor von der Recke of Westphalia.

[45] G[eheime] S[taats]A[rchiv] Berlin-Dahlem, Rep.77, Titel 2523, No. 1 Anhang 1: Minutes from a meeting by the local governor in Essen on 1 June 1912. See also Henning (1987) p.158.

[46] CA, Potsdam III, R 43, film signature 12425–12426. War Minister von Heeringen in the Reichstag, 23 January 1911.

[47] Cit. Craig (1955) p. 254.

[48] Minutes from the Reichstag, 15 December 1898. Cit. Klückmann (1978) p. 23.

[49] Cit. Kurt von Priisdorf, *Soldatischs Führertum*, Hamburg 1942, entry on Walther Bronsart von Schellendorff, No. 2676.

[50] CA, Potsdam III, R 43, film signature 12425–12426 (documents 88–89): Draft for von Heeringen's speech before the *Reichstag* in January 1911.

[51] HSA, Münster, OP 6095 (documents 206–215). Instructions of 8 February 1912 from War Minister von Heeringen to the commanding generals.

[52] Alfred von Waldersee, *Aus dem Briefwechsel des General-Feldmarschalls Alfred Graf von Waldersee*, Berlin: Mittler, 1927, pp. 288–289: Letter of 11 May 1889 from General von Albedyll to General von Waldersee.

[53] Waldersee (1927) p. 288: Letter of 11 May 1889 from General von Albedyll to General von Waldersee.

[54] Waldersee (1927) p. 289: Letter of 11 May 1889 from General von Albedyll to General von Waldersee.

[55] HSA, Münster, OP 2847b (documents 7–9): Letter of 11 June 1889 from General von Albedyll to Wilhelm II.

[56] Waldersee (1927) pp. 367–368: Letter of 24 April 1890 from General von Loë to General von Waldersee.

[57] HSA, Münster, OP 6095 (document 71): Letter of 6 April 1906 from General von Bissing to Province Governor von der Recke of Westphalia.

[58] Waldersee (1922) Vol. 2, p. 200.

[59] Waldersee (1922) Diary entry of 29 November 1896.

[60] MA, Freiburg, PH2/14 (documents 176–183): Letter of 22 January 1897 from General von Waldersee to Wilhelm II.

[61] Karl von Einem, *Erinnerungen eines Soldaten 1853–1933*, Leipzig: Koehler, 1933, pp. 165–168.

[62] HSA, Münster, Regierung Münster, VII–14 vol.1 /32–1 (documents 5–10): Report of 20 May 1912 from the district governor of Münster to Interior Minister von Dallwitz. Ibid. (documents 102–103): Letter of 14 March 1912 from the district governor of Münster which not only indicates in details where to send the troops, but also how many. HSA, Münster, Regierung Arnsberg, 14325: similarly, for the district of Arnsberg.

[63] See Chapters 7 and 9.

[64] Evans (1987) p. 61; Mommsen (1995) p. 142.

[65] Christopher Clark, *Kaiser Wilhelm II*, London: Longman, 2000, p. 71.

[66] CA, Potsdam III, R 43, film signature 11971–11972 (document 2): Telegram of 6 May 1889 from the Military Cabinet to the War Ministry.

[67] MA, Freiburg PH2 /14 (documents 188–189): Telegram of 28 June 1899 from General von Mikusch-Buchberg, army corps commander in Münster, to Wilhem II.

[68] MA, Freiburg, PH2 /14 (document 185): Telegram of 28 June 1899 from Wilhelm II to General von Mikusch-Buchberg; ibid. (document 187): Telegram of 28 June 1899 from Wilhelm II to the Military Cabinet.

[69] HSA, Münster, Regierung Arnsberg, 14325: Telegrams of 10 and 13 March 1912 from the local governors and municipal police officers to the district governor of Arnsberg.

[70] MA, Freiburg, N 324 /64: Personal Papers of General von Einem.

[71] CA, Potsdam III, R 43, film signature 11971–11972 (document 2): Telegram of 5 May 1889 from General von Hahnke, head of the Military Cabinet in Berlin, to War Minister Verdy du Vernois.

[72] CA, Potsdam III, R 43, film signature 11971–11972: Letter of 5 May 1889 from War Minister Verdy du Vernois to General Albedyll, army corps commander in Münster: "His Majesty, the Emperor and King, orders that, unless an ending to the on-going conflict is soon in sight, your Excellency shall prevent further expansion of the movement through the mobilisation of the largest possible number of troops".

[73] MA, Freiburg, N 324 /64, Personal Papers of General von Einem: Telegram of 13 March 1912 from Wilhelm II: "Where force is necessary, shoot without mercy! Use both machine guns and artillery! Waste no time watching the situation or negotiating. Wilhelm R."

[74] MA, Freiburg, N 324 /64, Personal Papers of General von Einem.

[75] Einem (1933) pp. 166–167.

[76] Sauer (1970) p. 433; Deist (1991, 1) p. 26.

Chapter 3

The Controversial Issue of Republican Order and Stability

Between civil liberties and public order maintenance

On May Day 1891, nine people were killed in the French industrial town of Fourmies in *département* 'Nord' when troops opened fire against a crowd of striking workers and young people celebrating May Day. Another five later died of their wounds. The shooting triggered a heated public debate on the use of troops for the policing of strikes and demonstrations. The debate continued in the National Assembly and the Senate with greater or lesser intensity throughout the 1890s until after the First World War. In the French debate on the domestic role of the army, the arguments and concerns were very similar to those raised in Germany about the practical and political disadvantages of using young conscript soldiers to maintain public order.

Successive French governments were painfully aware that military involvement in protest policing could easily be used by the forces on the extreme left and the extreme right who sought to undermine the legitimacy of the regime. However, their policies of public order maintenance were conceived with particular historical experiences in mind. Violent protests and the repeated overthrow of regimes had profoundly marked the fears and expectations of government ministers and bureaucrats. Even for a rather liberal regime such as the Third Republic, government policies on strategies for the maintenance of public order – even for small-scale protest – had to strike a delicate balance between civil liberties and the need to defend the existing political order.

The army was a particularly awkward factor in that equation, as the marriage of convenience between the Third Republic and the French army was an inharmonious match, characterised by mutual suspicion of disloyalty and ill intentions. Nevertheless, in their political calculations on how to police popular protest, successive Interior Ministers seemed to reach the same conclusion: that the army was an indispensable element in keeping the fragile social and political order intact. Thus, successive French heads of government, from Freycinet to Briand, made increasingly extensive use of military troops to police strikes and demonstrations: spontaneous protest as well as peaceful gatherings in public.

On the surface, the continued and intensified use of troops against civilians appeared to be nothing but a traditional response to popular protest; and critics never failed to note the discrepancies between the principles that constituted the ideological basis of the Republican regime and certain practices inherited from the Second Empire and further developed during the Third Republic.[1] Historians who are sympathetic to the centre-left governments of the first decade of the 20th century nevertheless tend to accept the official justification for the extensive use of troops, namely that these measures were necessary in order to defend the Republic against extremism from the far left as well as from the far right.[2] However, when historians, whose political sympathies are on the side of the workers' movement, suggest that policing measures and most particularly the military involvement were often out of proportion, they make a point that is difficult to refute.[3]

Scholars working specifically on French policing or the French army have wondered why successive governments, from the Conservative opportunists to the centre-left governments of the early 20th century, did not make serious efforts to find alternative ways of policing public protest.[4] Two main lines of argument have been developed, which are not mutually exclusive.

Jauffret and Carrot have looked at the question of why it proved impossible to obtain a political majority for establishing a special riot unit to relieve the army from its role in policing.[5] They see the repeated failures of establishing a riot unit as the result of a particular political constellation in the National Assembly. It was impossible to reach an agreement about major reforms to the organisation of public forces which were costly and which were, in the eyes of many liberals and for the radical and socialist left, no less controversial than the use of soldiers.

At the same time, there is general agreement among historians that the municipal police and *gendarmerie* forces, particularly in rural areas, were too weak to handle the incidents of mass protest which took place during the 1890s and the early 20th century.[6] However, while French police and *gendarmerie* forces were undeniably understaffed and badly trained compared to later periods, it is worth noting that, in comparison with Prussia, French towns and rural areas were actually slightly better provided with police and *gendarmerie* both by the early 1890s and by the outbreak of the First World War.[7]

Seen in the light of the demilitarisation policy pursued by Prussian authorities, the continued use of troops in France presents three paradoxes. In the first place, military involvement in the policing of protest continued in France despite the fact that it was potentially more damaging for the Republican regime than for the German Empire. Secondly, as noted above, French towns and rural areas were generally better provided with police and *gendarmerie* than Prussian areas. Thirdly, while France did experience some major protest movements between 1890 and 1914, the majority of incidents in which the French army was mobilised in Nord-Pas-de-Calais could not by any stretch of the imagination be described as threatening to the regime. It is therefore remarkable that politicians as different as Freycinet, Waldeck-Rousseau, Combes and Clemenceau all eventually came to regard military involvement as preferable to trying to handle crises with police and *gendarmerie* alone.

Recent research on French policing in the late 19th and early 20th centuries describes the increasingly frequent use of troops in French provinces as the continuation of a traditionally repressive approach to disturbances of the public order. This is contrasted with what is described as the modern policing techniques and strategies developed in Paris by Police Prefect Lépine.[8]

However, it is worth observing how Lépine's strategic principles, which were based on prevention and containment of violence, came to influence the national plans for military participation in the policing of large-scale protest which were developed within the Interior Ministry from 1897 onwards. The strategies reflected in the ministerial plans show remarkable similarities with the Lépinean principles for crowd management. Moreover, a close analysis of the function of the military troops which participated in the maintenance of public order in Nord-Pas-de-Calais reveals similar parallels.[9]

The linkage between Lépine's preventive policing strategies, and the measures developed and implemented to maintain public order in areas outside Paris, adds an important aspect to our understanding of why French Interior Ministers and prefects consistently involved the army in the maintenance of public order.

This modifies the immediate correlation which is otherwise drawn between military presence at strikes and demonstrations and 'violent repression' of these. Despite several notorious incidents that deteriorated into bloody confrontation, the role of military troops in protest policing gradually moved away from traditional confrontation and repression, adopting more sophisticated measures for crowd management.

Political debates on the domestic role of the French army

In France – as in Prussia – rethinking of forms of protest policing was linked to rising awareness among politicians and government authorities of the urgency for social reform. The great miners' strikes of the 1880s – the miners' strikes in Anzin (1884) and in Decazeville (1886) – sharpened the sensitivity of leading politicians such as Freycinet and Waldeck-Rousseau towards issues affecting industrial workers.[10] After the 1884 strike in Anzin, Waldeck-Rousseau supported legislation that recognised the right of workers to organise themselves in trade unions.[11] In 1899, as Prime Minister, he intervened personally to act as arbitrator in the first major strike among the metal workers of the Schneider factories, and in 1901 he made efforts to liberalise the legislation that facilitated workers' access to take action against employers.[12]

With the establishment of the first Centre-Left government under Waldeck-Rousseau in 1899 and with the victory of the *Bloc des Gauches* in 1902, there were great expectations among workers for a change in the balance of power in labour disputes and an assumption that the new government was on their side.[13] Given the high expectations and increasingly radical demands from the trade unions, it was difficult for the Radicals in government not to disappoint such hopes. At the same time, these governments had to reassure potentially anti-Republican forces about their capacity to defend the existing social and economic order against pressures from the extreme left. In particular, they had to prove that they were not under the influence of the trade unions, as claimed by the conservative press. One of the main priorities of whoever held the post of Interior Minister was therefore to make sure that the government and the provincial administration at no time lost control of public unrest. A badly managed crisis would allow the political right to describe the Republic as suffering from anarchy and to criticise the government for lack of authority and will to defend the existing social and economic order. Similarly, loss of control might undermine the government's authority among the workers, and strengthen the position of extra-parliamentary movements on the extreme left.

Increasing governmental involvement in the maintenance of order:
Commitment to the protection of private property and personal safety

In its policing policies, the Republican regime was, as Berlière rightly observes, caught between the financial need to maintain the decentralised structures where police forces were organised at the municipal level, and a strong wish to maintain tight control over the ways in which public order was handled by municipal authorities.[14] At the same time, central government and its provincial administration became increasingly involved in conflicts between employers and employees.

The French Republican regime had made certain guarantees to its citizens which were not easily compatible. With the law of 1884 on local government, municipal authorities were made financially responsible for damage to private property due to riots and popular protest, unless the municipal authorities could demonstrate that all adequate policing measures had been taken to protect persons and property.[15] Politically it was essential to convince the wealthy middle and upper classes that the Republic did not tolerate attacks on private property. Articles 106 and 108 of the law on local government therefore effectively committed central government to delivering supplementary forces for the protection of property and personal safety of its citizens if the local police could not provide reasonable protection with its own forces.

At the same time, it was very difficult for French governments to distance themselves from the responsibility of policing labour disputes. The law recognised the workers' right to strike[16] but it also guaranteed the right of workers to continue working. Yet in many cases the protection of strike-breakers outside the workplace was not a priority for the municipal authorities, in particular in communities where the city hall was dominated by Socialists and Radicals who had little sympathy for strike-breakers. Distrustful of the neutrality of municipal police, the prefects often preferred to make use of their right to take responsibility for all policing measures.[17] Moreover, if a conflict had implications for the order and safety in neighbouring municipalities, the prefect or sub-prefect would be often be urged to ensure their protection by granting additional *gendarmes*. French governments and prefects were therefore under political pressure to intervene by taking on responsibility for policing whenever a major conflict broke out.

As a result of the 1892 law on arbitration in labour disputes, French prefects also played an increasingly important role as negotiators between employers and employees. Between 1890 and 1914, the rate of arbitration through prefects and sub-prefects surpassed thirty per cent.[18] Attempts by prefects to end strikes through negotiation could easily be stifled by clumsy actions by municipal police forces, which were in many cases controlled by local industrialists. In order for the prefect to appear credible, both in the eyes of the employers and the workers, it was important to avoid biased police intervention against strikers whilst at the same time keeping incidents of disorder under strict control. This was yet another reason for the prefects to take over the responsibility for all policing measures, even when public order was not seriously threatened.

When a prefect took over the responsibility for policing measures he could dispose of the local police forces, he could reinforce these with *gendarmerie* forces directly under his authority, and he could call for military assistance. Given that the municipal police, particularly in small communities, tended to be understaffed, badly trained and easily influenced by the politicians in charge of the local institutions, prefects, when taking over responsibility for policing measures, generally preferred to rely primarily on the *gendarmerie*, and increasingly on military assistance.

Pressures to demilitarise the policing of public protest

Whilst the domestic use of the French army was intensified between the 1890s and the outbreak of the First World War, successive French governments faced increasing pressures from various sides to abandon this practice. The shooting at Fourmies on May Day 1891 became a key event fuelling the demands for more appropriate ways of policing the increasing number of long-lasting mass strikes and organised protests.[19] As incidents continued to occur where troops opened fire on strikers and demonstrators, the names of Fourmies, Narbonne, Draveil and Villeneuve-St-Georges acquired almost symbolic status as testimony to the inadequacy of troops performing as riot police.[20]

The arguments put forward in the French debate on the future role of the army were remarkably similar to those put forward by the Prussian Interior Ministry as justification for its attempts to demilitarise the policing of protest. In France, however, it was the Interior Ministry that continued this practice, despite continuous criticisms from all sides of the political spectrum. Over the years, politicians of all political tendencies, from Socialists and Radicals to liberal Republicans and pro-military conservatives, joined the calls for demilitarising the policing of protest.

For critics whose sympathies were with the protesters, it was the military presence itself that was the source of violence. This was not simply because the army in their view served as an instrument of repression, but also because the very appearance of soldiers on the scene of conflict was likely to provoke protesters and thereby increase the potential for violent clashes. According to the left-wing critics troops were, by the nature of their training, confrontational and too rigid in their handling sensitive situations. This was all the more problematic since the soldiers who were mobilised to police strikes and demonstrations were young, inexperienced conscripts with little personal authority. These young soldiers might easily start shooting in panic or frustration when confronted with a crowd of excited and angry protesters.

Instead, it was argued, the policing of sensitive situations required experienced men who could impose order by their personal authority and ward off potential outbreaks of open confrontation. In addition to these strategic objections came the ideological concerns. Republicans feared the alienation of industrial workers and agricultural labourers from the Republic that a frequent military presence at strikes was most likely to produce. As a regime that based its legitimacy on a mandate from the French people, this was a development that the Republic could ill afford. Similarly, it was argued that Republican attempts to turn the French army into an institution of national integration would be undermined if important groups of the French nation found themselves repeatedly confronted with 'the army of the nation'.[21]

From a different political perspective, conservatively minded politicians argued against the use of troops, fearing that conscript soldiers called out to maintain and restore public order might themselves join the protesters and turn their weapons against those whom they were supposed to protect.[22] Although there were very few incidents of the kind during the entire period, the prospect of soldiers refusing to obey orders, or even joining the ranks of the protesters, was a nightmare vision that critics of military involvement in protest policing never failed to point out.[23] This view was linked to a wider argument against universal conscription, which held that it was unwise to teach the revolutionary classes how to use weapons which they could eventually use to rebel against the established order.

Finally, politicians with close links to the military establishment repeatedly voiced concerns that frequent military presence at labour conflicts, which sometimes dragged on for weeks and months, gradually drained the army's resources, broke up military training schedules and undermined the health and morale of soldiers and officers.[24] The pro-military opposition to the use of troops was concerned with the potential damage to the prestige of the army in the wider population, as well as with the proper functioning of the military organisation: fighting street battles against crowds of men, women and children was not a worthy activity for the glorious French army.[25]

In defence of the Republic: official justifications for the continued use of troops

The Interior Ministry did not deny that military involvement in protest policing was indeed provocative, dangerous and expensive. However, successive Interior Ministers, who made extensive use of the army, pointed to the immediate political situation to justify their repeated calls for military assistance from the police and the *gendarmerie*. According to their official justifications, the military presence was necessary in order to defend the Republic against forces on the far left and the far right that threatened to undermine it. Certainly, the first decade of the 20th century was characterised by political instability, large-scale protest and labour disputes. The wounds were still fresh from the Dreyfus Affair that had split the French nation down the middle, and there were conflicts over the separation of the French State and the Catholic Church, which followed almost the same fault-lines. At the same time, political agitators on the far left and on the far right did their best to destabilise successive governments and to undermine the authority of the regime. In particular, the promotion of 'Revolutionary Trade Unionism' by the Communist trade union (C.G.T), with their encouragement of sabotage and physical attacks on strike-breakers, seemed to give credit to the official justification of government policies.[26]

Yet some historians have questioned the extent to which the Republic was actually threatened by revolutionary trade unionism, at least not until the great conflicts of the years 1906 to 1909.[27] The political branch of the Socialist movement and the trade union C.G.T. were in permanent mutual conflict, and the C.G.T. only adopted its revolutionary strategies by the Congress of Amiens in October 1906. Yet, by 1906, the practice of preventive mobilisation of large numbers of troops was already firmly in place. Furthermore, the majority of strikes to which the army was called were not organised by the Communist C.G.T. trade union. It is also worth noting that the vast majority of incidents which triggered military intervention in Nord-Pas-de-Calais could not, by any stretch of the imagination, be described as threatening internal stability.[28]

A discrepancy thus seems to exist between the official argument concerning the threat to the stability of the Republican regime, on the one hand, and, on the other, the fact that the majority of incidents to which the army was mobilised proceeded in a quite peaceful manner. Furthermore the remarkable conversion of Interior Ministers, like Combes and Clemenceau, to the military solution calls for an explanation. Both had spent their previous political careers vigorously opposing military involvement in the policing of protest, and both changed their minds strikingly quickly once they took up post at the Interior Ministry. It is therefore worthwhile considering the advantages that made successive Interior Ministers opt for the military solution despite continuous criticism.

The ministerial strategies for protest policing: prevention and containment

Whilst the frequent mobilisation of soldiers appeared to be simply a traditional military solution to problems of public disorder, important changes took place between 1891 and 1914 in the Interior Ministry's approach to protest policing. During the 1890s, new practices and procedures emerged around the use of troops which became formalised standard practice around the turn of the 20th century. In the first place, a practice developed of mobilising military troops preventively, so that soldiers were already present at the scene of conflict by the time a major strike was expected to break out. Secondly, very large numbers of men were mobilised. Finally, the function of the infantry underwent important changes.

Preventive mobilisation was not a new phenomenon; what was new was the consistent application of this measure, often organised on a nationwide scale by the Interior Ministry. One of the early examples of the uniform application of preventive mobilisation was for the annual May Day celebrations. In 1891, as in 1890, the government's response to the celebration of May Day was to forbid marches and gatherings in public. At both occasions, the government made sure that all over France troops were kept in their garrisons, ready for intervention.[29] According to the prefect of Pas-de-Calais, Gabriel Alapetite, there was some disagreement between Freycinet, War Minister and Head of Government, who feared the reaction from the left-wing opposition in the National Assembly, and his Interior Minister Constans who pressed hard for facilitating the deployment of troops.[30] In April 1891, Freycinet asked the commanding generals to make preparations for military mobilisation on May Day at any location within the national territory. Accordingly, not only prefects, but sub-prefects and mayors, got the green light from Paris to request military assistance to police May Day protests.[31] For each of the following years, the preventive measures for the May Day celebrations were discussed between the government, the prefects and military authorities.[32] The requisition of troops to Fourmies on May Day 1891, which ended in the shooting of fourteen workers, was not – as later inquiries claimed – simply the fault of local factory owners or the over-reaction of an inexperienced sub-prefect and local mayor, who was himself a factory owner.[33] It was a measure that had been sanctioned by the government.

After the shooting at Fourmies, and despite vigorous protests against military involvement in the policing of French citizens, Freycinet showed no intention of changing this strategy. Thus, year after year from the 1890s until the eve of the First World War, successive Interior Ministers recommended the preventive mobilisation of troops for May Day.[34] Similarly, in November 1891, during a strike among the gas workers in Le Havre, the Interior Minister asked War Minister Freycinet whether the military authorities could be contacted, just to prepare themselves for the possible outbreak of a strike. The War Minister answered in the affirmative.[35] Neither Freycinet nor later Interior Ministers seriously tried to change this practice, and preventive mobilisation became a standard measure for any conflict which contained potential for unrest.

It was also Freycinet who introduced the practice of mobilising significant numbers of soldiers compared to the number of protesters. French authorities had previously mobilised considerable numbers of men for particularly sensitive conflicts, but it was in the early 1890s that this became standard practice, also including for minor incidents of protest. The mobilisation of many soldiers, compared to the number of protesters, was a measure contrary to the lesson drawn by many public commentators in their analysis of 'what went wrong at Fourmies'. According to a widely held view, it was the strong military presence which had been seen as provocative and thereby escalated confrontation with the striking workers. However, the opposite lesson was drawn both by Freycinet, by Vel-Durand, prefect of the *département* 'Nord', and by General Loizillon, the army corps commander who had been responsible for the military intervention at Fourmies.[36] If troops were to intervene, they had to be present in great numbers. Insufficient military force might, on the one hand, provoke the population and on the other, troops would be at risk of losing control, thus making even more violent measures necessary to restore order.

Development and formalisation of the military participation through the Plans for Protection

Under Waldeck-Rousseau, 1899–1902, the strategies initiated by Freycinet were developed and formalised, with the establishment of a series of detailed plans for the protection of public order. Waldeck-Rousseau's attitude towards military involvement in the policing of labour conflicts merits attention. In terms of demilitarising the maintenance of public order, Waldeck-Rousseau started with the best of intentions. In February 1884, as Interior Minister during the miners' strike in Anzin, he stressed, in a circular letter to the prefects, that no troops were to be mobilised unless violence or riots had actually taken place.[37] Eventually, troops were called to restore order in Anzin, but only after more than a month's strike.

In October 1901, Waldeck-Rousseau again became responsible for the maintenance of order during a great miners' strike. In his biography on Waldeck-Rousseau, Pierre Sorlin describes his attitude towards this nation-wide miners' strike in 1901 as far more liberal and relaxed compared to his handling of the miners' strike in Anzin 1884.[38] However, if Waldeck-Rousseau in 1901 had become more confident as to the possibility of negotiating social peace with the representatives of the labour organisations, his policing measures can hardly be described as more relaxed and confident. In contrast to the reluctance shown in 1884 towards military presence in Anzin, the Waldeck-Rousseau administration in 1901 took the initiative of preparing a forceful response as early as June 1901 when rumours began to circulate that a nation-wide strike in the mining sector was about to break out.[39] In early October 1901, Waldeck-Rousseau told the prefects in Macon and Saint Etienne not to request troops until violent action had actually taken place.[40] However, his attitude changed with the development of the strike. By the beginning of November, the prefect of Pas-de-Calais was severely criticised for hesitating in calling for troops. The message was clear: if miners did not turn up at work, it was time to call in the army.[41] Similar instructions were given to the prefects in the other *départements* affected by the miners' strike.[42]

According to the Plans for Protection that were first developed for the policing of the miners' strike of October 1901, the requisition of military assistance was made solely on the basis of the type of conflict (i.e. a strike among rail workers, miners, or dock workers) with no regard to the degree of violence, actual or potential. If strikes were announced which were expected to be joined by a significant number of people over a widespread territory, the army would be requested to be present from the very outbreak of the strike. The Plans also turned away from the incremental approach to unrest, whereby the presence of soldiers, as well as their number, depended on the course of the conflict. Instead, the Plans formalised and gave priority to the existing practice of mobilising troops preventively. In addition, the Plans operated with very large numbers of troops compared to the number of potential strikers.

The Plans for Protection also made significant changes with respect to the function of the troops. In the 1880s and 1890s, the task of military troops was to patrol the wider area, to break up gatherings and marches, and to be present at sensitive locations where unrest was likely to occur. In the 1901 Plans, patrols were abandoned on the grounds of being ineffective and confrontational; instead the troops were to occupy sensitive locations around the clock for as long as the dispute lasted. In his instructions for the implementation of the plans, Waldeck-Rousseau also made clear that when confronted with a crowd of protesters, soldiers were to be placed in lines behind the police and *gendarmerie*, with the first lines of soldiers being unarmed. The soldiers should form a human wall to prevent protesters from approaching sensitive locations (such as a town hall, a prefecture, a factory, mine or port). At the same time, the soldiers were ordered not to react unless someone tried to break through their lines, even when abused or targeted with stones or bottles. The presence of a wall of soldiers behind the police and *gendarmes* was expected to allow the latter to move more freely and to intervene against individuals who committed acts of violence or vandalism. The cavalry was assigned the same task of keeping protesters at a distance, in order to allow *gendarmes* and police to move freely, although the instructions were much less specific on this point.[43]

Waldeck-Rousseau's measures for military involvement in the policing of large-scale unrest were not new. Indeed much was a continuation of measures developed by Freycinet and, as we shall later see, by the police prefect of Paris, Louis Lépine. However, through the Plans for Protection, these measures became formalised and were established with the participation of very senior military commanders. The Plans for Protection from 1901 eventually developed into a series of detailed plans for the policing of major strikes involving not only rail workers and miners, but also strikes among dock workers as well as post and telegraph personnel. Between 1901 and 1914 the plans were updated and extended to deal with any form of significant internal unrest.[44] The hesitation expressed by Waldeck-Rousseau in 1884 about calling on troops preventively was sacrificed in the name of efficiency and security.

The continuation of established practice under Combes and Clemenceau

When Emile Combes became Interior Minister and Head of Government in June 1902, he inherited a system in which the preventive mobilisation of large numbers of soldiers was already becoming standard practice. Combes had spent decades in opposition criticising this use of the army, and during his early days in office, he made some attempts to avoid military presence at a number of occasions.[45] In particular, he criticised the policing measures implemented by Waldeck-Rousseau during the miners' strike of October 1901 as being vastly exaggerated.[46]

However, Combes' first months at the Interior Ministry were marked by the largest miners' strike seen so far in France, with more than 100,000 miners on strike nationwide.[47] Confronted with a strike of this magnitude, Combes stepped down from his original intentions of avoiding military involvement and implemented the provisions from the Waldeck-Rousseau plans to their full potential. Later in his political speeches and in his memoirs, he played down the extent of military involvement and declared that the display of military force at the 1902 miners' strike was limited to the strictly necessary, with no significant display of troops.[48] These claims are sadly contradicted by the numbers of soldiers mobilised. In addition to the police and *gendarmerie* that were moved to the conflict areas, 15,948 soldiers and 767 officers were mobilised in Nord-Pas-de-Calais alone. With a total number of miners in Nord-Pas-de-Calais in 1901 being approximately 87,000, this makes one soldier for every seven *potential* strikers.[49]

In the summer of 1904, Combes tried again to manage a major strike without calling for military assistance, when thousands of agricultural labourers went on strike in the south of France. In a circular letter to the prefects, Combes repeated that he preferred to see labour disputes taking place without the presence of public forces altogether – whether police, *gendarmes* or soldiers.[50] At first, Combes declared before the National Assembly that this strike was a role model of a social protest.[51] However, just a few weeks later he asked the prefects in the *départements* concerned to make all preparations for a military intervention.[52] Just as the situation seemed to be about to go out of control, the administrative-military apparatus was in place, ready to ensure the effective defence of public order. Combes never felt confident about his use of troops; however he gradually surrendered to the apparent imperatives of bureaucratic efficiency.

A similar retreat from life-long opposition to military involvement in protest policing was made by Clemenceau. In 1891, during the debates following the shooting at Fourmies, Clemenceau warned that sending troops against striking workers would create a situation of quasi-civil war that future generations would have to sort out.[53] Historians and admirers of Clemenceau have often been at pains to explain why he developed into one of the most authoritarian Interior Ministers, who used the military apparatus not only to maintain order but also in his struggle against the trade unions. Clemenceau's biographers spend much time explaining the necessity of his political turns,[54] and even a Marxist historian such as Maurice Agulhon goes a long way in his attempt to rehabilitate his hero.[55]

Clemenceau's reversal of position began shortly after entering the Interior Ministry in March 1906. In the wake of a catastrophe in the mines of Courrière in which more than 1,100 miners were killed, a major strike broke out in Nord-Pas-de-Calais in protest against dangerous working conditions. At first, Clemenceau promised 33,000 striking miners in Lens that he would refrain from sending the army if they avoided riots and violence.

> I assure you that as Interior Minister I will make an effort to apply the policy that I have brought forward in my newspaper. I am and I will remain against the preventive mobilisation of soldiers to labour conflicts.[56]

> I commit myself not to confront the strikers with military troops...Please show yourself worthy of this measure which has not been implemented in previous conflicts.[57]

By addressing the miners in these terms, Clemenceau put the responsibility for military intervention on those leaders of the strike who were in favour of 'direct action' as a means of obtaining reforms. However, by doing so, he also committed the government to send in troops if the violent faction among the leaders of the strike took over.

Between 17 and 19 March 1906, Basly, Socialist deputy and mayor of Lens, lost control over the strikers. On 20 March the region was occupied by a military force of a size never previously seen in France. The figure mentioned in the secondary literature is that 20,000 soldiers were present in Lens on 20 March, whilst the records from the military headquarters in Lille mention a figure of over 38,000 soldiers in the region; the ministerial documents show that, at the peak of the crisis, 52,000 soldiers were mobilised in the region.[58]

In April, Clemenceau went back to his original attempt to limit military involvement. He sent a circular letter to the prefects in which he explicitly forbade them to use troops preventively or to mobilise soldiers only on the grounds that a strike had been declared.[59] However, two weeks later, on 1 May 1906, no less than 45,000 soldiers were preventively mobilised from all over France to ensure the maintenance of order in the capital during the May Day celebrations.[60]

If Clemenceau declared himself against the preventive mobilisation of troops in the spring of 1906, he had lost all inhibitions by the end of the year. In November 1906 government action was taken to implement highly unpopular anti-Catholic legislation. The registration of property owned by Catholic institutions had been initiated already in January–February 1906, but was met with such massive demonstrations in many parts of the country that its completion had to be postponed. When the registration was restarted in November, the government took no chances. Clemenceau made clear to the prefects that they had the authority to use soldiers if there was no other way of forcing through the policy of the government.[61] The crises of 1906 were followed by a strike among Parisian electricians in March 1907, and later the same year a major revolt among wine growers in the South, as well as the first joint strike of postal workers and rail personnel. The government's response to these conflicts was repeatedly to mobilise soldiers on a very large scale.

In the later years of Clemenceau's time as Interior Minister, soldiers were repeatedly used as strike-breakers in disputes between the government and public employees. He reshaped the role of the army to cover functions that could in no way be defined as maintenance of public order. Clemenceau himself argued that this use of troops was necessary in order to defend the continued functioning of French society which would otherwise be taken hostage by public employees on strike. Famously declaring himself to be *'le premier flic de France'*, Clemenceau made no further attempts to excuse or justify his extensive use of military troops, whether to maintain public order or to prevent trade unions from obstructing the functioning of ordinary society. Clemenceau's use of troops arguably reflected his increasingly authoritarian character.[62] It is however important to stress that in his use of soldiers as riot police, he implemented the very same preventive strategies that had been developed by his predecessors.

A number of violent confrontations between public forces and striking workers earned Clemenceau a reputation for being authoritarian, and for allowing and encouraging public forces to intervene against strikers with unrestricted brutality.[63] Nevertheless, however authoritarian Clemenceau appeared as Interior Minister, his use of troops must also be seen in the context of the changes which had taken place since the 1890s in the concept of means and aims in protest policing. Behind his uninhibited display of military troops, policing through the army in 1906 was very different from what it had been in 1891. A close look at the changes which took place in the ways of using soldiers for protest policing show remarkable similarities with the new approach to protest policing which developed during the 1890s in the French capital.

Lépine and the rise of a modern concept for protest policing in France

There are striking similarities between the measures developed for the Plans for Protection and the standard procedures for military participation in maintenance of order in Nord-Pas-de-Calais, on the one hand, and on the other, the strategic principles for the policing of Paris which were developed during the 1890s by Police Prefect Lépine. This correlation is generally overlooked. Whereas the military involvement is generally understood as the continuation of a traditional violent and repressive approach to popular protest, Lépine is often described as the father of modern French techniques for crowd management, because of the concern that he showed for containing violence through preventive policing strategies for mass gatherings and protest.[64] However both in terms of the proportions of forces mobilised, the preventive mobilisation, and the function of the troops, the parallels are numerous and hardly coincidental.

Louis Lépine took over the post of police prefect of Paris in 1893 after a series of heavy-handed police interventions that had aroused much public criticism. He remained in that post for almost twenty years, during which time he fundamentally changed the concept of protest policing. Lépine's approach constituted a radical break with previous practice in Paris. During the 1870s and 1880s, the purpose of protest policing had been to prevent people from gathering, by bullying and forcing them away from public places. The police had two way of operating. One was to intimidate potential protesters by filling the squares and streets where protesters were supposed to meet, with police and *gendarmes*, mostly horsemen. Protesters who assembled regardless were at serious risk of being beaten up by the police. Another policing strategy was to place small units of policemen in the side streets around the square where protesters were about to meet. Once people were gathered, police would arrive from all sides and attack whoever happened to be within the area, thereby dispersing the crowd. Distinction was rarely made between those who intended to join the protest and occasional bystanders who were unfortunate enough to be in the wrong place at the wrong time. Unsurprisingly this earned the Paris police a reputation for mindless brutality.

Lépine shared the fear of French bureaucrats of small-scale protest developing into full-scale revolt and was obsessed with the control and management of gatherings in public. On the other hand, he was very critical of the unrestrained and purposeless brutality of the Parisian police.[65] The innovation of Lépine, in terms of protest policing, was his development of strategies that provided a maximum of control with limited display of violence. Lépine's strategy consisted of a few main principles. The first was to implement rigorously the provisions described by the 1848 law on gatherings in public. The law stated that before being dispersed with force, people should be warned and have time to walk away. The police and the *gendarmerie* would then only intervene against those who refused to move. This simple prescription, designed to prevent violent actions against peaceful bystanders, had been generally ignored during previous decades.

Secondly, Lépine considered that police brutality was difficult to avoid if the police intervened in small units. His point was that a weak policeman is a violent policeman. Instead, he wanted public forces to appear in much greater numbers. This would create better conditions for a measured police response to provocation or attacks from the protesters.

His third principle was that sensitive locations should be occupied before the protesters arrived, since it would create less confrontation to prevent protesters from coming close to sensitive areas than trying to move them once they were there. Police forces were therefore to be placed in front of sensitive locations, at the entry to squares and side streets, so that the protesters were 'guided' along routes defined by the police and split into smaller groups.[66]

The virtue of Lépine's approach to crowd management was that it created space for police discretion. This allowed a certain degree of flexibility and permissiveness towards protesters and gave French policemen and *gendarmes* the space to distinguish between peaceful demonstrators and people who could be arrested for actual offences. This did not mean that French policemen and *gendarmes* did not continue to intervene against protesters with heavy handed methods. They often did. But because they were not immediately at risk of losing control, they had space for moderation and could deploy a series of strategies before reaching open confrontation.

The correlation between these strategic principles and the measures described by Waldeck-Rousseau in the 1901 Plans for Protection appears both in the preventive mobilisation of large numbers of troops, in the occupation of sensitive locations, and in the formation of a 'human wall' of soldiers when confronted with groups of protesters. Similarly there are clear correlations between Lépine's use of cavalry units to prevent the gathering of larger crowds and General Picquart's instructions from 1907. It was these strategic principles which became entrenched as standard policing measures in the particularly conflict ridden area of Nord-Pas-de-Calais. The problem about the policing strategies conceived by Lépine and taken up by Waldeck-Rousseau was that they required very large numbers of men. In Paris, the police was sufficiently strong to manage the majority of strikes and demonstrations alone. Outside Paris, however, there was only one organisation capable of delivering the number of men necessary to implement these preventive measures – and that was the army. This point is clearly made by Louis Vincent, prefect of *département* 'Nord', in an exchange with Lépine.[67] Insofar as Lépine's innovations in the forms of protest policing in Paris can be described as the basis of modern French protest policing due to their concern for containment of violence and detailed planning of crowd control, it is relevant to see the preventive mobilisation of large numbers of troops as closely linked to the same process of modernisation, rather than its opposition.

The advantages and conditions of the Lépinean strategic principles

The correlation between Lépine's policing strategies for Paris and the changes in the forms of policing in Nord-Pas-de-Calais may appear paradoxical, since Lépine declared that the purposes of the police and the army were largely incompatible and contrary to each other.[68] In his handling of maintenance of order in Paris, Lépine attempted to limit military involvement and was highly critical of the uninhibited use of the military in protest policing in areas outside Paris.

However, while he sought to limit military involvement to a minimum, he frequently used the mounted *gendarmerie* unit of Paris, the Republican Guard. He also had no qualms about calling for military assistance from the garrison of Vincennes for particularly sensitive situations with great potential for violence and riots. At the same time, Lépine was very clear that if the army were to be involved, it should be used appropriately. The mounted officers were to be used in a way that would limit direct contact with protesters; when infantry was called out to assist the Paris police, they were to be placed behind the police, out of direct contact with protesters and not too visible.[69]

The similarity between the rationale of Lépine's strategies, and the measures described in the Plans for Protection, was by no means accidental. Between 1907 and 1909 Lépine was himself a member of the committee responsible for the development and updating of the national Plans for Protection. Here he worked together with the prefects of the *départements* 'Nord' and 'Pas-de-Calais' as well as with the army corps commander responsible for this turbulent region. During this period the Plans were significantly extended to operate with large-scale military mobilisation for virtually any type of popular protest of significance.

When assessing the nature of French protest policing in the areas outside Paris during the decade and a half that preceded the outbreak of the First World War, an important distinction therefore needs to be made between the fact that troops continued to be involved, on the one hand, and, on the other, the nature of the strategies that these troops were supposed to follow. The extent to which these strategies actually reduced the level of violent confrontations is of course impossible to state. It is nevertheless worth noting that Louis Lépine was not the only French official who declared with pride that no one was killed in disorders within his jurisdiction during his years in office.[70] So did Louis Vincent, who was prefect in the *département* 'Nord' during the twelve most turbulent years of the period and who was responsible for the unprecedented use of troops for the maintenance of order. When leaving office in 1911 he declared with satisfaction that he had no blood on his hands, a fact that he ascribed to his 'energetic, cautious and preventive policing measures'.[71] Thus, the French Interior Ministry, as well as the prefects and military commanders from the most turbulent areas, seemed to believe that the preventive mobilisation of large numbers of soldiers was indeed the most effective way to prevent violent clashes with protesters.

It is therefore relevant to ask the question to what extent they were justified in this belief. Certainly, the aim of containing violent confrontations was not always met and at numerous occasions strikes and demonstrations deteriorated into generalised battles between protesters and public forces. Between 1891 and 1908, no less than thirty-seven protesters were killed in France in confrontations with public forces.[72] Historians and contemporary critics of military involvement in protest policing never failed to notice the high number of casualties outside Paris as the ultimate proof that the presence of soldiers was bound to result in violence and death.[73]

The immediate and almost inevitable link between military presence and bloody confrontations needs certain modifications. Eighty-eight per cent of the casualties between 1890 and 1920 occurred in areas outside Paris; however, this was also where ninety-three per cent of the French population lived. It is also worth noting that the single incident at Fourmies in 1891 accounts for fourteen of the casualties. In addition, the five casualties at Châlon-sur-Saône in 1900 and at Draveil-Vigneux in 1908 occurred in confrontation with the *gendarmerie* – not with the regular army. During the same period, at least twenty-two people were killed in the German Empire in clashes between public forces and protesters, despite the marginal involvement of the army.[74] Similarly, even though the French army participated extremely frequently in the maintenance of order, the number of casualties in clashes between public forces and protesters was much lower than for countries like Italy[75] or Russia.[76] Military involvement in protest policing in France was of a different nature.

Insofar as Lépine's strategies can be described as the basis of modern French protest policing, in their concern for containment of violence and detailed planning of crowd control, the practice of preventive mobilisation of large numbers of troops must be seen as closely linked to the same process of modernisation, rather than its opposite. Accordingly it is important to stress that one of the rationales behind the frequent use of troops in areas outside Paris, rather than being simply traditional military repression, was due to the implementation of preventive measures for crowd-management.

Rejection of alternative gendarmerie forces

If the key rationale behind the use of troops was prevention rather than repression, it helps in understanding why men like Combes and Clemenceau both made remarkable policy reversals once they became Interior Minister. The belief that the mobilisation of large number of troops was the most effective way of limiting the potential for violent confrontations adds to the debate about why French governments apparently did their best to jeopardise various projects for the establishment of a special police or *gendarmerie* force to handle protests and riots.[77] Between 1895 and 1913, several projects were discussed in the National Assembly concerning a mobile *gendarmerie* unit that could take over responsibility for policing large-scale protest anywhere in France. However, when presented with such initiatives, whether from deputies, senators or from various branches of the War Ministry, successive interior ministers seemed to do their best to oppose such projects, either by anticipating them with their own plans, or by shelving and eventually forgetting them.[78]

The first project was presented by Freycinet in the wake of the shooting at Fourmies in 1891. It operated with a mobile force of *gendarmes*, with the specific task of ensuring public order. However, as Jauffret rightly observes, Freycinet's suggestion of ensuring public order in the entire French territory with a force of one hundred mounted *gendarmes* could hardly be seriously meant, considering how many men were normally mobilised to police protest.[79] Between 1902 and 1907, a Senator de Montfort presented a series of projects proposing the establishment of a mobile force of state police of 2,000 to 3,000 men. However his projects were either shelved or anticipated by a similar government initiative. Another project, enthusiastically promoted by War Minister Etienne in April 1906, was not well received in the Interior Ministry and did not lead to any actual proposal. The project was later recalled only by the opposition, who still waited for the government to take action. After February 1907, there was no more talk about organising a mobile force of *gendarmes* to take over the responsibility for the maintenance of internal order.[80]

The replacement of military troops with a specialised riot unit of 2,000 to 5,000 men to police the whole of France was obviously expensive. There were undoubtedly important financial reasons for the government to refrain from establishing such a unit. At the same time, substituting the very significant number of soldiers with a small force of mounted *gendarmes* to handle conflicts all over France was unlikely to be attractive to government authorities and the provincial administration. Both had become used to operating with much more manpower. It would mean a much lower degree of control and protection than the military solution. Most importantly, the establishment of a small riot unit was also incompatible with Lépine's preventive approach and would require a complete rethink of existing policing strategies.

Modern policing strategies through traditional agents

The continued use of troops by French governments, from Freycinet to Clemenceau, was of course developed against the background of the high levels of social and political protest that took place in the late 19th and early 20th centuries. However the scale and forms of military involvement in protest policing seemed to go far beyond what could be justified as necessary in the face of extreme violence and riots. Instead, military troops became an integral part of the strategies for the policing of any form of mass protest.

The question is why successive Interior Ministers came to prefer military involvement, despite the political contentiousness of the use of troops. According to Gabriel Alapetite, Clemenceau admitted that the events of 1906 and 1907 had convinced him of the advantages of preventive military intervention as a way of avoiding bloodshed.[81] Lépine noted with satisfaction in his memoirs that, despite Clemenceau's initial attempts to avoid military involvement in maintenance of order, he very soon came to accept the advantages of preventive policing strategies and during his time in the Interior Ministry forged a surprisingly effective working relationship with Lépine.[82]

Undoubtedly, the fears of politicians and bureaucrats of small-scale unrest developing into full-blown revolt were central to the development of policing measures that relied heavily on military assistance. The military provided the government with the feeling of being in absolute control. However the similarities between the Lépinean strategies for crowd management in Paris and the strategies for the use of troops as reflected in the Plans for Protection gives a more sophisticated twist to the interpretation. It suggests that rather than being simply a handy tool for control and repression, the extended use of troops was just as much an attempt to develop policing strategies that reduced the potential for violent confrontations through preventive measures. Due to the scarcity of police and *gendarmerie* forces in areas outside Paris, the Lépinean strategies could only be implemented with the backing of soldiers.

French interior ministers often faced difficulties when trying politically to justify the massive presence of *gendarmes* and soldiers for quite peaceful incidents of protest; Clemenceau in particular earned a reputation for unrepentant authoritarianism, due to his belligerent tone and his open hostility towards the trade unions. Nevertheless, after the turn of the 20th century the basic character of the use of troops was preventive rather than repressive. This marks a fundamental change from the policing strategies of the period prior to 1890.

Paradoxically, the increasing military involvement in protest policing was closely linked to attempts to change the approach to protest policing through strategies based on prevention and containment. Behind the governmental obsession with prevention, containment and control of protesters was the fear that if control was lost order could only be restored through unrestricted military repression. This was the ultimate nightmare for government authorities and provincial administrators since the French Republic could ill afford major violent confrontations. A full-scale military repression of a protest movement that had gone out of control might easily spell the end of the Republic. The civil-warlike repression of the *Commune* was still fresh in the collective memory, and even bloody confrontation at a much smaller scale, such as the shooting at Fourmies, threatened to destroy the fragile consensus among the different groups supporting the Republican institutions.

In Prussia, government ministers, provincial administrators and local authorities were similarly alarmed about the increasing frequency of large-scale strikes and other forms of protest. However, compared to their French counterparts, the Prussian authorities were prepared to live with a higher degree of risk of losing control over small-scale unrest. This was the price for keeping the army away from most incidents of social and political unrest. At the same time, the Prussian authorities still kept open the possibility of repressing unrest by unrestricted military means, in case a situation were to get out of hand. The Prussian Interior Ministry was prepared to take greater risks, which allowed it to embark on its demilitarisation policy.

Notes

[1] Particularly on this problem, see Machelon (1976) pp. 7–8.

[2] Georges Wormser, *La République de Clemenceau*, Paris: Presses Universitaires de France, 1961, pp. 210–211; Pierre Sorlin, *Waldeck-Rousseau*, Paris: Armand Colin, 1966, pp. 473–474; Philippe Erlanger, *Clemenceau*, Paris: Grasset, 1968, p. 357; Miquel (1996) pp. 42–45; Rémond (2002) pp. 228–232. Maurice Agulhon has

a very ambiguous position towards Clemenceau whose policies he defends, arguing that Clemenceau had seriously wished to avoid using troops against civilians, but that the situation went out of hand and he had to react firmly in order to save the Republic. Agulhon (1993) pp. 121–125.

[3] Julliard (1965) p. 21; Rebérioux (1989) pp. 264–265; idem. (1994) pp. 15–17; Trempé (1995) pp. 324–335.

[4] Serman (1982) pp. 59–62; Jauffret (1983) p. 111; Berlière (1996) p. 129; Bruneteaux (1996) pp. 52–54.

[5] Jauffret (1983) pp. 115–125; Carrot (1984) p. 653.

[6] Serman (1982) pp. 58–63, Berlière (1996) pp. 17–18; Bruneteaux (1993) p. 32; idem. (1996) pp. 21–22.

[7] See Chapter 5.

[8] Berlière (1991) pp. 1001–1006; idem. (1996) pp. 121–126, Bruneteaux (1996) p. 98.

[9] Roynette-Gland notes the similarities between Lépine's strategies and the forms of military intervention in Nord-Pas-de-Calais, but she does not develop this point. Roynette-Gland (1997) footnote 61.

[10] Charles de Freycinet, *Souvenirs*, (vol. 2, 1878–1893) Paris: Delagrave, 1913, p. 355; Sorlin (1966) p. 264.

[11] Law of 21 March 1884.

[12] Sorlin (1966) pp. 477–479.

[13] Sorlin (1966) p. 470.

[14] Berlière (1991) p. 461.

[15] Law on municipal powers of 5 April 1884 Articles 106 & 108. See further details in Chapter 7.

[16] Law of 25 May 1864.

[17] Law on municipal powers of 5 April 1884 Art. 99.

[18] Tilly and Shorter (1974) p. 41.

[19] Jauffret (1983) p. 111; Berlière (1994) p. 185.

[20] Rebérioux (1989) p. 264; Serman (1982) p. 60; Agulhon (1993) pp. 217–218; Berlière (1994) pp. 185–186; idem. (1996) p. 120.

[21] Gohier (1898); Jaurès (1911); Krumeich (1994) p. 142.

[22] On this debate see 'La crise de viticole' and later 'Les événements du Midi', *La France Militaire* 13–22 July 1907; similarly Francis Charmes, 'Chronique de la quinzaine', in *Revue des Deux Mondes* of 1 July 1907 p. 233. At the same time, Georges Yvetot's call for conscript soldiers to 'go on strike' (i.e. disobey orders) was repeated regularly in *La voix du peuple* mouthpiece of the CGT and in the periodical of Urbain Gohier *La guerre sociale*.

[23] Already in 1891 after the shooting at Fourmies there were rumours that a soldier had refused to shoot because he was himself from Fourmies (N[ational] A[rchive], Paris, F 7 12527: Report of 14 June 1891 from the Special Commission investigating the events at Fourmies on May Day 1891; newspaper article entitled 'On ne tire pas!' from *Le Cri du Travailleur* of 17 May 1891). Similarly, two infantry units committed mutiny during the 1907 revolt of wine growers in the south of France.

[24] Ernest Lamy, 'L'armée et la démocratie', *Revue des deux mondes*, 1885 (69) p. 872; Francis Charmes, 'Chronique de la quinzaine', *Revue des deux mondes* of 1 July 1907 p. 234; see also the debate in the National Assembly of 13 April 1906 (*Journal official* 1905–1906, p. 1783–3); Jules Lewal, *Les troupes colonials*, (1894); Raoul-Marie Donop, *Le rôle social de l'officier*, (1908); Lucien Thile *Pouvoir civil et pouvoir militaire* (1914).

[25] Girardet (1953) pp. 249–256; Serman (1982) pp. 59–62.

[26] See details Chapter 4.

[27] Azéma and Winock (1970) pp. 121, 148; Julliard (1965) p. 21; Rebérioux (1989) pp. 249–255; Bernstein and Milza (1999) pp. 32–44. The raising of barricades in Lens and Liévin 17–20 April 1906, the May Day demonstrations in Paris 1906 and the 'Revolte' of winegrowers in the South of France in the summer of 1907 raised serious fears of Revolution. However, Rebérioux and Berlière both argue that despite many agitated protests which sometimes produced violence, none of these incidents could be described as 'truly revolutioary' (Rebérioux (1989) p. 248; Berlière (1996) p. 125).

[28] See details in Chapter 6.

[29] D[epartmental] A[rchive], Lille, M 159 /1: Confidential letter of 2 April 1890 from the Interior Minister to the prefects; DA, Lille, M 159 /1: Telegrams of 30 April 1890 from the Prefect in Lille to the Army Corps Commander; DA, Lille, M 159/1–3: Telegrams of 29 and 30 April 1891 from the Prefect in Lille to the Army Corps Commander.

[30] Gabriel Alapetite, 'Grève des mineurs et convention d'Arras', (extracts from Alapetite's memoirs) *Le Mouvement Social*, vol. 164, 1993, p. 18.

[31] MA, Vincennes, 1st A.C. /2.I.328: Letter of 26 April 1891 from War Minister Freycinet to the army corps commanders.

[32] MA, Vincennes, 1st A.C. /2.I.328; MA, Vincennes, 1st A.C./2.I.331.

[33] NA, Paris, F 7 12527: Report of 4 May 1891 from the Special Commissioner of Anon; NA, Paris, F 7 12527: Report of 6 May 1891 from Vel-Durand, prefect of *département* Nord, to Interior Minister Constans; NA Paris, F 7 12527, Report of 14 June 1891 from the Special Commission investigating the events at Fourmies on May Day 1891.

[34] NA, Paris, F 7 12528: 'Premier mai 1898–1911'.

[35] NA, Paris, F 7 12773: Letter of 9 November 1891 from War Minister Freycinet, war minister and head of cabinet, to Interior Minister Constans.

[36] NA, Paris, F 7 12773: Letter of 14 November 1891 from Freycinet, war minister and head of cabinet, to Interior Minister Constans; MA, Vincennes, 5 N 2: Letter of 19 April 1892 from Freycinet to the military governors and army corps commanders.

[37] NA, Paris, F 7 12773: Confidential circular of 27 February 1884 from Interior Minister Waldeck-Rousseau to the prefects.

[38] Sorlin (1966) p. 473.

[39] Émile Combes, *Mon Ministère, Mémoires 1902–1905*, Paris: Plon, 1956, pp. 56–57.

[40] NA, Paris, F 7 12778: Telegram of 1 October 1901 from Interior Minister Waldeck-Rousseau to the prefect in Macon; ibid.: Letter of 5 November 1901 from Interior Minister Waldeck-Rousseau to the prefect in Saint Étienne.

[41] NA, Paris, F 7 12778: Letter of 9 November 1901 from Interior Minister Waldeck-Rousseau to Jules Duréault, prefect of Pas-de-Calais.

[42] NA, Paris, F 7 12778: Letter of 9 November 1901 from Interior Minister Waldeck-Rousseau to the French prefects.

[43] NA, Paris, F 7 12778: Instructions of 16 October 1901 from Interior Minister Waldeck-Rousseau to the prefects.

[44] NA, Paris, F 7 12774–12780. See further analysis Chapter 9.

[45] Jacques Risse, *Le petit Père Combes*, Paris: Harmattan, 1994, pp. 153–154.

[46] Combes (1956) pp. 56–57.

[47] *Statistique des Grèves* 1901 and 1902.

[48] Combes (1956) pp. 56–57: "The unrest was concentrated within a few regions; we only implemented the plans there and only to the extent that we considered necessary. (…) The government could maintain order without going to excesses and even without operating with a very significant display of troops."

[49] Cooper-Richet (1987) p. 402.

[50] NA, Paris, F 7 12773: Circular of 4 August 1904.

[51] NA, Paris, F 7 12773: Intervention before the National Assembly of 11 July 1904.

[52] NA, Paris, F 7 12773: Circular of 4 August 1904.

[53] *Journal Officiel*, 8 May 1891, pp. 815–186.

[54] Wormser (1961) pp. 210–211; Erlanger (1968) pp. 353–359, 369–370; Jean-Baptiste Duroselle, *Clemenceau*, Paris: Fayard, 1988, pp. 509–521; Pierre Guiral, *Clemenceau en son temps*, Paris: Grasset, 1994, pp. 175–178.

[55] Agulhon (1993) pp. 121–123.

[56] Cit. Wormser (1961) p. 224.

[57] Cit. Erlanger (1968) pp. 356–157.

[58] See Chapter 7 for details.

[59] NA, Paris, F 7 12773: Circular of 16 April 1906 from Interior Minister Clemenceau to the prefects.

[60] Gaston Monnerville, *Clemenceau*, Paris: Fayard, 1968, p. 296.

[61] NA, Paris, F 7 12399: Letter of 11 November 1906 from Interior Minister Clemenceau to the prefects.

[62] Duroselle (1988) pp. 510–518; Guiral (1994) pp. 173–178.

[63] Julliard (1965) p. 17.

[64] Carrot (1984) pp. 663–665; Berlière (1993) p. 162; idem. (1994) p. 185; idem. (1996) pp. 94–104.

[65] Lépine (1929) p. 82.

[66] Berlière (1994) pp. 190–192; idem. (1996) pp. 123–125.

[67] Louis Lépine, *Mes Souvenirs*, Paris: 1929, p. 130; similarly in an exchange with Louis Vincent, prefect of *département* Nord (NA, Paris, F 7 12913: Minutes from a meeting, on 8 June 1907, in the *'Commission pour révision de l'instruction relative à la participation de l'armée au maintien de l'ordre public'*).

[68] Bruneteaux (1996) p. 56.
[69] Berlière (1994) p. 193; idem. (1996) p. 124.
[70] Berlière (1996) pp. 122–124.
[71] DA, Lille, M 6 /20 Personal Papers of Louis Vincent. Short unpublished biography dated November 1911.
[72] Carrot (1984) pp. 864–865.
[73] Rebérioux (1989) p. 264; Serman (1982) p. 60; Agulhon (1993) pp. 217–218; Berlière (1994) p. 196; idem. (1996) p. 125.
[74] See details Chapter 4.
[75] The intervention of the Italian army in Sicily 1894 cost the lives of ninety-eight peasants, while four years later more than eighty striking workers were killed in Milan. Indeed, soldiers opening fire against civilians appears to have been a common phenomenon when the Italian army was involved in protest policing (Jonathan Dunnage, 'Law and Order in Giolittian Italy', *European History Quarterly*, vol. 25, 1995, p. 396). According to Karl Liebknecht seventy-eight Italian protesters were killed in twenty-three separate incidents between June 1901 and May 1906. Liebknecht (1907) pp. 56–57.
[76] Russian official figures recognise that at least sixty workers were killed in 1892 in a confrontation between striking workers and Cossacks in the Donet Basin. Unofficial sources set the death toll at nearly two hundred. Similarly, in the clashes between strikers and public forces in St. Petersburg in February 1905, official sources estimate 130 dead and 450 wounded; however, these figures are challenged as being far too low. (Bushnell (1985) pp. 24–27; Christian (1997) p. 143).
[77] Jauffret (1983) pp. 115–128; Bruneteaux (1993) pp. 38–40.
[78] This is the main argument in Jauffret's article on the debate about special troops for maintenance of public order between 1870 and 1919. Jauffret (1983).
[79] Jauffret (1983) pp. 112–113.
[80] Jauffret (1983) p. 118.
[81] Alapetite (1993) p. 21.
[82] Lépine (1929) pp. 253–254.

PART II

POPULAR PROTEST AND RIOT POLICING

Chapter 4

Violent Encounters and Challenges to the Public Order

Industrial workers, labour disputes and popular protest

Mobilising the army to handle disturbances among a civilian population was always described by the authorities as a measure of last resort. Prussian government authorities and provincial administrators, as well as successive French Interior Ministers from Waldeck-Rousseau to Clemenceau and Briand, justified any involvement of troops in the maintenance of public order by pointing to the 'extreme urgency' of the particular conflict. Yet the bureaucratic definition of what constituted a situation of 'extreme urgency' came to differ significantly among French and Prussian bureaucrats during the 1890s. Protesters, for their part, almost invariably described the military involvement in the policing of strikes and demonstrations as inappropriate, and disproportionate in relation to the threat posed by any particular incident of protest.

The comparison of the use of troops in Westphalia and Nord-Pas-de-Calais allows the otherwise highly normative notions of 'extreme urgency' and of 'proportionality' to be placed in context. Several factors need to be considered. The first concerns the levels of disorder generated by protesters. If there was a particular tradition for violent protest in France – as some studies seem to indicate[1] – how did this manifest itself in Nord-Pas-de-Calais? And how did this compare to Westphalia? And were the differences so great that they could account for the much more frequent involvement of military troops in Nord-Pas-de-Calais?

In order to compare the scale of violent protest in the two areas we need to look at the size of the two regions, their populations – in particular the working population – and the forms of protest which took place. Comparing levels of violence poses obvious methodological problems. However it is possible to address the question of whether the potential for violent protest amongst the population in Nord-Pas-de-Calais was so much greater than the potential for violence and unrest amongst Westphalian workers that it accounted for the very significant dissimilarities in the degree of military involvement in policing.

The working population in Nord-Pas-de-Calais and Westphalia

The region of Nord-Pas-de-Calais was one of the most turbulent areas of France. The annual statistics on labour conflicts published by the French Labour Ministry since 1893[2] show that the *départements* of 'Nord' and 'Pas-de-Calais' were among the most strike-prone areas of France both in terms of the number of strikes and of strikers. The combination of large mining areas, the textile industry, and three important ports (Dunkirk, Calais, and Boulogne-sur-Mer) made this region particularly turbulent even when compared to other industrial regions, such as Le Creusot, Saint Etienne, and the area of Longwy, or to the main cities of Paris, Lyons and Marseilles.

The Province of Westphalia, which covered the major part of the industrial Ruhr District, was also a very turbulent area. In terms of violent protests recorded by the German press between 1882 and 1913, Westphalia had the second highest number of incidents, only outnumbered by the neighbouring Rhine Province.[3] It was because of the particular risk of popular unrest in the Ruhr District that the entire area, including the district of Düsseldorf, was covered by the military authorities in Münster, although the district of Düsseldorf was, in administrative terms, a part of the Rhine Province. Among Prussian provinces, Westphalia also experienced the highest number of military interventions between 1889 and 1914. Like Nord-Pas-de-Calais, the Westphalian Ruhr district was an important centre for the textile industry and coal mining. Following the industrial boom of the 1860s and 1870s, the Ruhr district also became the centre for the rapidly expanding steel industry.

With its 20,214 square kilometres, Westphalia's territory was considerably larger than Nord-Pas-de-Calais, which covered merely 12,414 square kilometres. But until the 1870s Westphalia was less densely populated than the area of Nord-Pas-de-Calais. This changed with the industrial boom and the German Unification, which led to considerable increases in the Westphalian population. With the second industrial upswing in the 1890s, the population grew at breathtaking speed. This was partly due to high birth rates in Westphalia and in Germany as a whole, and to large-scale migration into Westphalia from other parts of Germany. In comparison, the population in Nord-Pas-de-Calais increased much more slowly, with the main industries (textile, mining and steel) drawing the majority of their employees from the surrounding rural areas.[4]

Table 4.1   Population of Westphalia and Nord-Pas-de-Calais

	Westphalia	Nord-Pas-de-Calais
1870	1,760,000	2,100,000
1895	2,500,000	2,600,000
1910	4,125,000	2,943,000*

* This figure is for 1906

Sources: Jacques Dupâquier, *Histoire de la population française, de 1789 à 1914, PUF*, 1988; Wehler (1995) pp. 9, 494; Jessen (1991) p. 359.

Between 1870 and 1910, when the Westphalian population increased with more than 2.3 million newcomers, there was also an important local migration from Westphalian rural areas to the industrialised areas around the River Ruhr. In 1892 there were only about 400,000 people living in urban areas in Westphalia. By 1913 the urban population had tripled to 1.2 million, mostly concentrated around the large industrial centres of Essen, Dortmund, Bochum, Bielefeld, Gelsenkirchen and Recklinghausen.[5]

Most of the newcomers were employed as industrial workers in the textile industry and in the rapidly expanding mining and steel industries. The Westphalian textile industry was only half the size of the textile industry centred around Lille, Roubaix, Tourcoing and Valenciennes with its more than 100,000 employees.[6] On the other hand, Westphalian heavy industry and mining was in rapid expansion, with the number of employees in the metal industry increasing from fewer than 17,000 in 1882 to 111,000 in 1907. A similarly spectacular growth can be observed in the Westphalian mining population, which tripled in size between 1880 and 1906.

Table 4.2   Miners in Westphalia and in Nord-Pas-de-Calais

	Westphalia	Nord-PdC
1880	117,000	45,000
1901	210,000	87,000
1906-1907	324,000	102,145

Sources: Tenfelde (1990, pp. 148–149); Sorlin (1966) p. 290; Cooper-Richet (1987) p. 402.

Although the mining industry in Nord-Pas-de-Calais was also in expansion, the number of its miners by 1906 had not even reached the size of the Westphalian mines of 1880. The dissimilar size of the mining industries in the two areas is significant because the miners posed particular problems of maintenance of order, both in everyday policing and during labour conflicts.

Patterns of protest and workers' mobilisation in France and Nord-Pas-de-Calais

Apart from the sheer size of the industrial sectors, what problems in terms of protest and popular unrest emerged in these areas? Throughout the 18th and 19th centuries the French had a particular reputation for engaging in collective protest – whether violent or non violent – against public authorities, local elites or employers.[7] Moreover, during the Third Republic, the people of Nord-Pas-de-Calais became known for their political activism. Participation in associations, demonstrations, marches, election rallies and public meetings was widespread among the workers in Nord-Pas-de-Calais.[8] In the 1880s, the political movement of the controversial former general, Georges Boulanger, was particularly strong in *département* 'Nord' where Boulanger presented himself as candidate for the elections to the National Assembly. The Boulanger movement in *département* 'Nord' developed into a law-and-order issue that involved military participation on several occasions between 1886 and 1888. While the Dreyfus Affair did not seem to generate major public order concerns, the conflict over the separation of Church and State in the early 1880s, and again in the years 1902–1906, also developed into major policing operations involving military troops on a very large scale.[9]

Notwithstanding the variety of protest movements in Nord-Pas-de-Calais, the vast majority of, and the most serious challenges to, public order came from industrial labour disputes. Throughout the 19th century legislators of successive regimes had done their best to place legal restrictions around the organisation and political activities of workers. Professional associations were dissolved by law during the French Revolution,[10] and Napoleon subsequently made striking a criminal offence, placing severe restrictions around any attempt to organise workers.[11] Strikes, as well as trade unions, were briefly legalised during the Second Republic,[12] before Napoleon III reintroduced new restrictions on workers' associations in 1852.[13] However, with the industrial boom of the Second Empire, the laws on professional associations were liberalised in an attempt to strike a deal with industrial workers. Strikes were decriminalised in 1864, but did not enjoy any legal protection; and during the 1860s workers' associations were increasingly tolerated insofar as they presented themselves as non-political organisations.[14] In the early 1880s, freedom of assembly was extended to political organisations and with the Waldeck-Rousseau law of 1884, trade unions were finally legalised.[15]

Yet protest movements, particularly those involving industrial workers, were still subject to many legal restrictions. Throughout the 19th century, it remained a criminal offence to prevent strike-breakers from working whether through obstructing entry to the workplace or by picket lines. Such 'violations of the freedom to work' could be prosecuted according to Articles 414 and 415 of the Penal Code.[16] During the great labour disputes of 1890–1914 the defence of 'freedom to work' was the most common justification for requesting military troops. Moreover, while the legal restrictions around the political and professional organisation of industrial workers were gradually removed, the legislation on public order – in particular the law on gatherings in public – could still be used in a variety of ways to obstruct and undermine industrial action.[17]

Notwithstanding the restrictions on political activism among industrial workers, or as a reaction to it, the Marxist branch of the socialist movement became particularly strong in *département* 'Nord'. Paul Lafargue, Marx's son-in-law, was elected deputy of Lille in 1891 and Jules Guesde, the leader of the communist faction of the French socialist movement was elected to the National Assembly from a Roubaix constituency in 1893. The Marxists were fiercely competing with other branches of the socialist movement and there were frequent fights between activists of different socialist groups, particularly during election campaigns. Military troops were often kept on high alert during election campaigns, but there are very few examples of troops actually being mobilised, and the infighting between competing socialist groups was generally dealt with by the police.

Patterns of protest in Westphalia and in Germany

Forms of protest in Westphalia differed in several respects. In the 1870s and 1880s, levels of organisation and political activism among industrial workers and agricultural labourers were low. Incidents of protest tended to be limited in scale, generally spontaneous and – with the exception of strikes – often without clearly defined goals. Incidents of popular protest, irrespective of their type and cause, were almost invariably described by the authorities as riots (*Tumulte, Excesse, Krawalle*). During the years of the *Kulturkampf* in the 1870s, the legislation on public order was repeatedly used to justify intervention against people gathered for religious purposes. Similarly, public gatherings based on ethnicity other than German were equally likely to be classified as disturbance of the public order.

Towards the turn of the 20th century, German political parties were becoming increasingly active. Yet associations and parties who sought support among the middle and upper strata of society did not use public space for their activities: such a course of action was widely regarded as improper and, further, was subject to numerous legal restrictions and police regulations. By contrast a culture of public protest developed notably around the Social Democratic movement. Political activists at the margins of mainstream politics became increasingly skilled in operating around the maze of police regulations and developed sophisticated ways of using the streets. In particular the Social Democratic organisers of marches and demonstrations placed much emphasis on the importance of self-discipline among the participants. Disorder and unruly behaviour was strongly discouraged as counterproductive; it would weaken whatever public support the cause might have in the wider public and would provide the police with an excuse for intervening against the movement. The powerful image of well-organised but peaceful demonstrations of mass discontent was carefully projected as the trademark of Social Democratic political culture. However, popular protest also took other, less disciplined, forms. In a turbulent area like Westphalia, there was scope for a great deal of spontaneous popular protest and public disorder, whether connected or not to a labour dispute or a political rally.

Labour conflicts in Germany were subject to even more legal restrictions than in France. In Prussia coalitions were made illegal by the General Code of Law (*Allgemeines Landrecht*) of 1794. After a long period, from 1836–1857, when the legislation against workers' coalitions was reinforced in many German states, the right of workers to form coalitions was finally recognised in 1869 by the *Gewerbeordnung* for the North German Confederation. Trade Unions were allowed to exist but they were treated as ordinary associations, submitted to close administrative regulation and police scrutiny, and there was no recognition of their authority to speak and negotiate on behalf of their members. Strikes existed in a legal limbo. Without being explicitly prohibited, strikes were not recognised by German law until after the First World War. Labour disputes were defined as private disputes between employers and employees which might involve the courts. However the only concern for the public authorities was the problems they might produce for public order. On the other hand it was a criminal offence to prevent strike-breakers from working and the maintenance of public order thereby intervened directly in the conflicts between strikers and strike-breakers.

Singled out by Bismarck and by Wilhelm II as the 'Enemy of Empire', the Social Democratic Party was subject to constant harassment from the public authorities including a total ban on the party and its activities from 1878. The anti-Socialist legislation was finally lifted in 1890 and the Social Democrats could resume their activities as a legal party. Many restrictions were still imposed, however, not least the legislation on public order. At the same time, extended powers were given to municipal authorities and local police, allowing them to implement their own rules and regulations for public order and to determine the working conditions for workers' associations. Prussian law required a police officer to be present at public meetings in order to report back to the authorities what was said. The police officer present at any public meeting also possessed a host of powers that allowed him to shape the meeting in various ways; for example imposing the German language on meetings in Polish associations or closing meetings at any moment, if he so pleased. The relationship between workers and the police was notoriously tense with workers feeling harassed and discriminated against by police officers using their discretionary powers and police regulations to obstruct what the workers regarded as perfectly legitimate activities.

The potential for mobilisation of workers

Despite important legal restrictions to which German protest movements were subject, and despite constant harassment from the Prussian authorities, Germans did not refrain from participating in strikes and demonstrations. Studies on labour conflicts in France and the German Empire from the 1890s to the outbreak of the First World War show that the German workforce became just as willing to go on strike as did the French workers. This was both in terms of the number of strikes and the number of workers participating. In addition to the number of German workers who willingly laid down their tools and joined a labour dispute, the authorities in charge of maintenance of order also had to reckon with the unrest generated by workers affected by lockouts. Between 1900 and 1913, an annual average of 75,000 German workers were excluded from their workplaces for shorter or longer periods.[18] In France, by contrast, lockouts were extremely rare and most labour conflicts took the form of workers refusing to work.

Friedhelm Böll's comparison of strike patterns in France, Germany and England shows that Germany experienced many more strikes and lost working days than France during the period 1899–1914, whilst in England strikes were far less frequent, but with many more working days lost per strike. In terms of extent, the vast majority of German labour conflicts occurred in small and medium sized workplaces and generally concerned fewer workers compared to labour conflicts in France.[19] On the average 109 workers were involved in German labour disputes whilst in France the average number of strikers per strike was 215 and in England labour disputes involved an average of 455 workers. On the other hand, the levels of mobilisation of workers for mass-strike were much greater in Germany than in France. During the 1890s, the German workforce also became the most unionised in Europe. Between 1891 and 1911 the Social Democratic Free Unions came to organise more than twice as many workers as all French trade unions put together.

Table 4.3   Levels of Trade Unionism

	France **All Trade Unions**	**Germany** **Social Dem. Free Unions**
1891	205,000	277,659
1901	589,000	677,510
1911	1,029,000	2,320,986

Sources: Tilly and Shorter (1974), Table 6; Groh (1978) Table 5, p. 380.

By the eve of the First World War, the Social Democratic Free Unions organised between twelve and nineteen per cent of all miners, twenty-four per cent of metal workers and thirteen per cent of textile workers.[20] However, trade unionism in Germany was not limited to the members of the Social Democratic Free Unions. Many German workers joined other trade unions, in particular Catholic trade unions and 'yellow unions' controlled by the employers.

The mobilisation of miners in Westphalia and Nord-Pas-de-Calais

The large working population in Westphalia combined with high levels of trade unionism provided significant potential for large scale mobilisation. In 1889, at the time of the first major miners' strike, when only a tiny minority of workers had any connection with trade unions, as many as 90,000 miners went on strike in Westphalia, and more than 110,000 miners nationwide. In January 1905, when three major trade unions joined forces, almost 200,000 miners went on strike and in March 1912 around 190,000 men joined the last major miners' strike before the War. When unions were split over the question whether or not to strike, it created tension between the members of different trade unions. The employers – particularly in the chemical, iron and steel industries – were very effective in their attempts to split the workforce through the establishment of 'yellow unions' and various forms of black-listings or privileges for sections of their employees.[21] Frustration and conflict among the workers were created, and during labour conflicts policing became not only a matter of protecting strike-breakers from strikers, but also keeping the members of different trade unions apart.

In Westphalia the proportion of workers joining in during major strikes greatly outnumbers even the most extended labour conflicts taking place in Nord-Pas-de-Calais. The number of registered strikers does not accurately reflect the actual number of protesters involved in marches and gatherings in front of the factory or mineshafts, since the striking workers were often joined by their entire family. However the figures do provide some indication of the comparative size of most extended strikes in Westphalia and Nord-Pas-de-Calais. Despite much effort from French trade unions to mobilise workers in general strikes, the levels of participation, even in the region of Nord-Pas-de-Calais, where trade unions were stronger than in most parts of France, never reached levels like those seen in Westphalia. During the turbulent year of 1902, which included a major miners' strike, there was a total of 87,000 registered strikers from all professional categories in the two *départements* of Nord and Pas-de-Calais. Even during the most extended strike movement taking place in Nord-Pas-de-Calais in March–May 1906, the total number of registered strikers did not exceed 92,000.[22] The last conflicts of mass-mobilisation before the outbreak of the First World War took place in 1912 and 1913 when miners and dock workers undertook highly organised 24-hour strikes. However the annual figures of strikers for 'Nord' and 'Pas-de-Calais' at 97,000 in 1912 and at 89,000 in 1913[23] do not come anywhere near the levels of mobilisation for large-scale labour disputes in Westphalia.

Strikes in transport and communication

As can be seen from these large-scale labour disputes, the most serious challenges to public order in Nord-Pas-de-Calais and Westphalia came from the employees in the mining industry. On the French side, strikes among dock workers, rail workers and communication personnel (post and telegraph) also frequently triggered military intervention. In France these were the industrial sectors where trade unions were strongest and which produced the most spectacular labour conflicts. In Nord-Pas-de-Calais the proportion of unionised miners was already twelve per cent in the 1890s.[24] Communication personnel (post and telegraph) and rail workers were also particularly influenced by trade unionism, with one in five rail workers being a member of a trade union. Accordingly, French rail workers and communication personnel attracted much attention from the authorities in charge of internal security despite the fact that strikes among French rail workers constituted less than ten per cent of all labour disputes.[25]

In France, the great coal mines of Nord-Pas-de-Calais were essential for the provision of fuel for all other industrial sectors. Similarly German industries depended on the coal provisions from the mines of the Ruhr district. Thus strikes among the miners in any of the two areas were capable of bringing the entire national industry to a standstill. Moreover, in France the large ports in Nord-Pas-de-Calais were central to foreign trade and during major strikes in the coal mines, the ports of Dunkirk, Calais and Boulogne-sur-Mer were vital for the import of British coal to keep French industry running. If the 4,000–6,000 dock workers in the main ports decided to join the miners in a strike, the whole of French society and its industrial output would be affected.

In both countries authorities were also painfully aware that industrial production and foreign trade depended on the continuous functioning of communications and railways. Strikes among communication personnel or rail workers might put national defence at risk because the army depended on the railways for the quick mobilisation of troops. The issue of public order – serious as it was – was only one aspect of the challenge to public authorities that came from strikes among miners, dock workers and railway and communication workers.

Strikes among textile workers

The textile workers of Nord-Pas-de-Calais also had a long tradition of labour activism and were by far the most strike-prone profession in France. They were far more strike-prone than the textile workers in Westphalia and the neighbouring Rhine Province, but workers' conditions and labour disputes in the French and German textile industries shared many features.

In both countries, it was difficult to organise effective strikes amongst textile workers. Like in the other highly strike-prone sectors, metal and construction workers, trade unionism among French textile workers remained as low as three to four per cent, throughout the period examined.[26]

During the same period of time, the proportion of German textile workers who joined the Social Democratic Free Unions increased from less than one per cent in 1892 to thirteen per cent in 1913.[27]

Yet in both countries coordinated strikes among textile workers were particularly difficult to organise because, within the workplace, the unskilled, semi-skilled and the specialised workers did not share the same working conditions and had conflicting interests; in particular there were conflicts of interest between the workforce at the lower levels of the hierarchy – predominantly women and children – and the specialised male workforce higher up. Moreover, during labour disputes, the unskilled workforce was easy to replace with strike-breakers and in areas dominated by the textile industry the majority of textile workers did not have many alternatives to the factory.

Strikes in the textile industry varied significantly in length. Most lasted only a few days, but sometimes they dragged on for weeks or even months. As time passed, frustration and tensions increased the potential for violence between strikers and public forces, and amongst strikers and strike-breakers. Yet, while the French textile industry produced twenty four per cent of all strikes, it only generated ten per cent of all recorded violent incidents. In comparison, strikes amongst French construction and transport workers produced respectively sixteen and twenty-one per cent of violent incidents.[28] At the same time, strikes among textile workers did not have the potential to affect wider society in the same way as did strikes among miners, transport workers and communication personnel.

French authorities therefore tended to be less anxious about the disorder generated by striking textile workers than among miners, dockers and rail workers. The French inter-ministerial commission that developed plans for protection to be implemented in case of major strikes in key professions never discussed establishing a specific plan for strikes in the textile industry.[29] A similar attitude was adopted towards strikes among metal workers and construction workers. Between 1907 and 1909, the inter-ministerial commission discussed whether specific plans should be developed for the case of a major strike among metal workers. The idea was quickly abandoned based on the argument that metal workers were too internally split to constitute a serious problem of maintenance of order.[30]

Nevertheless, despite the complacency amongst French authorities concerning the threat presented by strikes and violence amongst textile or metal workers they still sent troops on a regular basis to police strikes among textile workers, metal workers or construction workers.

Forms of protest and levels of violence

The policing measures implemented by French and Prussian authorities were developed in the expectation of violence; not only the forms and levels of violence which occurred during strikes and demonstrations, but also the type that was common in everyday interactions between police and the public. Similarly levels of inter-personal violence between members of the public were crucial in shaping the expectations upon which public authorities developed measures for riot policing.

Research on policing of popular protest in France and Germany sometimes tends to dismiss the security concerns of the wider community as exaggerated, and totally unjustified; some German historians describe fears of violence and disorder as nothing but cynical attempts from local elite groups to attract more *gendarmerie* and troops in order to protect private property as well as to bully and intimidate people from legitimate protest actions.[31]

At the same time, violence by protesters is sometimes justified by sympathetic historians as legitimate responses to social injustice and political exclusion.[32] To these historians the violence on the part of protesters was dwarfed by the disproportionate and heavy-handed treatment that protesters often suffered from the forces in charge of policing.[33] Yet in order to understand the policing measures that were implemented in Westphalia and Nord-Pas-de-Calais it is important to recognise that local authorities and civil servants in charge of policing measures had reason to expect significant levels of violence.

Expectations of violence and the politicisation of violence

In France, the expectation of violence was influenced not least by the revolutionary rhetoric of the most radical elements within the French trade union movement who actively encouraged violence and sabotage. It was only by the Congress of Amiens in October 1906 that the communist C.G.T. trade union formally adopted revolutionary syndicalism as its main strategy in the fight for social and political change; however many of the leaders of the C.G.T., including Pouget and Pelloutier had long engaged in rhetoric of 'revolutionary syndicalism' linking strike action to revolution.

The extent to which the violent actions that took place in Nord-Pas-de-Calais could be linked to the promotion of revolutionary syndicalism is, of course, difficult to assess. Recent historical accounts tend to downplay the actual influence of 'revolutionary syndicalism' on the actions of striking workers.[34] Membership of the C.G.T. remained low, organising less than six per cent of French employees when it was at its highest.[35] More importantly, the sympathies and loyalties of French workers were highly diverse and not easily won over to the radical camp of the Socialist movement.[36]

On the other hand, the C.G.T. was very influential in Nord-Pas-de-Calais, particularly among the miners, and between 1891 and 1898 the Marxist *Parti Ouvrier Français* got about a third of its votes in the *département* Nord. There can be little doubt that even in sectors where membership among employees was low, the workers were well acquainted with the rhetoric of radical trade unionists. The rhetoric of 'revolutionary syndicalism' undoubtedly backfired on protesters because it increased the authorities' expectations of violence and at the same time provided public authorities with a justification for imposing very restrictive policing measures and frequent military intervention.

At the same time, violence between protesters and policing forces became highly politicised with successive French governments being in constant competition with the left-wing opposition in eliciting the sympathy of the wider public. As a result the instructions given by the French Interior Ministry and military commanders to the *gendarmes*, soldiers and officers increasingly stressed the need to show 'moderation', 'tact' and '*sang-froid*'.[37] From 1901 the War Ministry even began to give medals and distinctions to *gendarmes* and soldiers who had managed particularly difficult situations without open confrontation with the protesters.[38] The French government had a clear interest in avoiding violent clashes with protesters because dead bodies had a major propaganda value for the left-wing opposition. Such incidents would only help to undermine the legitimacy of the government and could furthermore be used to justify violent opposition to the existing government and regime.

On the German side, violent incidents during social and political protest were also highly politicised. However, here it was not the government but the protesters who were on the defence. As in France, the Prussian government and the conservative press would use any incident of window smashing or violent confrontation between protesters and public forces to de-legitimise the protest and describe the protesters as being out of control.

The active discouragement by Social Democratic leaders of violence and disorder has reinforced the impression of popular protest in Imperial Germany as peaceful and disciplined. To be sure, many large-scale protests organised by the Social Democrats were remarkably disciplined. However any study of popular protest in Imperial Germany also provides evidence of very violent actions on the part of protesters.[39] In Westphalia strikes and protests also produced a good deal of violence, from window smashing and stone throwing to physical attacks on perceived opponents and fist-fights with the police. At least one Prussian police commissioner and one *gendarme* were killed in confrontations with protesters.[40]

The significant level of violence on the part of the protesters needs to be recognised, even if protesters were also the victims of systematic and vicious attacks on the part of the police. The brutality of Prussian police officers was legendary, and testified to not only by the Social Democratic press but by numerous complaints from people with no loyalties to the protest movements in which they were caught up as unfortunate bystanders.[41]

The Social Democratic leaders' active discouragement of violence and their refrain from revolutionary rhetoric undoubtedly helped those in the Prussian Interior Ministry and the provincial administration who sought to avoid military involvement. It also strengthened the position of those who expressed confidence in the ability of the police and the *gendarmerie* to handle sensitive situations without military assistance, while weakening the arguments of local authorities and industrialists who called for military intervention. On the other hand, in their preparations for the policing of large-scale protest, the Prussian Interior Ministry and the provincial administration always started out from the assumption that there might be significant levels of violence against persons and property.[42]

Levels of inter-personal violence

Amongst workers the potential for violence tended to be high both during labour disputes and in times of peace and quiet. This was the case in Nord-Pas-de-Calais as well as in Westphalia. Social and political protest was often generated by long-standing grievances and the personal costs of engaging in labour disputes tended to be high. This was particularly true in Westphalia, where employers operated with well-developed systems of blacklisting actual and presumed militants and agitators, union members or simply workers joining a strike. Moreover striking workers and their families suffered serious personal hardship and each conflict created acrimonious rifts between colleagues more or less committed to the action. Thus, those responsible for policing measures had good reasons for expecting a good deal of random violence.[43]

Many of these contentious conflicts affected groups who were already singled out by the police and public authorities for unruliness and high potential for interpersonal violence even under normal circumstances. This was not simply due to middle-class panic in the face of the 'dangerous classes'. In the roughest industrial areas of Westphalia life was hard and dangerous, working conditions extremely poor, and frequent accidents often resulted in loss of limbs or lives. In the years preceding the outbreak of the First World War, six people on average were killed in accidents every day (Sundays and holidays included) in the German mining industry.[44] This generated a sub-culture hailing toughness and violent masculinity.

The levels of inter-personal violence were sustained by the high proportion of young single men among the working population. Within this volatile masculine population, marriage or even girlfriends might have acted as a moderating factor. However for many young men in the Westphalian Ruhr District this was hardly an option, since the male population aged between eighteen and twenty outnumbered the female population by three to one, and competition for girls therefore had the opposite effect. More than half the newcomers to Westphalian industrial areas were migrant workers, mainly from the Eastern provinces, and poorly integrated in local society.

Amongst the migrant workers, it was undoubtedly the Poles who faced the most serious problems of exclusion and as a group remained badly integrated in Westphalian society. The number of Polish workers in Westphalia grew from 33,000 in 1890 to reach a critical mass of almost 300,000 in 1910.[45] More than eighty-eight per cent of Poles in Westphalia were employed as unskilled workers in the mining sector and in heavy industry, where they found themselves at the bottom of the workplace hierarchy.[46] As an ethnic and linguistic minority their ties to other communities were weak and as Catholics they were openly discriminated against by the Prussian authorities, who kept a close eye on their cultural and religious activities. Poles also seem often to have been particularly targeted by the Westphalian police for violation of petty administrative rules.[47]

It is not a surprise that a macho sub-culture thrived particularly in the mining communities. Evans describes how in a mining town like Hamborn, men often gathered to socialise in groups of forty or fifty, which not infrequently resulted in brawls.[48] Crimes of violence made up more than twenty-two per cent of reported crime figures in 1900–1908, but behind that figure one has to assume much higher levels of unreported violent encounters. Police officers on patrol frequently reported that they had been attacked while carrying out their duties,[49] and mining towns, like Hamborn, were simply 'no-go areas' for the police; similarly many foremen carried revolvers, even in times of peace and quiet.[50] Guns were common among the workers as well. It was said at the time that the first thing a young miner would buy for himself was a watch, the second a revolver. The description of migrant workers as knife-wielding and gun-happy undoubtedly has a ring of xenophobia, as several historians observe.[51] However the possession of firearms was obviously widespread in Westphalia. Between 1898 and 1900 there were no less than 1,339 prosecutions for violation of firearms regulations in the county of Essen alone, and this constituted only forty-two per cent of prosecuted firearms violations within the county of Düsseldorf.[52]

In Nord-Pas-de-Calais, the rapid growth of industrial sectors with poor conditions in the workplace and in the crowded living quarters also brought about high levels of inter-personal violence. The industrial population was characterised by a large turnover of workers, and local migration from the countryside to and between cities. Many of the industrial workers coming from neighbouring rural areas had difficulty in adapting themselves to the conditions of modern industry.[53]

While the majority of the employees in the mining industry of Pas-de-Calais were recruited in the surrounding rural areas and were for the most part married family men, who were well integrated in the local community, the *département* 'Nord' also had a substantial group of young single males migrating from other French regions, from Italy and from across the Belgian border. Nord-Pas-de-Calais was until 1911 the area with the highest proportion of foreign workers.[54]

Workers from outside the local area were the occasional target of physical and verbal abuse from the local population, and incidents of local youths fighting with groups of young Belgians or Italians were commonplace. Yet compared to the exclusion of Poles in Westphalian society, the position of Belgian and Italian workers in Nord-Pas-de-Calais was better in several respects. The majority of migrant workers from Belgium and Italy were Catholics like the local population and they generally spoke fluent French. Moreover a significant proportion of the Belgians and Italians were skilled or semi-skilled workers employed in the textile, metal or mining industries; as a result some held important positions within the workplace.

Given the volatile workforce in some of the industrial areas of Westphalia and Nord-Pas-de-Calais, the authorities in charge of policing of popular protest had to reckon with a significant potential for violence. During labour conflicts or in situations of popular unrest this might erupt and be directed either against the policing forces or against those within the local community who were singled out as opponents.

Protest and the dynamics of violence

How was this reflected in the levels of violence during strikes and demonstrations? In the first place the comparative study on violent protest in France, Italy and Germany by Charles Tilly, Louise Tilly and Richard Tilly provides some important clues about the differences between France and Germany generally. Their investigations are limited to incidents reported in the press of 'violent protest' defined as a group of at least fifty people involved in a protest action during which some persons or objects were either damaged or seized.[55] However their study provides an indication of the differences in the number of violent protests that occurred in France and Germany between 1830 and 1930.

While the number of recorded protests in France between 1882 and 1913 exceeded 20,000 only some 520 to 525 of these incidents could be described as violent.[56] Charles Tilly observes that the vast majority of French strikes and demonstrations identified by the study did not generate violence beyond minor pushing and shoving.[57] On the basis of similar research methods and definitions of collective action, Richard Tilly found merely 214 incidents of violent protest occurring within the German Empire over thirty-one years between 1882 and 1913.[58] Richard Tilly therefore describes the Imperial Era as a period of low violence compared to France, or to the levels of violence during the Weimar Republic.[59]

However, these figures could be seen from another angle. The 214 incidents of violent protest might well be described as a 'low' figure and earn Wilhelmine Germany the label of a particularly peaceful period; yet in comparison with the 525 incidents recorded in France the difference appears surprisingly limited; the period between 1882 and 1914 is, after all, considered to be an extremely turbulent period in the history of the French Third Republic – covering the Boulanger movement, the continuous challenges from the far right, the Dreyfus Affair, the struggle over the implementation of anti-Catholic legislation, as well as an increasing number of labour conflicts, widespread social and political protest among industrial workers and major disturbances generated by the crisis in the agricultural sector. If the research by Charles and Richard Tilly only identifies two and a half times as many incidents of violent protest in France as in Germany, we may need to rethink the interpretation of the 'rebellious French' as opposed to the 'orderly Germans'. After all, the 214 incidents of violent protest between 1882 and 1913 indicate that there was still scope for a good deal of violent protest in Wilhelmine Germany. Between 1900 and 1913 there were twenty-three incidents of major disturbances involving on average 847 people.[60]

This is not to argue that there was not in France a particular culture of violent protests or to question the fact that many protest actions in Germany took place in a remarkably disciplined manner, given the number of people involved. Yet we need to ask the question whether, particularly in the case of Germany, historians have not been too ready to accept the accounts of the protesters and dismiss the accounts of local authorities, police and employers.[61]

To be sure, accounts from local police authorities, mayors, and industrialists may often be wildly exaggerated and conspicuously distinguished by private interests. Even the civil servants in the provincial administration were keenly aware of the particular interests behind the demand for more police and military intervention.[62] Yet the discrepancy between the levels of violent protest France and Germany is not sufficiently large to account for the highly dissimilar use of troops in the two countries.

Armed confrontations and people killed: the dynamics of violence

The number of people killed in confrontations between protesters and public forces in France and Germany also points towards similarities rather than differences. The most eye-catching outcome of fights between protesters and policing forces was that in both countries it was the protesters who accounted for the highest number of casualties. On the side of the policing agencies, there were five casualties amongst French police officers, *gendarmes* and troops,[63] whilst at least one Prussian *gendarme* and one police commissioner were killed in fights with protesters.[64]

The thirty-seven protesters killed in confrontation with the French police, *gendarmerie* or troops between 1889 and 1914 are all well documented incidents. On the German side any quantification remains uncertain; this study identified twenty-two deaths amongst German protesters in the entire Empire between 1889 and 1914; this however must be regarded as a minimum, while the actual figure is likely to be higher.[65]

The higher number of deaths among protesters is not surprising when one considers the arms involved. Both the French and Prussian *gendarmes* carried guns and bayonets as well as swords. Similarly, the Prussian police officer on patrol was armed as if for a war, as the American Raymond Fosdick observed in 1913.[66] The Royal Guards, who policed many Prussian cities, carried firearms similar to those used by infantry soldiers as part of the outfit for ordinary patrols, and after 1910 they also carried revolvers.[67] For Prussian municipal police officers the main weapon was a sword but after the turn of the century guns became widely available and were specifically used for major operations of protest policing. In France, municipal police officers also carried swords and in the 1890s the truncheon was introduced to the Paris police.[68]

There were many common features in terms of the small-scale violence generated by protesters in Westphalia and Nord-Pas-de-Calais: window breaking and stone throwing against police and *gendarmerie* being commonplace; in both areas there was also a good deal of pushing and shoving, which not infrequently developed into fist-fights, particularly when a policeman or *gendarme* attempted to make an arrest. During labour disputes, serious intimidation was used by strikers to keep potential strike-breakers in line: verbal abuses, violence or threats of violence against those who continued working, were as much a part of any labour dispute in Westphalia as it was in Nord-Pas-de-Calais. Strike-breakers were targeted on their way in or out of the workplace, but most attacks happened on the way from home to the work place or in their own home.[69]

Nevertheless, towards the end of the 19th century some important differences can be traced in the conditions under which protest could take place. In Nord-Pas-de-Calais until the late 1880s, occupying the factory or mine was a widespread form of obstruction of the continuation of production. During the 1890s, with the building of fences and walls around mines and factories, and with the introduction of preventive policing measures, striking workers were more effectively barred from entering the premises of their workplace. Instead the protest moved out into the streets.

In Nord-Pas-de-Calais – as in Westphalia – it was therefore the area in front of the workplace that became the centre for gatherings face-to-face with the forces in charge of policing. Protest movements frequently spilled over into wider areas, so that a labour conflict or other type of protest easily dominated the entire public space in a small or middle-sized town. It was in the face-to-face stand-offs between protesters and public forces that violence might escalate from shouting abuse and stone throwing and isolated incidents of pushing and shoving involving a few individuals, to violent physical confrontation between the two groups.

It is from the moment when confrontations went beyond the level of minor pushing and shoving that important differences appear on the French and German side. Whereas in Nord-Pas-de-Calais protesters fought to get access to locations occupied by the police, *gendarmerie* and troops, in Westphalia the conflict area was the one occupied by protesters. German protesters pushed, shoved and threw stones until the police and *gendarmes* were ordered to 'clear the street' by attacking protesters indiscriminately with their sword or bayonet. Those who did not run fast enough or were otherwise prevented from getting away would be given a very bad beating, sometimes with fatal consequences. In Westphalia confrontations also occurred when police or troops arrived in locations that were already occupied by protesters, and then sought to force the protesters away.

In the light of the large number of guns among the working population in the Westphalian Ruhr, it is hardly surprising that there were numerous incidents of alleged shooting against the police or troops, particularly during contentious labour conflicts. However these never seemed to take place as direct confrontation, but were reported as revolver shots from windows or from unidentified persons in the dark.[70]

In France, revolvers were widespread among workers as well as amongst employers and foremen since there were no rules limiting the possession of firearms. Firearms were occasionally reported to have been used against the police in Paris and there were several incidents of shooting during the great agricultural unrest in the South of France during the summer of 1907 and during confrontations in Villeneuve-Saint-Georges in July 1908.[71] In Nord-Pas-de-Calais, however, the protests did not seem to be characterised by widespread use of firearms on the side of the protesters.

On the other hand, in stand-offs face-to-face with police, *gendarmes* or military troops, protesters in Nord-Pas-de-Calais tended to be remarkably bold in comparison with protesters in Westphalia. Apart from the general shoving and stone- and bottle-throwing, protesters often directly challenged the forces by trying to break through their lines. Such attempts seriously raised the stakes, by forcing the police and front line soldiers into fist-fights. It was then that mounted *gendarmes*, or cavalry armed with swords, would be sent in to attack those who attempted to break through. Officers and *gendarmes* were ordered to use only the blunt side of the sword, but numerous serious wounds received by the protesters show that this order was often ignored. In most cases the intervention with mounted *gendarmerie* and cavalry was enough to prevent further attempts by protesters to reach areas closed off by the police. However when this failed, the situation immediately became very chaotic and dangerous. The police and troops were no longer in charge and violence could spin out of control within a matter of minutes, with soldiers shooting into the crowd.

Berlière and Bruneteaux both argue that it was the presence of military troops in itself that produced the violence, because the military intervention was provocative and escalated confrontation.[72] This was undoubtedly the case in some conflicts in Nord-Pas-de-Calais during the 1890s. However, after the turn of the century, the linkage between military presence and high levels of violence and casualties became far more complex. The use of the military to police popular unrest has two aspects. The soldiers of course have the means to repress any disorder with unrestricted use of force. In many cases the military troops should not need to proceed to violence, because the very presence of heavily armed soldiers carries an implicit threat of immediate destruction of opposition. In Germany, this simple logic was perfectly understood by protesters. During major protest movements, the Westphalian population was warned that policemen, *gendarmes* and soldiers had orders to shoot,[73] and only the most audacious hothead would dare to challenge a Prussian military unit openly.

In Nord-Pas-de-Calais however the rules of the game were more complex. When troops appeared in the town of Fourmies on May Day 1891 there was still a widespread assumption among workers that troops acting on behalf of the Republican regime would not shoot on unarmed civilians; indeed some protesters even doubted that the guns were loaded with real ammunition; those expectations proved unfounded with fourteen people killed and many more injured. Agulhon describes the shooting at Fourmies as the breakdown of trust in troops acting with moderation towards workers.[74] However, when looking at Nord-Pas-de-Calais it is worth noting that protesters in subsequent years were remarkably audacious in their interaction with troops. Yet protesters could be in no doubt that the soldiers' guns were loaded: soldiers had previously opened fire and the government had then backed the army.

If protesters in Nord-Pas-de-Calais still dared to challenge the troops it was because some unwritten rules seemed to have emerged for how far protesters could go when confronted with soldiers. Many who participated in strikes and demonstrations had been soldiers themselves and knew the orders that were given to troops: not to react to provocation and to show moderation. Moreover, striking workers knew that many of the conscripts were themselves workers, and could assume some sympathy from their side. Protesters could therefore assume that they could challenge and harass the soldiers with relative impunity, up to the point where they tried to break through the lines. And even at that stage there was room for toeing-the-line before the situation reached a really critical point. This mutual understanding between soldiers and protesters seemed to work up to a certain point; but it was a dangerous game, for when it broke down soldiers possessed extremely effective means to injure and kill.

Despite the extremely frequent military involvement in protest policing, there were only seven occasions between 1891 and 1914 where soldiers opened fire against protesters. On the other hand, it was not simply the presence of soldiers that was responsible for fatal confrontations. Amongst the thirty-seven French protesters who died in the years between the shooting at Fourmies in 1891 and the outbreak of the First World War, five were killed in confrontations with the police or *gendarmerie*.

A similar observation could be made for Germany. Among the twenty-two people who were killed between 1889 and 1914 in confrontation with public forces, fourteen were killed by soldiers; the remaining eight were killed in confrontations with police and *gendarmerie*, including the deaths occurring during the military interventions in Herne in June 1899 and during the miners' strike of March 1912.

Undoubtedly there was in France a particular culture of violent protest, which was different from the manner of protest in Germany. The studies of Charles and Richard Tilly seem to confirm this. Yet their figures also indicate that the difference is not significant enough to account for the highly dissimilar frequency of military involvement in the policing of popular protest in the two countries. Looking specifically at Westphalia, it is worth observing that its working population was larger, and the potential for large-scale mobilisation much higher than was the case in Nord-Pas-de-Calais. This was particularly significant for the highly volatile and strike-prone mining industry.

In terms of violence occurring during labour disputes, certain radicals among the French Trade Union Movement actively encouraged violent protest as a means to achieve their desired ends. This conscious use of violent protest was not limited to workers linked to the communist C.G.T. It reflected a political culture where violent protest was easily justified not only among disaffected workers or political radicals on the extreme left or the extreme right, but also among middle-class supporters of the Catholic Church.

Despite the rhetoric in French political culture that often legitimised and even glorified violent protest, it is important not to exaggerate the actual levels of violence taking place. In fact, during the vast majority of labour conflicts in Nord-Pas-de-Calais the confrontation remained at the level of pushing and shoving. Even the incidents to which the army was called out were often described by civilian and military authorities alike as being fairly peaceful with protesters doing nothing more serious than shouting abuse and throwing stones and bottles.

It is similarly important to stress, that despite the proverbial orderliness of Germans, there was considerable potential for violence amongst the population of Westphalia, particularly in the industrial areas around the River Ruhr. Attacks on strike-breakers and the throwing of stones against the police and *gendarmerie* were as commonplace as in Nord-Pas-de-Calais. This was despite the Social Democratic leaders and the trade unions actively discouraging violence and sabotage as counterproductive.

At the same time, despite the low number of military interventions in Westphalia the Prussian authorities can hardly be described as more relaxed about the prospect of violence than their French counterparts. Local authorities in charge of policing, as well as the senior civil servants in the provincial administration, reckoned with significant potential for random violence. What distinguished the senior administrators in Westphalia from their counterparts in Nord-Pas-de-Calais was not so much their expectation of violent popular protest as their strategic approach to policing: confrontation or prevention and containment. The different strategic approaches to protest policing in the two areas also resulted in the highly dissimilar dynamics between protesters and public forces when confronting each other face-to-face.

Notes

[1] Charles Tilly's contribution to Tilly, Tilly and Tilly (1975). See also Charles Tilly (1986).

[2] The French Labour Ministry, *Statistique des greves*, (Annual publication, 1893–1913).

[3] Richard Tilly and Gerd Hohorst, 'Sozialer Protest in Deutschland im 19. Jahrhundert: Skizze eines Forschungsansatzes', in Konrad Jarausch (ed.), *Quantifizierung in der Geschichtswissenschaft. Probleme und Möglichkeiten*, Düsseldorf: Droste, 1976, p. 267.

[4] Trempé (1995) pp. 249–250.

[5] Calculated on the basis of figures provided by Jessen (1991) Table 5.

[6] Jacques Dupâquier, *Histoire de la population française, d 1789 à 1914*, Paris: Presses Universitaires de France, 1988, p. 259; Groh (1978) p. 359; Tenfelde (1990) pp. 148–149.

[7] Despite methodological difficulties in comparing the figures, the study of Tilly, Tilly and Tilly on protest in France, Germany and Italy between 1830–1930 seems to provide some quantitative evidence to support that reputation. Tilly, Tilly and Tilly (1975) pp. 17–29.

[8] Charles Tilly (1986) pp. 271–272.

[9] See Chapter 9.

[10] Law of 14–17 June 1791 banning professional associations.

[11] The prohibition of strikes stated in the law of 22 Germinal of year XI (12 April 1803) was reinforced by the articles 414, 415 and 416 of the Napoleonic Criminal Code of 1810.

[12] Decree of 25–29 February 1848 on freedom of association; law of 27 November 1849 legalising concerted actions by employers as well as by employees.

[13] Decree of 25 March 1852.

[14] Laws of 25 May 1864 and of 11 July 1868.

[15] The 'Naquet Law' of 30 June 1881 recognising political organisations and trade unions. The 'Waldeck-Rousseau Law' of 21 March 1884 legalising trade unions.

[16] Machelon (1976) p. 200.

[17] See Chapter 1.

[18] Calculated on the basis of the figures of Groh (1978) p. 380.

[19] In Germany there was an annual average of 2,058 strikes with 4,650 working days lost; for France the annual average was 970 strikes with 2,760 lost working days, and in England there were only 640 strikes but an annual average of 7,409 working days lost. Böll (1992) pp. 101–102; see also Friedhelm Böll, 'Changing forms of labor conflict: secular development or strike waves?' in Leopold Haimson and Charles Tilly (eds.), *Strike, Wars, and Revolutions in an International Perspective*, Cambridge: Cambridge University Press, 1989, p. 62; Perrot (1974) p. 51; *Statistique des grèves*, 1899–1913.

[20] Groh (1978) p. 359.

[21] Geary (1993) pp. 141–143.

[22] The total number of strikers recoded in the two *départements* 'Nord' and 'Pas-de-Calais' for the entire year of 1906 was 92,191. *Statistique des grèves* 1906.

[23] *Statistique des grèves* 1893–1913.

[24] Tilly and Shorter (1974) p. 151.

[25] Tilly and Shorter (1974) p. 195.

[26] Tilly and Shorter (1974) p. 151.

[27] Calculated on the basis of Groh (1978) p. 359.

[28] Charles Tilly and Edward Shorter, 'Déclin de la grève violente en France, 1890–1935', *Le Mouvement Social*, 1971, p. 110.

[29] See Chapter 9.

[30] NA, Paris, F 7 12912: Letter of 8 May 1909 from the State Council to the Prime Minister includes an eight pages rapport from the sub-commission in charge of estimating the potential for unrest among metal workers.

[31] Saul (1981) pp. 215, 231–233; Jessen (1991) pp. 75–76.

[32] Rebérioux (1989) pp. 245, 264.

[33] On police and *gendarmerie* violence against protesters, see Funk (1986) pp. 284–301; on France see Berlière (1991) pp. 1011–1016.

[34] Marcel van der Linden and Wayne Thorpe, 'Essor et declin du syndicalisme révolutionnaire', *Le Mouvement Social*, vol. 159, 1992, p. 11.

[35] Michel Dreyfus, *Histoire de la C.G.T.*, Paris: Editions complexe, 1995, p. 63.

[36] Edward J. Arnold, 'Counter-Revolutionary Themes and the Working Class in France of the Belle Epoque: The Case of the "Syndicats jaunes", 1899-1912', *French History*, vol. 13 /2, 1999, pp. 99–133; Colin Heywood, 'Mobilising the Workers in fin-de-siècle France', *French History*, vol. 12 /2, 1998, pp. 172–194; Magraw (2002) pp. 104–106.

[37] One simply needs to look through the General Orders issued by the army corps commander to identify the buzz words. MA, Vincennes, 1st A.C. /2 I 227, *Ordres généraux*, 1893–1904 and 1909–1913.

[38] MA, Vincennes, 1st A.C. /2 I 227, *Ordres généraux*, 1893–1904 and 1909–1913 contains numerous lists of soldiers and *gendarmes* designated for gold, silver and bronze medals. See also Chapter 9.

[39] Erhard Lucas, James Wickham and Karl-Heinz Roth, *Arbeiter-Radikalismus und die 'andere' Arbeiterbewegung*, Bochum: Edition Egalite, 1977; David F. Crew 'Steel, Sabotage and Socialism: the strike at the Dortmund "Union" steel work in 1911', in Richard Evans (ed.), *The German Working Class 1888–1933*, London: Croom Helm, 1982; Lindenberger (1993) pp. 47–68.

[40] One *gendarme* was shot in 1890 during unrest in Köpenick near Berlin, and in 1907, a police commissioner in Düsseldorf was fatally wounded during a street fight by a violent blow to his head. MA, Freiburg, PH2 /14 (document 96): Telegram of 21 March 1890 from General Bronsart von Schellendorf to Wilhelm II; GSA, Berlin, HA1, Rep. 77, Titel 505–3, vol. 6, (document 203) on the death of Police Commissioner Eidam in July 1907.

[41] GSA, Berlin, HA1, Rep. 77, Titel 508–4, Beiheft 4. This collection of 228 documents brings together police reports, press cuttings from the social democratic press as well as complaints from 'pillars of society'. From their different viewpoint they describe the violence on the side of both protesters and police during a number of confrontations in Gelsenkirchen, Hagen and Dortmund in connection with the provincial elections to the *Reichstag* in June 1903. The documents provide particularly detailed descriptions of patterns of behaviour that are typical for numerous other incidents of clashes between police and protesters.

[42] GSA, Berlin, HA1, Rep. 77, Titel 2513–1, Beiheft 9 (documents 124–130): Report from a meeting on 7 July 1904 between authorities in the Düsseldorf District concerning policing measures in the case of a major miners' strike; HSA, Münster, VII–14, vol.1 /32–1: Minutes from a meeting on 1 June 1912 by the Local Governor in Essen on future policing measures after the great miners' strike of March 1912.

[43] Berlière also makes this point in his analysis of the policing of Paris under Lépine. Berlière (1991) pp. 1006–1007.

[44] According to Hobsbawn (1987, p. 306), on average 1,430 British miners were killed every year (almost four a day) between 1910 and 1914, while 165,000 were reported injured. The casualties in Britain, however, were only two-thirds the rate of persons killed and injured in the German mining sector.

[45] Stephen Hickey, 'The shaping of the German Labour movement: miners in the Ruhr', in Richard Evans (ed.), *Society and Politics in Wilhelmine Germany*, London: Croom Helm, 1978, p. 217; Ritter and Tenfelde (1992) p. 25.

[46] Jessen (1991) p. 245.

[47] Jessen (1991) pp. 245–246.

[48] Evans (1987) p. 172.

[49] GSA, HA1, Rep. 77, Titel 505/ 3, vol. 6 (documents 203–207); Reports relating to a case where a police commissioner who was knocked unconscious and later died; GSA, Berlin, HA1, Rep. 77, Titel 508/ 4 Beiheft 4: this collection contains typical accounts of accusations and counter-accusations of violence against the police and police violence against protesters and innocent bystanders during

demonstrations in Gelsenkirchen, Hagen and Dortmund in June 1903; Jessen (1991) pp. 266–267.

[50] Evans (1987) p. 172.

[51] Klaus Tenfelde, 'Die "Krawalle von Herne" im Jahre 1899', *Internationale wissenschaftliche Korrespondenz zur Geschichte deutschen Arbeiterbewegung*, vol. 15, 1979, p. 90; Jessen (1991) p. 66; Spencer (1992) p. 113.

[52] Spencer (1992) pp. 113–114.

[53] Haupt (1986) p. 248.

[54] Trempé (1995) p. 236; Yves Léquin, '*La Mosaïque France*', Paris: Larousse, 1988.

[55] Tilly, Tilly and Tilly (1975) p. 56.

[56] Tilly, Tilly and Tilly (1975) p. 57. Unfortunately Charles Tilly does not provide the exact numbers, but a careful reading of his graphs leads to this figure.

[57] Tilly, Tilly and Tilly (1975) p. 249.

[58] This compares to 319 incidents during the thirty-one-year period between 1816 and 1847 and 236 recorded incidents between 1850 and 1881. Tilly, Tilly and Tilly (1975) pp. 212 and 226.

[59] Tilly, Tilly and Tilly (1975) p. 245.

[60] Tilly, Tilly and Tilly (1975) p. 213.

[61] Several historians working on German policing mention the need to revise the idea of the 'orderly' and subservient Germans and the ability of the Prussian authorities to successfully domesticate the industrial towns of the Ruhr area: Evans (1987) pp. 171–174; Jessen (1991) p. 263; Spencer (1992) p. 164; Blackbourn (1997) pp. 370–374.

[62] See Chapter 7.

[63] Figures established by Carrot (1984) p. 865; Berlière (1996) footnote 180. See also Chapter 3.

[64] MA, Freiburg, PH2 /14 (document 96): Telegram of 21 March 1890 from General Bronsart von Schellendorf to Wilhelm II; GSA, Berlin, HA1, Rep. 77, Titel 505 /3, vol. 6, (document 203): on the death of police commissioner Eidam.

[65] According to Liebknecht it was impossible to form any clear idea of how many people had died in the hands of the Prussian police. (Liebknecht (1973) pp. 59–61.) Eleven people were reported to have died during the great miners' strike of 1889; three were killed during a military intervention in October 1894; two were killed by police and *gendarmes* during the Westphalian miners' strike of 1899; at least three people were killed in clashes with the Hamburg police in January 1906; another two were killed the same year during clashes with Berlin police in the so-called Moabit Riots of 1910; and a young miner was shot in the head by police during the Westphalian miners' strike of 1912.

[66] Fosdick (1969) p. 231.

[67] Funk (1986) footnote 108.

[68] Berlière (1991) pp. 1006–1016.

[69] HSA, Münster, Regierung Arnsberg, 14321: Telegram of 27 June 1899 from the Local Governor in Bochum to the District Governor of Arnsberg; HSA, Münster, Regierung Münster, VII–14 vol.1 /32–1 (document 120): Letter of 20 May 1912

from the District Governor in Münster to the Interior Minister von Dallwitz. After the miners' strike in 1912, the district governor reported that while there had been no attacks on the mining installations, many strike-breakers were assaulted in their homes or on their way to work. Moreover, the police had been powerless in the face of the riots taking place in the towns when thousands of people were gathered.

[70] HSA, Münster, Regierung Arnsberg 14321: Letter of 14 July 1899 from Province Governor von der Recke in Münster to the District Governor of Arnsberg; HSA, Münster, Regierung Arnsberg 14321: Report of 17 July 1899 from the District Governor of Arnsberg on the miners strike in Herne, June 1899; MA, Freiburg, PH2 /14 (document 194): Telegram of 30 July 1899 from General von Mikusch-Buckberg to Wilhelm II; GSA, Berlin, HA1, Rep. 77, Titel 2523–1, vol. 17 (documents 67–69): Letter of 12 March 1912 from the District Governor in Düsseldorf to Interior Minister von Dallwitz; HSA, Münster, Regierung Arnsberg 14325 (document 120): Telegram of 13 March 1912 from the police in Bochum; HSA, Münster, Regierung Münster VII–14 vol. 1/ 32–1 (documents 5–10): Letter of 20 May 1912 from the District Governor in Münster to Interior Minister von Dallwitz; GSA, Berlin, HA1, Rep. 77, Titel 508–4, Beiheft 4: this contains several mentionings of gunshots against the police during the election unrests in Gelsenkirchen, Herne and Dortmund June 1903.

[71] Carrot (1984) p. 686; Berlière (1991) p. 1013; idem. (1996) p. 119; Bruneteaux (1996) p. 44.

[72] Rebérioux (1975) p. 113; Bruneteaux (1996) pp. 44–47; Berlière (1996) p. 199.

[73] HSA, Münster, OP 6095 (documents 22–23): Letter of 22 June 1895 from Interior Minister von der Recke to Westphalia Province Governor Studt; GSA, Berlin, HA1, Rep. 77, Titel 2523, 1 (document 200): 'Mahnung an die Bevölkerung!' of 11 March 1912; HSA, Münster, Regierung Münster, VII–14, vol. 1 / 32–1: Minutes from a meeting by the Local Governor in Essen on 1 June 1912.

[74] Agulhon (1993) p. 55.

Chapter 5

The Extension of Police and *Gendarmerie* Forces

The demilitarisation of the maintenance of public order

During the second half of the 19th century the rapid industrialisation and urbanisation of many areas created new challenges in terms of policing. In urban areas, everyday policing implied not only crime fighting and maintenance of public order; in France and Germany the police and the *gendarmerie* were also given the responsibility for carrying out an increasing number of administrative tasks and the enforcement of numerous regulations concerning traffic, health and safety. At the same time, expectations of effective policing were rising in rural communities. In both France and Prussia, central government and local authorities agreed about the urgent need for more manpower in the forces and for improving the quality of policemen and *gendarmes*. Accordingly, the numbers of French and Prussian policemen and *gendarmes* increased markedly between 1890 and 1914, despite constant political battles between governmental and local authorities about financing and control over these forces.[1]

In the case of Prussia, the strengthening of police and *gendarmerie* forces is seen as the precondition for the subsequent detachment of the regular army from its traditional role in the policing of popular protest,[2] although Funk admits that police and *gendarmerie* forces remained too weak to entirely avoid occasional military assistance.[3] Interpretations of the French case also focus on the number of policemen and *gendarmerie* officers arguing that the insufficient number of police and *gendarmerie* forces was one of the main reasons for the continued reliance on support from military troops.[4] Yet when comparing Nord-Pas-de-Calais with Westphalia, the question arises of how much police presence was 'sufficient' to maintain public order. Whether or not military assistance was 'necessary', is after all a highly normative assessment. In Prussia the governmental and local authorities differed over the question, and their positions often changed when confronted with situations of imminent crisis. Opinions also differ between historians. Tenfelde and Saul see requisitions for the Prussian army during the miners' strikes of 1899, and again in 1912, as unnecessarily authoritarian measures indicating an attempt to provoke violent confrontations with the workers.[5] Jessen, Henning and Spencer, on the other hand, all admit that Prussian administrators made serious attempts to avoid involving the army. Thus they see the military interventions on those occasions as marking the limits of how far public order policing could be demilitarised during major social or political conflicts.[6]

In the literature on protest and policing in France, there seem to be even greater difficulties in handling the normative question of what constitutes 'sufficient' police forces and in which situations military assistance could be described as appropriate. In order to explain why the French army was so frequently involved in protest policing between 1890 and 1914, three lines of argument prevail. These three positions are not mutually exclusive and are often presented side by side, although given different degrees of importance. While some historians argue that military assistance to police and *gendarmerie* was in many cases necessary due to inadequate police and *gendarmerie* forces,[7] those who insist that the display of force was often excessive make a point that is difficult to refute.[8] Exactly where the distinction lies between the 'necessary' and the 'excessive' military interventions is rarely touched upon. The third argument (which is linked to the second) explains that frequent military involvement in protest policing became necessary because of the inability of the National Assembly and successive governments to reach a compromise over the establishment of a special riot unit.[9]

The comparison of the police and *gendarmerie* forces available for protest policing in Nord-Pas-de-Calais and in Westphalia places the measures implemented in France and Prussia in a different context. The fact that the French authorities had more police and *gendarmerie* available for riot policing than their Prussian counterparts challenges the immediate correlation between understaffed police and *gendarmerie* forces on the one hand and the involvement of military troops on the other.

Comparing the police and *gendarmerie* forces available for maintenance of order in case of major conflict requires a careful consideration of three factors. In the first place, we need to look at the number of men employed in the various forces (municipal police forces, national police forces, *gendarmerie*, and, in the case of Prussia, also private security corps). Secondly we have to consider how many of these forces were actually available for maintenance of order, since not all would be called on for operations outside their own area. Finally it is worthwhile looking at how many forces were actually mobilised during the most extended conflicts that took place during this period.

The development of municipal police, and *gendarmerie* 1889–1914

Since 1800 any French town with more than 5,000 inhabitants was obliged by law to organise and finance a municipal police force.[10] Already by the end of the Second Empire there were more than 12,000 municipal policemen in France,[11] though in many towns the municipal police corps only comprised one or two policemen. The mayor was the head of the local police force, although the prefect or sub-prefect could at any moment intervene on policing matters.[12] In towns of more than 40,000 inhabitants the municipal police force was under the command of a police master accountable to the mayor. When the Third Republic established local governments with elected mayors, the Interior Ministry lost the control it had previously exercised when mayors were government appointees.

According to the 1884 law on local government the municipal authorities were responsible for the funding of a police force capable of defending persons and property within the community.[13] While the financial responsibility was firmly placed with the municipal authorities, central government still sought to control the use of municipal police forces through the prefects and sub-prefects. Thus, although not directly responsible for policing in urban communities, the prefect was empowered to take over responsibility for law-and-order measures if he considered the policing measures taken by the mayor inadequate.[14]

When the prefect and sub-prefect took responsibility for maintaining public order in urban areas they could draw not only on municipal police forces but also on the local *gendarmerie*. Although technically a military corps, the *gendarmerie* was established with the purpose of policing rural areas. Within the *département* or *arrondissement*, the *gendarmerie* was first and foremost at the disposition of the prefect or sub-prefect, who had ultimate authority to determine the use of these forces in rural as well as in urban areas. Local *gendarmerie* units could be solicited by any public authority – mayor, assistant mayor or police authorities – however the prefect or sub-prefect could, at any moment, invalidate requisitions of *gendarmes* issued by local police or any municipal authority. This allowed prefects and sub-prefects to implement policing measures across municipal boundaries, without depending on municipal police forces.

In the largest urban areas – Paris, Lyons and from 1908, Marseilles – the police forces were partly nationalised. Although financed by the municipality, they were directly subject to government control through their chiefs – the Paris Police Prefect and the Prefects of the *départements* 'Rhône' and 'Bouche-du-Rhône' – who were appointed by the Interior Minister and accountable to him only.

In the German Empire, police forces were organised by each of the federal states according to its particular laws and constitution. In Prussia, as in France, the responsibility for policing was distributed between municipal and government authorities.

Conditions for municipal police forces were first described in the Prussian General Code of Law (*Allgemeine Landrecht*) of 1794[15] and further elaborated in the *Städteordnung* of 1808. As in France, towns of more than 5,000 inhabitants were obliged by law to keep a police force capable of maintaining public order and defending persons and property. However during most of the 19th century, many Prussian towns were policed by a handful of night watchmen; it was only during the Wilhelmine era that municipal police forces increased in numbers and strength.[16]

In rural communities law-and-order was in the hands of the Prussian *gendarmerie*, established in 1812 and inspired by the French *gendarmerie*.[17] As in France, it was the ministerial appointees in the area, the local governor, the district governor and the province governor, who had responsibility for the use of this force.

For major policing operations the Prussian provincial administration could also draw upon the state police: the Royal Guards (*Königliche Schutzmänner*). The Royal Guards were originally the police force of Berlin, but during the second half of the 19th century they policed an increasing number of large towns. Like the *gendarmerie*, the Royal Guards were organised at national level and could, in case of major unrest, operate anywhere within Prussian territory.

During the 1890s, the province governors and district governors worked increasingly closely with municipal authorities in organising the management of major unrest, by coordinating strategies and the various police and *gendarmerie* forces within the entire province. Although the number of police and *gendarmerie* forces increased, large-scale coordination was difficult because of the high level of fragmentation between the corps. In cases where popular unrest extended over several municipalities and administrative entities, the state-appointed governors organised the coordination of policing measures at the level of the *Kreis*, the district or the entire province. However the Prussian governors did not have the same extended powers as the French prefects to intervene directly in the operations of the municipal police. Moreover, unlike their French counterparts, who could manage many situations with their own *gendarmerie* forces, the Prussian province and district governors did not have a major unified force directly at their disposition because the Prussian *gendarmerie* was a tiny force compared to the French.

The distribution of police and *gendarmerie* forces

While the Prussian and French populations were roughly the same size, the number of police and *gendarmerie* forces differed. In 1889, the number of municipal policemen in Prussia was as low as 2,393.[18] By 1910 this figure had spectacularly increased to more than 17,000.[19] Similar increases took place in the number of Royal Guards. In 1889 there were 5,444 Royal Guards policing seventeen major towns; by 1913 the corps comprised 16,501 police officers present in twenty major towns and cities.[20]

Despite growth in police numbers in the main Prussian towns it did not surpass the levels of police density in France, which was notoriously high by European standards. In 1888, the density of police in larger French towns was generally much higher than that in the Prussian cities. Between 1890 and 1907, the number of French police increased less dramatically than in Prussia. Nevertheless, due to the unfavourable starting point in Prussia and its rapidly growing urban population, most Prussian large towns only reached French levels of police density by 1907–1908.

Table 5.1   Ratio of inhabitants per police officer in major cities

	1888	1908		1889	1907
Berlin	367	288	Paris	358	316
Königsberg	1,315	637	Lyons	-	575
Danzig	1,098	613	Marseilles	775	604
Stettin	1,204	675	Bordeaux	525	-
Posen	1,063	649	Lille	960	822
Magdeburg	1,315	632	Toulouse	820	617
Hanover	1,492	531	Nantes	817	615
Kiel	1,315	552	Saint Etienne	1,100	829
Wiesbaden	1,030	645	Roubaix	993	806
Frankfurt a.M.	685	520	Le Havre	-	530
Fulda	2,040	980	Reims	1,009	963
Hanau	1,449	751	Nice	673	-
Kassel	1,265	653			
Köln	1,818	637			
Koblenz	1,786	752			
Aachen	1,493	588			
Average	1,296	631	Average	803	650
Without Berlin	1,358	654	Without Paris	852	692

Sources: Jessen (1991) p. 357; Berlière (1991) pp. 500–504; idem. (1996) pp. 26–28.

Unfortunately there are no comprehensive data for police densities in smaller towns of Westphalia and Nord-Pas-de-Calais. A comparison of the ratio of police officers to the population in the main industrial towns, however, shows a similar pattern to that of the larger cities. Already by 1889, the density of policing was generally higher in the main towns of Nord-Pas-de-Calais compared to those of Westphalia.

Although the total numbers of police in Westphalia increased sevenfold, the population in some of the main industrial areas, like Essen or Gelsenkirchen, increased four- or five-fold. Given the poor state of police density in 1889, it was difficult to catch up, despite important increases in numbers of police.

Table 5.2 Ratio of inhabitants for every police officer in the main towns of Westphalia and in Nord-Pas-de-Calais

Westphalia	1889–1890	1907–1910	Nord-Pas-de-Calais	1889	1907
Düsseldorf	-	886	Lille	960	822*
Dortmund	1,333	1,041	Roubaix	993	806
Essen	-	821	Calais	1154	-
Bochum	1,250	925	Tourcoing	1380	-
Oberhausen	-	1,630	Boulogne	956	-
Hagen	1,666	862	Dunkerque	1000	406
Gelsenkirchen	3,225	1,020	Douai	1363	-
Recklinghausen	2,272	1,010	Armentières	1473	-
			Valenciennes	1314	882
			Arras	1076	-
			Cambrai	1405	-
Average	1,949	1,024		1,189	729

* Figure for the year 1898

Sources: Berlière (1991) p. 498ff.; idem. (1996) pp. 26–28; Jessen (1991) pp. 63, 357; Spencer (1985) p. 311; GSA, Berlin, HA1, Rep 77, Titel 2513/1 Beiheft 12, (documents 378–379).

By 1907–1908 the number of inhabitants per policeman in the Westphalian towns was down to the same level as that of many towns in Nord-Pas-de-Calais in 1888; yet by that time, police density in the main industrial towns of Nord-Pas-de-Calais had also increased markedly. By the outbreak of the

First World War the available police forces in the main Westphalian industrial towns still lagged slightly behind levels of density in the main towns in Nord-Pas-de-Calais.

The gendarmerie *in the two industrial regions*

The most remarkable difference between the French and the Prussian police forces was the size of the *gendarmerie* that policed rural areas, and functioned as a supplementary force in case of popular unrest. By 1872, the French *gendarmerie* comprised more than 18,000 officers, organised into units of five and placed in rural communities all over national territory.[21] By the turn of the 20th century, there were more than 20,000 French *gendarmerie* officers,[22] and by 1907 their numbers had increased to 26,000, thus constituting the single most important force.[23]

Compared to the French *gendarmerie*, the Prussian force was, and remained, of modest size. Between 1873 and 1882, the Prussian *gendarmerie* comprised only 3,500 men. From 1889 to 1913, the number of *gendarmes* increased from 4,698 to 5,802[24] thus still only a fifth of the size of the French equivalent.

These differences were also noticeable in Westphalia and Nord-Pas-de-Calais. The first *gendarmerie* legion, which covered the *départements* of Nord and Pas-de-Calais comprised 397 mounted *gendarmes* and 449 *gendarmes* on foot.[25] Throughout the period, French authorities constantly complained that a total of 846 *gendarmes* was completely inadequate to police the rural communities of the region with its important mining areas. The problem was particularly acute because significant numbers of the local *gendarmes* were sometimes mobilised for weeks or even months to act as supplementary forces in conflict areas within or outside the region.

Yet the comparison with Westphalia speaks for itself. Whilst rural communities in Nord-Pas-de-Calais had a local force of 846 *gendarmes*, there were only 544 Prussian *gendarmes* in Westphalia in 1913. Given that the population in Westphalia was more than twenty-five per cent larger than the population of Nord-Pas-de-Calais and its territory much larger in size, it becomes clear just how stretched the Westphalian *gendarmerie* forces were.[26]

Together with the 534 Royal Guards who policed some of the large urban areas in Westphalia,[27] the forces directly under the authority of the Prussian government and provincial administration, in all 1,078 Royal Guards and Prussian *gendarmes*, outnumbered the 846 French *gendarmes* based in Nord-Pas-de-Calais.

In relative terms, however, there was only one Royal Guard or Prussian *gendarme* for every 3,827 inhabitants in Westphalia by 1913, as opposed to one French *gendarme* per 3,389 inhabitants in Nord-Pas-de-Calais already by 1901.

Prussian authorities regularly complained about the inadequate numbers of *gendarmes*, particularly after the great miners' strike of 1905. However, in the wake of the strike when the Province Governor of Westphalia asked for the number of *gendarmes* that could be mobilised to Westphalia to be raised to at least 1,250 this demand was not met.[28] Despite some increases, the number of *gendarmes* and Royal Guards in the province could not keep pace with the rapidly growing population and the *gendarmerie* and Royal Guards remained hopelessly inadequate in numbers to deal with major unrest.

This appears clearly from the number of *gendarmes* and Royal Guards available during the last great mining conflict in Westphalia of March 1912. In the county of Lüdinghausen, where 2,000 miners out of 2,800 went on strike, the total number of *gendarmes* and police was eighteen, including those mobilised from other provinces.[29] In the county of Recklinghausen, one of the great centres of the mining industry with a population including 44,000–46,000 miners and a strike rate of 21,000–24,000, there were less than one hundred men to police twenty-eight mines.[30] In a report of 14 March 1912, the District Governor in Münster told the Interior Minister that until the military requisition of two days before, the six local policemen faced the impossible task of maintaining order during a demonstration involving 8,000–10,000 people.[31]

Private security corps

While the lack of sufficient police and *gendarmerie* forces was more acute in Westphalia than in Nord-Pas-de-Calais, the policing of major strikes in Westphalia, particularly in the mining sector, became increasingly characterised by the presence of private security forces.

The *Zechenschutzwehre* were organised by the individual mining company or factory, drawing on 'reliable' workers whose main task was to defend the property of the company against sabotage from striking workers. No comparable force existed in France, where the idea of breaking with the state's monopoly of violence was never popular within the provincial administration or the Interior Ministry.[32]

In Prussia however, the idea of privately financed policing was not new. Earlier in the 19th century, there had been a significant element of privatisation of the civil forces in Westphalia.[33] Private companies financed municipal police or even *gendarmes*. Thus in the 1870s, six local *gendarmes* were financed by the Krupp company.[34]

The main task of these privately financed officers was to be entirely devoted to the policing of the factory or mine during periods of conflict. In times of peace and calm these forces would be at the disposition of the local authorities. This practice was stopped during the 1880s, but the idea of some privatisation of policing reappeared in the 1890s when the Interior Ministry and the provincial administrators in Westphalia began to encourage private companies – particularly the mining companies – to organise private security corps who would be granted some authority within the areas belonging to the company.

The Interior Ministry saw this as a way of boosting the number of police forces without incurring public expense. In situations of major conflict the private security corps could remove an important part of the burden from the municipal police and *gendarmerie*. Although some private companies were initially reluctant to accept the extra costs,[35] these corps became an important feature in the policing of major labour conflicts after the turn of the 20th century. In 1904, there were forty-three corps with more than 1,000 members; during the mining strike of 1905, this number increased to 2,562 security guards in 117 mining companies, thus with an average of twenty-two guards per mining company.[36]

In the early 20th century, private security corps became an indispensable element in the attempts by the Prussian Interior Ministry and provincial administration to manage larger cases of conflict without military assistance. On the other hand, the private security corps were still insufficient in numbers to compensate for the serious problems of understaffed police forces. This becomes clear when comparing the total number of forces that could be mobilised in Westphalia and Nord-Pas-de-Calais during major labour conflicts.

Forces mobilised in industrial areas in cases of conflict

In both countries the Interior Ministry and the provincial administration were involved in organising the coordination of the police and *gendarmerie* forces to be mobilised to any particular area in the case of major popular unrest.

In France it was the 20,000–26,000-strong *gendarmerie* that constituted the single most important provider of supplementary forces. This heavy reliance on the *gendarmerie* was exacerbated by the fact that French prefects and sub-prefects were very reluctant to use municipal police forces to any great extent. Other large forces were those of Paris, Lyons and Marseilles, comprising in total 8,000–10,000 men; however these forces never operated outside their home areas. Even the prefects of the *départements* of 'Rhône' and 'Bouche-du-Rhône', who headed the police corps of Lyons and Marseilles, could not mobilise these police officers to areas of conflict in other parts of their *département*.

In coordinating the *gendarmerie* forces nationwide, the French authorities operated with two lists detailing the number of *gendarmes* within each military region who could be mobilised to other regions in cases of major unrest. In 1901, the number of *gendarmes* who could be transferred to other regions, without disrupting the regular service, was set at 1,819 men on foot and 1,850 mounted *gendarmes*. In the case of urgent need, a total force at 6,300 *gendarmes* could be gathered from the entire country.[37] Such a drain on the forces from other regions was supposed to last for no longer than ten to twelve days. Nevertheless on several occasions the number of mobilised forces went beyond 6,300 and sometimes continued for months.[38]

In practice, the number of *gendarmes* actually available entirely depended on whether there were several on-going conflicts in different parts of the country. Prefects and local authorities could therefore never count upon a full force of external *gendarmes*. Moreover even though the number of *gendarmes* increased with 6,000 men between 1901 and 1913, this number still fell seriously behind the very important numbers of forces which were regarded as necessary for the implementation of the French Interior Ministry's protection plans.

The Prussian forces that could be mobilised to an area of conflict comprised a variety of corps including *gendarmes* and Royal Guards as well as municipal police. However, in comparison with the forces available in France, it is clear that the Prussian forces remained desperately understaffed. In Prussia it was the Royal Guards, and to a lesser extent the *gendarmerie*, that functioned as mobile riot police forces. By 1913 they constituted together a force of 22,500 men[39] and were thus inferior in numbers to the 26,000 strong French *gendarmerie*. Moreover, when Prussian Royal Guards were mobilised for major policing tasks they were drawn away from their ordinary tasks of policing the large cities. In contrast when French *gendarmes* were called to conflict areas they were mobilised from rural communities. This was bad enough, and many French prefects and local authorities vigorously complained when rural communities in large parts of the country were left without adequate police presence for long periods of time; but these problems were all the more serious in Prussia where it was the large urban areas that provided the majority of supplementary police forces.

Like their French counterparts, the Prussian authorities also established lists detailing the number of *gendarmes* and Royal Guards who could be sent to any particular province or district in the event of major conflict. In the wake of the great miners' strike of 1889, the number of designated *gendarmes* that could be sent to the Westphalian mining areas in case of unrest increased from 170 in 1890 to 227 in 1893,[40] before rising to 493 in 1906.[41] At the same time, the number of police from outside the province who could be sent to Westphalia only increased from 205 in 1889 to 255 by 1905. After the great miners' strike of 1905 the number of external police forces increased to 1,051,[42] and in 1911, the Ministry of the Interior operated with an external force of 1,167 men including *gendarmes*, Royal Guards and municipal police. Together with local forces of 2,155 *gendarmes*, Royal Guards and municipal police, this brought the maximum available policing force to 3,322 men.[43]

During the most extended police operation in Westphalia before the First World War, the miners' strike of March 1912, when all forces that could be spared elsewhere had been mobilised to the province, there was a total of 5,658 policemen and *gendarmes*.[44] This was less than the French *gendarmerie* was capable of mobilising from its own forces according to the plans of the Interior Ministry.

The use of troops as structural necessity or bureaucratic choice

Thus French authorities made more frequent use of military troops than did their Prussian counterparts, despite the fact that they were generally better provided with police and *gendarmerie* forces. Similarly, the demilitarisation policy in Prussia was implemented despite the fact that problems of understaffed police and *gendarmerie* forces were even more acute in Prussia than in France. This was the situation in 1889 and to some extent this still remained the case by 1914, despite increases in the number of Prussian police and *gendarmerie*.

In spite of the French authorities' complaints about inadequate *gendarmerie* forces, the French *gendarmerie* corps was in fact capable of mobilising as many men in its own forces as the Royal Guards and the Prussian *gendarmerie* combined. In France, major police operations took place without even drawing upon the police forces of the larger cities or the municipal police forces, neither of which were taken account of in the plans of the French Interior Ministry. The heavy reliance on the French *gendarmerie* would of course stretch the French *gendarmerie* to its limits and leave vast rural areas with very few *gendarmes* for weeks or months on end, but it shows the significant manpower available to French authorities even before the army became involved.

In France the main riot unit was the *gendarmerie*: a single unified corps of militarily trained and highly professional officers. In Prussia, by contrast, the forces that operated as riot police were fragmented and with very uneven levels of professional training and discipline; moreover, an important part of the men involved in policing during major labour conflicts were not even professional police or *gendarmerie* officers, but simply 'reliable' workers without any adequate training. Viewed from a comparative perspective, the increasingly frequent use of troops in France therefore appears to be a political and administrative choice rather than a structural problem of insufficient police and *gendarmerie* forces.

Notes

[1] Funk (1986) pp. 211–233; Jessen (1991) pp. 75–91; Berlière (1991) pp. 498–510.
[2] Spencer (1985) pp. 310–311; idem. (1992) pp. 86–87; Henning (1987) pp. 140ff.
[3] Funk (1986) p. 234.
[4] Jauffret (1983) pp. 111–128; Carrot (1984) p. 656; Berlière (1996) pp. 118–119; Bruneteaux (1996) pp. 46–47.
[5] Tenfelde (1979) pp. 88–89; Saul (1981) p. 232.
[6] Jessen (1991) pp. 132–134; Henning (1987) p. 141; Spencer (1984) pp. 100, 126.
[7] Berlière (1991) p. 493; idem. (1993, 1) p. 9; idem. (1996) p. 118; Bruneteaux (1993) p. 32; idem. (1996) p. 47; Roynette (1997) p. 33.
[8] Julliard (1965) pp. 21–25; Rebérioux (1989) pp. 264–265; Alary (2000) p. 105; Magraw (2002) pp. 99–103; Michel Winock, *La Belle Epoque: France de 1900 à 1914*, Paris: Perrin, 2002, pp. 148–149.
[9] Bruneteaux (1993) p. 32; Carrot (1984) p. 653; Jauffret (1983) pp. 143–144.
[10] Law of 28 pluviôse in Year VIII (1800).
[11] Haupt (1986) p. 244.
[12] Law of 5 April 1884 on municipal powers, Article 91.
[13] Law of 5 April 1884 on municipal powers, Article 92.
[14] Law of 5 April 1884 on municipal powers, Article 99.
[15] Prussian General Code, Part II, Chapter 17, Articles 10–14.
[16] Jessen (1991) p. 28; Funk (1986) pp. 26–27.
[17] Emsley (1999) p. 208.
[18] Funk (1986) p. 213.
[19] Jessen (1991) p. 359.
[20] Funk (1986) p. 213. There is a slight degree of incongruity between the figure for 1913 provided by Funk and the number provided by Jessen, who sets the number of Royal Guards at 16,801 in 1913. Jessen (1991) p. 359.

[21] Carrot (1984) p. 654.

[22] The first plans from 1901 concerning a potential nationwide strike in the mining sector operated with a *gendarmerie* force of 20,849 officers. NA, Paris, F 7 12780. Plan of October 1901 from the French Interior Ministry *'Etat des forces de gendarmerie disponibles'*.

[23] Carrot (1984) p. 654.

[24] Funk (1986) p. 213; Jessen (1991) p. 359.

[25] NA, Paris, F.7.12780. Plan of October 1901 from the French Interior Ministry *'Etat des forces de gendarmerie disponibles'*.

[26] Jessen (1991) p. 358.

[27] Jessen (1991) p. 358.

[28] HSA, Münster, Regierung Münster VII–57, vol. 4 (documents 23–24). Letter of 12 March 1906 from the Province Governor in Münster to the Interior Minister.

[29] HSA, Münster, Regierung Münster VII–14, vol. 3 / 37–1 (documents 104–105). Letter of 14 March 1912 from the District Governor in Münster to the Army Corps Commander General von Einem.

[30] HSA, Münster, Regierung Münster, VII–14, vol. 5 / 37–3 (documents 86–89, 91–93). Daily Reports from the Local Governor in Recklinghausen of 12 March and 15 March 1912.

[31] HSA, Münster, Regierung Münster VII–14, vol. 3: Report of 14 March 1912 from the District Governor in Münster to the Interior Minister.

[32] Machelon (1976) p. 84.

[33] Jessen (1991) pp. 120–125.

[34] Jessen (1991) pp. 120–121.

[35] GSA, Berlin, HA1, Rep. 77, Titel 2513, vol. 4: Letter of 8 September 1894 from the District Governor in Arnsberg to the Interior Minister.

[36] GSA, Berlin, HA1, Rep. 77, Titel 2513, vol. 4: Reports from December 1907.

[37] NA, Paris, F 7 12780: Plan of October 1901 from the French Interior Ministry *'Etat des forces de gendarmerie disponibles'*.

[38] After the strike in Montceau-les-Mines in October 1901, the last external *gendarmes* were only demobilised in June 1902. Similarly, after the great uprising in Southern France during the summer of 1907, vast contingents of *gendarmes* from all over the country remained in place until October.

[39] Jessen (1991) Table 6.

[40] HSA, Münster, County Lüdinghausen, Arnsberg /389: *Übersicht über die designierten Detachements für die Kohlengebiete 1890*; HSA, Münster, Regierung Münster, VII–57, vol. 1: *Designierten Gendarmerie-mannschaften*, 1893.

[41] HSA, Münster, Regierung Münster, VII-57, vol. 4 (documents 23–34).

[42] Jessen (1991) p. 361.

[43] Funk (1986) p. 308. During the Westpahlian miners' strike of 1912 when a maximum police force was drawn to the areas there was a total of 5,658 policemen and *gendarmes*.

[44] See details in Chapter 6.

Chapter 6

Patterns of Military Involvement in the Policing of Protest

Estimating the frequency of military intervention

Until the mid-19th century, the patterns of domestic military intervention in France and Prussia seem to share features. In towns and rural areas, unrest of any importance required assistance from the nearest garrison, and in many areas the army was the only force of order. The army continued to assume the responsibility for keeping public order until after 1848.[1] However, after the repression of the revolutionary movements of 1848–1850, there appears to be a gradual decline in the number of military interventions in both France and the German countries.

Estimating the frequency of military intervention in Prussia and the German Empire between 1889 and 1914 is complicated due to the lack of consistent recording of military mobilisation for policing purposes.[2] The documents from the Prussian War Ministry and Interior Ministry contain information about some of the incidents, but there are important gaps, particularly in the material from the military authorities; the documents in the Interior Ministry are compiled from the viewpoint of information about labour conflicts rather than about whether troops were present or not. However, cases of even very minor military interventions do appear among the papers in the Interior Ministry and there is a high degree of convergence between the incidents found among the papers of the two ministries. The military interventions in Westphalia that can be identified through the ministerial records are also the only ones appearing in the bureaucratic correspondence from administrators at the provincial, district and local levels, and from what remains from the offices of the army corps commanders.[3]

In the case of France, it is extremely difficult to estimate the frequency of military intervention with any level of certainty. As in Prussia, there seems to have been no consistent recording of the mobilisation of troops. However, most fortunately for historians, the documents which were kept in the office of the army corps commander in Lille were hidden away when

German troops approached the town in the autumn of 1914, only to be found again in the 1970s. The military operations in the area of Nord-Pas-de-Calais are therefore extremely well documented from the viewpoint of the military authorities from the 1880s to August 1914.[4] Even without any consistent recording of military involvement in protest policing, the high number of identified incidents amply testifies to the much higher frequency of military intervention in France compared to Westphalia.

Another problem in estimating the number of military interventions arises from the fact that it is sometimes difficult to distinguish between instances where soldiers were actually mobilised and those where the troops were only kept ready for intervention, never leaving the garrison. In both countries, similarly, the non-military documents often fail to make the distinction between the use of *gendarmes* and the use of regular soldiers and officers. In non-military sources, references to 'troops' and 'military' may just as well apply to *gendarmes* as to soldiers. Moreover, due to the political significance of a military presence at strikes and demonstrations, the press sometimes mentions the presence of troops where the military documents reveal that in fact none had been mobilised. References to a military presence, appearing in the press, are therefore not taken into account here unless they are confirmed by documents from the military authorities. During major conflicts, military intervention consisted of many requisitions, for different areas and at different times. The same military unit was often moved around within a large territory in order to assist police and *gendarmerie* at different points of conflict. Yet, it makes sense to treat these multiple requisitions as one single incident of military intervention.

In Westphalia these incidents of military mobilisation had a clear start and a clear end-date, with long periods of time in between each incident. In Nord-Pas-de-Calais, by contrast, distinguishing one case of military intervention from another poses particular problems. A strike starting in one location or professional sector could easily develop into strikes in other branches or areas, so that several independent strikes might trigger a string of separate military interventions. French troops requested for one conflict were often directly transferred to another once when the former strike appeared to be over. The military authorities could have troops called out for policing purposes for weeks or months on end for what were in effect separate protest movements. Such 'chains' of requisition will be treated here as one single incident of military intervention. However, even when counting military intervention in successive conflicts as a single case, the number identified in Nord-Pas-de-Calais is still much higher than in Westphalia.

The decline in domestic military intervention in Prussia

A rough estimate of the extent of military involvement in the policing of popular unrest in Germany is provided by the studies of Richard Tilly, based on the incidents appearing in the German press. Through careful scrutiny Richard Tilly identifies thirty-three cases between 1882 and 1913 where military troops were involved in violent clashes with civilians.[5] This is an important decline compared to the period 1850–1881 where military troops were involved in at least sixty-six incidents of confrontation with protesters.[6] The figures derived from a study of the press need to be regarded, of course, with a good deal of caution; however as military involvement in the policing of civilian conflicts became less frequent during the 1890s it is all the more likely that even minor incidents where troops appeared on the scene of conflict would be mentioned in the press.

The figures provided by Richard Tilly cover the entire German Empire beginning from 1882. It is worth noting that the number of incidents recorded in the press for the entire German Empire from 1882–1913 seems to be reasonably in accord with the seventeen incidents of military intervention which appear in the documents from the Prussian Interior Ministry and the War Ministry[7] for the years 1889–1913. In addition, study of ministerial documents also reveal twelve incidents where the military authorities were contacted and troops were kept ready for intervention, but never mobilised.[8] Together the study of the German press and the documents from the Prussian Ministries indicate that the total number of interventions with military troops between 1889 and 1913 probably did not exceed thirty for the entire German Empire.

The rather limited number of military interventions for the German Empire as a whole seems to be confirmed by the numbers recorded in Westphalia between 1889 and 1914. Being one of the most turbulent amongst the Prussian provinces, Westphalia experienced military intervention on three occasions: May 1889, June 1899 and March 1912. On three more occasions, January 1890, April 1891 and again in January 1893, contacts were made by the Province Governor asking the military authorities to keep troops ready for intervention. In none of these cases were troops ever mobilised.

The documents from the Westphalian administration at the provincial and local level refer to the military interventions in 1889, 1899 and 1912 as the only incidents of this kind,[9] and General von Einem, who held the post as army corps commander in Münster between 1909 and 1914, describes the mining strike of 1912 as the only military intervention during his time in office.[10]

The increasing frequency of military involvement in the policing of Nord-Pas-de-Calais

The development in France was quite different. The Second Empire and the Third Republic were both established with extensive use of military force. However, during the Second Empire and the early Third Republic most incidents of popular disorder were dealt with by local police, by the *gendarmerie* and by the National Guard. Apart from a series of bloody interventions during the strike-wave of 1866–1869, the French army did not play a major role in the maintenance of order during the 1860s.

After the bloody repression of the *Commune*, military interventions against civilians were only very occasional in France. In her work on labour conflicts during the years 1870–1890, Michelle Perrot estimates a rate of military intervention (including cases where only the *gendarmerie* intervened) which fluctuated from approximately thirteen cases of public disorder in every thousand in 1872, falling to three cases in every thousand by 1882.

This gradual decline in military involvement in protest policing began to reverse by the mid-1880s. With the military intervention in a miners' strike at Decazeville in 1886, and following turbulence linked to the political campaign of General Boulanger, military interventions increased from ten in one thousand cases of public unrest in 1886 to fifteen in every thousand by 1890.[11] The years 1889–1893 were characterised by waves of strikes with several major conflicts that involved the army.

After 1893 there was a gradual decline in military interventions in Paris, when Police Prefect Louis Lépine began to experiment with new approaches to crowd control and maintenance of public order.[12] During the 1890s the presence of soldiers at strikes and demonstrations became primarily a phenomenon of the areas outside Paris. The documents left by the French Interior Ministry indicate that the frequency of military involvement in the policing of protest was particularly common in the industrial centres of Nord and Pas-de-Calais, of Le Creusot and Longwy, as well as in the main provincial towns (Marseilles, Bordeaux and Saint Etienne).[13]

The correspondence of the Army Corps Commander in Lille provides some indication of the frequency of military participation in the policing of the area of Nord-Pas-de-Calais.[14] In the early 1880s, there were a few incidents of military intervention, mainly linked to a major strike among the textile workers in Tourcoing, Roubaix and Armentière in 1880 and a great miners' strike in Anzin in 1884.[15]

This all changed in 1886, when the army was requested no less than ten times, mainly due to strikes in the local textile industries and to major strikes and unrest on the other side of the Belgian border.[16] The following year, when the controversial General Boulanger launched his right-wing populist movement, this triggered a series of military interventions in *département* Nord where the Boulanger movement was particularly strong.

This was only the beginning. Between 1889 and 1914, no less than eighty-four separate incidents have been identified where the military authorities in Nord-Pas-de-Calais were contacted to provide troops for the maintenance of public order somewhere in the region. In sixty-eight of these cases troops were actually mobilised while in the other sixteen occasions troops were only kept ready for intervention but never mobilised. Seventy-six of the eighty-four identified incidents occurred after 1900, but this extreme bias may be partly explained by better documentation for the latter period.

Given that the documents only provide a very incomplete picture, and that long-lasting mobilisation for 'chaining' conflicts only counts as one, the actual number of military interventions is likely to be a great deal higher.

The extreme frequency of military involvement in the policing of Nord-Pas-de-Calais is well illustrated by a letter from the Army Corps Commander in Lille informing the Prefect that during the year 1904, from January to November, there had not been one single day when troops were not mobilised somewhere in the region.[17]

Compared to the three incidents which took place in Westphalia over the same period of time, the sixty-eight incidents of military intervention in Nord-Pas-de-Calais not only indicate very dissimilar patterns of requisition. A closer look at the patters of military presence during the military interventions in Nord-Pas-de-Calais and Westphalia reveals distinctly different ways of using the troops as supplementary police forces.

Types of conflict triggering military intervention

In addition to the more frequent mobilisation of troops for policing purposes in Nord-Pas-de-Calais, considerable differences developed in the types of conflict which triggered military intervention in Westphalia and in Nord-Pas-de-Calais.

This was not the case prior to 1889, when the military authorities in both Westphalia and Nord-Pas-de-Calais were requested to provide troops in a variety of situations of greater or smaller unrest. These included social protest movements, local riots, smaller strikes in all types of industry, and protests linked to the implementation of unpopular anti-Catholic legislation in Germany during the *Kulturkampf* of the 1870s and in France during the Gambetta government of the early 1880s.

Military intervention in Imperial Germany

In Germany, as military involvement in the maintenance of public order became increasingly rare, the incidents of military intervention tended to occur in relation to a few types of conflict. Out of the twenty-eight cases from the entire German Empire (excluding Bavaria) where the military authorities were either mobilised or kept ready for intervention, ten were linked to conflicts in the mining sector.

In Westphalia all the cases of military intervention since the late 1880s were linked to conflicts in the mining sector, both in the great miners' strike of May 1889, the Herne strike among young Polish miners in June 1899 and the last great miners' strike of March 1912. Similarly, the three incidents where military troops were kept ready to intervene in January 1890, April 1891, and January 1893 were all linked to labour conflicts among the Westphalian miners.

Outside Westphalia there were four incidents of military intervention during labour conflicts in other professional categories. These were strikes among construction workers, electricians, and factory workers, with one incident due to 'unrest among workers' without further specification. On three occasions, troops were mobilised to patrol the national borders when conflicts were taking place in a neighbouring country (the Habsburg Empire, Russia, and France). The purpose of the military participation was to prevent striking workers in these countries from crossing the border so drawing German workers into their conflict.

Finally, a few incidents were interventions against political protest rather than labour disputes. Four cases were linked to political demonstrations, another four incidents were related to unspecified public disorder (*Krawall*), and in one case the nature of the conflict was not stated. In contrast to Nord-Pas-de-Calais, military intervention by the Prussian army was a measure implemented *ad hoc* with scarcely preconceived planning. This was the case in 1889 and was still the case at the outset of the First World War.[18]

The conflicts occurring in Westphalia, where the Prussian troops were mobilised or were kept ready for intervention, were all significantly larger than the incidents that triggered military intervention in Nord-Pas-de-Calais. The great strike of 1889 mobilised approximately 90,000 miners in

Westphalia and, together with the conflicts in the other great mining areas in Saarland and Silesia, the number of participant miners is estimated to have been close to 150,000.[19] In April 1891, 12,000 miners were on strike in Westphalia and in January 1893, the Westphalian authorities expected a strike of a similar size to that in 1889 to break out.

The unrest among young Polish miners in June 1899 remained within a geographically limited area around the mining town of Herne; it involved 3,500 out of the 18,000 workers in the local mines. During the miners' strike of 1905, almost 195,000 miners out of 268,000 went on strike. In 1912, the number of strikers was 190,000 but, due to expansions in the mining sector, the number of workers employed in the Westphalian mines had by that time been extended to 322,000 men. In comparison, by far the most extended conflict occurring in Nord-Pas-de-Calais was the strike movement in the spring of 1906, which mobilised at most 92,000 strikers.[20]

At the same time, several major labour conflicts took place in the German Empire involving significant numbers of protesters without triggering a military intervention. During a two-month strike from November 1896 to January 1897 among 33,000 Hamburg dock workers, the military authorities were never contacted. The same was true during the Westphalian miners' strike of January 1905, when close to 200,000 workers went on strike. There was great unrest among Westphalian miners in September–October 1906, in May 1907 and again in June 1911 yet without the authorities seriously considering calling upon military assistance.

Similarly some major incidents of mass demonstration were handled by the police or the *gendarmerie* alone. In March 1906, during the nationwide Social Democratic demonstrations for the extension of the franchise to the Prussian Diet, no troops were called upon. The so-called *Moabit* unrest in Berlin of March 1910, with the participation of more than 150,000 demonstrators, was handled entirely by the Berlin police including the violent confrontations with the demonstrators; no evidence has been found of contacts being made with the military authorities on that occasion.

Types of incidents entailing military participation in Nord-Pas-de-Calais

In Nord-Pas-de-Calais, the eighty-four recorded incidents where the army was mobilised for policing purposes reflect a wide range of events from ordinary crowd management to major incidents of popular unrest.

Although the recorded cases constitute a very incomplete picture, they provide some clear indications of the diversity of incidents to which troops were called out.

The pattern of military intervention was, to some extent, influenced by the waves of strikes that hit the region, with military intervention often lasting for months. This happened during the three great strikes in the mining sector of Nord-Pas-de-Calais during October to November 1889, November 1891, and September to November 1893. This was also the case during the nationwide strikes in the mining and transport sectors, of October 1901 and of October to-November 1902.

The years 1903, 1904 and particularly 1906 were characterised by great strikes in the textile industry, the mining industry and confrontations over the implementation of the government's anti-Catholic legislation.

The years 1907–1910 saw a series of nationwide strikes among public employees (postal and telegraph workers) and public service personnel, notably rail and tram workers, and gas and electricity employees. Finally the year 1911 was characterised by widespread food riots which are also reflected among the incidents of military involvement in policing.

Thirty-four of the recorded incidents were situations with some significant potential for unrest. In twenty cases troops were mobilised for more than one month, in eight cases the conflict lasted between two and six months.

In addition to the incidents linked to the major social and political conflicts of the day, half of the recorded incidents of mobilisation must be described as ordinary policing tasks or maintenance of order during very minor or local conflicts. All but one of the recorded incidents of troops performing ordinary police tasks occurred after 1900. These included maintaining order during a religious procession in the port towns of Dunkirk or St. Pol (nine incidents); at the occasion of an election or a political demonstration (two incidents); during a public execution (two incidents) or a public feast (one incident).

The practice of using troops for ordinary crowd management continued up until the eve of the First World War. As late as 1911, the Interior Minister told the prefects not to request military assistance for the maintenance of order during horse races.[21] Compared to the mobilisation of thousands of troops for sensitive incidents of popular protest, crowd management never involved more than six hundred soldiers.

In addition to the mobilisation for crowd management, there were three recorded incidents where soldiers were called upon to undertake strike-bound work, to ensure essential services of railways, ports, and energy supply. Similarly soldiers were ordered to unload boats during labour disputes in the great ports and in October 1911 they were asked to remove rubbish from the streets during a strike among dustmen.

Troops were also mobilised on a regular basis to ensure the security of VIPs, including eight incidents where troops were called out when foreign heads of state were passing through the region to take the boat to Britain from Dunkirk. The port of Dunkirk was one of the areas that experienced a military presence most often. Troops were requested repeatedly to ensure the protection of port installations, even for such minor incidents as 350 dock workers going on strike for three days in September 1905 or to a strike among Icelandic sailors from a ship harboured in the port of Dunkirk in February 1910.[22]

When it came to dock workers and miners, the authorities took no chances, and strikes involving almost any number of workers would trigger military intervention. Thus on twelve occasions, troops were mobilised for strikes that involved less than 5,000 workers.

Compared to the pattern of military involvement in Westphalia, it is clear that in Nord-Pas-de-Calais troops were not only requested far more frequently, but also for much smaller incidents than was the case in Prussia. However there were also important differences in the ways in which troops were used in the two areas.

The numbers of forces mobilised

A particularly significant difference between the use of troops in the two areas was the number of troops considered necessary to police strikes and demonstrations. In Nord-Pas-de-Calais the civilian and military authorities consistently mobilised many more soldiers than their Westphalian counterparts.

The discrepancy between the practices becomes apparent when we compare the number of mobilised forces with the number of registered strikers during the major labour disputes that took place in Nord-Pas-de-Calais and Westphalia. Both in France and Prussia, the official registration of strikers tended to be on the low side, so the numbers mentioned below are based on estimates of the highest possible number of participants. The figures are meant to provide a basis for comparison with the great labour conflicts in Westphalia.

However, the actual number of persons involved in marches and gatherings during the strikes would be significantly higher, because such events also involved family members and sympathisers who were not registered among the strikers.

Table 6.1   Major conflicts occurring in Nord-Pas-de-Calais

	Number of Strikers	Number of Troops	Ratio: Soldier /Strikers
1889, Oct.–Nov. (miners)	c. 13,000	1,600	1 / 8
1891, Sept.–Nov. (miners)	c.15,000	1,987	1 / 7.5
1893, Sept.–Nov. (strike wave)	c. 40,000	min. 4,160	1 / 10
1901, Oct.–Nov. (strike wave)	max. 14,700	6,150–8,000*	1 / 1.8 – 1 / 2.3
1902, Aug. (miners, Anzin)	1,529	286	1 / 5.3
1902, Oct.–Dec. (miners/dockers)	71,000 miners 5,000 dockers	16,715	1 / 4.5
1903, Sept.–Nov. (textile)	50,000	12,600	1 / 4
Dec.1903–April 1904 (textile)	15,000	5,700	1 / 2.6
1905, March (dockers, Dunkirk)	4,000	775	1 / 5
1906, March–May (strike wave)	max. 92,000	35-38,000	1 / 2.6
1909, Oct. (textile)	2,400	500	1 / 4.8
1912, July (dockers, Dunkirk)	4,500	2,300	1 / 1.7

* 61½ infantry companies and 21 cavalry squadrons were mobilised. Each unit comprised between 75 and 100 men

The most extended conflict that took place in the area of Nord-Pas-de-Calais between 1889 and 1914 was the wave of protest that hit the region in the winter and spring of 1906. It beats all records both in terms of the number of protesters and the number of forces called out to maintain public order.

The protests began in January–February 1906 when the government tried to implement some highly unpopular anti-Catholic laws. This triggered nationwide protests to which military assistance was requested on a massive scale. In both larger and middle-sized towns such as Roubaix (121,017 inhabitants) and Wattreloos (27,000 inhabitants), more than 1,000 infantry soldiers and cavalry officers participated in forcing their way through protesters and barricaded churches.[23]

In early March there was a major explosion in one of the large mines at Courrière (Pas-de-Calais) that caused more than 1,100 deaths. This gave rise to spontaneous strikes among miners throughout the entire region against their degrading working conditions. The strikes spread to other professions and developed into the greatest strike movement in Nord-Pas-de-Calais throughout the period 1889 and 1914. Due to the large number of individual strikes in many different professions, it is difficult to give an estimate of the number of workers participating in the strikes between March and early May.

According to official statistics the year 1906 beat all records with more than 438,000 registered strikers in all France. The total number of strikers in the two *départements* Nord and Pas-de-Calais was 92,191 for the entire year of 1906.[24]

The military forces called to the region between March and May also reached unprecedented levels. Military documents reveal a figure of more than 35,000 soldiers and officers.[25] In Lens alone 20,000 troops were mobilised on the 20 March. In addition, at least 591 *gendarmes* were called to the *département* Nord,[26] and a similar number is likely to have been present in Pas-de-Calais. In addition, an unknown number of municipal policemen participated in the policing of the area. A source from the Interior Ministry mentions that a total of 52,000 forces (troops, *gendarmerie*, police) were present in Nord-Pas-de-Calais when the conflict reached its peak.[27]

In November 1906, the government made a second attempt to implement the unpopular anti-Catholic laws that the authorities had been forced to give up in February. In November the civilian and military authorities took no chances and significant numbers of military troops were employed to back government officials. In the *arrondissement* of Lille, 1,708 soldiers and officers were mobilised on 20 November; 754 soldiers and officers mobilised the next day; some 1,668 on the 22 November and 1,370 on the last day of the campaign. Similarly, villages with a total population of 1,000–3,000 inhabitants received a military presence around their local church of 150–200 infantry soldiers, between twenty-five and fifty cavalry officers and between twenty-five and forty *gendarmes*.[28]

Both the implementation of the anti-Catholic laws, and the handling of the great strike movement of March–May 1906, indicate the levels of manpower that the French authorities were prepared to mobilise for the policing of sensitive conflicts. However, when looking at the ratio of troops in relation to the number of protesters during other conflicts, great and small, it is worth noting that the high police and military presence at the particularly sensitive conflicts of 1906 are perfectly in line with general bureaucratic practice.

The number of forces mobilised in Westphalia 1889, 1899, 1905 and 1912

In comparison, the number of forces mobilised in Westphalia appears remarkably low. As in France, we cannot know the exact size of each military unit;[29] however estimating the highest possible figures for soldiers mobilised in Westphalia, there were still significantly fewer troops mobilised there compared to Nord-Pas-de-Calais, even when the numbers of police officers, *gendarmes* and private security forces are taken into account. Only during the 1899 riots in Herne did the Prussian authorities mobilise a very large number of men compared to the strikers. At its peak, the strike comprised approximately 3,500 young Polish workers[30] out of the 18,000 men employed in eleven large mines around the town of Herne. The conflict developed into riots and violence and within less than a week the military moved in with three battalions of infantry and 140 cavalry soldiers.[31]

Similarly, looking at the large-scale labour conflicts in Westphalia, the numbers of troops mobilised compared to the number of strikers tended to be significantly lower than in Nord-Pas-de-Calais. In the great Westphalian miners' strike of 1889, General von Albedyll mobilised ten battalions of infantry – between 6,000 and 8,000 soldiers and eight squadrons of 1,600–2,000 cavalry officers, to police 90,000 striking miners.[32] In 1893, when a new miners' strike broke out in Westphalia that threatened to become as extended as the strike of 1889, General von Albedyll kept a force of 6,800–8,000 infantry soldiers and 1,050 cavalry officers ready for intervention.[33]

During the great miners' strike of January 1905, which involved nearly 200,000 strikers, no troops were mobilised. The entire Westphalian mining district was policed by 1,220 *gendarmes*, 2,313 policemen, and 2,562

Patterns of Military Involvement

private security guards (*Zechenwehrleute*).[34] The low number of police and *gendarmerie* may not be surprising since this strike was a prime example of discipline and orderly behaviour on the part of the striking miners. During this strike, the potential for violence between the workers was limited since all the major trade unions supported the action; public opinion showed much sympathy for the action, partly because of the intransigent attitude of the mining companies but also because of the absence of any notable level of disorder.

Seven years later, during the miners' strike of March 1912, when the government took a much firmer stand against the 190,000 strikers and the 322,000 Westphalian miners were themselves deeply split, the number of policemen and *gendarmes* mobilised amounted to 5,658 and 2,000–3,000 private security guards.[35] In the light of the extended policing aims set for the conflict of March 1912, the provincial administration and local police forces seem to have mobilised as many policemen and *gendarmes* as they could possibly draw from within and from outside the region. However, when it became clear that these forces were not capable of handling the situation without military assistance, the number of soldiers mobilised amounted to a total of merely 5,000.

Table 6.2   Protesters and forces mobilised during main conflicts in Westphalia

	Number of Strikers	Policemen and *Gendarmes*	Number of Soldiers	Ratio: Soldiers/ Strikers
1889 Miners	90,000	(unknown)	6–8,000 infantry 1,250 cavalry	1/10 – 1/13
1899 Miners	3,500	(unknown)	2–3,000 infantry 140 cavalry	1/1.1 – 1/1.8
1905 Miners	195,000	255 *gendarme*s 1,135 police 704 external police 2562 private guards	(none)	1/43
1912 Miners	190,000	5,658 police and *gendarmes* 2–3000 private guards	5,000 infantry	1/14

The duration of mobilisations

Significant differences also appear in the length of time during which troops were mobilised for any particular conflict in Nord-Pas-de-Calais and Westphalia. The troops were generally mobilised for longer periods in Nord-Pas-de-Calais at least until after 1906, whereas in Westphalia the number of days of military mobilisation decreased from one conflict to the next. Military intervention in the great strikes in Nord-Pas-de-Calais of 1889, 1891 and 1893 each lasted for twenty to twenty-five days. Military interventions in the major conflicts of the first decade of the 20th century lasted for significantly longer. In 1901, troops were mobilised for at least forty-four days, in 1902 for fifty days, and, in the spring of 1906, the army was mobilised for forty-seven days.

In Westphalia, by contrast, the number of days of military intervention constantly declined. During the conflict of 1889, troops were mobilised for eighteen days in Westphalia and for sixteen days in the Saarland. In 1899, during the Polish riots in Herne, troops were mobilised for thirteen days, and in March 1912 the military intervention lasted for only seven days. The only breach with this pattern, in Prussia between 1889 and 1914, was the intervention in the Mansfeld coal areas in October–November 1909 that lasted for twenty-six days.

The long periods of military mobilisation in Nord-Pas-de-Calais were the result of the increasing practice of mobilising troops from the outset of a strike, sometimes even from the moment it was declared. Similarly, the troops were not sent back until the strike or protest had effectively ended. In Westphalia, a more reactive approach was taken and troops were only present for part of the period of conflict The Prussian army was requested only at the point when a province or district governor considered that the civil forces could no longer manage on their own, normally when the conflict had already been going on for some time. In the same way, the troops were sent back to their garrisons as soon as the authorities believed the situation to be sufficiently calm for the police and *gendarme*rie to handle the conflict on their own.

Patterns of military involvement and the structural conditions for the policing of mass protest

What we observe in Westphalia and Nord-Pas-de-Calais are completely dissimilar patterns of military involvement in protest policing. This appears not only from the frequency of military intervention with merely three incidents in Westphalia between 1889 and 1914, while there were at least sixty-eight separate incidents in Nord-Pas-de-Calais. On the French side, soldiers were involved both in the policing of strikes and demonstrations and deployed for ordinary crowd management. Moreover, compared to the incidents in Westphalia, the French authorities generally mobilised troops in very great numbers.

The more frequent and extended military involvement in Nord-Pas-de-Calais cannot be explained simply by the size of the conflicts. The number of protesters joining even the most extended conflicts occurring in Nord-Pas-de-Calais was much lower than the number of people involved in the major strikes in Westphalia. Nor can it be explained simply in terms of the Nord-Pas-de-Calais protests being particularly violent, since troops were normally mobilised as a preventive measure at the very beginning of conflicts. Indeed, in many cases the military authorities later reported no unrest whatsoever during the conflict.

The pattern of military involvement in Nord-Pas-de-Calais reflects both the principles developed during the 1890s by Police Prefect Louis Lépine for the maintenance of public order in Paris, and the strategic thinking behind the Plans for Protection developed for large-scale unrest established by the inter-ministerial committee under successive French Interior Ministers.[36]

While the logic behind the French approach was prevention and containment of violence, even if this aim was not always met, the Prussian approach was reactive and at its core confrontational. Even if the reputation of Prussian police and *gendarmes* for unrestrained brutality and having a military mindset, may occasionally have been overstated by contemporary critics and historians sympathetic to the workers' movement (as Spencer suggests[37]), there can be little doubt that their approach to protesters was extremely aggressive.[38] Yet this aggressive and confrontational policing was not simply due to the military background of Prussian police officers: it was central to the strategies expressed in the plans and preparations developed between 1889 and 1912 among ministerial, regional and local authorities in Westphalia.[39] Even if attempts had been made to encourage a less aggressive approach, this would have been extremely difficult, due to the structural constraints faced by seriously understaffed police and *gendarmerie* forces.

The comparison with Nord-Pas-de-Calais provides some insight into the extent of the difficulties faced by Westphalian police and *gendarmerie* officers who were given the responsibility for handling mass protest with very understaffed forces. The virtue of the French strategies of prevention and containment was the space they created for police discretion. In Nord-

Pas-de-Calais, the police and *gendarmerie* were – in all sensitive situations – backed by a large number of forces. This allowed a certain degree of flexibility, moderation and permissiveness towards protesters, and gave French policemen and *gendarmes* the space to distinguish between peaceful demonstrators and people who could be arrested for actual offences. This did not mean that French policemen and *gendarmes* did not intervene against protesters with heavy handed methods. They often did. But because they were not immediately at risk of losing control, they had space to deploy a series of strategies before reaching open confrontation.

In the Prussian situation, there was very little room for flexible or permissive approaches to crowd management, and the individual policeman or *gendarme* had few resources at his disposal when facing an overwhelming number of protesters. He had to make use of his personal authority, ordering people away from sensitive locations, and threatening them with violent attack and arrest if they did not follow instructions. A handful of policemen facing hundreds or thousands of protesters were obviously in a weak position, and their authority was easily challenged. The police officers, individually and collectively, were constantly at risk of losing control. If this happened there were few alternatives to indiscriminate and unrestrained brutality against whoever crossed their path.[40]

The policing measures we have observed in Westphalia and Nord-Pas-de-Calais reflect the dissimilar approaches to military involvement in protest policing that came to prevail in the Prussian and French Interior Ministries during the 1890s. However one question remains unanswered. In both countries there were important disagreements over the issue amongst politicians, ministers, senior members of civil service and the army; it is, therefore, remarkable that the particular approach adopted by the French and Prussian Interior Ministries was implemented with such consistency. Moreover, in the light of the important economic interests at stake, one might have expected the Prussian policy of demilitarisation to have been repeatedly overruled by powerful forces linked to large industries and big business. Similarly, in the French situation, it could have been expected that prefects might depart from the ministerial approach due to their concerns for the political sensitivity of certain conflicts.

In order, therefore, to understand the high levels of consistency in the measures adopted, it is necessary to look at the men, in Westphalia and Nord-Pas-de-Calais, who were making the decisions about whether, and how, to involve military troops in the policing of major protest.

Notes

[1] Lüdtke (1982) p. 238ff; Funk (1986) p. 47.

[2] The most comprehensive documentation are the files in the Prussian War Ministry, which contain document on most of the incidents (MA, Freiburg, PH2/14). The Prussian Interior Ministry has what seems to be a comprehensive collection of documents over the use of either *gendarme*s or military troops, but only for the policing of labour disputes (GSA, Berlin, HA1, Rep. 77, Titel 2513 /1 Beiheft 4–15; GSA, Berlin, HA1, Rep. 77, Titel 2523).

[3] HSA, Münster, OP 6095 *'Notstandsmassnahmen: Requisition militärischer Hülfe und Waffengebrauch, 1822, 1840–1851, 1876–1929'*.

[4] MA, Vincennes, Special Collection from the 1st Army Corps.

[5] Tilly and Hohorst (1976) p. 252.

[6] Tilly, Tilly and Tilly (1975) pp. 212, 226.

[7] The Prussian War Ministry was responsible for military operations in all parts of the German Empire except Bavaria.

[8] GSA, Berlin, HA1, Rep. 77, Titel 2513 /1; Idem. HA1, Rep. 77, Titel 2523; MA, Freiburg, PH2 /14.

[9] HSA, Münster, OP 685; OP 6095; OP 6681; OP 6889. Similarly the monthly reports from the local governors to the Province Governor.

[10] Einem (1933) pp. 165–168.

[11] Perrot (1974) pp. 83, 195.

[12] Berlière (1993) p. 9.

[13] NA, Paris, F 7 12773–12794 (Police générale) and F 7 12912–12920 (Sûreté générale).

[14] MA, Vincennes, 1st A.C. /2.I.2.: Confidential correspondence from the General Commander's Office, 1880–1889.

[15] The military authorities were also contacted at the occasion of a textile strike in March 1883 and in relation to expected trouble in Roubaix after the general elections of 1885.

[16] Twice that year in March–April and again in October 1886 the prefect in Lille requested the army to patrol the Belgian borders because of major strikes and other trouble in Belgium. During the summer and autumn small units were called out to Fourmies (June 7), to Lille (June 11), to Hesdin (June 11), to Armentière (August 1), to Roubaix (August 1–11), to Lille again (August 14), and to Calais (October 7). In November, 250 infantry soldiers were requested to ensure public order during the visit of a minister; later the same month, all the troops of the first military region were also kept in a state of preparedness because of the elections.

[17] MA, Vincennes, 1st A.C. /2.I.325: Letter of 13 November 1904 from General Laplace, army corps commander in Lille to Louis Vincent, Prefect of *département* Nord.

[18] See details Chapter 10.

[19] Spencer (1992) pp. 86–87.

[20] *'Statistique des grèves'* (1906). See details below.

[21] NA, Paris, F 7 12722: Two telegrams of 21 March and 21 December 1911 from Interior Minister Caillaux to the prefects in 'Loiret' and 'Alpes Maritimes'. A similar request was issued by War Minister Briand in an instruction of 23 August 1910.

[22] For details see appendix 2.

[23] NA, Paris, F 7 12399: Letter of 3 March 1906 from Louis Vincent, prefect of *département* Nord, to the Interior Ministry.

[24] *'Statistique des grèves'* (1906).

[25] Figures from the Interior Ministry mentions that 129 infantry companies and 45 cavalry squadrons were mobilised to *département* Nord, while 176½ infantry companies and 37 cavalry squadrons were called out to Pas-de-Calais. Depending on the size of these units, this brings the number of soldiers and officers to somewhere between 30,000 and 38,000. (NA, Paris, F 7 12912: Report of 10 October 1907 entitled *'Commission Chargée d'étudier la révision de l'exercice du droit de réquisition de la force armée par les autorités civiles et du plan de protection établi pour le cas de grèves dans les départements'*.)

[26] DA, Lille, M 626 /60: An undated document from around May 1906 detailing the number of mobilised troops in *département* Nord.

[27] NA, Paris, F 7 12913: Minutes from a meeting of 8 June 1907 in the inter-ministerial Commission revising the Instructions on Military Participation in the Maintenance of Public Order.

[28] MA, Vincennes, 1st A.C. /2.I.335: a collection entitled 'Inventaires des églises 1906' contains documents from many different towns and areas with details of how many soldiers and *gendarmes* were mobilised for this particular operation.

[29] The military authorities often only refer to the number of military units (squadrons, companies, and battalions), without mentioning the number of men per unit. A Prussian battalion would comprise between 600 and 1,000 infantry soldiers, whereas a French battalion only comprised 400–500 men. During the period 1901–1914, when the French army was particularly busy delivering forces for the maintenance of public order the size of a French battalion was reduced to 375 men, while squadrons were reduced from 100 to 80 men.

[30] Tenfelde (1979) pp. 71–104. We here operate with Tenfelde's estimate of 3,500 strikers, although a local newspaper mentions figures as high as 6,000 strikers when the conflict was at its peak. HSA, Münster, Regierung Arnsberg 14323 (documents 2–4): *Rheinisch-Westphälischen Zeitung* of 30 June 1899.

[31] MA, Freiburg, PH2/14, (documents 209–211): Report of 2 July 1899 from General von Mikusch, army corps commander in Münster, to Wilhelm II.

[32] CA, Potsdam III, R 43, film signature 11971–11972, (documents 71–90) or HSA, Münster, OP 14317, (documents 53–73): Report from the meeting in Dortmund of 10 May 1889 between Interior Minister Herrfurth and the Westphalian civil authorities.

[33] MA, Freiburg, PH2 /14, (document 155): Letter of 10 January 1893 from General von Albedyll, army corps commander in Münster to Wilhelm II.

[34] Figures gathered from the correspondence between the Interior Ministry and the province governor of Westphalia: HSA, Münster, Regierung Münster, VII–57 Vol.2 /40–2 and GSA, Berlin, HA1, Rep. 77, Titel 2523 /1, vols. 11–12.

[35] Figures provided by Jessen (1991) pp. 136–137 and HSA, Münster, Regierung Münster VII–14, vol.1 /32–1 or GSA, Berlin, Rep. 77, Titel 2523 /1 (Appendix 1), vol. 20: Report from a meeting in Essen on 1 July 1912.

[36] See Chapter 3.

[37] Spencer (1992) p. 164.

[38] Funk (1986) pp. 284–301; Jessen (1991) pp. 158–170.

[39] CA, Potsdam III, R 43, film signature 11971–11972, (documents 71–90) or HSA, Münster, OP 14317, (documents 53–73): Report from the meeting in Dortmund on 10 May 1889 between Interior Minister Herrfurth and the Westphalian civilian authorities; GSA, Berlin, HA1, Rep. 77, Titel 2513 /1, Beiheft 9, (documents 124–130): Minutes from a meeting on 7 July 1904 by the District Governor in Düsseldorf between regional and ministerial authorities; GSA, Berlin, HA1, Rep. 77, Titel 2523 /1 No.1, vol. 20: Minutes from a meeting on 1 July 1912 by the local governor in Essen between local, regional and ministerial authorities.

[40] Jensen and Dunnage have made similar observation with respect to protest policing in Italy of the 1890s. Ralph Bach Jensen, *Liberty and Order: The Theory and Practice of Italian Public Security Police, 1848 to the Crisis of the 1890s*, New York: Garland, 1991, pp. 180–181; Jonathan Dunnage, 'Law and Order in Giolittian Italy. A case study of the Province of Bologna', *European History Quarterly*, vol. 25, 1995, p. 383.

PART III

BUREAUCRATS, GENERALS AND ELITES IN WESTPHALIA AND NORD-PAS-DE-CALAIS

Chapter 7

Local Influences on the Requisition of Troops

Elite relations and elite cooperation in Imperial Germany and the French Third Republic

From the perspective of the protesters who found themselves face-to-face with rows of soldiers, it mattered little whether it was the local mayor, the police master or the head of the provincial administration who had decided to call upon the army. The presence of military troops was, by its very nature, to the advantage of those who sought to protect their industrial interests and private property, because it seriously limited the scope for effective protest. Accordingly historians sometimes assume that the decision to request troops was either a direct result of pressure from industrialists, or at least indicates the willingness of government and their regional representatives to accommodate to the interests of employers against strikers and local elites against popular protest.[1] This was certainly the case earlier in the 19th century.[2] However, during the 1890s requests for military troops became less of a local decision.

When military troops were requested to maintain or restore public order in Westphalia and Nord-Pas-de-Calais, the interests of the central governments in Paris and Berlin, their provincial administration and the army were not identical – or at least only partly coincided – with those of municipal authorities and industrialists.[3] When it came to involving the army in policing, the municipal authorities, the senior bureaucrats of the provincial or *départmental* administration and the military authorities all had their particular interests at heart. The French and Prussian-German governments, and their provincial administrations, were both concerned with maintaining law and order; avoiding the disruption of wider society; supporting trade and industry and ultimately with maintaining the existing social and political order. While the French and Prussian armies were both concerned with defending the regime against the challenge from working-class movements, their primary concern was the narrow interests of the military organisation. For both the army and the provincial administration the achievement of these aims, with or without military involvement in policing, was a careful balancing of risks and benefits. For those, by contrast, who were concerned with the protection of their private property, personal safety or industrial interests there were clear advantages in gaining as much military protection as possible.

In the light of the highly dissimilar degree of military involvement in the two countries, the question emerges whether the extremely frequent calls upon military assistance in Nord-Pas-de-Calais was due – in part at least – to local elites in Nord-Pas-de-Calais having better access to obtaining military protection, either through their control over the municipal authorities or by the pressure they were able to put on the prefects in Lille and Arras. We therefore need to look at the decision-making process: who had power to influence decisions and how did the authorities involved cooperate with each other.

The local influence on the requisition of troops in Westphalia

Since the maintenance of public order was the responsibility of municipal authorities – in the first instance at least – local elites and industrialists often held great influence over the measures implemented by municipal police and the *gendarmerie*.[4] Not surprisingly, factory owners and mining companies sought to obtain protection of strike-breakers and to disperse crowds of strikers blocking entry to the workplace. The Interior Ministry and provincial administration were up against very powerful forces when embarking on their demilitarisation policy. German heavy industry – coal, iron and steel – were far better organised than their French counterparts. Organisations like the Central Association of German Manufacturers or the Rhineland-Westphalia Coal Syndicate formed very effective pressure groups who successfully lobbied for state subventions and the tariffs to support the home market against foreign competitors. *Reichstag* members, government officials and senior bureaucrats of the provincial administration were all targeted with a sophisticated system involving informal approaches as well as direct pressures.[5] However when it came to obtaining military protection, even the great industrial associations were increasingly ostracised, by both the provincial administration and the military authorities.

Until the 1880s Westphalian industrialists still tended to take military protection of mines and factories for granted. During the 1889 miners' strike, mining companies sent requests directly to the government, describing in detail the type of military protection that they considered appropriate. In many cases their requests were supported by the local governors, who held meetings with representatives from the mining companies. During the 1889 miners' strike, von Baltz, the local governor in Gelsenkirchen, sent a letter to the Interior Minister putting forward the wishes of the mining companies about changing the previous military dispositions in order to obtain permanent military guards at plants and frequent military patrols.[6]

Yet nothing came of these demands. Although the army was mobilised during the 1889 strike, requests from individual mining companies were seriously frowned upon. Whenever the army was involved industrialists, as well as local governors, found themselves up against not only the heads of the provincial administration and the Interior Ministry but also powerful military commanders who had their own agendas.[7] Moreover, throughout the strike, the Central Association of German Manufacturers appealed in vain to the government to declare a state of siege. The request was turned down despite the fact that many of the strikebound mines – particularly those in the Saarland – were owned by the state. Similarly, in 1905 and again in 1912, the mining companies appealed to the province governor of Westphalia, and directly to the government, to provide an impressive show of military force.[8] Their requests were not fulfilled, despite their attempts to present the problem of strikes in the mining sector as involving the interests and responsibility of the state.[9]

During the 1890s a division becomes noticeable between the local governors and the province and district governors over the issue of military involvement in protest policing. Local governors held a key position in implementing measures to ensure public order whenever unrest spread beyond the borders of a municipal police district; until the 1890s, it was primarily the local governor who determined whether and when troops were to be requested from the nearest garrison. Local governors often supported the pleas for military protection coming from municipal authorities and they were generally keen on requesting troops long before the district and province governors were prepared to take this step. This may be because the local governors were often closely associated with the groups and individuals, who were directly or indirectly targeted by protesters. Similarly, in many cases the local governor had vested interests as landowner, as member of local assemblies or was involved in local industries.[10] However even if industrialists, municipal authorities and local governors may have acted out of consideration for their own interests, this does not exclude that local governors, being closer to the conflict, were also genuinely alarmed by the prospect of police and *gendarmerie* losing control over highly volatile and potentially violent conflicts.

The position of the heads of the provincial administration and the military establishment

The general failure of industrial pressure groups, even with the support of the local governor, to persuade the province and district governors to accommodate the wishes of heavy industry was linked both to the self-perception of Prussian bureaucrats and to the professional relationship between the provincial administration and the military authorities.

Members of the Prussian administration generally showed a very self-assertive attitude towards industrialists and businessmen, even if the days had gone when state bureaucrats could look down upon them as 'self-interested merchants'.[11] As civil servants appointed by the Interior Minister, and only responsible to the government in Berlin, Prussian civil servants generally saw themselves as defenders of the interests of the King and the Prussian State, independent of any private interests.[12]

This did not prevent leaders of the provincial administration from supporting industrial interests, particularly in disputes with striking workers. Yet they were very particular about not giving any impression of simply accommodating the wishes of businessmen and industrialists. Military involvement in the policing of protest was an issue where leaders of the provincial administration saw opposition between the interests of great industry and the Prussian State.

Comparing the attitude of senior civil servants before and after the great miners' strike of 1889, it appears that senior state administrators tended to increasingly distance themselves from the industrialists. In 1889, the predominant attitude among civil servants was that strikes were unacceptable and that a forceful response to public disturbance was the only appropriate way of dealing with it. However, the 1889 strike was also the first in which some senior administrators began to doubt the justification of the employers' continued refusal to negotiate with the workers.

The District Governor in Düsseldorf, von Berlepsch, expressed his frustration about the intransigent attitude of mine-owners.[13] It was not that von Berlepsch was prepared to accept anything that smacked of Social Democratism or trade unionism; it was rather an element of criticism of the private companies for being irresponsible in their provocation of labour confrontations. A certain tone of bitterness can be discerned in von Berlepsch's account of private companies and their pursuit of particular interests that put public order at risk and exposed the entire community to the threat of violent clashes.[14]

Similar considerations emerged at the time of the miners' strike of 1905. Reports from province and district governors to the Interior Ministry showed exasperation with companies whose actions deliberately obstructed police measures being taken by the state administration.[15] The demands for military intervention coming from local police authorities, under strong pressure from private companies, convinced some leaders of the provincial administration of the need to keep the requisition for military troops under strict control.[16] In their justification to the Interior Ministry for not yielding to pressure from the mining companies, senior civil servants showed that they were perfectly aware of the underlying agenda when private companies and local police authorities described widespread violence and riots.[17] Indeed they bluntly described the claims of the mining companies as irresponsible, and their demands for forces as highly unrealistic.[18] Unlike the mining companies, some senior civil servants also began to accept that, insofar as the workers' organisations controlled the strikers, labour disputes could take place without serious incidents of violent unrest.[19]

Senior bureaucrats in the Westphalian provincial administration had several reasons for distancing themselves from pressure by industrialists who called for crackdowns on workers on strike. In the correspondence between the Province and District Governors and the Interior Ministry, the claims of workers are occasionally recognised as reasonable and justified, despite the strong aversion among Prussian civil servants to the Social Democratic movement.

In the same way, a certain recognition of workers' organisations developed, especially those holding a mandate from workers to negotiate on their behalf. As for the protection of private property and workers who continued to work, the state administration insisted that it was primarily the responsibility of the private companies to finance private security forces and to pay for expenses in the case of a military intervention.[20]

Another important reason for province and district governors to avoid military involvement was the difficult relationship with the military authorities. Like their French counterparts, Prussian civil servants had a tradition of underlining their independence from the military authorities. Since the reform era at the beginning of the 19th century, the provincial administration had tried to assert its independence from military interference in civilian affairs, attempting to exclude the military authorities from functioning as a co-executive.[21]

The Prussian army was an awkward partner; yet, the dismissive attitude of Prussian commanders towards industrial interests had the beneficial side-effect of helping leaders of the provincial administration to enforce the demilitarisation of protest policing. Thus, successive army corps commanders seemed to be in full agreement with the province governors on at least one issue: restricting the right of local governors to approach local garrison commanders to obtain military protection.

If province and district governors were not always capable of controlling the local governors' use of their right to requisition, senior military commanders did the job. During the conflicts of the 1890s, there were still examples of mayors addressing their requisitions directly to a local commander instead of passing through the province or district governor.[22] This procedure was effectively stopped by army corps commanders increasingly forbidding their subordinate commanders to mobilise troops without an explicit order from the army corps commander. General von Albedyll was strongly disinclined to let local police commissioners have access to the requisition of military troops.[23] Like Albedyll, General von Bissing argued that local authorities could not be trusted to call for military assistance, because in a situation where many strikes broke out in different localities, such a procedure of requisitioning could only lead to chaos.[24] Thus in 1906, General von Bissing wrote to the provincial administration that requisitions needed to be coordinated by the province and district governors before being presented to the army corps commander.[25] This was confirmed in 1910 by a meeting among civilian authorities during which it was also stipulated that it was no longer possible to ask for protection of particular factories or mines.[26] It therefore became standard practice that when a local military commander received a requisition from a local authority he needed to ask the army corps commander for permission to mobilise; the army corps commander would then contact the province governor to check the seriousness of the case and the appropriateness of intervening with troops.

The result of these administrative adjustments was a *de facto* transfer of authority from local to regional level that seriously reduced the access of local governors to request military assistance. Only during the short periods troops were already mobilised within a county or district was there direct communication between the local governors, municipal authorities and the military commander sent to the area.

Government authorities and civil servants were generally attentive to the wishes of industrialists and used the police and *gendarmerie* to allow the continuation of production during labour disputes. Yet, when it came to involving the army, there were opposing interests at stake. The wishes expressed by employers and municipal authorities to obtain effective protection of private property coincided neither with the provincial administration's desire to avoid military involvement, nor with the particular interests of the army; in this debate, the military authorities had the upper hand.

The position of the industrial elites: social exclusion and financial considerations

As local governors were gradually being marginalised from decisions on whether or not to involve military troops, industrialists lost their most important source of informal influence. Henceforth individual industrialists and their pressure groups had to make their case before province governors and army corps commanders. Whilst local governors were often approachable through informal social contact, province governors and senior military commanders belonged to a social *milieu* from which the industrial bourgeoisie was generally excluded.

Whilst businessmen and industrialists seemed to have very close social ties amongst themselves,[27] studies of Rhineland-Westphalian industrialists all emphasise the social separation of the industrial magnates and wealthy businessmen from the local nobility.[28] Kaudelka-Hanisch's study reaches the same conclusion in relation to businessmen holding a semi-official status.[29] Whilst some members of the Rhineland nobility were occasionally invited by the Krupps to balls at *Villa Hügel*, such invitations were normally declined.[30] The other munitions manufacturing magnate, Heinrich Ehrhardt, received frequent visits from the Duke of Saxe-Coburg Gotha, but such social contacts between members of the landed nobility and Rheinish-Westphalian magnates of heavy industry were highly exceptional.

In Berlin and Hamburg wealthy businessmen formed social networks amongst themselves and successfully integrated senior civil servants and politicians in their social circles. Such informal social connections between industrial magnates and civil servants did not characterise local elites structures in Westphalia and the Rhine Province.[31] Here the wealthy bourgeoisie and industrial magnates socialised much less with the members of the provincial administration, and contacts were far more likely to involve only civil servants who had not yet moved into the ranks of the nobility. In terms of networking, the wealthy businessmen and industrial magnates preferred to court politicians and officials in Berlin.

Hardly any of the industrialists of the Rhineland-Westphalia area enjoyed personal friendships with military officers.[32] One notorious exception, which in itself was significant, was the Krupp family. Apart from their private affiliations with at least one province governor, Konrad Studt,[33] Alfred and Fritz Krupp enjoyed privileged relations with several senior commanders. Senior commanders were regular private guests at the

Krupp residence, *Villa Hügel* in Essen. However the position of the Krupps with their personal access to the *Kaiser* was, as Dolores Augustine points out, highly unusual.[34] In 1906 Wilhelm II even attended the wedding of the heir to the Krupp industries together with a string of senior members of the military establishment.[35] However, the direct access of Krupp to the military leaders was – as General von Deimling explains in his memoirs – entirely due to Krupp being the main provider of weaponry to the army.[36] It is also worth noting that the Krupps never sought military protection of their factories despite the direct and privileged access of the Krupps to top generals, and regardless of the Krupp firm financing six local *gendarmes* between 1870 and 1910.[37] The Krupp firm had other ways of keeping their workforce firmly away from engaging in labour disputes.[38]

Whilst the leaders of the provincial administration and the army did their best to restrict the access of local authorities to the army, the local pressure for military protection also changed. Until the early 1890s, there was strong pressure from local authorities and private citizens to call for military assistance in order to put down strikes and popular disorder.[39] It therefore appears paradoxical that while labour conflicts became more extended, more organised and more effective, the pressure on the provincial administration and the military authorities to provide a significant display of force against strikers and public unrest became less direct. The main reason for this change in approach was the question of finance.

The expenses of any military intervention were to be covered by the local community who had asked for protection. Similarly when factory owners or a mining company asked the municipal authorities to call for military troops, they took responsibility upon themselves for the expenses incurred. Previously, in the 19th century, when public disorder could be managed with a limited number of soldiers mobilised for a few days, the costs of military protection were still within the financial reach of smaller communities or medium-sized industries. However, as labour disputes became extended, requiring a considerable number of forces for a conflict that could last for weeks or months, the costs soon exceeded the financial capacities of most municipalities or industries. After 1889, private companies therefore seldom called directly for military intervention, with the exception of those industries – such as mining and heavy industry – which were supported by financially powerful organisations. Smaller private companies generally addressed their demands for protection to the municipal authorities or local governor without specifying the type of force that they needed, whilst stressing the potential for violence among the strikers and the disorder spinning out of control. By this indirect approach they sought to persuade municipal authorities or the local governor to request military assistance at their own expense.

However, municipal authorities also had to calculate the financial implications of such a move. If they issued a requisition, the community would have to carry the costs of military intervention which would weigh heavily on the municipal budget for years to come. Even with municipal institutions being firmly in the hands of the property owners, a mayor seeking re-election might think twice about demanding military protection, if the military presence only benefited a minority of the electorate. If, on the other hand, a requisition for military intervention was finally issued by the province or district governor, there was always the possibility of negotiating with the provincial administration about the state taking over at least some of the costs. Demands from municipal authorities for military intervention accordingly became less frequent during the 1890s, and generally more hesitant than they had been previously.

A similarly hesitant approach became discernable in the petitions from the Provincial Assembly. In 1912, a few days before troops were mobilised in the Ruhr district to police the greatest miners' strike since 1905, the Westphalian Province Assembly sent a petition to the Interior Minister, urging the government to intervene in order to protect employers and to prevent workers from being bullied into joining the strike. However, instead of directly mentioning military intervention, the petition simply demanded that all necessary measures be taken to protect the strike breakers.[40] The hint was hardly to be misunderstood, although not clearly expressed.

With the technical exclusion of local governors and municipal authorities from requesting troops from local garrisons, the decision was firmly in the hands of the province governors and army corps commanders; and these tended to prefer that strikes and demonstrations were handled with police and *gendarmerie* alone. Yet, if troops were eventually mobilised it was on the initiative of the province governor and the expenses were primarily covered by the state.

The French concentration of decision-making on the use of troops

The comparison with Nord-Pas-de-Calais raises two questions. The first is whether the more frequent military involvement in protest policing here was linked – in part at least – to French prefects having difficulties controlling local authorities' use of their right to request troops. Secondly, we need to investigate whether French prefects were more easily put under pressure to provide military protection than their Prussian counterparts.

In the first place it is worth noting that French prefects exercised influence over policing measures in local communities to a much greater extent than their Prussian counterparts. Westphalian province and district governors acquired some degree of influence over the policing measures by organising close cooperation between the various municipal police organisations. Negotiations between municipalities and coordination of policing strategies were facilitated by the fact that the vast majority Prussian municipalities were firmly controlled by conservative forces as a result of the three-class voting system. Attitudes and interests in matters of maintenance of order therefore did not vary significantly between the local communities.[41] The situation was very different in Nord-Pas-de-Calais which was politically highly diverse. Accordingly policing policies varied significantly from one municipality to another, depending on the political composition of each community. Although the majority of municipalities in the *départements* 'Nord' and 'Pas-de-Calais' had a comfortable majority to the right of the centre-left governments throughout the period 1898–1914, the socialists were gaining ground. Elections to the National Assembly show that left-wing candidates received sixteen to eighteen per cent of the votes in 1902, increasing to twenty-five to thirty per cent of the votes in 1914.[42] Wealthy middle-class candidates might successfully stand for municipal or parliamentary elections in the predominantly industrial constituencies of Roubaix, Tourcoing or Lens, but they depended on the workers' votes for re-election.[43]

With some municipalities being solidly conservative and others firmly socialist, mayors implemented very different policing policies and were fundamentally divided over the issue of military presence. From the early 1890s onwards, this patchwork of administrative units with mayors of opposing sympathies towards labour conflicts and dissimilar policies towards public unrest threatened to create mayhem. Some mayors would seek military protection at a very early stage whilst others would do their best to implement only the most basic measures. In situations where a conflict spread beyond the municipal borders, this made any coordination of municipal forces almost impossible. In October 1902, for instance, when the miners from the entire region went on strike, the mayors of Bethune and of the surrounding suburban municipalities urged the prefect of Pas-de-Calais to request military assistance. At the same time, the mayor of Avion, who belonged to the French Labour Party, and the Socialist mayors of Lens and Denain, protested vigorously against the idea of military intervention and threatened to resign if troops were called upon.[44]

When French municipal authorities requested military assistance, the military commanders were obliged by law to deliver troops.[45] However, when confronted with large-scale conflict concerning several municipalities, the prefects also had power to take responsibility for all policing measures and thereby ensure coherent management. Prefects had two ways of imposing their authority. One was to strip mayors of their policing responsibility and take authority for maintaining order through the *gendarmerie* and perhaps by calling upon the army.[46] In addition, prefects were empowered to invalidate requisitions issued by a subordinate authority by making a counter-requisition; this allowed the prefect to limit or to specify the terms under which the army was requested. Effectively, no military intervention could take place against the will of the prefect.

The dilemma of municipal authorities

While prefects became increasingly inclined to assume responsibility for all decisions concerning the use of troops this was matched by increasing hesitation from mayors to call directly for military protection. As in Prussia there were both financial and political considerations to take into account. In 1891, in the wake of the bloody incidents at Fourmies, Henri Vel-Durand, prefect of *département* Nord, wrote to the Interior Minister that the responsibilities of the mayors and the prefects in terms of maintenance of public order were becoming increasingly difficult, since they were constantly being exposed to criticism from opposing groups within local society.[47]

Within their constituencies, the mayors were in a difficult position for reasons very similar to those confronting Westphalian mayors: no matter what decision a mayor might take, the municipality risked ending up with a huge bill. The 1884 law on local government made communities financially responsible for damage to public and private property if the municipal authorities had not used all available resources to ensure the maintenance of public order.[48] The expense of a requisition for supplementary *gendarmerie* forces or military troops would also fall upon the local community unless the *gendarmes* were requested on the prefect's initiative, in which case the community only bore the cost of accommodation and food for men and horses.

Socialist mayors frequently complained about bearing expenses for *gendarmes* and troops that they had not called for, and in many cases, the question of financial responsibility was merely one element of a politically motivated opposition to military presence.[49] In other cases the timing of the formal request for military assistance was carefully calculated by the mayors in order to square their responsibility for maintaining order with their political opposition to the presence of soldiers or *gendarmes*. One mayor called for supplementary forces only at the moment when he knew that the prefect could hardly spare any more *gendarmes*. The reason for this was bluntly admitted. By making a request for more forces and calculating that the prefect would refuse, the local community was discharged from its financial responsibility for private property damaged by rioters or striking workers.[50]

Conversely, mayors who based their political power on the well-to-do often faced strong pressure from mine and factory owners to call for substantial military forces. These mayors were very vulnerable to criticism for not having done enough if a situation got out of control. In 1903, for instance, the owner of a textile factory in Armentière considered taking legal action against the municipality which he accused of not taking all measures necessary to prevent violent attacks on his private property.[51] At the same time, striking workers, as well as some of the locals who were not involved in the ongoing conflicts, would complain about the expense of troops and tended to consider military presence a costly and exaggerated measure.

The result was that, during the early days of a conflict, both the military commanders as well as sub-prefects and the prefect would receive a large number of requisitions issued by the municipalities, some of which were clearly exaggerated, while others appeared to be issued merely in order to discharge a municipality from its legal and financial obligations. Increasingly, therefore, prefects preferred to take over the responsibility for law-and-order measures, thus marginalising the municipal authorities. In cases where the military was asked to intervene, requisitions would come to the army corps commander through the prefect, who had received information about the situation on the spot from sources independent of the local authorities (i.e. the sub-prefect, the local *gendarmes* or the agents of the surveillance police, the *commissaires spéciales*).

Until the outbreak of the First World War, there were still occasional incidents of mayors requesting troops directly from the local military authorities. This, however, was only for incidents of minor unrest or simple crowd management. In these cases, a local commander would be directly requested by a mayor or – in the case of Dunkirk – by the civil governor. In these minor cases, the local commander would order his troops to mobilise, and only afterwards inform the army corps commander through the ordinary bureaucratic channels. It normally took four days for such a message to pass from a local commander through the commander of the section, the commander of the sub-division, and the division commander, before it landed on the army corps commander's desk in Lille. If the local commander was uncertain about the measures to be taken or about the potential for trouble, he sometimes warned the army corps commander by telegram in order to obtain his informal approval. However, these local requisitions always took place under close supervision from the prefect.

No decision could therefore be taken without the prefect's knowledge. Directly or indirectly, the prefect was always in charge of the conflicts involving the army. During the years between 1890 and 1914, the prefect became the single most important authority of any decision concerning the use of troops within his *département*. The powers of French prefects to strip mayors of their policing responsibility as well as their access for requesting military protection placed the prefects firmly in control of any use of troops within their *départements*. The prefects in 'Nord' and 'Pas-de-Calais' could therefore hardly be described as less capable than their Westphalian counterparts of controlling the municipal authorities' use of their right to request military troops.

Were the prefects subject to local pressures?

This still leaves open the question concerning the extent to which prefects were exposed to pressure from influential groups and individuals within the local society. In the General Council, the most powerful elected body at the *départemental* level, the measures of protest policing were hardly ever on the agenda. The minutes from the General Council in Lille show that the issue was only raised three times between 1891 and 1913. Complaints from the elected representatives attracted little interest and had scarcely any effect. In 1893, when three members proposed a resolution inviting the government to refrain from mobilising the army for labour conflicts, the prefect simply asked the Council not to discuss an issue which fell outside its competence.[52] Similar resolutions were presented to the General Council in April 1904 and again in May 1905. These resolutions were briefly discussed, one motion failed, the other passed. However, this resolution from the General Council was a simple statement with no political consequence.

At the same time, however, prefects needed a significant degree of goodwill among the members of locally elected bodies in order to function effectively as the government's executive representative in a *département*. During the early Third Republic prefects were particularly vulnerable to pressure from local representatives (i.e. deputies, senators, mayors, and members of the regional council).[53] One of the most important sources of potential pressure on the prefects came from politically powerful mayors who were also deputies to the National Assembly or held other important positions in the central political institutions. Due to the notorious instability of governments during the early Third Republic and because of the ever-changing and fragile alliances in the National Assembly, any threat from a powerful local politician to withdraw his support for the government could easily place a prefect in a difficult position. Such tactics were widely used in France to put provincial administrators under pressure.[54] The position of prefects was notoriously fragile and a prefect who brought down a government by annoying powerful local politicians was most likely to be sacked or transferred to another *département*.

It is therefore worth noting that prefects in Nord and Pas-de-Calais were remarkably less exposed to sacking or transfer than the prefects of other French *départements*. If the position as prefect in the two *départements* of Nord and Pas-de-Calais had been at stake over the issue of protest policing this would undoubtedly have resulted in a high turnover of prefects because of the strong pressures from both Conservative and Socialist mayors. However, the opposite was the case. While the average time in service for French prefects was less than three years, the *départements* Nord and Pas-de-Calais had the highest degree of prefectorial stability, only comparable to the *département* Seine that covered Paris. Seven out of ten prefects in Nord and Pas-de-Calais served for more than seven years and often it was the same prefects who served first in Pas-de-Calais and were then promoted to the more prestigious *département* Nord. Gabriel Vel-Durand served for fourteen years altogether in the region; Gabriel Alapetite and Jean-Baptiste Trépont served for a total of ten years each, while Louis Vincent remained prefect in *département* Nord from 1899 to 1911 during the twelve most turbulent years of this period.

This remarkable degree of prefectorial stability indicates that successive interior ministers were more inclined to maintain a strong prefect, someone who could impose himself in a difficult region, rather than to sacrifice him for the sake of political alliances in the National Assembly.

Another factor indicating that the prefects in Lille and Arras were not easily put under pressure on public order issues is the consistency with which policing measures were implemented. This is remarkable because of the polarisation of local politics between the traditionally influential conservative bourgeoisie supporting industrial interests, and the Radicals and Socialists supported by the ever-growing group of industrial workers. If the prefects' public order policies had been heavily influenced by pressure from local representatives, one would expect policing measures – in particular the use of troops – to change significantly from one conflict to another, depending on the location of the conflicts and on the national political power constellations of the day.

It is also worth noting that the number of military interventions rose sharply under the Waldeck-Rousseau, Combes and Clemenceau administrations.[55] These governments depended more than any previous government on the support of political groups who were the most likely to oppose military intervention. This indicates that, in questions concerning the maintenance of public order, the policies pursued by the prefects were not a reflection of horse-trading with regard to national politics, but that the prefects had the power to impose their policing measures and could allow themselves to disregard pressure from local groups or individuals.

Prefects and local elites

In Nord and Pas-de-Calais, the position of the prefects on policing issues was further strengthened by the weakness of the employers' organisations. Individually the owners of the mines and manufacturing industries in Nord-Pas-de-Calais were no less hard-nosed and uncompromising towards striking workers than their Westphalian counterparts.[56] However, French industrialists tended to be suspicious of each other as competitors and of state involvement in industrial affairs. The most powerful employers' organisation 'The National Coal Employers' Federation' was much less cohesive and effective than its German counterpart and had difficulties reconciling opposing interests within the industry. While it was mostly concerned with lobbying government authorities in Paris, it did not seek to shape policing policies at the regional level.

In labour disputes, the prefects sometimes fulfilled the double function of mediators whilst at the same time being responsible for the maintenance of public order. In order to appear credible as a negotiator in labour disputes, it was essential to appear neutral in the implementation of policing measures. Yet often the prefects did not trust the neutrality of the local authorities and suspected individual mayors of being either too repressive or too indulgent, depending on their political sympathies.[57] Prefects were constantly confronted with attempts by mayors or directors of private companies to exaggerate the extent of violence and riots to persuade them to provide the maximum display of force. In the early 1890s, the prefects in Lille often complained about companies who seemed to regard the public forces – including the army – as their private security service.[58] At that time, it was not uncommon for mining companies to send requests to the prefect stating how many soldiers they needed for the protection of their plants. During the miners' strike of September 1893 private companies had no hesitation of asking for military protection and the number of soldiers they demanded was considerable. One mining company requested no less than 401 soldiers, infantry and cavalry, to protect its five mineshafts and an administration building.[59] The irritation of the prefects over private companies was reinforced by battles over bills, and the problems of making the private companies, who claimed that their property had been insufficiently protected, cover their share of expenses.[60]

The suspicion and irritation of the prefects over local industrialists using public forces for their own particular interests emerge quite strongly in the accounts provided to the Interior Ministry about the shooting at Fourmies in 1891. In a report from the special commission that had been investigating the incident for the Interior Ministry, accusations against the local authorities and the industrialists were numerous. The blame for the disorder that had broken out during the May Day demonstrations lay, according to the special commission, largely with local industrialists with their intransigent attitude towards their employees.[61] Moreover, the mayor and local councillors – most of whom were mine or factory owners – were criticised for using public forces to protect their own property, while showing only a semblance of consideration for the maintenance of public order within the rest of the community.[62]

A similar account was given by the prefect of *département* Nord, Vel-Durand. He saw the call for troops and the escalation of an otherwise peaceful demonstration into violent encounters between the armed forces and the strikers as the result of pressure from local industrialists to protect their particular interests. He stressed that demands for protection coming from private companies were often exaggerated, and described the unfortunate incident as the result of an irresponsible and self-interested mayor and an inexperienced sub-prefect.[63] Arguing that he could not intervene against decisions already made by the sub-prefect, Vel-Durand managed to avoid responsibility for the shooting at Fourmies. However, in subsequent years, prefects in the *départements* Nord and Pas-de-Calais were generally very keen on remaining in charge of the maintenance of public order when military troops were involved and indeed sought to supervise closely the requisitions issued by mayors and sub-prefects.

If the prefects became increasingly suspicious about the neutrality of the mayors who were closely connected to mine and factory owners, a similar attitude was apparent in relation to mayors whose sympathies lay with the labour movement. Among civil servants and governmental authorities alike, there was little sympathy for the trade unions that were about to establish themselves outside the control of the politicians in the National Assembly. In particular, the communist C.G.T. trade union, with its revolutionary rhetoric, was regarded with much suspicion.[64] The prefects therefore saw attempts by Socialist mayors to protect strikers from police intervention – and ultimately from military intervention – as an irresponsible policy that put public order seriously at risk. This became particularly apparent during the turbulent spring of 1906, when Socialist mayors – in particular Basly, mayor of Lens – joined the demonstrations against the military intervention. Similarly, the trouble in South France over the summer of 1907 showed the opposition from mayors who were sympathetic to the protest movement of the wine growers, and who resigned in great numbers in protest against the military intervention.

The difficult relationship between industrialists and military authorities

The French military commanders who became involved in the policing of strikes and demonstrations were even less inclined than the prefects to feel sympathy or understanding for the needs and interests of municipal authorities or industrialists. Senior commanders tended to share the prefects' strong prejudices against municipal authorities and industrialists who demanded military protection. This negative military attitude towards private companies significantly sharpened between 1890 and 1914, as the army became increasingly involved in the policing of labour disputes.

In the 1880s, when the use of troops was still decided primarily between municipal authorities and local garrisons, the mine and factory owners had often treated both the police and the army as their private security corps and simply expected them to perform according to their particular wishes and needs. As in Prussia, there were private companies offering extra bonuses to the *gendarmes* or soldiers. On their side, the military authorities became increasingly irritated about the exaggerated reports emanating from the private companies, and commanders expressed frustration when rushing to communities where private companies had described widespread violence and riots only to find the situation much calmer than indicated.[65] Particularly during the great miners' strike of 1901, complaints were expressed through the War Ministry about exaggerated demands for military protection a long time after the strike had effectively ended.[66]

Like their Prussian counterparts, French military commanders were very reluctant to become an extended police force and were very careful not to be seen as a private security force for local industrialists.[67] The mining companies were supposed to pay for expenses incurred, such as accommodation, food and supplies for officers, soldiers and horses; however, the military authorities vigorously refused the idea that a supplementary payment to the officers and soldiers should be paid by the private companies, thus employing the troops virtually as a private security corps. It was, as one general commander put it, a matter of honour.[68] Similarly, in the few cases in which mining companies addressed their plea for military protection directly to the army corps commander, the request was immediately handed over to the prefect who had been bypassed. Apart from the slightly derogative tone with which the general refers to 'un sieur Portier', thus indicating that no previous connections had existed between the mining director and the military commander, General Jamont preferred to send the question to be investigated by the prefect in whose judgement he obviously had more confidence.[69]

Despite the frequent mobilisation, the French military authorities continued to complain that the private companies did not provide appropriate accommodation and food for soldiers and horses. In some cases the inadequate provision for soldiers and horses was used by municipal authorities as a way to demonstrate dissatisfaction with the measures imposed on them by the prefect. The mayor of Hazebrouck – who was against military intervention to enforce the anti-Catholic legislation in March 1906 and again in November the same year – used the question of provisions and accommodation for the troops mobilised as a way of demonstrating his discontent.[70] This type of deliberate obstruction happened often, in particular when Socialist mayors protested against the prefect sending troops to their municipalities during labour conflicts. Such protests were primarily aimed at the prefect rather than turned against the army. However, any incident of inadequate provisions to soldiers and horses just added to the grudge felt by the military authorities against municipal authorities and private companies.

In the years following the great strikes of the spring of 1906, the military authorities complained particularly about companies being unwilling to follow the suggestions made jointly by the prefect and the general staff about how to make their factory or mine easier to protect during strikes. From 1907 onwards, the ministerial protection plans contained whole sections with recommendations to the mining companies and factory owners about making their installations easier to protect against striking workers. These included constructing walls around the plant or factory, investment in electric lighting during the night, and the organisation of private security corps to ensure entry to the site and the protection of strike-breakers. These provisions were later repeated in a secret circular letter of 20 July 1909 from the Interior Ministry.[71] Yet, in subsequent years, the military authorities repeatedly complained that private companies had done nothing to make their sites less exposed to invasion or sabotage from striking workers.[72]

Given that the military commanders were legally obliged to deliver troops whenever requested, they were vulnerable to numerous and uncoordinated calls issued by municipal authorities. Being unable to refuse to become involved in protest policing, their best option was to support the attempts of the prefects to tightly control the municipal authorities' use of their right to requisition, and to work together with the Interior Ministry about national coordination of measures and distribution of troops.

In Nord-Pas-de-Calais as well as in Westphalia any decision concerning the mobilisation of troops rested firmly in the hands of the prefects, the province governors and the army corps commanders. If there were differences between the prefects and the military authorities over the role of the army in protest policing, it was not a conflict on which the municipal authorities could capitalise to gain better access to military protection. Despite the complex interactions between local and national politics in the French Third Republic the prefects serving in the *départements* Nord and Pas-de-Calais appear no less capable than their Westphalian counterparts of withstanding pressure from local elites and industrialists and imposing their own policing measures. If the far more frequent use of troops in France had been due to the greater ability of local authorities and industrialists to exercise influence, this would have been discernable in far more reluctance from the prefects and attempts from the prefects to reduce the military element. However the frequent mobilisation of great numbers of men was a practice generated by the prefects, and implemented – willingly or reluctantly – by the army corps commanders.

Notes

[1] Tenfelde (1979) p. 77; Saul (1981) p. 210; Rebérioux (1975) p. 90; idem. (1994) pp. 15–17; Trempé (1995) p. 365.
[2] Lüdtke (1982) p. 291; Perrot (1975) vol. 1 pp. 75–76; Magraw (2002) pp. 83–89.
[3] See Chapter 2 and Chapter 3.
[4] Twenty-two per cent of Westphalian manufacturers of heavy industry were involved in municipal politics. (Toni Pierenkemper, *Die Westfälischen Schwerindustriellen 1852-1913: Soziale Struktur und unternehmerischer Erfolg*, Göttingen: Vandenhoeck & Ruprecht, 1979, p. 62.)
[5] Hans-Peter Ullmann, *Der Bund der Industriellen*, Göttingen: Vandenhoeck & Ruprecht, 1976, pp. 116–130; Jürgen Kocka, *Industrial culture and bourgeois society: business, labor and bureaucracy in modern Germany*, Oxford: Berghahn Books, 1999, pp. 201–203.
[6] GSA, Berlin, HA1, Rep. 77, Titel 2513 /1 Beiheft 2: Letter of 13 May 1889 from the Local Governor in Gelsenkirchen to Interior Minister Herrfurth; GSA, Berlin, HA1, Rep. 77, Titel 2523 /1 (documents 129–133): Telegram of 19 January 1905

from the Ruhr *Zechencentrum*; Bergbau Archive, Bochum, 32 /4277: minutes from a meeting on 18 January 1905 in the Bochum Strike Insurance Association.

[7] CA, Potsdam III, R 43, film signature 11971-11972 (documents 71–90) or HSA, Münster, OP 14317 (documents 53–73): Report of 10 May 1889 from a meeting in Dortmund between civilian authorities concerned by the miners' strike; Waldersee (1927) pp. 288–289: Letter of 11 May 1889 from General von Albedyll to General von Waldersee.

[8] GSA, Berlin, HA1, Rep. 77, Titel 2523 /1, vol. 11 (documents 129–133): Telegram of 19 January 1905 from the mining company '*Zechencentrum*' to the Interior Ministry; GSA, Berlin, HA1, Rep. 77, Titel 2523 /1, vol. 11 (documents 213–214): Letter of 18 January 1905 from the District Governor in Münster to Interior Minister von Hammerstein.

[9] GSA, Berlin, HA1, Rep. 77, Titel 2523 /1, vol. 12 (documents 17–18): Letter of 21 January 1905 from the mining company 'König Ludwig' to the District Governor in Münster.

[10] Similar observations have been made for the entire German Empire: Funk (1986) Footnote 307; See also Johnson (1995) pp. 20–21.

[11] Born (1957) p. 82; Elaine Glovka Spencer, 'Businessmen, Bureaucrats and Social control in the Ruhr, 1914' in H-U Wehler (ed.), *Sozialgeschichte heute*, Göttingen: Vandenhoeck & Ruprecht, 1974, pp. 452–466.

[12] Born (1957) p. 82; Henning (1987) pp. 141–144.

[13] Berlepsch (1925) pp. 19–20.

[14] Berlepsch (1925) p. 25.

[15] GSA, Berlin, HA1, Rep. 77, Titel 2523 /1, vol. 12 (documents 2–3): Letter of 23 January 1905 from the District Governor in Münster to Interior Minister von Hammerstein.

[16] GSA, Berlin, HA1, Rep. 77, Titel 2523 /1, vol. 12 (documents 19–20): Letter of 23 January 1905 from the District Governor in Münster to the mining company *König Ludwig*.

[17] GSA, Berlin, HA1, Rep. 77, Titel 2523 /1, vol. 11 (documents 213–214): Letter of 18 January 1905 from the District Governor in Münster to Interior Minister von Hammerstein. GSA, Berlin, HA1, Rep. 77, Titel 2523 /1, vol. 11 (document 185): Telegram of 19 January 1905 from the District Governor in Düsseldorf to Interior Minister von Hammerstein. GSA, Berlin, HA1, Rep. 77, Titel 2523 /1, vol. 11 (documents 269–271): Letter of 20 February 1905 from the District Governor in Münster to Interior Minister von Hammerstein; HSA, Münster, OP 6095 (documents 107–112): Minutes from a meeting by the Local Governor in Essen on 21 December 1910.

[18] HSA, Münster, OP 2849, vol. 2 (document 93): Letter of 15 January 1905 from the District Governor of Arnsberg to Province Governor von der Recke of Westphalia; GSA, Berlin, HA1, Rep. 77, Titel 2523 /1 (documents 33–35): Letter of 15 January 1905 from the District Governor in Düsseldorf to Interior Minister von Hammerstein; HSA, Münster, OP 2849, vol. 2 (documents 246–247): Report of 16 January 1905 from the District Governor in Düsseldorf to Interior Minister von Hammerstein; GSA, Berlin, HA1, Rep. 77, Titel 2523 /1, vol. 11 (documents

269–271): Letter of 20 February 1905 from the District Governor in Münster to Interior Minister von Hammerstein.

[19] GSA, Berlin, HA1, Rep. 77, Titel 2523 /1, vol. 11 (documents 269–271): Letter of 20 February 1905 from the District Governor in Münster to Interior Minister von Hammerstein.

[20] Jessen (1991) pp. 142–144.

[21] Lüdtke (1982) pp. 291–293; Funk (1986) pp. 30, 47.

[22] Jessen (1991) pp. 133–134.

[23] Waldersee (1927) pp. 288–289: Letter of 11 May 1889.

[24] HSA, Münster, OP 6896 (document 46–50): Letter of 4 October 1904 from the District Governor in Arnsberg to Province Governor von der Recke in Münster; HSA, Münster, OP 6095 (document 71): Letter of 6 April 1906 from General von Bissing to Province Governor von der Recke.

[25] HSA, Münster, OP 6095 (document 71): Letter of 6 April 1906 from General von Bissing to Province Governor von der Recke.

[26] HSA, Münster, OP 6095 (documents 107–112): Minutes from a meeting by the local governor in Essen on 21 December 1910.

[27] Kaudelka-Hanisch (1993) p. 89; Dolores Augustine, 'Arriving in the upper class: the wealthy business elite of Wilhelmine Germany' in David Blackbourn and Richard J. Evans (eds.), *The German Bourgeoisie*, London: Routledge, 1993, p. 69.

[28] Friedrich Zunkel, *Der Rheinisch-Westfälische Unternehmer*, Cologne, 1962; Pierenkempter (1979); Hans-Jürgen Teuteberg, *Westfälische Textilunternehmer in derIndustrialisierung. Sozialer Status und betriebliches Verhalten im 19. Jahrhundert*, Dortmund: Gesellschaft für Westfälische Wirtschaftsgeschichte, 1980.

[29] Kaudelka-Hanisch (1993) pp. 89–90.

[30] Augustine (1993) pp. 69–72.

[31] Dolores Augustine, *Patricians and Parvenus: Wealth and High Society in Wilhelmine Germany*, Oxford: Berg, 1984, p. 226.

[32] Augustine (1993) p. 69.

[33] GSA, Berlin, Private Papers of Konrad von Studt (vol. 8).

[34] Augustine (1984) p. 202.

[35] Berthold von Deimling, *Aus der alten in die neue Zeit*, Berlin: Verlag Ullstein, 1930, p. 141; MA, Freiburg, N 550, Private Papers of General von Kluck (vol. 6) contains several documents showing this connection.

[36] Deimling (1930) p. 141; Augustine (1993) p. 69.

[37] Jessen (1991) p. 120.

[38] Lothar Gall, *Krupp: Der Aufstieg eines Industrieimperiums*, Munich: Siedler, 2000, pp. 217–231.

[39] Lüdtke (1982) p. 285; Spencer (1985) pp. 305–306.

[40] GSA, Berlin, HA1, Rep. 77, Titel 2523 /1, vol. 17 (document 14): Petition of 12 March 1912 from the Westphalian Province Assembly.

[41] Spencer (1992) p. 162. The election in 1903 of a Social Democratic mayor in the Arnsberg District gave rise to serious discussions about turning the municipal police in this area into state police. Jessen (1991) pp. 93–94.

[42] François Goguel, *Géographie des elections françaises sous la Troisième et la Quatrième République*, Paris: Armand Colin, 1970, pp. 36–45, 64–73; Danielle Delmare, 'Entre Socialisme et Catholicisme: Le Nord' in Pierre Birnbaum (ed.) *La France de l'Affaire Dreyfus*, Paris: Gallimard, 1994, p. 174.
[43] David Gordon, 'Liberalism and Socialism in the Nord', *French History*, Vol. 3 /3, 1989, pp. 312–341.
[44] Haupt (1986) p. 246; Cooper-Richet (1987) p. 409.
[45] See Chapter 1.
[46] Law on municipal powers of 5 April 1884, Articles 95 & 99.
[47] NA, Paris, F 7 12525: Report of 6 May 1891 from Vel-Durand, prefect of *département* Nord to the Interior Ministry.
[48] Law on Local Government of 5 April 1884, Articles 106 & 108.
[49] D[epartmental] A[rchive], Arras, M 4865: Minutes from the session on 20 November 1891 of the municipal council of Beuvry; DA, Arras, M 4865: Letter of 13 September 1893 from the mayor of Lens to Gabriel Alapetite, prefect of Pas-de-Calais; DA, Arras, M 4862 'Grève générale dans le bassin houiller 1893. Renseignements, Instructions, correspondance'. DA, Lille, M 625 /9: Letter of 8 October 1903 from the mayor of Houpline to Louis Vincent, prefect of *département* Nord.
[50] DA, Arras, M 1231: Letter of 8 November 1889 from the mayor in Leforest in the *arrondissement* of Béthune to Vel-Durand, prefect of Pas-de-Calais.
[51] DA, Lille, M 625 /4: Letter of 3 December 1903 from Interior Minister Combes to Louis Vincent, prefect of *département* Nord .
[52] DA, Lille, 1 N 135–158: 'Délibérations du Conseil Général,1891-1913', session of 11 April 1893.
[53] Chapman (1955) pp. 49–54; Siweck-Pouydesseau (1969) pp. 35–38; Wright (1994) pp. 298–299.
[54] Siweck-Pouydesseau (1969) pp. 35–38; Chapman (1955) pp. 49–54.
[55] See detailed figures Chapter 6.
[56] Roger Magraw, 'Management, Labour and the State in France, 1871–1939: Industrial relations in the Third Republic' in Peter Mathias and John A. Davis (eds.), *The Nature of Industrialisaiton*, Oxford: Blackwell, 1996, pp. 83–105.
[57] Berlière (1996) pp. 85–86.
[58] DA, Arras, M 1231: Letter of 12 October 1889 from the managing engineer of the mining company Meurchin-Bauvin to Vel-Durand, prefect of Pas-de-Calais; DA, Arras, M 4862: Letter of 30 October 1893 from a company engineer to the directing manager of the Courrière Mining Company.
[59] DA, Arras, M 4862: Letter of 13 September 1893 from the director of the *'Mines de Bruay'* to Gabriel Alapetite, prefect of Pas-de-Calais; similarly letter of 17 September 1893, from the company *'Vicoigne & Noeux'* to the prefect of Pas-de-Calais; letter of 17 September 1893 from the mining company *'Vendin-Lez-Béthune'*, and letter of 18 September 1893 from *'La compagnie des mines de Drocourt'* .
[60] DA, Arras, M 1231: Letter of 22 October 1889 from Vel-Durand, prefect of Pas-de-Calais to the senior manager of *'La Compagnies de Béthune'*.

[61] NA, Paris, F 7 12527: Report of 14 June 1891 by the *Commission spéciale adjoinet* to the Ministry of the Interior.
[62] NA, Paris, F 7 12527: Report of 14 June 1891 by the *Commission spéciale adjointe* to the Ministry of the Interior.
[63] NA, Paris, F 7 12525: Report of 6 May 1891 by Vel-Durand, prefect of *département* Nord to the Interior Ministry.
[64] Sorlin (1966) pp. 470–471; Agulhon (1993) p. 219.
[65] DA, Arras, M 1231: Letter of 25 October 1889 from the General Commander in Lens to Vel-Durand, prefect of Pas-de-Calais.
[66] NA, Paris, F 7 12779: Letters of 11 January and 16 May 1902 from War Minister André to Interior Minister Waldeck-Rousseau; NA, Paris, F 7 12779: Letter of 20 June 1902 from the General Staff to Interior Minister Combes.
[67] General de France, Instructions of 15 February 1893 to the First Army Corps.
[68] MA, Vincennes, 1st A.C. /2.I.331: Letter of 28 October 1880 from a division commander to General Lefebvre, army corps commander in Lille. (ibid.): Letter of 11 April 1884 from General Billot, army corps commander in Lille to the commander of the first division.
[69] DA, Arras, M 1231: Letter of 16 October 1889 from General Jamont, army corps commander in Lille, to the prefects of Nord and Pas-de-Calais.
[70] MA, Vincennes, 1st A.C. /2.I.335, 'Inventaires des Eglises, 1906' contains much evidence to this effect.
[71] NA, Paris, F 7 12912: 'Rapport de la commission chargée d'étudier la révision de l'exercice du droit de réquisition de la force armée par les autorités civiles et du plan de protection établi pour le cas de grèves dans les départements' 10 October 1907; See also NA, Paris, F 7 12779: Circular letter of 26 July 1909 from Interior Minister Briand on strikes in the mining sector; NA, Paris, F 7 12912, 'Projets de lois: Mesures de protection 1884–1907'.
[72] NA, Paris, F 7 12779: Letters of 27 July 1911 and of 17 January 1912 from War Minister Messimy to Interior Minister Caillaux.

Chapter 8

Civilian and Military Elites: Social Backgrounds and Interactions

If French municipal authorities and industrialists did not exercise significantly more influence over the use of military troops in Nord-Pas-de-Calais than their counterparts in Westphalia, this places the focus specifically on the senior civil servants and army corps commanders who were at the centre of the decision-making process. Who were they and how did they relate to each other as the most senior representatives of the central government in the region? Significant differences appear between Westphalia and Nord-Pas-de-Calais. Yet, whilst there was more professional cooperation between French prefects and military commanders than between their Prussian counterparts, this observation seems strangely counter-intuitive. It appears at odds with the fact that the social and political basis for cooperation between the provincial administration and the army was much more favourable in Prussia than in France.

The senior members of the Republican civil service and the French army were generally recruited from among different social groups and had limited social contact with each other. Furthermore, the vast majority of senior army officers had little or no sympathy for the Republican regime that they were supposed to defend against its internal as well as its foreign enemies. French military commanders were at best moderately sympathetic to the Republican regime and at worst fiercely hostile. The government authorities and their representatives at the *départemental* level were painfully aware of the lack of enthusiasm for the Republic within the military establishment and asked the prefects to keep a watchful eye on the activities and acquaintances of individual army officers.

This mutual suspicion was not an ideal basis for cooperation between the civilian administration of the *départements* and the army, as the literature on French civil-military relations and social elites never fails to point out.[1] Scholars working on civil-military relations in France therefore tend to focus on the elements of conflict, highlighting the complaints from the military establishment about the role of the army in the policing of protest.[2] At the same time the active involvement of some French senior generals in the development and implementation of policing strategies based on massive military assistance is rarely dwelt upon or is written off. It is explained as French officers simply performing their professional duty in submitting to the will of the civilian authorities. Yet compared to Prussia, the extent of French civil-military cooperation is remarkable.

The social profiles of Prussian bureaucratic elites and of the general corps, by contrast, were far more auspicious as a basis for close cooperation, due to the social affinities between these two professional corps.[3] Many belonged to the Prussian nobility and the same family names appear frequently among senior civil servants and the senior generals. Whether noble or not, the majority also came from families which had been in the service of the Prussian state for generations, either through the state administration or the army. Whilst the senior members of the Prussian provincial administration and army were much more closely connected than their French counterparts, they also shared an unreserved allegiance to the Hohenzollern dynasty and to the Imperial regime.

Moreover with their conservative political outlook, these senior civil servants and general commanders were equally committed to resisting any attempt to challenge the existing social and political order. The social connections of senior civil servants and general commanders to the landed nobility were arguably most pronounced in the predominantly agrarian areas east of the River Elbe. However, in all areas of the German Empire, including the industrialised areas in Westphalia and the Rhineland, province governors and military commanders appeared to form a pillar of stability and a solid front against any form of popular protest, with the army styling itself as the ever present iron fist behind the provincial administration.[4]

On the one hand, the senior members of the Prussian provincial administration and military establishment had all good reasons for working together in maintaining the existing social and political order against challenges from popular protest, in particular from the Social Democrats. The policing of strikes and demonstrations would therefore have been a natural point of cooperation between these two groups. On the other hand, the Prussian-German State was characterised by high levels of fragmentation and institutional compartmentalism. Bismarck had created a political system with himself as the only coordinating point between the different sections of the State. It needed a strong person at the centre who could impose his will and create coherent policies against the particular interests of powerful agencies within the Prussian-German state organisation. With the downfall of Bismarck, it became extremely difficult to ensure any kind of cohesion, and the Prussian-German system was increasingly characterised by 'polycratic chaos'.[5]

Although there has been much debate about the extent to which Wilhelm II was in control, there is general agreement that governmental policy-making of the Wilhelmine era was characterised by lack of coordination and different branches of the Prussian State working in opposite directions.[6]

When looking at the civil-military relations in Westphalia it is therefore worth noting which of the two tendencies prevailed at the provincial level: the elite cooperation or the institutional fragmentation. The comparison with France provides a useful measure for estimating levels of cooperation and fragmentation.

The social basis for civil-military relations in Imperial Germany

Prussian nobility, by the late 19th century, has been described as one of the European noble groups that managed most successfully to maintain its social and political position within the German-Prussian State and society, through a combination of exclusion and integration of new members.[7] Yet, during the Wilhelmine era both the senior positions in the provincial administration and the upper ranks of the military hierarchy were being penetrated by newcomers.[8] Moreover, even the civil servants and military commanders who belonged to the old Prussian noble families were for the most part several generations away from the landed nobility and were by then only distantly related to those braches of their family who continued to live as great estate owners.[9]

Newly ennobled members of the civil service or the officer corps most often adopted the same cultural outlook as the members of the old *Junker* families. On the other hand, even Prussian old noble families were rapidly adapting themselves to a new reality and integrating elements which are otherwise seen as characterising bourgeois capitalist culture.[10]

Irrespective of formal status – noble, ennobled or non-noble – the senior members of the provincial administration and the army were highly conscious of belonging to a small, tightly knit and socially cohesive group of top state officials. The self-awareness as members of a bureaucratic elite corps in the service of the Prussian King and the German Empire was the most significant feature of Prussian province governors and army corps commanders alike. This was how they saw themselves and this was how they were seen by the surrounding society.

The Province Governors of Westphalia: between social and professional elites

The senior civil servants and military commanders who served in Westphalia as province governors and army corps commanders reflect both the increasing diversity of social origin and the close personal affiliations between these two most senior representative groups of Berlin at the provincial level. That province governors and army corps commanders should share political outlook is hardly surprising, given that no one displaying anything but highly conventional arch-conservative views would be promoted to the senior posts of Prussian state institutions. Prominent social status undoubtedly improved the chances for promotion within the provincial administration even if nobility was not a precondition for reaching the senior positions. More than ninety per cent of civil servants holding positions as province governors between 1882 and 1914 formally belonged to the nobility. Nevertheless, an increasing number of this group were commoners by birth, who had been ennobled during their career. In fact, twenty-seven per cent of the province governors appointed by Wilhelm II were commoners by birth.[11] Some were ennobled before reaching the top posts, others only immediately before retirement, after having attained the most senior positions as commoners. The prospect of ennoblement at some point during a bureaucratic career helped to ensure a high level of loyalty and conformism among the non-noble members of the administrative corps.

The bureaucrats who occupied the position as province governor of Westphalia reflect the rise of commoners as well as the persistence of ancient noble families within the corps. Two out of the five senior civil servants who served as province governor of Westphalia between 1871 and 1914 were commoners by birth. Friedrich (von) Kühlwetter, who had been a government minister during a brief period in 1848, was only ennobled in 1866 before being promoted to the post as province governor of Westphalia in 1871. Similarly, Konrad Studt remained a commoner throughout his ten years (1889–1899) as province governor of Westphalia; he was only ennobled in 1906 after having served for seven years as government minister for religious affairs and public education.

In the 1880s there had been a deliberate policy by Interior Minister von Puttkamer to stop the influx of commoners among senior civil servants, but this policy was reversed by Puttkamer's successor as Interior Minister, Ludwig von Herrfurth, who was accused of promoting too many commoners. Herrfurth's successors in the Prussian Interior Ministry may have been less clear in their preferences for nobles or commoners than

Puttkamer and Herrfurth, however their choices of province governor to Westphalia were remarkably distinguished. The last two of the pre-war period belonged to the highest aristocracy by any standard: Baron Gustav von der Recke von der Horst was of ancient Westphalian nobility and retired to the post as province governor in Münster after having served as Prussian Interior Minister. His successor as province governor, Karl von Ratibor und Corvey, Prince of Hohenlohe-Schillingfürst, belonged to a royal dynasty and was linked by family to the Reich Chancellor, Chlodowig, Prince of Hohenlohe-Schillingfürst.

Whatever differences there were in the social standing of the Westphalian province governors, there were also important common aspects. In the first place, the heads of the provincial administration were all highly professionalised career bureaucrats, and the requirement of appropriate legal training and administrative experience was generally applied scrupulously. During the early days of his reign, Wilhelm II sought to fill the senior positions in the eastern provinces with political appointees without appropriate professional qualifications, however this policy was abandoned alongside Wilhelm's gradual retreat from 'personal rule'.[12]

All the senor civil servants who served as province governors in Münster held doctorates in law and had pursued many years of professional training and administrative careers before attaining their posts. Irrespective of their noble background, the men appointed to the senior posts in the provincial administration were all closely linked to the political elite in Berlin, or at least came from families traditionally in the service of the Prussian state through the civil service or the army.

The social and professional profile of the army corps commanders

Although the public image of an exclusively noble officer corps was carefully upheld throughout the Imperial era, the Prussian army did make important concessions to this principle and a few commoners did in fact reach the most senior military posts. Amongst 137 army corps commanders serving between 1871 and 1914 twenty-two were born commoners; the majority of these were promoted by Wilhelm II. With sixteen per cent of recently ennobled general officers,[13] the proportion of commoners by birth among the army elite was still lower than in the civil service where more than twenty-seven per cent of province governors promoted between 1866 and 1918 were commoners by birth.[14] Out of eight army corps commanders serving in Westphalia, two – General von Mikusch-Buckberg and General von Bernhardi – were commoners by birth while General von Einem was of recent nobility.

Commoners or noble, the 137 generals serving as army corps commanders between 1871 and 1914 were closely linked to the groups most closely associated with the Prussian State or belonged to one of the ruling dynasties. The profile of the army corps commanders resembles that of the civil servants in the provincial administration[15] in that more than seventy per cent had a father who had either made his career in the army or in the civil service, or was registered as a landowner, in many cases both.

The army corps commanders obtained their posts at the very end of their careers, sometimes after having occupied the most influential positions in the central institutions, including War Minister, head of the General Staff or leader of the politically influential Military Cabinet. In some cases appointment to army corps commander seemed to be an elegant way of easing senior generals out of leading posts in the central institutions by seeming to give promotion. This was particularly clear during the attempts by the young Wilhelm II in 1888–1890 to rejuvenate the corps of generals who were occupying the leading military posts in Berlin. Thus, General von Albedyll, then head of the Military Cabinet, was 'promoted' to army corps commander in Westphalia in 1889 in order to clear the way for the *Kaiser*'s candidate General von Hahnke. This, at least, was how the transfer of General von Albedyll to Münster was perceived by some of his colleagues.[16] This was also how General von Waldersee saw his own transfer in 1891 from chief of the General Staff to army corps commander in Altona.[17]

A few appointments appeared to result from political horse-trading amongst the military leaders in Berlin, but the majority of promotions of generals to the provincial army corps seem to have been increasingly conducted with primary consideration for professional qualifications. Most notably was this the case with the appointment of General Kluck – a commoner by birth and not from the Prussian heartland – to the extremely prestigious post as commander in Königsberg in the most eastern part of Prussia.

Insiders and outsiders: social interactions within the local elites

The men who served in Westphalia as province governors or as army corps commanders were clearly the representatives of Berlin. One of the key functions of such representatives of central power at the regional level was to mediate between Berlin and local elite groups and create a fruitful relationship with the local elites.[18] The Province of Westphalia was only integrated into the Prussian kingdom after the Napoleonic Wars and the relationship between the Westphalian nobility and Berlin contained significant potential for conflict. By the establishment of the Empire, the Westphalian population was almost equally divided between Roman Catholics and Protestants. Whilst a considerable proportion of Protestants belonged to the urban middle classes and upper bourgeoisie, the Westphalian nobility was predominantly Catholic. During the 1870s, Westphalia became one of the strongholds of the rising Catholic Centre Party and was particularly targeted by the anti-Catholic legislation of the years of the *Kulturkampf*. In the process of national integration after the establishment of the Empire, attempts were made by Berlin to appoint civil servants and general commanders who were likely to fit well into the elites of each province. Later in the Wilhelmine era, however, appointments to posts as province governors and army corps commanders reflect little or no priority given to matching the social or religious profile of the state representatives to the local population.

The province governors and general commanders sent to Westphalia were outsiders to the local society; in particular, as non-nobles and as Lutherans, several were at odds with the predominantly Catholic Westphalian nobility. One of the few exceptions was Province Governor von Kühlwetter who was appointed to the province during the early years of the Empire when attempts to national integration were activity sought. He was born in Düsseldorf and spent most of his career in Westphalia.[19] As a local and as a Catholic, it is most likely that he was originally chosen for the post in an attempt to mediate between the authorities in Berlin and the Westphalian Catholics. How effective this mediation was is difficult to say, but Kühlwetter managed to remain in this post throughout the decade of the *Kulturkampf* – whilst many other senior civil servants of Catholic confession were sacked because of their reluctant implementation of anti-Catholic legislation.[20] This indicates that Kühlwetter belonged to the group of Catholic civil servants who were so zealous in showing their loyalty to the government in Berlin that they were prepared to estrange themselves from local society. By contrast, his successors von Hagenmeister and Konrad Studt were both Lutheran with roots in the eastern provinces who had spent most of their career in the eastern provinces.

Like their civilian counterparts, the generals who occupied posts as army corps commanders in Münster were outsiders to the local Westphalia society. None originated from the province and, although the post was often the last before retirement, only one settled in Westphalia after his retirement.[21] The only Catholic army corps commander in Westphalia was General Count zu Stolberg-Wernigerode (1871–1882) who, like the Catholic province governor von Kühlwetter, served during the decade of unification and *Kulturkampf*. All following army corps commanders in Westphalia were Lutherans.

During their service in Westphalia province governors and army corps commanders became part of a social *milieu* that mostly included the otherwise very exclusive Westphalian nobility. By virtue of their positions as the highest representatives of the Prussian State at the provincial level, the army corps commander and the province governor belonged to a social stratum where members of royal dynasties and the noble elites met at private dinners, birthday parties and *soirées*, society balls as well as any public or private celebration. The position of province governor or army corps commander seemed to compensate for whatever the individual holder of these posts might lack in terms of social standing. Even the commoner Konrad Studt had many social contacts among the local nobility. He participated in dinner parties and went hunting with members of the Westphalian nobility. After leaving the province, Studt remained on very friendly terms with Baron von Landsberg-Velen, a distinguished member of the local noble families and president of the Westphalian Provincial Assembly.[22]

Memoirs and letters from persons who frequented these *milieux*, provide an excellent insight into who was considered an appropriate social acquaintance for military commanders and for senior civil servants. In particular the memoirs and biographies of senior military officers define the social boundaries that surrounded military commanders. They provide a clear indication of the inclusion and exclusion of social groups within these particular *milieux*. Of course the leaders of the provincial administration were expected to have professional contacts with a variety of groups, including the great industrialists and the leaders of local traders' associations. The private social contacts of province governors and army corps commanders, in contrast, seemed to be limited to the highly exclusive social circles around the Westphalian nobility.

Generally Prussian military commanders tended to restrict their social acquaintance to very narrow groups. Some army corps commanders took upon themselves what they described as a 'cultural mission' by making contacts with influential locals in order to win over reluctant notables in non-Prussian areas to fully embrace the Imperial regime. This 'cultural mission' was attributed a great deal of importance and the relations with local elites is a recurrent theme in the memoirs and biographies of general commanders.[23] Similar attempts can be observed in the case of Westphalia. In 1889, General von Albedyll, who had just been moved to the post of army corps commander in Münster, endeavoured to create a good relationship with the predominantly Catholic nobility in Westphalia, whose enthusiasm for the Prussians was particularly limited. On the other hand, he saw the industrial magnates as people who were to be carefully watched and tamed.[24] Later, General von Bernhardi and General von Einem indicated similar patterns of social links in Münster.[25]

This 'cultural mission' and 'duty of military representation' could only take place within the narrow conventions for appropriate social acquaintances of a senior military commander. The groups of appropriate social acquaintance included members of the local nobility, and, if relevant, members of the royal dynasties.

Depending upon the personal inclination of the individual army corps commander, generals also socialised with senior members of the clergy, both Protestant and Catholic.[26] Guest lists and table plans show that it was only at very large dinner parties that army corps commanders were part of a wider social circle including senior magistrates, university professors and representatives of locally elected bodies (city mayors, members of the upper chamber of the Prussian Diet, and perhaps certain distinguished members of the Provincial Assembly).

Province governors and army corps commanders: social and professional relations

In Prussian garrison towns civilian officials and military commanders were expected to socialise, and in a similar manner the army corps commander would be personally acquainted and closely associated with the province governor in his area.[27] In memoirs, letters and biographies, the relationship with the province governor was attributed a great deal of importance by the senior military commanders, and the excellent relationship with the province governor is a theme which is very often dwelt upon. The province governor, who is almost invariably described as an excellent and highly cultivated man, is often the only member of the local community who enjoys a separate mention in the generals' autobiographies.[28]

In professional matters, however, the relationship between members of the provincial administration and the army corps commanders was less cordial. The Prussian generals were of course ready to defend the Prussian system and its institutions with all their might – however it had to be on the terms defined by the army itself. If the perceived interests of the military organisation conflicted with the needs of the provincial administration, it was the interests of the army that prevailed.

Despite declarations from commanding generals about the excellent relationship with the Province Governor, the attitude of the military commanders towards the state administrators was often arrogant and dismissive, particularly when it came to requests for military protection. Despite the cordial relationship between general commanders and province governors, the latter were after all civilians, and as such regarded as an inferior species of humanity.

Even if requisitions were sullenly followed, commanding generals often complained that the civil servants exaggerated problems and that there was no real threat of serious trouble. During the great miners' strike 1889, General von Albedyll described in a letter to Waldersee how frightened civil servants and industrialists completely overreacted and telegraphed him every ten minutes claiming that a major revolution had broken out in their area; in Albedyll's view the soldiers wasted their time because when arriving on the scene the incidents were not of a kind that required military intervention.[29] Similarly General von Loë, when solicited to provide soldiers for the policing of the May Day demonstrations in 1890, complained about being misused by the state administration and by the mayors of the larger cities.[30]

Military commanders also complained that the civilian authorities were too soft, obsessed with legal formalities and concerns for citizens' rights. Moreover, certain generals expressed very little respect for the legal distribution of authority between the state administration and military authorities.[31] In particular, the Zabern affair of 1913 revealed the complete disregard shown by many officers towards the civilian authorities. General von Deimling, in his justification of the military intervention without civilian requisition in Zabern refers to the incompetence and lack of energy of the civilian administration in Zabern, who failed to provide sufficient police and *gendarmerie* to deal with the anti-military demonstrations.[32]

Province governors and senior commanders went to the same dinner parties and were on cordial terms within the local elite groups, yet this did not lead to close professional connections even over the issue of defending the social and political order that both were a product of and strongly committed to.

French prefects and military commanders: social separation and clash of culture

The relationship between the civilian representatives of the Republican regime and the French army in Nord-Pas-de-Calais was perceived by prefects and military commanders alike to be an unholy alliance. The relationship between regime and army was plagued by conflict and mutual suspicion of ill-intent, with very few enthusiastic Republicans among the senior officer corps. When General Galliffet took over the War Ministry in the middle of the Dreyfus Affair, he put all his enormous prestige within the military establishment behind a reconciliation of the officer corps with the Republic.[33] However, throughout the pre-War period, the relationship between the French officer corps and the Republic continued to rest on fragile mutual acceptance.

Mutual understanding and trust was further weakened by the fact that prefects and senior military officers were recruited from different social groups. The Third Republic, and in particular the centre-left governments of the first decade of the 20th century, recruited and promoted men outside the traditional families in the service of the State. During the Second Empire, more than twenty per cent of the prefects had a father in the army.[34] Amongst the prefects serving between 1890 and 1914, fewer than six per cent were sons of military officers. Instead, the majority of prefects were sons of civil servants or lawyers, doctors and university professors. A significant number had a very humble background, with fathers who were peasants, shopkeepers, craftsmen, coachmen, or even labourers.[35] These were the men made by the Republic, and their self-awareness and political loyalty was committed to the Republican regime.

The social background and political outlook of French senior officers was very different. Almost forty per cent of generals were recruited from families with close ties either to the army or to the landed elites.[36] If not born into these groups, they could of course always marry into them. Accordingly, almost half of the generals – forty-nine per cent – married a woman whose father was either in the army or a landowner.[37] Only ten per cent of French generals had a father who held a public office,[38] and only fifteen per cent married a woman whose father was a public employee.[39] The vast majority of generals were recruited from groups with no connection to the civil service. At the same time, many military officers were linked to traditionalist Catholic *milieux*. Even if the French officer corps could hardly be described as characterised by religious zeal, the profession of Catholic sympathies nevertheless became a widespread political statement among military officers and one of the clearest divisions that existed between the army and the other branches of the French state.[40]

The insulated military establishment

Military officers lived in separate social circles, based in garrison accommodation together with other officers and their families. Professional activities as well as social events took place within the walls of the garrison largely separated from local society and the social connections of officers and their families were guided by strict rules of appropriate and acceptable conduct. In the first decades of the Republican era, a senior general could still get away with befriending politicians and frequenting circles which did not support the Republican regime;[41] after the Dreyfus Affair and the rise to power of the Radical Republicans, more restrictions were imposed on the social acquaintances of senior military officers, and there were increasing expectations for individual officers to remain strictly neutral in political matters.

In small provincial towns the social affiliations, as well as the political sympathies and religious practices of senior military commanders and their families, were under constant scrutiny from all sides. Senior officers complained about being under observation by the prefectoral and sub-prefectoral authorities who would monitor their appearances in public, their social acquaintances and their affiliations with the Catholic Church.

Even for very senior officers, self-imposed social isolation was well-regarded and often considered the only safe way to avoid trouble from superiors.[42] Links with the local civilian population were strictly limited and the generals commanding the eighteen regional army corps were almost always outsiders to the region in which they served. Their time in office was limited by law to three years, and compared with Prussian commanders they had few opportunities to participate in the social life of local elites.

Members of the officer corps were formally prohibited from participating in civil organisations or private clubs; they were only allowed to join music associations, cultural societies, or charity organisations. Depending on the position of power of an individual general, he could allow himself acquaintances who carried some degree of political sensitivity, in particular connections with the senior clergy of the Catholic Church; to pay respects to the local bishop was just about acceptable; to accept a dinner invitation from the bishop was controversial.

Any public appearances of a military officer, including the army corps commander, had to be approved by the prefect. A collection of correspondence between the army corps commander in Lille with the prefects and mayors gives an insight into the type of social event which was considered appropriate for a senior commander.[43] As the head of the local military organisation, general commanders were involved in a considerable number of associations with links to the army, mainly charitable societies, sports clubs, or veterans' associations. Some cooperation was occasionally established with the local university so that officers were allowed to give public lectures on topics such as natural science or geography. Interestingly, senior commanders sometimes accepted invitations to preside over the distribution of school prizes at the local *lycée*; this may have served as a way of demonstrating sympathy for the Republican school system, whereas any military officer would be strongly criticised, and even risked ruining his career, if he accepted an invitation to preside over a similar event in a Catholic educational institution.

Similarly, even very senior commanders had to be extremely careful about not being seen with local industrialists because this would put them under immediate suspicion of favouring private interests. Army corps commanders occasionally accepted to preside over the distribution of the *Médaille Agricole*. This seemed to be acceptable as long as the medal was issued by a public authority and not by a private organisation. However, occasional invitations to preside over events linked to trade and industry were always politely turned down.

Socialising between senior military commanders and the prefect were very occasional and seem to have depended on the individual prefect and general commander. Dinner invitations from the prefect to the army corps commander show that such events tended to be small gentlemen's parties, involving mainly the senior representatives of the government based in the area.[44]

Prefects and Army Corps Commanders: surveillance and lack of public recognition

The fragile relationship between the French Republic and its army was stretched to its limits in November 1904, when it was revealed that the War Minister, General André – one of the few fervent Republicans amongst the senior generals – had been collecting data on almost 25,000 military officers, stating their presumed political sympathies and their religious practices, as well as those of their close families. This information had been used as the basis for appointments and promotion in an attempt to 'republicanise' the military elite. Thus officers considered politically reliable were promoted, while 'suspect' officers were to be passed over. General André himself claimed that the information came primarily from civil servants,[45] and, indeed, certain prefects and sub-prefects had been involved as informers in their capacity as freemasons. Although the actual involvement of civil servants was probably marginal,[46] the damage was done. Many members of the military establishment saw this as the ultimate proof that prefects were engaged in spying on them and became increasingly suspicious towards the representatives of the Republican regime.

General André resigned over the scandal of the Secret Files but the two following war ministers were civilians for whom it was difficult to repair the damage. The rift between the politically appointed head of the army and the military establishment was not improved between 1906 and 1909 when the post was occupied by General Picquart, the officer who had first blown the whistle about the miscarriage of justice against Captain Dreyfus, and who was widely regarded as a traitor amongst military officers. Throughout that time prefects continued to provide some general information on senior officers, a practice that was only abandoned in 1912.[47]

The bitterness among military officers was exacerbated by the revision in 1907 of the official protocol for honours and ranks. The Napoleonic rules for '*Honneurs et Préséances*' from 24 Messidor Year XII were replaced with a more 'Republican' ranking in which the military commanders and the clergy were significantly downgraded, while elected representatives and public officials at all levels were upgraded. Even high-ranking officers – including the army corps commanders of whom many were former war ministers – were placed behind middle ranking civilian officials.

The revised official protocol was received with a great deal of resentment in the military establishment as an intolerable degradation of them as officers, and as a general attack on the prestige of the army within wider society. Gone were the days when a prefect could be forced to leave his post after having committed the blunder of stepping out in front of a division commander.[48] General Jourdy bitterly noted his inferior status when compared to a young prefect 'owing his position to the favours of some politician in Paris',[49] and *La France Militaire* reported on the embarrassing position of senior generals and on the devastating impact that this was having on the authority of army commanders in the eyes of their subordinate officers and soldiers, as well as the prestige of the army in wider society.

The military debate on the use of troops for the policing of protest

Against this background, the frequent requisition of troops for protest policing only added to the military grievances. Within the military establishment there was widespread resentment against the use of troops as riot police: not only did it absorb many military resources, it further fuelled the indignation of many officers that the army was not being sufficiently honoured and respected by the Republican regime. The role of the army in protest policing was therefore a major issue in the on-going debate within the French military establishment, and many were the reasons for senior commanders to prefer withdrawing from civilian conflicts, concentrating on the defence of the national borders.

From the early days of the Third Republic, some senior military officers reflected on the future role of the national army in relation to the reorganisation of the French army after 1871.[50] In the wake of the shooting at Fourmies in 1891 a former war minister, General Lewal, expressed the view that, although the army was responsible for domestic order as well as for national security, the current conflicts between employers and employees were not matters for the armed forces.[51] Along the same lines, a famous article from 1895 by the later Marshal Lyautey argued strongly in favour of concentrating the attention of the military on defence of the national borders.[52] The critical military voices mainly came from retired officers and officers at the lower level of the military hierarchy, namely those in command in the actual situation of disorder.[53]

Between 1899 and 1906 *La France Militaire*, the semi-official mouthpiece of the War Ministry, published twenty-two articles arguing against military involvement in protest policing and in favour of the establishment of a mobile force to relieve the army from this task. During the turbulent spring of 1906, the newspaper also published several articles describing how the frequent military involvement in protest policing tarnished the prestige of the army and undermined its authority in the eyes of the wider population.[54] The most common military arguments against the domestic use of troops were that frequent use of the army broke up the military schedule and damaged the training of recruits, but there was great concern for the negative effects of long-lasting mobilisations on the discipline and health of soldiers and horses.

French civil-military cooperation against all odds

It was in this climate of military hostility towards the Republican government and its representatives that close civil-military cooperation on protest policing emerged. Undoubtedly it was primarily the French prefects and the French Interior Ministry who generated the frequent military involvement, whilst the military commanders were under legal obligation to deliver troops whenever requested. This contrasted to the situation in Prussia, where one of the driving forces in the policy of the Interior Ministry and the provincial administration was the urge to distinguish themselves from a powerful army organisation and uncooperative military commanders.

In France the constellation of powers was inverted. Interpretations of the French army of the Third Republic tend to highlight the crisis of professional conscience felt amongst French officers, and historians often describe the attitude of French commanders towards their involvement in protest policing as 'submission under protest'.[55] The fact that there are only few examples of open military opposition is explained simply by referring to the professional principle among French officers of respecting the authority of any legal government.[56] The accommodating position may be linked to the fact that the French military establishment was in a weak position following the Dreyfus Affair, and had little moral authority to oppose the civil authorities.[57]

The literature, nevertheless, tend to underestimate the extent to which those French senior commanders who were most involved in the planning and implementation of large-scale policing operations actually engaged positively with their civilian counterparts.[58] The French Interior Ministry and its prefects at the *départemental* level depended strongly on the cooperation from the military authorities. Indeed, successive governments would not have been able to make such extensive use of military troops had there been only reluctant cooperation from the military leaders. Local commanders possessed great potential for obstruction and they could undermine the effectiveness of any strategy through bureaucratic resistance. As Carrot rightly points out: the legislation and formal definition of powers left plenty of issues open to discussion and to potential conflicts between civil and military authorities.[59]

Looking at the accounts written by some generals, there is no doubt that they were perfectly aware of the extent to which the prefects depended on a good relationship with the military authorities; they knew they were in a position to force the civilian authorities to concessions, if they so wished. General Millet remarks revealingly about his relationship with local civilian authorities: '*An order to a subordinate officer is an order; an order to an equal is a matter of negotiation*'.[60] Similarly, the not very respectful description of a local prefect provided as late as 1913 by General Jourdy indicates that the submission of French generals was a highly delicate matter, depending more on the individual commander than on legal-constitutional arrangements or textbook definitions of the obligation of an officer to submit to civil authorities.[61]

It is therefore worth stressing that the documents from Nord-Pas-de-Calais show remarkably little disagreement on practical matters, and a generally good understanding between the prefects and the army corps commander about the need for efficient responses to public disorder. The documents from the army corps commander in Lille, for the most part internal military correspondence, suggest that the conflicts with the prefectoral authorities were rare and all concerned minor issues. The most frequent type of disagreement is where commanders complain about the poor quality of the accommodation and food supply provided by local communities during a period of mobilisation. The commanding generals did not contravene the policies of the civilian authorities; they very seldom insisted on their formal right to determine the number of men to be mobilised or questioned the measures to be implemented with military assistance. On the contrary, the military commanders willingly participated in the gathering of information for the current updating of the ministerial Protection Plans and made suggestions for the more effective use of troops. The suggestions made by military commanders indeed rarely questioned the basic definitions concerning the types of conflicts where military involvement was seen as appropriate or attempted to significantly reduce the number of troops to be mobilised.

In the majority of cases, the predominantly conservative-minded senior officers were often inclined to agree with the government and the state administration about the seriousness of the challenges presented by public unrest, and the necessity in certain situations for the state to maintain control. Compared with their Prussian counterparts, there was also a higher degree of alarmism among French military leaders. French political history during the 19th century had shown that the army was not always capable of putting down a full-scale revolt with military force. The military authorities therefore recognised that even small cases of public unrest constituted a potential threat to the existing social and political order. Given the difficult balance between peaceful control and violent coercion, the French general commanders who participated in the development of large-scale policing measures seemed ready to accept the rationale behind the Interior Ministry's plans for protection: it was better to mobilise troops preventively and in great numbers, rather than having to repress a revolt later through traditional military means. Unlike their Prussian counterparts, they did not nourish ideas of waging open war against the left-wing opposition and did not have the same confidence as the Prussian commanders in their capacity to win such a battle.

The only important incident of widespread military obstruction to delivering protection against protesters came in January–February 1906 during the implementation of anti-Catholic legislation. Significantly, the active opposition came primarily from lower ranking officers and garrison commanders. The reluctance of individual officers and local commanders was so manifest that it developed into serious problems of military discipline. Yet, it was not the first time that the army had participated in the implementation of anti-Catholic laws. In the 1880s, when the government closed down mainly Jesuit institutions, the army was mobilised at several occasions. Similarly troops were repeatedly requested between 1902 and 1905 for the implementation of the ban on religious processions and unauthorised events organised by the Catholic Church.[62] It therefore came as a surprise when there was widespread obstruction amongst lower ranking officers to become involved in the recording in January–February 1906 of the possessions of the Catholic Church.

The crisis around the implementation of the anti-Catholic legislation in January–February 1906 is often pointed to as the incident that shows the level of exasperation among military officers towards their role in protest policing.[63] On the other hand, the incidents surrounding the 'Inventories' also indicate the capacity of the army to obstruct requisitions from the civil authorities. If the full potential of military obstruction was not put into practice, this can only be explained by the division which existed within the military establishment at the regional level: the lower ranking officers who rebelled against their role as enforcer of governmental policies were not backed by their senior commanders.

Most general commanders were undoubtedly sympathetic to the resentment of the officers against the task with which they had been charged, which is indicated by the rather mild disciplinary sanctions enforced by the military courts. However, the senior commanders were above all concerned with the problem of keeping discipline among the officers and of avoiding giving the impression to the French public and foreign powers that the French army was about to disintegrate under weak leadership. Thus successive army corps commanders repeated again and again to their subordinate commanders, officers and soldiers that the decrees and service regulations[64] were to be strictly observed.[65]

Despite their dissimilar social backgrounds, political differences and mutual suspicion between the prefects and the senior military commanders in Nord-Pas-de-Calais, close practical cooperation was established around the issue of controlling popular protest. Whilst military commanders occasionally complained about the ways in which soldiers were used, the question of order maintenance was rarely turned into an inter-institutional battle. On their side, the Interior Ministry and the prefects in Lille and Arras were not apparently worried about granting the military authorities a significant degree of influence in decisions over public order – matters from which they were formally excluded – despite the constant rumours in Paris about a military conspiracy against the Republic.

In France, the effective and continuous cooperation took place against all the odds. This was very different from Prussia, where there was little professional exchange despite the much better conditions for cooperation between the province governors and the army due to their common commitment to the Prussian state, their similar outlook and their personal acquaintance as members of the same social *milieux*.

The close civil-military cooperation became possible in Nord-Pas-de-Calais in ways that had little to do with social affiliations or shared political values, and everything to do with the inner logic of bureaucratic practice. In order to understand the importance of bureaucratic practices and how it shaped French and Prussian policing policies, we need to focus on the gradual institutionalisation and entrenchment of standard procedures and the patterns of cooperation or non-cooperation between the provincial administration and the military authorities in Nord-Pas-de-Calais and Westphalia.

Notes

[1] Girardet (1953) pp. 189–192; Ralston (1967) p. 33; Serman (1994) pp. 213–216; Jerôme Hélie, 'L'Arche Sainte fracturée' in Pierre Birnbaum (ed.), *La France de l'Affaire Dreyfus*, Paris: Gallimard, 1994, pp. 246–247; Bruneteaux (1996) pp. 45–47; Chaussinand-Nogaret (1991) pp. 363–367.

[2] Serman (1982) pp. 59–61; Jauffret (1983) p. 98; Bruneteaux (1996) pp. 45–47.

[3] Messerschmidt (1994) pp. 260–261; Wehler (1995) pp. 823–825; Berghahn (1994) pp. 257–258.

[4] Nipperdey (1992) pp. 203–204; Berghahn (1994) p. 257; Wehler (1995) pp. 805–825.

[5] The expression was coined by Wehler in his influential 1973 interpretation of the German Empire Wehler (1985) p. 62; idem. (1995) pp. 1000–1020.

[6] Nipperdey (1992) pp. 217–218; Berghahn (1994) pp. 195–196; Mommsen, (1995) pp. 142–147; John Röhl, *The Kaiser and his Court: Wilhelm II and the Government of Germany*, Cambridge: CUP, 1997, pp. 116–117; Blackbourn (1997) p. 404.

[7] Mayer (1985); Wehler (1995) pp. 805–825.

[8] Preradovich (1955) pp. 106–108, 126–131; Demeter (1965) pp. 25–32; Brocke (1981) pp. 254–256.

[9] Demeter (1965) p. 26.

[10] Heinz Reif, *Adel im 19. und 20. Jahrhundert*, Munich: Oldenburg, 1999.

[11] Brocke (1981) p. 269.

[12] Brocke (1981) p. 267.

[13] Figures based on information gathered by Ottomar von Krug. MA, Freiburg, MSg 109: Unpublished collection of biographical data on the Prussian-German general corps.

[14] Brocke (1981) p. 269.

[15] Wehler (1995) p. 1024.

[16] Waldersee (1927) pp. 229–230: Letter of 3 March 1889 from General von Loë to General von Waldersee.

[17] Waldersee (1922) vol. 2, p. 177. Diary of 26 January 1891.
[18] Brocke (1981) p. 266.
[19] Dietrich Wegmann, *Die leitenden staatsliche Verwaltungsbeamten der Provinz Westphalen, 1815-1918*, Münster: Aschenforffsche Verlag, 1969: 'Kühlwetter'.
[20] The district governor of Arnsberg was obliged to resign in 1875 whilst ten out of eighteen Catholic local governors were sacked during the *Kulturkampf.* Blackbourn (1993) p. 261.
[21] General von Witzendorff (1882–1888) was born in Lüneburg and died in Göttingen; General von Albedyll (1888–1893) was born in Brandenburg and retired to Potsdam; General von Goetze (1893–1898) originated from Posen and retired to Hannover; General von Mikusch-Buckberg (1898–1900) also originated from Posen but retired to Baden; General von Bülow (1900–1901) was born in and retired to Hannover; General von Bissing (1901–1907) originated from Silesia; General von Bernhardi (1907–1909), who spend his childhood in Russia, retired to Silesia. Only General von Einem (1909–1913) who originated from Braunschweig retired to Westphalia.
[22] GSA, Berlin, Personal Papers from Konrad (von) Studt (1868–1920). HSA, Münster, Papers of Baron von Landsberg-Velen. K. Landmann, *Konrad von Studt, ein preußischer Kultusminister*, Berlin, 1908.
[23] This also relates to General von Kluck when he was promoted to headmaster at the Military Academy in Baden in 1888. E. Wolbe, *Alexander von Kluck*, Leipzig: Otto Spamer, 1917, p. 48, pp. 66–67. Similarly, General von Deimling mentions his frustrated attempts to establish contacts to the local elites in Mulhouse. Deimling (1930) p. 130.
[24] Waldersee (1927) pp. 229–230: Letter of 3 March 1889 from General Loë to General von Waldersee.
[25] Friedrich von Bernhardi, *Denkwürdigkeiten aus meinem Leben*, Berlin: Mittler, 1927, p. 299. Einem (1933) pp. 167–168.
[26] Einem (1933) p. 165; E. von Witzleben, *Adolf von Deines. Lebensbild 1845-1911*, Berlin: Verlag der Liebelschen Buchhandelung, 1913, p. 264; Alexander von Kluck, *Wanderjahre – Kriege – Gestalten*, Berlin: Eisenschmidt, 1929, p. 105.
[27] Walther von Bremen, *Denkwürdigkeiten des Preussischen Generals der Infanterie Eduard von Fransecky*, Bielefeld, Leipzig: Velhagen & Klasig, 1901, p. 571.
[28] Witzleben (1913) p. 264; Bruno Clemenz, *General-Feldmarschal von Woyrsch und seine Schlesier. Eigenhändige Auszüge aus seinem Kriegestagebuch*, Berlin: Carl Flemming, 1919, p. 40; Einem (1933) pp. 165–168. Waldersee (1927) pp. 367–368: Letter of 24 April 1890 from General von Loë to Waldersee.
[29] Waldersee (1927) pp. 288–289: Letter of 11 March 1889 from General von Albedyll to General von Waldersee. "…I cannot promise each and every district governor and mine owner to maintain complete calm in his area, since even an entire company before their bedroom door would not be enough (to reassure them)."
[30] Waldersee (1927) pp. 367–368: Letter of 24 April 1890.
[31] Waldersee (1922), p. 200: Diary of 15 March 1891.

[32] Deimling (1930) p. 147.
[33] MA, Vincennes, 5 N 5: Letter of 25 November 1899 from War Minister Galliffet to the army corps commanders and military governors.
[34] Le Clère and Wright (1973) pp. 315–334.
[35] Information gathered from biographical information on individual prefects in Bargeton (1994).
[36] Barge (1982) p. 51.
[37] Barge (1982) p. 263.
[38] Twenty-one working for local government, nineteen for the national government, and three were employed by a departmental government. Barge (1982) p. 51.
[39] Seven per cent of the generals' wives had a father working for the national government, less than six per cent were employed by local government, and hardly two per cent of the generals' wives had a father employed by a departmental government. Barge (1982) p. 263.
[40] Serman (1982) pp. 101–108; Ralston (1953) pp. 257–266.
[41] For instance, General Brugière, who was a very moderate Republican, undertook private acquaintances with far-right political movements where he met Deroulède, while he was at the same time chief of the military staff at the Elysée Palais under Jules Grévy.
[42] After being accused of being indiscreet in his acquaintances, General Bixard declared not to have any contacts whatsoever outside the military circle. MA, Vincennes, 1st A.C. /2.I.333: Report of 12 June 1910 from General Bixard, commander in Cambrai, to the army corps commander in Lille.
[43] MA, Vincennes, 1st A.C. /2.I.217: 'Correspondance entre le commandant du corps d'armée et préfets et maires, 1905–1912'.
[44] NA, Paris, AP 270: private papers of General Chanzy; MA, Vincennes, 1st A.C. /2.I.211: correspondence from the army corps commander in Lille; MA, Vincennes, 1st A.C. /2.I.217: 'Correspondance avec les Préfets et les maires 1905–1912'; MA, Vincennes, 1st A.C. /2.I.21, 'Correspondance générale, Général Jeannerod' August 1898 to June 1900.
[45] General André, *Cinq ans de ministère*, Paris: Louis Michaud, 1906, p. 311.
[46] Serman (1982) p. 80.
[47] Serman (1982) p. 84.
[48] Le Clère and Wright (1973) p. 88.
[49] MA, Vincennes, 392/GD/3: Private papers of General Jourdy, *Mes Souvenir* (unpublished memoirs, ca. 1913), pp. 607–608; similarly, Lucien Thile, *Pouvoir civil et pouvoir militaire*, Paris: Rousseau, 1914, pp. 148–149.
[50] General Faidherbe, *Bases d'un projet de réorganisation d'une armée nationale*, (1871); General Charenton, *Projet motivé de réorganisation de l'état militaire de la France*, (1871); General Davout, Duc d'Auerstædt, *Projet de réorganisation militaire*, (1871).
[51] General Lewal, *Les troupes colonials*, Paris, 1894: "On voudrait que les soldats ne fussent plus obligés d'intervenir dans les conflits entre patrons et grévistes. Ce n'est pas le rôle de l'armée. Elle y subit des injures, elle y reçoit des coups et des

blessures, on l'outrage quand elle se défend. C'est du sang francais et du meilleur que l'on perd (...) on n'a pas le droit de le répandre pour la protection d'intérêts privés. Il importerait donc d'avoir des agents spéciaux pour ce service de police, des volontaires rétribués 'constables' à pied et à cheval pour contenir et apaiser les conflits industriels." Cit. Jauffret (1983) p. 114.

[52] Hubert Lyautey, 'Le rôle social de l'officier', *Révue des Deux Mondes* March, 1891.

[53] Anonymous, *L'armée et l'ordre public*, Paris, 1891; anonymous, *L'armée sous le régime civil et les questions militaires pendants*, Paris: Henri Charles-Lavauzelle, 1894; Commandant Francfort, *Les Corps d'officiers des principales armées européennes*, Paris, 1895; Commandant Sila, *Une vie infernale. Mémoires d'un officier de cavalerie*, Paris, 1907; Le lieutenant Z., *L'armée aux grèves, grèves générale des mineurs, oct-nov 1902*, Paris, 1904.

[54] Anonymous front page article entitled 'Faiblesse et energie', *La France militaire*, 28 April 1906; General Lamiraux, 'Armée contre l'Anarchie', *La France militaire*, 12 May 1906.

[55] Girardet (1953) pp. 262–264, Ralston (1967) pp. 281–282; Jauffret (1983) p. 99; Carrot (1984) pp. 657–658, Serman (1982) pp. 58–63; Bruneteaux (1993) p. 37.

[56] Raoul Girardet, 'Civil and Military Power in the Fourth Republic', in Samuel Huntington (ed.), *Changing Patterns of Military Politics*, Glencoe: Free Press, 1962, p. 121.

[57] Ralston (1967) pp. 250–251, Hélie (1994) pp. 227–229.

[58] See details Chapter 9.

[59] Carrot (1984) p. 647.

[60] MA, Vincennes, 1 K mi 9: General Millet *'Souvenirs'* unpublished manuscript (c. 1913).

[61] MA, Vincennes, 392 /GD /3: General Emile Jourdy *'Souvenirs'* unpublished memoirs (c. 1913).

[62] MA, Vincennes, MR 2172 or REC 2172: 'Application des lois des congrégations'.

[63] Girardet (1953) p. 264; Ralston (1967) pp. 280–283; Serman (1982) pp. 61–62.

[64] Law of 27 July–3 August 1791 on the requisition of soldiers for the maintenance of public order; Decree of 4 October 1891 on civilian and military authorities in garrison towns; Instructions of 24 June 1903 on the participation of the army in the maintenance of public order; Instructions of 20 August 1907 on the participation of the army in the maintenance of public order.

[65] MA, Vincennes, 1st A.C. /2.I.328: Order of 18 September 1903 from General Jeannerod. Similarly General de France 'Instructions en cas de grève ou de troubles' of 15 February1893.

Chapter 9

Civil-Military Cooperation in Nord-Pas-de-Calais

The origins of civil-military cooperation in France

In the early 1890s, the mobilisation of troops in Nord-Pas-de-Calais always brought up a number of issues to be negotiated between the prefect and the army corps commander and between the Interior and War Ministries; by the outbreak of the First World War, military assistance to the civilian authorities in Nord-Pas-de-Calais worked remarkably smoothly. In Westphalia, by contrast, where civil-military relations were kept to the absolute minimum, any inter-institutional cooperation was difficult and unpredictable; this was the case in 1889 and it was even more so in 1914.

The development towards close civil-military cooperation in France, as well as the entrenchment in Prussia of the demilitarisation of protest policing, provide excellent examples of the phenomenon that political scientists describe as 'path dependency'[1]: that one type of solution to any particular problem gradually becomes institutionalised and internalised in the bureaucratic procedures, thus making it increasingly difficult to change approach. What we observe in both Nord-Pas-de-Calais and Westphalia are self-sustaining dynamics in the bureaucratic procedures that developed during these years. In Nord-Pas-de-Calais this made the military involvement in the policing of public protest not only an attractive option, but gradually the most viable solution. Due to the logistical imperatives in the organisation of large-scale policing operations, any breach with standard procedures would have required total rethinking of strategies and objectives.

A comparison of the bureaucratic procedures within the two systems also shows that certain bureaucratic procedures which facilitated civil-military cooperation in Nord-Pas-de-Calais were virtually absent in Westphalia. This provides some important clues about why the Prussian provincial administration became increasingly reluctant to consider military involvement even for the policing of major incidents of popular protest. In order to understand how these dissimilar structures came about in

Westphalia and Nord-Pas-de-Calais, it is important to look closely at the bureaucratic practices that developed between French civilian and military authorities. These were particularly noticeable in Nord-Pas-de-Calais, because of the frequent military involvement in the handling of strikes, popular protest and mass gatherings in public.

In the 1880s and the early 1890s intervention by military troops in Nord-Pas-de-Calais was characterised by a lack of coherent strategy and consistency in the procedures from one incident to another. The number of soldiers to be mobilised, their role in the policing operation, the measures to be implemented and the locations to be protected were all issues decided on the spot while the conflict was developing. Disagreements with the military authorities were dealt with at the municipal level between mayors, local police authorities, and the commander of the nearest garrison. Even when sub-prefects and prefects were involved, each military unit operated largely independently with limited overall strategy or coherent management. Many details in the formal distribution of powers were ambiguous and open to interpretation, leaving plenty of issues as potential sources of conflict. After the turn of the 20th century a completely different pattern emerges, with high levels of consistency in the procedures followed and the strategies implemented. Each time troops were requested for a specific type of conflict in an area where it had happened before (for instance, a miners' strike in the industrial basin of Douai, a textile strike in Roubaix, or a dockers' strike in Dunkirk), similar measures were implemented as before. This covered issues such as the role of the troops, the number of soldiers mobilised, their transport, the locations to be protected, and the provision of food and accommodation.

The emergence of these standard operating procedures was partly due to the frequent military intervention in the region which created strong precedents for measures, responsibilities and lines of communication between civilian and military authorities. At the same time, the standard operating procedures, even for small-scale policing operations with military participation, were strongly shaped by the measures and strategies formulated in the Plans for Protection developed jointly by the Interior and the War Ministries between 1897 and 1913.

The institutionalisation of civil-military cooperation

It is difficult to underestimate the importance of the inter-ministerial planning in shaping civil-military cooperation after the turn of the 20th century. The inter-ministerial Plans for Protection defined not only the conflicts appropriate for military involvement, the approximate number of troops to be mobilised and the measures to be implemented; they also detailed the responsibilities and the lines of communication between civilian and military authorities. The procedures followed during military interventions in Nord-Pas-de-Calais show that the framework established by the Plans for Protection was also adhered to when troops were called out for small-scale policing operations. The inter-ministerial planning committee, with representatives from the civilian as well as the military authorities, constituted an institutionalised forum for debate and exchange of information, where experience and problems from previous operations could be analysed. The inter-ministerial committee was vital in integrating the military authorities into the decision-making process. Bringing together representatives from various ministries in Paris as well as those at *départmental* level provided senior military staff with the opportunity to express their concerns and to negotiate directly with their counterparts from the Interior Ministry about the particular problems and needs of the troops.

The early stages in the coordination of civil and military strategies were designed to determine the military authority to which each civilian authority was to address a requisition in the case of an imminent crisis. Demands for the formalisation of this issue appeared for the first time in 1893, when the Interior Minister asked each prefect to settle with the army corps commander in his region the exact lines of command between local authorities and military garrisons.[2]

In 1897–1898, the first general instructions were drawn up to cover the event of a nationwide strike among rail workers. Civilian and military authorities in all *départements* and military regions were asked to designate locations to be protected and numbers of soldiers to be mobilised. The initiative for these special plans was taken by the Interior Ministry. The justification for involving the army in labour disputes between private rail companies and their employees was the importance of the railway system for national defence. This was clearly stated in the first communication from the War Ministry to the army corps commanders which described the devastating effects such a strike could have for national defence.[3]

The first draft from the War Ministry consisted simply of a list of locations which were particularly vulnerable to sabotage in case of a major strike among the rail workers. In July 1897, all prefects and army corps commanders were asked by their respective ministries to sit down with the chief engineer in their *département*, as well as with representatives from the rail companies in their region, to study the necessary protection of the local railway infrastructure.[4] These meetings resulted in the first nation-wide Plans for Protection of July 1898.[5]

In the early Plans, the role of the army was limited to the protection of the communication infrastructure (telephone, telegraph and railways). The purpose of the military involvement was justified solely in terms of the importance of the railway system to national defence. The General Staff of the War Ministry, however, already toyed with the idea of ensuring the basic rail services by replacing striking workers with soldiers from the engineers. When presented with a report on the subject War Minister Billot preferred to keep such suggestions strictly confidential.[6] These nationwide provisions were put into action for the first time during a major strike among rail personnel in October 1898 and were described by both civilian and military authorities as a great success.[7]

Three years later, in July 1901, when confronted with the prospect of a nation-wide strike in the French mining industry, Interior Minister Waldeck-Rousseau and the War Minister, General André, took the initiative of revising the 1898 plans for strikes among rail workers and establishing similar plans for the mining industry.[8] In contrast to the previous plans, these were concerned primarily with the maintenance of order and the protection of strike-breakers and private property. They made no attempt to justify military involvement by reference to national defence. These plans were implemented during the first nationwide miners' strike of October–November 1901. Already in March 1902, in the face of renewed trouble in the mining sector, the Interior Ministry took the initiative of updating and extending the plans which had been put into practice only six months before. The new plans also covered possible strikes among workers in all the main ports.[9] Although developed with particular professional sectors in mind, it soon became clear that the provisions were easily applicable to strikes in other industries, such as metal or textile.[10]

After 1901–1902, the Plans for Protection were updated and improved several times. The updating that took place between 1907 and 1909 was particularly detailed.[11] This was due partly to the unprecedented strikes during the spring of 1906 and the revolt among wine growers in the South of France over the summer of 1907; partly also to the introduction in 1905 of the two-year conscription laws which significantly reduced the number of soldiers available and made a revision of the previous plans necessary.

With the revision of 1907, the role of the army was slightly extended. The new justification of its role in the Plans for Protection was now to prevent a general strike in vital professions from affecting wider society. This included the defence of the import of foreign coal to ensure the continuous functioning of other industrial sectors.[12] It also meant ensuring basic provisions for ordinary people (dairies, water supply, electricity) when the personnel of vital sectors went on strike.

In the 1909 revision, new professional groups were added, namely the postal and telegraph workers. In the last revisions in 1911, 1913 and 1914, the plans for particular professional groups were integrated into general plans for internal unrest and could be applied to strikes in any professional branch or any organised disturbance of public order.[13] The revised Plans for Protection of 1913 described the main objectives of military involvement primarily as protecting the interests of wider society by 'ensuring the circulation and communication,' 'protecting persons and goods,' and 'protecting the equipment of public utilities'.[14]

Inter-ministerial cooperation between the Interior Ministry and the War Ministry

From the initial stages, the Plans for Protection were an inter-ministerial initiative between the Interior Ministry and the War Ministry. Throughout the period, these two Ministries remained the key actors in organising the meetings and coordinating the reports from the ministerial representatives at the regional level.

Nevertheless, between the first plans of 1897–1898 and the extended plans of 1901, the relationship between the Interior Ministry and the War Ministry underwent important changes. In 1897–1898 France was still governed by conservative Republicans who entertained a carefully cosy relationship with the military establishment in which the army was allowed significant degrees of institutional independence.

In 1899 the political landscape changed when centre-left politicians were brought to power on the back of their fierce criticism of the military establishment over the Dreyfus Affair. The most extended civil-military cooperation on military involvement in the policing of major strikes and popular unrest took place during the years when the relationship between the government and the army was at its lowest point and at a time when the position of the military establishment was as weak as ever. Yet judging from the members of the Planning Committee, there can be little doubt that both the Interior and War Ministries came to consider the Commission to be of major importance.

The Commission responsible for the development of the 1901 plans comprised only nine members: Apart from Interior Minister Waldeck-Rousseau, there were two representatives from the General Security Department of the Interior Ministry, two middle ranking representatives from the War Ministry (a lieutenant colonel and a general staff officer), three chief engineers from the Ministry of Public Works, and one representative from the Ministry responsible for the main ports.

Six years later the Commission had increased to twenty-three members representing five ministries including many very senior bureaucrats and military commanders: Célestin Hennion, head of the General Security Department of the Interior Ministry participated, together with Paris Police Prefect Lépine and the prefects from three particularly unruly regions (Vincent, prefect of *département* Nord; Trépont, prefect of Pas-de-Calais and Luteaud, prefect of the *départment* Rhône). The four military representatives included General Lebon, army corps commander in Lille, and General Desoille, Military Governor in Reims, as well as two lieutenant colonels from the General Staff of the War Ministry. The Ministry of Public Works sent three chief engineers from the mining inspection and from the rail services. The Ministry of Naval Affairs was represented by a vice-admiral, a naval captain, and two senior administrators from the Ministry. Finally, the Justice Ministry was represented by a vice-president of the State Council, together with a head of department from the Justice Ministry and an attorney general from the Supreme Court of Appeal.[15]

There was a high degree of continuity in the membership of the Inter-ministerial Commission for each revision of the Plans for Protection. Thus fifteen out of the twenty-three members of the 1907 commission were still in the Commission in 1909.[16] It is worth noting that the two general commanders who became permanent members of the inter-ministerial Committee were both members of the most prestigious military body, the Supreme War Council (*Conseil supérieur de la guerre*). Some members of the Supreme War Council obtained a particular influence on the development of strategies for the policing of civilians, which had already been observed in 1894.[17]

That Waldeck-Rousseau thought of the Plans for Protection as a way of limiting the military commanders' freedom of action appears clearly in his answer to some of his prefects who, in October 1901, wondered whether it was necessary to follow all the prescriptions of the Plans.[18] The existence of plans established jointly by the Interior and War Ministries, involving prefects and army corps commanders, made it very difficult for individual military commanders to question the appropriateness of the strategic principles and the estimated numbers of soldiers to be mobilised. Once settled, it also became extremely difficult to back down and change the practice of preventive mobilisation or to reduce the number of soldiers. The Plans for Protection themselves amounted to recognition by both civilian and military authorities that these types of strikes presented a sufficiently serious threat to the public order that they required military assistance.

Moreover, the plans created the basis for very specific expectations of the degree of security provided by the army.

Since these plans established the entire concept of military participation in dealing with internal disorder, the integration of senior military commanders in the elaboration of measures against internal unrest was an effective way of ensuring the consent and willing cooperation of the army. The military members of the commission had ample opportunity to shape the role of the army. It is therefore worth noting that General Lebon and General Desoille did not seek to reduce the military involvement in protest policing. Instead they both participated actively in the discussions of how to respond to public disorder and how to improve the effectiveness of civil-military cooperation.[19]

The repercussions in Nord-Pas-de-Calais

In Nord-Pas-de-Calais, the standard operating procedures that arose from the Plans for Protection, and from the frequent implementation of the same measures, brought about a particular bureaucratic mind-set that seemed to be shared by successive prefects and military commanders. This bureaucratic mind-set included the common acceptance of the strategies adopted, the notions of appropriate response to public unrest, and the distribution of powers and responsibilities between the two institutions. These norms and expectations established clear limits on the professional behaviour of senior military commanders, since any deviation from the standard operating procedures would need to be justified.

This was demonstrated when, shortly after the establishment of the 1901 Plans for Protection for the port of Dunkirk, Louis Vincent, the prefect in Lille, complained to the Interior Minister that he had not been informed about some minor changes made by the army corps commander and demanded to be immediately informed about any further changes that the military authorities might want to make.[20] It was also difficult for the army corps commander to withdraw from the implementation of plans that he himself, or his predecessor, had negotiated with the civil administration.

This helps to explain why military commanders actively participated in the implementation even of policies of which many of them were likely to strongly disapprove. This was particularly important during the military involvement in the implementation of the anti-Catholic legislation of the years 1902 to 1906. It also helps to explain how military commanders could cooperate effectively with representatives of governments that were apparently attempting to break the power and the social standing of the army elite.

Given the mutual suspiciousness between civil and military authorities after the Dreyfus Affair and the *Affaire des Fiches* of 1904,[21] it was of major importance that politically sensitive decisions were taken jointly by the prefect and the army corps commander.

Towards joint decision-making between civil and military authorities

The inter-ministerial Commission with its numerous sub-commissions was also closely connected to the inter-ministerial Commission in charge of revising the legislation on military involvement in maintenance of public order. Here the overlapping of members and the important participation of military representatives is particularly noticeable. Amongst the ten members of the commission revising the 'Instructions on Military Participation in the Maintenance of Public Order' there were three senior military commanders. The commission was chaired by the same General Lebon, member of the Supreme War Council, who also participated in the establishment of Plans for Protection in his capacity as army corps commander in Lille.

The military establishment thereby acquired direct influence on the new formal rules, defining its own sphere of action in relation to the civilian authorities. Just as the involvement of senior commanders in the development of the Plans for Protection helped to bind the military commanders to the provisions of these plans, their inclusion in the formulation of new instructions on military participation in the maintenance of order must be seen as an attempt to facilitate the acceptance of the revised legislation. The involvement of senior generals in these commissions may also have been intended to compensate for the lack of authority of War Minister Picquart within the military establishment.

The 1907 revision made some important adjustments to the legislation dating from 1791. The former right of the military commander to determine all military measures[22] was transformed into a new duty of the military authorities to prepare for the execution of the measures decided together with the civilian authorities.[23] The demand for cooperation between civil and military authorities was stated already in the 1791 legislation on participation of the armed forces in maintaining public order. However, the nature of cooperation was not defined. During the 1890s when strike movements began to extend over several administrative units and required unprecedented numbers of forces, the prefects tended to ask for instructions from the Interior Minister.[24] As a result of this, the need for exchange of information between the civil and military authorities became a recurrent theme in the instructions from the Interior and War Ministries to their representatives at the *départemental* level. Both the Interior Ministry and the War Ministry repeatedly urged prefects and army corps commanders to communicate with each other, rather than turning to their respective ministries for instructions.[25]

The insertion in the 1907 Instructions of a formal demand for exchange of information and joint decision–making between civilian and military authorities marks an important break with former institutional barriers. In the 1890s the military authorities had insisted on the importance of being allowed to determine the means and measures in dealing with popular unrest.[26] In 1893 General de France stressed the principle enshrined in legislation and in the decree of 4 October 1891, which was that when requested by a competent civil authority, the military authority alone determined the means and measures needed to maintain public order.[27] Yet from the early 1890s successive Interior Ministers and War Ministers began to instruct their respective authorities at the regional level that prefects and army corps commanders were to communicate as early as possible in the course of a conflict about the possible requisition of military troops.[28] During the following years, it became a requirement that the prefect and the army corps commander reached an agreement (*se concerter*) about all important decisions.

As the Interior Ministry and the War Ministry increasingly encouraged prefects and the army corps commanders to sort out these questions between themselves within the framework of the Plans for Protection and the Ministerial Instructions, practical issues concerning military participation in the policing of minor incidents or protest or simple crowd control were dealt with entirely between the prefect and the army corps commander.[29] In December 1902 War Minister André wrote to the army corps commander in Lille concerning the ending of the military intervention in the great miners' strike and the strike among the dock workers in Dunkirk and Calais. In his letter, War Minister André stated that any decision concerning the ending of a military intervention was to be taken jointly by the army corps commander and the prefect.[30] It was not only the War Minister who allowed his general commander to participate in such decisions; the message from the Interior Ministry was the same: cooperation, joint decision-making between the prefects and the military commander, and a demand for a continuous exchange of information.

The demand for decision-making at regional level by the prefectoral authority and the army corps commander was finally formalised in the 1907 Instructions on Military Participation in the Maintenance of Public Order.[31] The Instructions of 20 August 1907 reaffirmed the principle of civil supremacy by stating which civil authorities were entitled to call for military assistance (Articles 2–6). Article 8 very briefly states that the civilian authorities alone were to determine the moment of intervention.[32] However, five substantial paragraphs (Articles 8, 9, 10, 11 and 14) demanded civil-military cooperation. Article 18 repeated the right of the military authorities to determine the measures to be implemented, but the following Articles 19–22 made it clear that any important measure was to be taken in agreement with the civil authorities, thus leaving little room for independent military decision-making.[33] Similarly, the ministerial circular letter concerning the application of the 1907 Instructions does not emphasise civilian supremacy over the military, but concentrates more on stressing the importance of joint decision-making between civil and military authorities. In contrast to the official text, the circular letter directly invited the military authorities to take the initiative of contacting the civil authorities and preparing themselves for intervention.[34]

At the same time, the civil-military cooperation ensured that senior commanders acquired significant influence over issues such as the time and the conditions for the mobilisation of troops, questions from which they were formally excluded. Given the important areas which were jointly determined by civil and military authorities, civilian supremacy was transformed more into a leading role in an inter-institutional relationship, where both the civil and military authorities were bound to operate within a sphere of mutual agreement.

Similar to the military engagement in the development of the Plans for Protection, the minutes from meetings in the commission revising the 'Instructions on Military Participation in the Maintenance of Public Order' reveal that General Lebon and Lieutenant-Colonel Bernhard were all too keen on improving the efficiency of military actions, and at no time did they express any wish to limit the engagement of the army in the settlement of labour disputes or other types of public disorder.[35] The military representatives accepted the increased importance placed on joint decision-making with civilian authorities – notably the prefect – rather than insisting on military independence.

The development of plans to deal with large-scale protest ensured the *de facto* integration of the civil authorities into what had formerly been an entirely military matter. At the same time, it provided the civilian authorities with continuous insights into the functioning of the army at regional and local level. It also gave senior military commanders influence over aspects of policing which were otherwise the realm of the civilian authorities.

The functioning of civil-military cooperation in Nord-Pas-de-Calais

The civil-military cooperation at ministerial level was replicated at regional level in Nord-Pas-de-Calais. The 1907 revision of the legislation on the role of the army in maintenance of public order, with its insistence on cooperation and exchange of information, did little other than formalising what had already become standard procedure over the past decade.

In Nord-Pas-de-Calais the prefects of Lille and Arras already sent copies to the army corps commander of any correspondence relevant to public order maintenance and copies of relevant correspondence were sent from the army corps commander's office to the prefects. This provided both civilian and military authorities with insights into the problems and complaints which were objects of communication between the authorities at local level and their superiors within the other organisation.

In addition to the direct communications between civilian and military authorities, they shared another source of information, namely the daily reports from the local *gendarmerie* units. These were sent simultaneously to the prefect, to the army corps commander, and to their respective Ministries, thus ensuring a regular flow of information about the state of affairs in local communities. By this means, the army corps commander was constantly informed of problems of popular discontent and conflicts in local communities, and was warned at an early stage about the possible outbreak of open protest. Arguably, this day-to-day stream of information increased the understanding among military commanders of the needs of the civilian authorities, in terms of military assistance.

The establishment of the Plans for Protection and their up-dating every two or three years between 1897 and 1914 also required the prefects and the army corps commanders in each military region to work closely together in making their recommendations to the inter-ministerial Commission about the locations to be protected and the troops available. This was a major administrative operation that allowed informal exchange of views and facts on policing issues between prefects and army corps commanders. At the same time, it provided insights into the needs and intentions of their counterparts.

In an area as turbulent as Nord-Pas-de-Calais, the civil-military correspondence on policing issues was particularly intense. Before each meeting of the inter-ministerial Commission, information was gathered from each *département* about the forces needed in a situation of crisis and the main locations to be protected. When establishing the first nation-wide plans from 1897–1898 in case of a major strike among rail workers, the Interior and War Ministries asked their representatives at regional level –

prefects and army corps commanders – to hold meetings with the chief mining engineer who represented the Ministry of Public Works at regional level. This procedure was repeated and developed in the 1901 plans.[36] This was followed by a circular letter from the Interior Ministry to the prefects urging them to contact their military counterparts in order to determine precisely the locations to be protected and the forces to be used.[37]

In 1901, the talks between the prefects and the army corps commanders included a general discussion about how the mines and the shafts could be maintained during a long interruption of work and what could be done in order to defend the mines from sabotage. At the regional level, a commission was charged with the establishment and regular revision of the list of locations to be protected and the number of troops to be mobilised in cases of conflict. The prefect and the army corps commanders were permanent members of these commissions, together with the most senior *gendarmerie* commander and the regional inspectors for mines, railway infrastructure and ports.

While municipal authorities and private companies were kept well away from influence on decisions concerning requisition of troops, some local authorities and private companies provided the civilian and military authorities with the information that was necessary for the development of policing measures for local areas. Mayors, local police authorities and representatives from industrial organisations thereby became indirectly involved through the information they provided about social, economic, industrial and topographic conditions within the local communities.

At local level, similar cooperation took place between the representatives of state authorities. In the large ports of Dunkirk, Calais and Saint Pol, the local military governor or garrison commander was in continuous communication with the sub-prefect, with the head of the maritime authorities and with the chief engineer. These local state officials were the first to recommend smaller changes or adjustments of the existing Plans for Protection. Most importantly the provisions stated in the plans became the standards for the number of troops and measures to be implemented for smaller conflicts. Accordingly, if one hundred dock workers or sailors went on strike in Dunkirk, a predetermined number of soldiers could be mobilised just to prevent sabotage of the most vulnerable parts of the port installations.

In 1902, during a major strike among the dock workers of Dunkirk and Calais, the division commander and the prefect of Pas-de-Calais asked their subordinates in Calais to develop a set of measures to ensure public order. On 23 October 1902, a meeting was held in the garrison of Calais between the local military commander, the sub-prefect of the *arrondissement* of

Boulogne-sur-Mer and the state police commissioner in order to decide the measures to be implemented.[38] Such examples of local integration of the military authorities into the planning process were not confined to the protection of ports. In June 1910, when the first rumours arose about a nationwide strike among rail workers, the commander of the garrison in Cambrai arranged a meeting in the local military headquarters with the deputy head of the sub-prefectoral offices of Cambrai (*Chef des Bureaux de la Sous-Prefecture*) and the state inspector of railways.[39] Similarly, in August 1911, when the authorities feared large demonstrations against rising prices, a meeting was held at the office of the military governor between the military governor of Maubeuge, the sub-prefect of Avesnes and the deputy mayor of Maubeuge with the purpose of determining detailed policing measures in case of mass demonstrations.[40]

In the wake of the great strike movements of 1902 and 1906 there were discussions between the prefects in Lille and Arras and the military authorities concerning experiences and possible improvements to the policing of future strikes and demonstrations.[41] The civil-military correspondence – both at the ministerial level and in Nord-Pas-de-Calais – reveals the intentions of the prefects and the army corps commanders to improve and intensify the use of the army for the policing of protest of any significance. Thus, for example, rather than trying to restrict the involvement of the army after the mass strikes of March–May 1906 or questioning the justification for future requisitions, General Lebon, army corps commander in Lille, wrote a report expressing his concern for a more efficient management of the troops in future policing operations.[42]

In the 1907 revision of the plans for a rail workers' strike, the government asked the regional authorities to limit the number of mobilised troops. This had become urgent after 1905, with the reduction of military service from three to two years. After conferring with the rail authorities of '*Compagnie du Nord*', the prefect of *département* Nord followed the wishes of the rail company and wrote to the Interior Minister that it was impossible to make changes to the locations to be protected or reduce the number of troops to be mobilised.[43] In a letter to the army corps commander, the prefect expressed his regret that he was unable to reduce the number of troops to be mobilised, but he could not take the responsibility for the maintenance of order with a reduced number of soldiers.[44] The number of troops stated in the plans from 1902 remained at the same high level in all later revisions.

The extensive correspondence between the different branches of the state amply testify to the multiple contacts and lines of communication between civilian and military authorities at regional as well as local levels during the years 1901–1914. This is remarkably different from the previous period, when decisions on the number of troops to be mobilised and measures to be implemented were taken almost entirely by the military authorities, often by the commander on the spot. It is also remarkably different from the practice in Westphalia where the civilian and military planning for large-scale policing was completely separate and mutually exclusive.

The outcome: greater inter-institutional confidence and limitation of misunderstanding

The detailed plans, the shared information, and the continuous correspondence were all important elements in overcoming the mutual suspiciousness which otherwise characterised the relationship between the Republican regime and the French military establishment.

Louis Vincent, who was prefect in Lille for twelve years from 1899 to 1911, developed a self-assured, but very courteous, relationship with successive army corps commanders. Vincent seemed to make a virtue of informing the army corps commander about the intentions of his administration. To his subordinate sub-prefects, he also insisted on the importance of always issuing formally correct requisitions so that the military commander could proceed with no risk of being accused afterwards of acting illegally. Similarly, Vincent was very keen on paying his respects to the officers and soldiers after the end of major cases of unrest, which gave him a reputation in the local press for making the army the auxiliary arm of his administration.[45]

The detailed planning also ensured that both were acquainted with the standard operating procedures for civil-military cooperation. This helped in great measure to limit the potential for disagreement and misunderstandings. Despite the extremely frequent mobilisation of troops in Nord-Pas-de-Calais, incidents of conflict are rare.

It is worth noting that the majority of incidents of conflict date from the 1880s and 1890s before the standard operating procedures for civil-military cooperation were properly settled. In those days there was considerable confusion about the formal rules, and the strategies proposed to deal with popular unrest were sometimes at the edge of legality or far beyond it. Thus in 1882, during a great miners' strike in Montceau-les-Mines, the prefect suggested that the local authorities should organise patrols which were entitled to interrogate suspects, to undertake searches in the homes of the strikers, and to arrest suspected leaders for twenty-four hours.[46]

In the 1880s, Interior and War Ministers also felt the need repeatedly to inform their subordinates about the most basic regulations and procedures relating to military participation in the policing of protest.[47] Similarly, in the 1890s prefects and army corps commanders still expressed uncertainty about the exact procedures to be followed as well as the legal definitions of civil and military authority. In 1893 the prefect of Allier complained to the Interior Ministry that the army corps commander in his region had ordered his subordinate commanders not to mobilise troops when requested by a civilian authority, but urged them to wait for an order directly from himself. The prefect admitted that the general had probably acted in good faith, and committed this error of procedure out of ignorance about the exact formal procedures.[48] During the first implementation of the 1897 Plans for Protection the Interior Minister complained that some of the prefects had issued requisitions with a signature, but without a date and indication of numbers of troops; the intention was that the military commander could fill in these details when necessary. This procedure was immediately banned by the Interior Ministry.[49] Similarly, in 1898, many prefects addressed themselves to the Interior Ministry because they were uncertain about how to proceed when calling for military assistance. Worst of all, the prefect of the Eastern Pyrenees addressed his list of locations to be protected directly to the War Ministry.[50]

After 1901 uncertainties about measures and procedures occurred almost exclusively in *départements* where military intervention was rare. As interior ministers both Waldeck-Rousseau and later Clemenceau complained of the hesitation about the standard operating procedures, but noted that most incidents of uncertainty occurred when troops were mobilised in areas where the civilian and military authorities had little experience in working together.[51] This was particularly notable during the implementation of the controversial Inventories in January–February 1906 and during the wine growers' revolt in the South of France over the summer of 1907.[52]

In the early 1890s, there was also much uncertainty even from the prefects in Lille and Arras about financial responsibility for requesting troops. This resulted in prefects hesitating with their requisitions. Until 1893, the financial responsibility was determined for each case individually. In principle it was the local community, or, in labour disputes, the factory or mine owner, who was asked to pay for the expenses incurred. However a decision of the State Council of 1893 stated that when troops were mobilised by the prefect for the purpose of maintenance of public order the French state would accept financial responsibility.[53] Once the state accepted responsibility for the costs, the prefects could call for military assistance without fearing months of problematic negotiations with local communities and private companies who refused to pay, or facing complaints from impatient military authorities who were eager to have their expenses covered.

Once the standard operating procedures were in place, any breach would often be commented on, but seldom had practical consequences. Military commanders sometimes frowned if a requisition mentioned that the troops were 'at the disposition' of the civil authorities. It would then be made clear by the army corps commander that the army could not legally be 'at the disposition' but could only 'deliver assistance' to the civil authorities.[54] Similar corrections might be made if a civil authority had been too explicit in its demands for troops, thus offending the professional pride of the military commander.

Such details of formulation rarely had any practical implications for the implementation of requisitions. Although the military commanders were obsessed with covering their own backs, they tended to follow even slightly incorrectly formulated requisitions, as long as they could do so without compromising themselves. Only after the end of the mobilisation would the military commander concerned address a formal protest to the prefect that the standard procedures had not been observed. The authority that had issued the requisition would then be urged to do it correctly next time.

It was only on a few occasions that questions of formality were used to obstruct requisitions for military assistance. Although General Loizillon had no qualms about challenging the prefect's assessment of the situation in Fourmies nearly two months after the bloody incidents on May Day, he did not proceed to acting against the wishes of the civilian authorities.[55] The problems resulting from the implementation of unpopular anti-Catholic legislation in January–February 1906 were a notorious exception to the otherwise smooth cooperation between prefects and army corps commanders. Since a large proportion of officers came from families with strong connections to the Catholic Church, they particularly resented their participation in the enforcement of the anti-Catholic legislation. A certain number of officers were driven to acts of disobedience or broke their military career over the issue. Similarly, several local military commanders who were strongly opposed to the government policies used issues of formality as a means of obstructing the participation of troops.

The civil-military confrontations on that occasion also indicate the importance of the pre-established consensus and mutual confidence. Normally, in politically sensitive situations when disorder was to be expected, contacts were made with the military authorities weeks or even months before the actual conflict broke out. This was possible when a major strike was announced. It was also possible at occasions such as the annual May Day celebrations, general elections, or political meetings. The importance of the previous contacts between prefects and senior commanders becomes clear when looking at the problems which arose in January–February 1906, during the implementation of this controversial piece of anti-Catholic legislation.

On the two previous occasions when military troops had participated in the implementation of controversial anti-Catholic legislation, the fact that many officers were also devout Catholics did not present major problems. In 1880, in his account to the prefects within the ninth army corps, General Galliffet, as responsible commander, admitted that there had been a few incidents during the expulsion of Jesuits, but these were due to misunderstandings between the civil and military authorities and inexperience in implementing a requisition of troops. [56]

When comparing the events of January–February 1906 with the other occasions where military troops were involved in the execution of the laws against the Catholic Church, it appears that on previous occasions the measures foreseen to maintain public order had involved the military authorities from the outset. During the implementation of the laws against unauthorised religious orders, in March 1880 and again in 1902–1903, the army corps commanders received instructions directly from the War Ministry about the possibility of requisitions from the civil authorities.[57] The army corps commanders had therefore instructed the local commanders about their duty to obey if a civilian authority requested assistance. These 'instructions' were to be considered as an order from a military superior.

The closing of illegal religious orders in 1902–1903 was in many respects far more controversial than the establishment of inventories of the possessions of the Catholic Church in 1906. The civilian authorities had therefore not expected such strong reactions from Catholics demonstrators and had not prepared the military authorities for the possible need for military assistance.[58] When troops were requested in panic, the requisitions came from the local civilian authorities and went directly to the local garrisons, and not, as was usually the case, came as an order from the division general or the army corps commander. As a result, a certain number of local commanders found an occasion to be difficult about the formalities in the requisitions, thus postponing or impeding the mobilisation of troops.

Confronted with important demonstrations and with these obstructions from local military commanders and individual officers, the government had to give up their attempts to establish the controversial lists, at least for some months. Eight months later, from 19–23 November 1906, the inventories were accomplished. Again this took place with a massive display of military force. However, this time, the campaign was carefully planned in cooperation with the army corps commanders. A circular letter from the War Ministry informed the army corps commanders by 15 November about the forthcoming action.[59] The requisitions sent from the prefects were pre-printed so that no doubt could arise about their legality, about the role of the military troops, or about the number of soldiers to be mobilised. This and the involvement of the army corps commanders in the procedure of requisition ensured that this time there were no problems of obstruction from local commanders or individual officers.

Logistical dependence on the army and the breakdown of the civil-military distinction

With the establishment of Plans for Protection based on strategies that required a massive military presence from the beginning of any sensitive conflict, the French civilian administration came to rely heavily on the army. For simple logistical reasons it became difficult to break away from the measures of the Plans, since this would require complete rethinking of the existing strategies and total reorganisation of the available police and *gendarmerie* forces.

Moreover between the late 1890s and the outbreak of the First World War, the French army also became indispensable in the implementation of the governmental policies by performing a variety of functions, both military and non-military. In situations when major labour disputes threatened to paralyse the entire society or impede continuous work in the wider industrial sector, the army was used to fulfil non-military tasks, thus ensuring the continuous functioning of public utilities and industries that were not involved in the conflict.

During the process of increasing cooperation, a series of formal barriers which should have ensured the separation of the military organisation from the civilian sectors of the state were transformed or undermined for the sake of efficient cooperation.

Similarly certain aspects of the military legislation and organisation were adjusted to fit the increasing number of domestic functions attributed to the army. One of these concerned the establishment of garrisons for the sake of efficient policing. In 1898, the War Ministry had vigorously rejected suggestions from the civil administration for establishing permanent military posts in some turbulent areas in order to ensure rapid military intervention whenever needed.[60] The War Minister's argument was that garrisons were to be established solely according to the strategic needs of national defence. Nevertheless, five years later, in 1903, a new garrison was established in the industrial area of the *département* Nord. This time, the Interior Minister and the prefect openly admitted that the location of the garrison was primarily due to considerations of military involvement in policing.[61]

At the same time, the institutional demarcation between the realms of the civilian administration and the military was gradually perforated between 1900 and 1914, for the sake of efficient cooperation. This was particularly relevant in Nord-Pas-de-Calais, but was in fact a phenomenon occurring in many areas of France. In his analysis of the French civil-military relations of the early Third Republic, Ralston stresses that the army and the civilian sectors of the state had their particular spheres of competence, each respected by the other.[62] This could describe the civil-military relations in many Western states, including the German Empire. Nevertheless, between 1890 and 1914 the separation of the 'civil' and the 'military' realms in France became significantly less clear cut than it was in Prussia. Whilst the French army was left with a high degree of autonomy when it came to strictly technical military issues,[63] the respect of successive governments increasingly diminished for the particular nature of the army as a separate institution primarily responsible for the defence of the national territory against a foreign enemy.

Compared to previous instructions and laws on the requisition of military assistance,[64] the 1907 instructions went a long way in breaking down a series of formal barriers that were meant to confine the army within strict institutional boundaries. In the first place, procedures were simplified so that the military commander could start mobilising the troops as soon as he received the telegram of request from a civil authority.[65] The increasingly easy access for the prefect and sub-prefect to initiate mobilisation of troops was undertaken for the sake of 'efficiency'.[66]

Another significant aspect of the breakdown of institutional barriers was the elimination – in part at least – of the distinction between a state of normality and a state of emergency through the permanent opening of the right to so-called 'military requisition'. Military requisition was the military authorities' right to obtain food supplies and accommodation from the local population during periods of mobilisation.[67] It should not be confused with the right of the civilian authorities to request military assistance. In principle the access of military authorities to obtain supplies in the local community was to be authorised by the War Minister only in the case of general mobilisation.[68]

During the long miners' strikes of 1891 and 1893, the right to military requisition was granted exceptionally to the troops which were called out in Nord-Pas-de-Calais.[69] However, by the turn of the century, the right to military requisition during major policing operations had become standard procedure and the Plans for Protection from 1901 operated with military requisition as the basis for accommodation and provisions for men and horses.

In principle the right to military requisition was supposed to last only for a limited period of time; an extension of this period required a renewed authorisation from the War Minister. During the great miners' strike of 1901, the right to military requisition was made available first for a period of two weeks, and was then prolonged by the War Minister as the conflict continued.[70] Yet, War Minister André soon recognised that the formal procedures around military requisitions still impeded efficient mobilisation. During subsequent incidents of military mobilisation, he therefore sent printed forms with his own signature to the commanding officers involved, right down to the level of garrison commanders. Thereafter, it was up to the commander of each unit to insert a new date if the right to military requisition needed to be prolonged. This step was taken for purely practical reasons, and with the full blessing of the Interior Ministry and the regional administration.[71]

A further step in the breakdown of the formal distinction between a 'state of normality' and a 'state of emergency' was yet to come. In December 1904, the army corps commander in Lille reported to the prefect of the *département* Nord that there had been no occasion to formally end the right to military requisition which had been made available for the entire *département* on 12 February 1904 and then prolonged throughout the year. Each extension of the right to military requisition had to be publicly announced in all municipalities concerned.

As strikes dragged on, this cumbersome practice was becoming annoying. General Laplace therefore suggested to the prefect that the right to military requisition should be opened permanently for the entire region of Nord-Pas-de-Calais.[72] Given the high frequency of mobilisation of troops in the region, the prefect of the *département* Nord agreed that they should ask their respective ministers to allow a permanent opening of the military right to requisition.[73]

This was granted by the government without further comment, so in following years, on every 1 January, the War Minister formally opened the right to military requisition for the entire year. Similar provisions were made for the *département* Pas-de-Calais after the great strikes in the spring of 1906.[74] By a ministerial decree of 17 December 1910, this practice was extended to the all French *départements*.[75] Thus year after year, the entire region of Nord-Pas-de-Calais, and after 1910 all French *départements*, were – with respect to this particular aspect – kept in a permanent state of emergency.

In addition to the increasing inter-penetration between the civilian and military authorities, soldiers were increasingly called upon to perform strictly non-military functions. The idea of using soldiers to fill in for striking workers had already arisen in the 1870s, when the War Minister allowed conscript soldiers, who were professional bakers in civilian life, to produce bread for the civilian population in the event of a strike among Parisian bakers.[76] The aim was to ward off the detrimental effects of strikes in the most essential professions. In following years, conscript soldiers were on several occasions ordered to undertake strikebound work. In 1889, 'baker-soldiers' were ordered to stand in during a bakers' strike in Marseilles; in December 1903, soldiers and military ovens were used when the bakers in Lille went on strike the day before Christmas.

If it was in the public interest to prevent bread shortage in the cities, it was not difficult to argue the case for using soldiers to ensure the continuation of public utilities in the case of labour disputes. In 1891 preparations were made for allowing soldiers to substitute for gas workers in a factory in Le Havre.[77] The 1897 Plans for a nationwide strike among rail workers, although primarily aimed at protecting the railway infrastructure, were also tied up with considerations concerning the possibility using soldiers from the engineers division to ensure the basic services.[78] This was implemented the following year during the first occasion of a nationwide rail strike.

Once a precedent had been established for this use of soldiers, the same justification was all too easily applicable to labour disputes in which the French state was the employer against public employees. In May 1899, during the first major strike among postal workers, soldiers were used to deliver the mail. The same measures were taken during the strike among postal workers in 1906 and in March and May 1909. When Parisian electricians went on strike in March 1907, Parisians had to spend one evening without electric light. When the electricians wanted to repeat their success in October 1910, the authorities had prepared themselves well beforehand for this eventuality, and called out the engineers to ensure the continuous functioning of the Parisian power stations.

The idea of using soldiers to stand in for striking electricians was already discussed in February 1905 apparently without any opposition from the military authorities.[79] The use of soldiers was equally convenient in situations where specific skills were needed to enforce governmental policies. Thus, during the establishment in 1906 of the Inventories of the possessions of the Catholic Church, conscript soldiers who were locksmiths by profession were used to unlock church doors which had been barred and barricaded by the local priest and parishioners.

The most inventive use of the army organisation occurred in October 1910 when rail workers from all over France went on strike. Instead of sending soldiers from the engineers to ensure basic services, as had happened in the rail strike of 1898, the conscription laws were used to prevent at least some of the rail employees from going on strike. Rail workers who were also army reservists were simply called upon for military service, only to be sent back to work under military orders. Failure to turn up or any refusal to work could then be treated as mutiny under military law. This type of measure had already been suggested during the first major strike among rail workers twelve years earlier.

In 1898, the suggestion of using conscript soldiers or reservists to stand in for striking rail workers had generated much discussion both within government and among legal specialists; there were serious doubts whether the army could be involved in labour disputes in this way and whether such a measure could be taken within the boundaries of the conscription laws of 15 July 1889.[80]

By 1910, the precedent already existed for the use of soldiers as strike-breakers. This facilitated the calling up of striking rail workers as military reservists, and the government went ahead with this highly controversial procedure, regardless of public outcry and amidst accusations of acting illegally and anti-constitutionally, even by Yves Guyot, a former Minister of Public Works who was otherwise known for his strong anti-Socialist views.[81]

From cooperation to inter-penetration and inter-dependence

As these examples show, the use of the French army went far beyond simple requisition of troops in cases of urgent need to restore order. The army increasingly became an integrated part of the strategies that the government, the Interior Ministry and its prefects employed to implement their policies. The procedures of cooperation with the military authorities were characterised by a high degree of institutional formalisation and practical organisation. This made the functioning of military assistance extremely efficient. On the other hand, it bound the civil administration to strategies that relied heavily on the army since all existing plans for the policing of popular protest and labour disputes of any significance operated with military assistance from the very beginning of a conflict.

In the face of the ambiguous sentiments among French officers about the army's role in protest policing, the establishment of Plans for Protection was crucial in facilitating cooperation between the military authorities and the Interior Ministry and its prefects. In the first place, the Planning Commission, with its sub-committees and numerous *départemental* committees, constituted a permanent forum where ministerial representatives, prefects, and other public authorities concerned with the maintenance of public order could meet with their military counterparts in informal discussions about their problems and needs in a situation of crisis.

The Plans for Protection also defined the types of conflict in which military involvement would be justified. Through these plans the civil and military authorities agreed on the numbers of troops which they considered appropriate for large-scale conflicts. Although the plans were conceived for large-scale policing operations, they were easily applicable for more limited conflicts, which explains the close correlation between the strategic principles stated in the plans and the measures implemented in Nord-Pas-de-Calais.

The existence of this detailed framework for large-scale policing also helps to explain the strong continuity in the measures implemented in Nord-Pas-de-Calais. The intensified exchange of information between civil and military authorities as well as the frequency with which troops were called out to assist municipal police and *gendarmerie* led to the development of standard procedures which limited the scope for misunderstandings and uncertainty about the measures to be implemented. With civil-military relations otherwise characterised by mutual suspicion, the repeated implementation and entrenchment of the same measures and procedures allowed for some level of mutual trust. By integrating the military authorities into the decision-making process and by agreeing all details in advance there was limited the scope for military obstruction. Once a senior military commander had accepted the basic principles in the Plans for Protection, it became difficult for his successors or subordinate commanders to break this pattern, even in situations where they might not consider military assistance strictly necessary.

The highly sensitive political and social situation in France during the first decade of the 20th century left little space for experiments in crisis management. This made the repeated implementation of the same measures and strategies attractive because they seemed safe and predictable. With civil-military authorities cooperating highly effectively, any change in strategy or approach became unattractive because it involved many unpredictable factors and high risk of losing control.

The increasingly frequent calls upon the army and the use of troops for even minor cases of potential unrest, the gradual breakdown in the distinction between the realm of civilian and military authorities, as well as the use of soldiers to perform non-military tasks, all indicate that inter-institutional cooperation between the civilian and military authorities functioned surprisingly effectively.

Yet, it is only when comparing the situation in Nord-Pas-de-Calais with the difficulties surrounding civil-military cooperation in Westphalia that we can fully appreciate the importance of the Plans for Protection, as well as the significance of institutionalised civil-military cooperation and the entrenchment of standard operating procedures into the bureaucratic practice.

Notes

[1] Since the 1980s, path dependency has been a central concept in the New Institutionalist approach to historical continuity in bureaucratic policy-making. (Peter Evans, Dietrich Rueschmeyer and Theda Skocpol, 'On the Road towards a more Adequate Understanding of the State', in Peter Evans, Dietrich Rueschmeyer and Theda Skocpol (eds.), *Bringing the State back in*, Cambridge: Cambridge University Press, 1989. For a theoretical discussion about the importance of long-term development in bureaucratic practices see March and Olsen (1989) pp. 53–63. See also Chapter 1 Footnote 83.

[2] MA, Vincennes, 5 N 5: Letter of 18 February 1893 from Interior Minister Ribot to the prefects, and letter of 23 February from War Minister Loizillon to the army corps commanders.

[3] NA, Paris, F 7 12774: Circular of 3 June 1897 from War Minister Billot to the army corps commanders.

[4] DA, Lille, M 622 /1: Circular of 25 July 1897 from Interior Minister Méline to the prefects.

[5] NA, Paris, F 7 12774: Circular letters of 3 June 1897 and 22 July 1898 on the measures to be taken in the case of a strike among rail workers. Idem.: A list dated 1897 detailing the distribution of troops nationwide.

[6] MA, Vincennes, 7 N 127: Report of 25 May 1898 from the General Staff of the War Ministry, including notes from the hand of War Minister Billot.

[7] DA, Lille, M 622 /2: Letter of 12 December 1898 from Interior Minister Dupuy to the prefects.

[8] MA, Vincennes, 7 N 100: Note of 27 July 1901 from the General Staff of the War Ministry. Idem.: Letter of 3 August 1901 from War Minister André to the army corps commanders. NA, Paris, F 7 12773: Letter of 16 October 1901 from Interior Minister Waldeck-Rousseau to the prefects.

[9] NA, Paris, F 7 12773: Letter of 15 March 1902 from Interior Minister Waldeck-Rousseau to the prefects.

[10] NA, Paris, F 7 12778: Letter of 5 March 1902 from Interior Minister Waldeck-Rousseau to the prefects of Moulins, Rody, Nîmes, Grenoble, Saint Etienne, Le Puy, Lille, Arras, Clermont-Ferrand, Mâcon, Albi.

[11] NA, Paris, F 7 12774: Confidential Instruction of 18 October 1907 concerning the implementation of the 1907 Plans for Protection.

[12] MA, Vincennes, 7 N 100: Note from the General Staff of the War Ministry of 27 July 1901 concerning the measures to be taken in case of a general strike in the mining sector. MA, Vincennes, 7 N 115: Circular letter of 1 February 1911 from the Interior Ministry to the prefects.

[13] MA, Vincennes, 7 N 115: Circular letter of 1 February 1911 and instructions of 27 June 1913 concerning the implementation of the Plans for Protection.

[14] MA, Vincennes, 7 N 115: Instructions of 27 June 1913 concerning the implementation of the Plans for Protection.

[15] NA, Paris, F 7 12913: Minutes from the meeting in the Interior Ministry on 5 February 1907.

[16] Hennion, head of the General Security Department of the Interior Ministry; Paris Police Prefect Lépine; the prefects Vincent, Trépont and Lutaud; Grumback and Capot from the Interior Ministry; the Generals Lébon and Desoille; Lieutenant Colonel Bernhard and Commander Fabia from the War Ministry; Coulon, vice-president of the State Council; Attorney General Manoël-Saumane, and two chief engineers from the Ministry of Public Works.

[17] Anonymous, *'L'armée sous le régime civil et les questions militaires pendantes'*, Paris: Henri Charles-Lavauzelle, 1894, pp. 84–85.

[18] NA, Paris, F 7 12778: Notes of 5 October 1901 from the hand of Interior Minister Waldeck-Rousseau.

[19] NA, Paris, F 7 12912: Confidential report of 15 May 1902 from the sub-commission preparing measures in the case of strikes among rail workers; DA, Lille, M 623: Letter of 12 April 1906 from General Lebon to Louis Vincent, Prefect of *département* Nord; NA, Paris, F 7 12913: Minutes from a meeting on 10 July 1907 in the sub-commission for the revision of the Plans for Protection in case of strikes among miners.

[20] DA, Lille, M 624 /7: Letter of 10 October 1901 from Louis Vincent, prefect in Lille, to Interior Minister Waldeck-Rousseau.

[21] See Chapter 7.

[22] Law of 26 July–3 August 179, Article 23.

[23] NA, Paris, F 7 12913: Minutes from a meeting of 13 April 1907 in the Commission revising the 'Instructions on Military Participation in the Maintenance of Public Order' uses the formulation "L'autorité militaire prépare les mesures d'exécution qui sont la conséquence de ces communications (avec l'autorité civile)."

[24] NA, Paris, F 7 12773: Letter of September 1893 from Interior Minister to the prefects.

[25] MA, Vincennes, 5 N 5: Circular letter of 15 May 1878 on the communications between the military authorities and the prefect and local authorities. Similarly, letter of 14 June 1882 from Interior Minister Freycinet to the prefects and letter of 29 January 1883 from War Minister Thibaudin to the army corps commanders.

[26] Carrot (1990) p. 60.

[27] Decree of 4 October 1891 on civilian and military authorities in garrison towns, Article 167: "Le choix et l'execution des mesures à prendre appartiennent exclusivement à l'autorité militaire, dont la responsabilité à cet égard reste entière." MA, Vincennes, 1.A.C. /2.I.330: 'Instructions en cas de grèves ou de troubles' of 15 February 1893 from General de France, army corps commander in Lille: "Le commandement des troupes sera toujours réglé et assuré par l'autorité militaire."

[28] MA, Vincennes, 5 N 5: Letter of 18 February 1893 from the Interior Minister to the prefects, and the letter of 23 February 1893 from War Minister Loizillon to the army corps commanders.

[29] MA, Vincennes, 1.A.C. /2.I.326: Letter of 17 December 1902 from War Minister André to Army Corps Commander Jeannerod in Lille; DA, Lille, M 624 /7: Letters from October 1901 from Louis Vincent, Prefect in Lille, to the Interior Minister.

[30] MA, Vincennes, 1.A.C. /2.I.326: Letter of 17 December 1902 from the War Minister to the Army Corps Commander in Lille.

[31] Instructions of 20 August 1907 on military participation in the maintenance of public order. Article 10.

[32] Instructions of 20 August 1907 on military participation in the maintenance of public order. Article 8: "L'autorité civile est seule juge du moment où la force armée doit être requise."

[33] MA, Vincennes, 5 N 6: Circular letter of 31 August 1907 on the application of the Instructions of 20 August 1907 on military participation in the maintenance of public order. War Minister Picquart comments on the Article 21 about the obligation of prefects and the army corps commanders to meet and determine together all policing measures involving the army: "Je ne saurais trop insister sur les prescriptions de cet article. Il faut qu'à tous les degrés de la hiérarchie, chacun s'inspire du but à atteindre et qu'il y contribue de toutes ses forces en mettant de côté toute question d'amour-propre."

[34] MA, Vincennes, 5 N 6: Circular letter of 31 August 1907 on the application of the Instructions of 20 August 1907 on military participation in the maintenance of public order. Articles 8 & 9.

[35] NA, Paris, F 7 12913: Minutes from meetings in the Commission revising the 'Instruction on Military Participation in the Maintenance of Public Order' on 13 April, 8 June, 11 June, 22 June, and 30 October 1907; 3 June 1908 and 27 February 1909.

[36] NA, Paris, F 7 12780: Letter of 18 June 1901 from Interior Minister Waldeck-Rousseau to War Minister André.

[37] NA, Paris, F 7 12780: Circular letter of 23 August 1901 from Interior Minister Waldeck-Rousseau to the prefects.

[38] MA, Vincennes, 1 A.C. /2.I.326: Report of 24 October 1902 from the military commander of Calais.

[39] MA, Vincennes, 1 A.C. /2.I.333: Letter of 12 June 1910 from the military commander in Cambrai to the Army Corps Commander in Lille.

[40] MA, Vincennes, 1.A.C. /2.I.330: Letter of 23 August 1911 from the military governor of Maubeuge to the Army Corps Commander in Lille.

[41] NA, Paris, F 7 12778: Letter of 5 March 1902 from Interior Minister Waldeck-Rousseau to the prefects; DA, Lille, M 626 /40: Letter of 6 March 1902 from Louis Vincent, Prefect in Lille, to the sub-prefects of *département* 'Nord'; MA, Vincennes, 1 A.C. /2.I.325: Letter of 30 October 1906 from War Minister Picquart to General Lebon, army corps commander in Lille.

[42] MA, Vincennes, 1 A.C. /2.I.149: Report of 4 October 1906 by General Lebon, army corps commander in Lille entitled 'Note concernant des questions ne se rattachant qu'indirectement à l'organisation des bassins industriels, mais réclamant une solution immédiate'. Similarly attempts to increase cooperation and coordination comes out in the correspondence between successive prefects and army corps commanders covering the years 1903–1910 (MA, Vincennes, 1 A.C. /2.I.332; 2.I.333; 2.I.334).

[43] DA, Lille, M 622 /2: Letter of 6 September 1907 from Louis Vincent, prefect of *département* Nord, to Interior Minister Clemenceau.

[44] DA, Lille, M 622 /2: Letter of 31 August 1907 from Louis Vincent, prefect of *département* Nord, to the Army Corps Commander.

[45] MA, Vincennes, 1.A.C. /2.I.325: Letter of 28 October 1903 from Louis Vincent, prefect of *département* Nord, to the Army Corps Commander Jeannerod; DA, Lille, M 6 /20: the personnel File of Louis Vincent contains several newspaper cuttings on this subject.

[46] NA, Paris, F 7 12526: Letter of 14 October 1882 from the Prefect of Saône-et-Loire to the Interior Minister.

[47] DA, Arras, M 1641: Letter of 4 December 1880 from the Interior Ministry to the prefects. MA, Vincennes, MR 2172 or REC 2172: Letter of 17 November 1880 from General Gallifet to the prefects of the *départements* 'Indre-et-loire', 'Indre', 'Vienne', 'Deux-Sèvres', and 'Maine-et-Loire'.

[48] NA, Paris, F 7 12773: Letter of 22 February 1893 from the prefect of Allier to the Interior Ministry.

[49] NA, Paris, F 7 12774: Note of 24 August 1897 from Interior Minister Méline.

[50] NA, Paris, F 7 12774: Letter of 10 November 1898 from War Minister Freycinet to Interior Minister Dupuy.

[51] NA, Paris, F 7 12778: Note dated 5 October 1901 addressed to Interior Minister Waldeck-Rousseau.

[52] NA, Paris, F 7 12399: Letter of 4 March 1906 from War Minister Étienne to Interior Minister Clemenceau.

[53] NA, Paris, F 7 12773: Decision from the State Council announced to the Interior Ministry on 18 July 1893.

[54] MA, Vincennes, 1.A.C. /2.I.335: Letter of 13 March 1906 from the division commander General Chomer to the Army Corps Commander, General Lebon.

[55] NA, Paris, F 7 12527: Letter of 27 June 1891 from Prefect Vel-Durand to the Interior Minister; Idem. Letter of 8 July 1891 from Interior Minister Constans to War Minister Freycinet.

[56] MA, Vincennes, REC 2172: Letter of 17 November 1880 from Army Corps Commander General Gallifet to the prefects of the *départements* of Indre-et-Loire, Indre, La Vienne, Les Deux-Sèvres, and Maine-et-Loire.

[57] MA, Vincennes, 1.A.C./2.I.325: Letter of 23 August 1903 from the commander in Cambrai to the division commander in Lille.

[58] In the instructions from the Interior Ministry to the prefects there is no suggestion of involving troops until late February 1906, although several violent confrontations had taken place in January between demonstrators and public forces. Only by 25 February 1906 did Interior Minister Rouvier recommend for the first time to call for military assistance in order to accomplish the 'Inventories'. NA, Paris, F 7 12399: Letter of 25 February 1906 from Interior Minister Rouvier to the prefects.

[59] MA, Vincennes, 1A.C. /2.I.335: Letter of 15 November 1906 from War Minister Picquart to the army corps commanders.

[60] NA, Paris, F 7 12774: Letter of 10 November 1898 from the War Minister to Interior Minister Dupuy concerning a suggestion from the prefect of the Eastern Pyrenees.

[61] NA, Paris, F 7 12780: Letter of 20 March 1903 from Louis Vincent, prefect of *département* Nord, to Interior Minister Combes.

[62] Ralston (1967) p. 135.

[63] This is Ralston's main conclusion. Ralston (1967) p. 373.

[64] Law of 27 July–3 August 1791 on the requisition of military assistance to civilian authorities; Decree of 4 October 1891 on civilian and military authorities in garrison towns; Instructions of 24 June 1903 on military participation in the maintenance of public order.

[65] Instructions of 20 August 1907. Articles 8, 9 & 13; A similar observation is made by Jauffret (1983) p. 127.

[66] MA, Vincennes, 1 A.C. /2.I.325: Letter of 3 January 1905 from Louis Vincent, prefect of *département* Nord, to the Army Corps Commander in Lille.

[67] This was defined by the law of 3 July 1877 on military requisition.

[68] Law of 3 July 1877 on Military Requisition, Article 1.

[69] DA, Arras, M 4865: Letter of 18 November 1891 from War Minister Freycinet to General Loizillon, army corps commander in Lille; DA, Arras, M 4862: Letter of 18 September 1893 from Gabriel Alapetite, prefect of 'Pas-de-Calais' to Interior Minister Dupuy.

[70] NA, Paris, F 7 12780: Letter of 11 October 1901 from War Minister André to Interior Minister Waldeck-Rousseau.

[71] NA, Paris, F 7 12780: Letter of 27 November 1901 from War Minister André to Interior Minister Waldeck-Rousseau also containing pre-printed forms to be filled in by local commanders.

[72] DA, Lille, M 624 /13: Letters of 12 December and 31 December 1904 from the Army Corps Commander to Louis Vincent, prefect of *département* Nord.

[73] DA, Lille, M 624 /13: Letter of 3 January 1905 from Louis Vincent, prefect of *département* Nord, to the Army Corps Commander.
[74] MA, Vincennes, 1 A.C. /2.I.325: Letter of 30 October 1906 to General Lebon, army corps commander in Lille.
[75] MA, Vincennes, 7 N 115: Note of 12 April 1912 from the General Staff of the War Ministry.
[76] NA, Paris, F 7 12773: Letter of 8 May 1876 from War Minister Cissey to the army corps commanders.
[77] NA, Paris, F 7 12773: Letter of 9 November 1891 from War Minister Freycinet to the Interior Minister.
[78] MA, Vincennes, 7 N 127: Report of 25 May 1898 from the General Staff of the War Ministry including a note of approval from War Minister Billot.
[79] MA, Vincennes, 1 A.C. /2.I.333: Letter of 4 February 1905 from the General Staff of the War Ministry to the army corps commanders; Idem.: Letter of 6 February 1905 from General Dessirier, Military Governor of Paris, to the army corps commander in Lille.
[80] MA, Vincennes, 7 N 127: Report of 25 May 1898 from the General Staff of the War Ministry including a note of approval from War Minister Billot; Ludovic Desveaux, *Les grèves des chemins de fer en France et à l'étranger*, Paris: Marchal & Billard, 1899.
[81] Yves Guyot, *Les chemins de fer et la grève*, Paris: Felix Alcan, 1911.

Chapter 10

Mutual Exclusion and Non-Cooperation in Westphalia

Operating in the borderland between civilian and military authorities

The extended planning and practical cooperation between French military authorities and the provincial administration contrast sharply with the situation in Westphalia. Prussian civil servants and military commanders sought the lowest possible degree of inter-institutional cooperation. Whereas civil-military cooperation in France was highly formalised with all important details carefully negotiated, the relationship between the provincial administration in Westphalia and the Prussian army was largely based on unwritten rules; it depended much on the inclinations of those who were province governors and army corps commanders. Where matters fell outside the clearly defined competencies of the civilian administration or the military authorities they had to be negotiated between the province governor and the army corps commander. Sometimes disagreeable issues relating to large scale policing were passed around the province governor, the Interior Ministry, the War Ministry and the army corps commander since the military authorities were generally unwilling to assume responsibility. Hansjoachim Henning, in his article on the attitude of the Prussian Interior Ministry towards military involvement in the policing of strikes and demonstrations, points to the lack of appropriate military preparation for their role in handling major popular unrest. He also shows the inability of the relevant military commanders to respond adequately to this type of challenge.[1] Analysing the major conflicts in Westphalia, this lack of military preparation was equally evident for all three incidents of military interventions: the great miners' strike of 1889, the 1899 riots in Herne, and the miners' strike of March 1912.

In Nord-Pas-de-Calais, the standard operation procedures for civil-military cooperation on protest policing ensured continuous exchange of information; in Westphalia, by contrast, the relationship between the provincial administration and the army was characterised by slow and infrequent communication. Moreover because the Prussian army was rarely involved in policing operations, lessons were not learned from one intervention to the next of how the military organisation should best handle large-scale policing operations. No precedents were established between the civilian and military authorities about procedures and the distribution of duties and responsibilities. Therefore each time the army was called upon to police major strikes or popular protest, all measures and procedures had to be re-established on the spot by the military commander in charge.

In Prussia there was no equivalent to the French Plans for Protection. Insofar as military plans existed, they were not coordinated with the plans drawn up by the provincial administration; indeed the provincial administration seemed to be unaware whether any military plans existed at all for situations of major unrest. Each time the Prussian army was called upon, there was general confusion among civil servants and military commanders at all levels about lines of communication and authority. There was also much confusion about the financial responsibility for a military intervention. All these issues often had to be negotiated while the crisis was unfolding. Despite these important areas of uncertainty and lack of preparation, the military interventions in 1899 and in 1912 did not give rise to major conflicts between the provincial administration and the military authorities. This was primarily because the commanders in charge of the operations tended to follow the recommendations of the civil administration. Even so, the civilian authorities could never be confident of getting support or being able to rely on the good-will of the military.

Calling on the army in Prussia implied a significant degree of uncertainty for provincial administrators as well as for the military commanders. This must be seen as a major incentive for the heads of the provincial administration to deal with public unrest without calling for military assistance, even when there was significant potential for violence and riots. In order to understand the consistent preference by the leaders of the Prussian provincial administration to demilitarisation of protest policing, it is worth paying attention to the high levels of compartmentalism that existed in the relationship between the provincial administration and the army.

Communication and non-communication

Like their French counterparts, the Prussian authorities were supposed to work together and sustain each other in order to safeguard the interests of the state; provide the military with a good local base to pursue their military training; recruit soldiers; and obtain food and material from local providers.

The principle of mutual support was stated repeatedly in the Cabinet Orders and instructions that defined the relationship between civil and military authorities at the provincial level.[2] This was also the message from War Minister Verdy du Vernois in his 1890 Instructions to the army corps commanders.[3] The service regulations issued by the War Ministry in 1899 also stressed the importance of cooperation[4] and was restated by War Minister von Heeringen in 1910.[5] The Prussian legislation also defined a series of situations in which the armed forces could be requested by the civil authorities to perform non-military functions. These included situations of natural disaster (flood, fire, hurricane) or searches for missing people, victims of accidents or crime, and escaped criminals.[6] The Prussian legislation was, in this respect, not essentially different from the non-military duties defined by the French legislation.[7] However the institutional practices in Westphalia differed significantly from those in Nord-Pas-de-Calais.

Although the province governor and the army corps commander were personally acquainted and in some cases claimed to be on excellent terms,[8] professional communications between the provincial administration and the military authorities were strictly limited. Most of the civil-military correspondence concerned minor practical issues, such as demands for allowing the local police to use equipment from the local garrison – everything from horses to chloroform or electric lamps in case of interruption of street lighting during a night operation. This type of correspondence was quite random and required nothing from the army corps commander except his formal acceptance. The issue of military assistance to police popular protest did not even appear prominently among the few issues that the provincial administration and the army did consult each other about.

Questions concerning the measures to be taken against Social Democrats, Anarchists, and other politically suspect individuals and organisations were also very marginal to the civil-military correspondence. When the ban against the Social Democratic Party was lifted in 1890, War Minister Verdy du Vernois had sought to involve the army corps commanders more actively than previously in the fight against the Social Democratic activities.[9] However, despite the intension to give the army corps commanders a more political role in the surveillance and repression of 'subversive elements',[10] this invitation was clearly not followed by the generals who were in charge of the most industrialised province of the Empire.

Instead, between 1890 and 1914, the division of labour between the provincial administration and the military authorities was increasingly strictly observed: the civilian authorities dealt with everything involving surveillance of the Social Democratic party and other suspect organisations and individuals; the military authorities were only concerned with the influence of Social Democratic ideas among recruits and reservists in the army. The correspondence between the provincial administration and the military authorities in Westphalia reveals that sharing of information and correspondence concerning measures against Social Democratic activities was remarkably marginal.

Army corps commanders were of course involved in pro-military propaganda through the Veteran Clubs and other charitable organisations linked to the provincial army corps, and they kept a watchful eye for Social Democratic influence in these organisations.[11] After 1891 soldiers were forbidden to frequent certain shops and taverns because the owner or inn keeper was known or suspected to have Social Democratic sympathies and to serve suspect customers. In the light of the highly interventionist measures implemented to shield young recruits from Social Democratic influence, it is remarkable how little enthusiasm the majority of the army corps commanders showed for gathering information from the civilian authorities, or even actively investigating the levels of Social Democratic influence among recruits and reservists. The yearly reports to the War Ministry on this particular subject mostly consist of one or two pages for each army corps explaining in general terms – and often with the same wording from year to year – that the men were motivated and that no strong sympathies for the Social Democratic Party could be traced among recruits and reservists.[12] Only in 1910 did the commanders of the most industrialised areas notice that the influence of Social Democratic ideas had become significant. It was as late as 1911 before the War Minister drew the conclusion that for the first time a significant influence of Socialist ideas had been noticed among recruits and reservists.[13]

This lack of enthusiasm among army corps commanders for reporting Social Democratic influence among recruits and reservists may be explained by their gradual realisation that attempts to immunise and isolate the soldiers from such influence were largely unsuccessful. In the early 1890s even a hard-liner such as Field Marshall von Waldersee did not consider the influx of Social Democrats into the army as a problem for the time being, but he did insist on his right to eliminate the few that he considered to be a potential problem.[14] Other senior commanders began to argue that there was no reason for excluding men from military service simply on the basis of their Social Democratic sympathies, since they most often proved to be loyal and disciplined soldiers.[15] General von Haenisch, the commander of the fourth army corps 1889–1897, went so far as to argue that the strong discipline among members of the Social Democratic party actually made them very good soldiers.[16] At the same time, the attempts in 1905 from General von Eichhorn, army corps commander in Frankfurt, to expose recruits to anti-Social Democrat propaganda were recognised in following years as having had little effect and possibly to have been counter-productive.[17] In 1907, Wilhelm II therefore decided that anti-Socialist instruction should no longer be part of the training of recruits and reservists.[18]

In his 1890 decree, War Minister Verdy du Vernois also urged the army corps commanders to stay continuously informed about Socialist activities in the local communities where they were based, including politically suspect organisations, their local leaders, and their press.[19] This information was supposed to be provided by the provincial administration who were in charge of monitoring potentially subversive elements in civil society. These included 'black-lists' with the names of persons who might constitute a threat in the case of war. These 'black-lists' were established by the police authorities, revised every six months, and sent by the province governor to the army corps commander. This information, however, was not followed up by further correspondence.

In November 1912, Interior Minister von Dallwitz told the Province Governor von Ratibor in Münster to contact the military authorities in order to establish lists of people to be arrested and of publishing houses to be closed in case of a state of siege during a major strike. This was a significant extension of the system of 'black-listing' since previously they had only included people 'suspect' in a situation of war and general mobilisation.[20]

Nothing came of this initiative because the military authorities were not interested. The Army Corps Commander in Münster, General von Einem, sent a quick reply to the Province Governor stating that it was unnecessary and a waste of time to send the lists of Social Democratic leaders and Anarchists to the military authorities. If a state of siege was declared due to popular unrest, it would be sufficient if these lists were made available to the military commanders by local police authorities.[21] A similar wish was expressed by the Army Corps Commander in Frankfurt when he was presented with a similar initiative from the Interior Ministry.[22]

Slow lines of communication

Despite repeated calls from the Prussian War Ministry for cooperation and exchange of relevant information, the provincial administration and the military authorities in Westphalia had much fewer inter-institutional connections than their counterparts in Nord-Pas-de-Calais. Nor were there, as existed in France, strong linkages at government level between the Interior and War Ministries that might have made up for the tendencies towards compartmentalism and ensured some degree of coordination of measures for the handling of major operations to handle popular unrest. Prussian authorities – both the provincial administration and the army – were extremely concerned with maintaining their institutional autonomy; any commitment to cooperation across institutional boundaries was seen as placing restrictions on the independent decision making of civilian as well as military authorities.

Similarly there was general reluctance within the Prussian system to exchange information between civilian and military authorities. Within the French system, inter-institutional correspondence was 'circular': the French Interior Ministry communicated continuously with the War Ministry as well as with the prefects, and both these authorities communicated regularly with the army corps commanders. Within the Prussian system, by contrast, communication was rather 'linear': the Interior Ministry corresponding with the province and district governors, while the War Ministry communicated with the army corps commanders. At government level, there was no regular correspondence between the Interior and War Ministries and exchange of information was limited. Most of the communications were issued by the Interior Ministry informing the War Ministry about activities that might concern the army. The War Ministry seems to have been given information mainly to ensure that the military authorities would not obstruct initiatives carried out by the civilian administration. Unlike the French system, the Interior Minister was not in a position of authority in relation to the War Minister, and neither the Interior Minister nor the Prussian *Ministerpräsident* were in a position to force the War Ministry to participate in inter-ministerial cooperation. This compartmentalism was exacerbated by the tendency of the War Ministry to jealously guard its semi-independent position within government and its insistence on the secret nature of many of its activities. Similarly the army corps commanders carefully watched over their own independence in relation to the War Ministry.

At regional level, too, exchange of information between province and district governors and the army corps commanders was occasional and slow. Unlike his French counterpart, the army corps commander in Westphalia received no regular information from the province and district governors about problems of policing in the area. The army corps commander in Münster was therefore much less prepared for policing operations than was his counterpart in Lille. French military commanders at all levels of the hierarchy had to sign and pass on the daily reports from local *gendarmerie* units; these provided the army corps commander with detailed information about policing issues within his region. This was a source of information he shared with the prefects in Lille and Arras since they received copies of the same *gendarmerie* reports. In contrast, the Prussian *gendarmerie* only reported to local civilian authorities and directly to the War Ministry. The Prussian army corps commanders' main source of information about the state of affairs in local communities was provided by local garrison commanders. Yet Westphalian garrisons were deliberately located in rural areas. For example, there was no permanent military unit in the entire district of Arnsberg, which was one of the main centres of labour conflict in the Ruhr area. The army corps commander of the Westphalian province was himself based far from the industrial centres in a quiet provincial town surrounded by rural areas. He could therefore easily be scarcely informed even of significant conflicts that took place in the industrial areas around the River Ruhr.

Whether in highly important issues, such as policing strategies that involved both civilian and military authorities or strictly trivial matters, the provincial administration and the army sometimes deliberately excluded each other from relevant information. The civilian authorities were not informed about military plans on dealing with major internal unrest. Whether or not military plans were developed at all depended entirely on the initiative of the individual army corps commander and his general staff; by the outbreak of the First World War, it seemed to be only those provinces which had experienced military intervention which had some form of military plans or instructions. Even in an area as turbulent as Westphalia, with its significant potential for extended labour conflicts, the only military planning up to 1907 appears to be the very vague instructions issued by General von Albedyll during the 1889 strike.

Such was the exclusion of information, that not only were the civilian authorities kept in the dark about the details of military planning but in most cases they did not even know whether the military authorities had made any plans or preparation at all for military intervention in a situation of major unrest. When the controversial instructions developed by General von Bissing for military intervention in the industrial areas of Westphalia became public in 1910, their existence came as much of a surprise to the Interior Ministry and the provincial administration as to the wider public.[23]

Insofar as the civilian authorities were informed at all about the existence of plans or instructions for major policing operations, the military authorities would insist on their secret nature and were very reluctant about providing any details. Thus, one of the few sets of instructions that defined the army's role in handling popular unrest was issued by the War Ministry to the army corps commanders in February 1912; yet it was only made available to the Interior Ministry in June 1913, and at first the War Ministry insisted that only the most senior civil servants should be allowed to know the details.[24]

For their part the provincial administration also sought to withhold information from the military authorities about the plans for large-scale policing which were elaborated in cooperation with local authorities. In January 1905 the Province Governor of the Rhine Province, von Nasse, even forbade his subordinates to provide information to the military authorities about the details of these plans.[25] Yet some aspects of the civilian planning for large-scale policing operations inevitably involved the army, for instance the use of military horses for police officers and *gendarmes* called to the area in case of great unrest, the designation of garrisons to which each civilian authority was to address requisitions in case of extreme urgency, as well as accommodation for soldiers and horses in case of requisition of troops. When determining such details, the normal procedure was that every aspect would first be discussed at length between the Interior Ministry and the province and district governors. Plans and instructions would then be presented to municipal and police authorities. Only when all details were settled between the various civilian authorities would the army corps commander be contacted.[26]

The low level of inter-institutional connections is well illustrated by the length of time it took for correspondence to move from the left wing of Münster Castle, which housed the offices of the province governor, to the right wing, where the army corps commander was based. In July 1904, a meeting took place between the District Governor of the Düsseldorf District, and twelve representatives from local and municipal authorities. The purpose was to determine how to handle a situation of a major strike among miners. One problem identified was that there seemed to be great uncertainty over which military authority should be contacted in case of immediate need for military assistance. It was agreed that the issue should be settled with the military authorities so that there would be no confusion in times of crisis. After the meeting, Province Governor von Nasse presented the matter to Interior Minister von Hammerstein, who then informed Province Governor von der Recke of Westphalia. The recommendation from the Minister was that the Province Governors of Westphalia and the Rhine Province should contact the military authorities within their respective provinces.[27] Instead, Province Governor von Nasse of the Rhine Province advised his colleague to discuss these suggestions with the district governors of his province, and not to contact the military authorities until all details were fully negotiated between the different sections of the provincial administration and the local authorities.[28]

Over the following seventeen months the matter was discussed at length. A plan was developed and agreed between the different ministerial, provincial and local authorities. It was not until the end of March 1906 that the military commanders of the Rhine Province and Westphalia were informed about the issue.[29] It would have saved a great deal of time and ink had the army corps commanders been contacted at an earlier stage, for it turned out that the Army Corps Commander of Westphalia, General von Bissing, was fiercely opposed to the idea that troops could be mobilised except on his explicit order.[30] By October 1906 it was clear that there would be no question of formally determining in advance the lines of communication between civil and military authorities at the local level, even in a case of extreme urgency.[31] It was now more than two years after the issue had first been raised by Province Governor von Nasse in Düsseldorf.

The correspondence is interesting because it shows how a relatively minor issue could be discussed for two years before being presented to the military authorities. It indicates how cumbersome and complicated it was to establish any inter-institutional coordination, let alone practical cooperation, between the provincial administration and the military authorities. Despite the physical proximity of the offices of the province governor and the army corps commander in Münster Castle, most information and correspondence between them went via Berlin. More surprisingly, during the twenty months from August 1904 to March 1906, when various branches of the provincial administration were discussing amongst themselves which garrisons might be approached by which local authority in case of extreme urgency, Westphalia experienced the greatest miners' strike since 1889. Yet even the miners' strike of January 1905, when many local authorities were pressing hard to obtain military protection, did not speed up the correspondence.

Slow correspondence was not uncommon. Nor does it seem to be specific to the province of Westphalia, since examples of infrequent communication even on important matters have been found in other provinces. A particularly remarkable incident of non-communication occurred in October 1903, when the local governor in Welten, near Potsdam, asked the local garrison commander to keep troops ready for intervention due to a strike that threatened to develop into riots. Without informing the local governor, the garrison commander requested a train from a private rail company to be kept on steam (*unter Dampf*) day and night, ready to transport the troops. Only after one month did the military authorities contact the local governor to ask whether he still needed the troops to be kept ready for intervention. The local governor had apparently forgotten that he had asked for troops to be kept ready and was not aware that a train had been kept on steam day and night for more than a month. The affair developed into a major row when the rail company sent a bill of 1,200 Marks that both the military authorities and the provincial administration refused to pay.[32] After this bill had passed between the Interior Ministry and the War Ministry for several months, the Interior Minister grudgingly accepted financial responsibility, but subsequently urged civil servants to be extremely careful when contacting the military authorities for assistance.[33]

Even information about the most important measures decided within the military organisation could take a significant time before reaching the relevant civilian authorities: The instructions from War Minister von Heeringen of 8 February 1912[34] on the role of the army in handling popular unrest was only released to the Interior Ministry in June 1913, fifteen months after it had been presented to the army corps commanders.[35] Again, the delay is remarkable because in March 1912, while the War Ministry still refrained from informing the Interior Ministry about this decree, troops were mobilised in Westphalia for the third time since 1889.

Military refusal of commitment to any practical cooperation

Generals like von Albedyll or von Bissing did not entirely reject the idea of military engagement in civilian conflicts: General von Bissing's infamous Instructions of 1907 show that he saw this as a highly likely possibility. It was rather a refusal to enter into a continuing relationship with the civilian authorities, thus avoiding any commitment or responsibility that might tie the hands of the military commander – were it even ever so slightly. The relationship with civilian authorities was therefore kept strictly *ad hoc*.

The attitude of General von Bissing seems to be characteristic of Prussian army corps commanders. Certainly, their helpfulness and attentiveness towards senior members of the provincial administration varied, depending on the particular inclination of individual army corps commander, and General von Bissing was known to be particularly difficult. General von Einem – being a former War Minister and far more politically minded – seemed to have a more courteous relationship with the Province Governor von Ratibor.[36] However, the degree of civil-military cooperation and exchange of information was as low under General von

Einem as it had been under very detached commanders such as General von Bissing or General von Albedyll.

In addition to the low degree of cooperation and exchange of information with the provincial administration, the military commanders adopted an attitude of strict observance of the borderline between the civil and military authorities. Early in March 1912, General von Einem sent a message to Province Governor von Ratibor asking him how many copies of the 'black-lists' were available from the local police authorities. It is interesting to note that General von Einem makes clear that the question was posed for purely military considerations in the hypothetical case of a declaration of war, and had no relation to the ongoing labour dispute in the mining sector.[37] This courteous avoidance of even touching upon the question of possible military intervention in an ongoing labour dispute took place only seven days before troops were mobilised for the most extended military intervention since 1889. As late as two days before the intervention, the daily report of 11 March 1912 from the Local Governor in Lüdinghausen to the District Governor in Münster reveals that, among the various measures to be taken in this county, no provisions had been made for the possibility of a military intervention.[38] Thus, even a Province Governor and an Army Corps Commander, who otherwise claimed to have an excellent professional and personal relationship,[39] carefully avoided mentioning the possibility of military involvement in the policing of a major strike or any other form of practical cooperation. This is all the more striking when compared to the intense correspondence between prefects and army corps commanders in Nord-Pas-de- Calais before, during and after any significant strike or politically sensitive situation.

The mutual exclusion, which can be observed in the exchange of information, equally characterised the establishment of Civilian Plans for Protection in the event of major unrest. In Nord-Pas-de-Calais, much of the communication and exchange of information between civil and military authorities was linked to the establishment and updating of the plans for protection. In Prussia, by contrast, there is no indication of civil-military cooperation on this issue, but much evidence to the contrary. In addition to the plans and instructions developed by some army corps commanders, there were civilian plans established by the province and district governors in cooperation with mayors and local police authorities; but unlike the French situation, the military authorities were conspicuously absent from involvement in this planning.

During the great Westphalian miners' strike of 1889, a meeting was held in Dortmund on 10 May to discuss the policing of the conflict, five days after the military intervention. All the authorities concerned with the maintenance of order were present at the meeting: Interior Minister von Herrfurth; the Province Governor of Westphalia, von Hagenmeister; the district governors of the three districts concerned (Münster, Arnsberg and Düsseldorf); a mining inspector; the city mayor of Dortmund; five local governors from the counties most concerned (Dortmund, Essen, Gelsenkirchen, Hörde, and Bochum) as well as the public prosecutors of Recklinghausen and Bochum.[40] Despite the fact that the army was already involved and had assumed supreme authority over all police and *gendarmerie* forces in the province, and despite the prospect of declaring a state of siege being discussed at length, there was no military representative present at the meeting. The army corps commander in charge of the military intervention, General von Albedyll, had sent a copy of his instructions to the military commanders, mainly so that the civil authorities would know what the military would not do and what they expected the civilian forces to deal with.[41]

After the end of each major strike in Westphalia between 1889 and 1914, representatives from various sections of the Interior Ministry, the provincial administration and local authorities got together in order to draw lessons from the crisis, and prepare for similar situations in the future. At least four conferences were held in the Interior Ministry at which Prussian province governors discussed the organisation and distribution of the police and *gendarmerie* forces in case of major popular unrest. The lists distributing police and *gendarmerie* forces nationwide which resulted from this cooperation were regularly updated and revised. In 1904, the district governor of Düsseldorf organised a meeting in order to determine the measures to be taken in case of a greater strike among the miners. Similarly, after the military intervention in March 1912, a meeting was held with representatives from all the civilian authorities involved. At neither meeting was there any representative from the military authorities. The complete absence of military representatives is surprising because, even with the Prussian Interior Ministry and provincial administration seeking to avoid military participation in policing operations, the possibility of military intervention was discussed at length as a likely option.[42]

In contrast to the detailed civilian planning for incidents of major unrest, military preparations were strikingly underdeveloped. In Westphalia, the orders issued by General von Albedyll during the 1889 strike seem to have remained the only form of military planning for a situation of major unrest until General von Bissing's Instructions of 1907.[43] The military planning suffered from a series of defects. In the first place, the orders issued by General von Albedyll, as well as the instructions from General von Bissing, were a series of indications rather than detailed plans. They contained no information about the topographical and demographical features of the industrial areas; such information had to be obtained by local authorities at the moment of intervention.

Military preparations – insofar as they existed at all – covered only the military regions, as there was no coordination of military plans at national level. As late as 1912, a suggestion from the Interior Ministry to coordinate the military forces at national level was rejected by War Minister von Heeringen as completely unnecessary. Instead he pointed to the paragraph in the military service regulations of 1899 that insisted on the independence of military preparations.[44] As the military plans were not coordinated with the civilian plans either, there was a gap between the two sets of plans. The civilian plans foresaw all possible situations that might occur, right up to the moment when military involvement would be required. This was where the civilian plans stopped and the military planning was supposed to take over. However, all military plans started from the assumption that a military state of siege had been declared. Since such a situation never occurred in the period between 1889 and 1914 in all cases of domestic military intervention the authorities operated within a vacuum that neither the civilian nor the military authorities had foreseen.

The lack of coordination is all the more striking since, in the case of a military intervention, the army corps commander also became responsible for the organisation and command of all the police and *gendarmerie* forces within the military region. Yet the military plans were only concerned with the role of the troops, making no arrangements whatsoever for the police and *gendarmerie* forces under their command. The military authorities had no detailed knowledge of the size and organisation of the numerous local police forces that would come under their command; moreover the civilian authorities were unable to inform the chiefs of the numerous police corps of their role in the case of military intervention, because the military planning was considered a military secret. Thus the police and *gendarmerie* officers had no idea about how the military authorities would use them in case of a major conflict.

Military obstruction of the wishes of the civilian administration

Another important aspect of the military involvement in civilian conflicts was the refusal of the military authorities to allow military personnel or organisations to support civilian authorities by undertaking non-military tasks. In Prussia the separation between the civil administration and the army remained very clear and became increasingly strict by the eve of the First World War. This strict institutional separation existed alongside the widespread militarisation of Prussian society which took place during the same decades and profoundly shaped German society and culture. At the same time, many Prussian army corps commanders did their best to prevent military personnel from being deployed according to the wishes and needs expressed by the provincial administration.

One example of this was the discussion about the location of garrisons. Traditionally garrisons were placed within the main towns, with the specific role of performing police tasks.[45] This changed in the 1890s, partly because the large cities, in particular industrial ones, were thought to have a negative influence on conscript soldiers and officers.[46] General Loë, army corps commander in the Rhine Province, expressed himself in very clear terms in a letter to Waldersee: if local communities wanted protection, they should organise a sufficient police force and pay for it.[47] A similar response was given to the Province Governor of Silesia immediately after the end of the miners' strike of 1889, when he suggested that a military garrison ought to be established in the Waldenburg coal mining area.[48] This request was refused from the War Ministry on the grounds that the military authorities saw no need for a military post in the district.[49] Thus, after 1889, new garrisons were to be established only according to strategic need and not out of consideration for the possibility of popular unrest. Accordingly, there was no garrison in the entire district of Arnsberg, which was one of the most turbulent areas in the entire German Empire and included several large industrial centres north of the River Ruhr (Dortmund, Essen, Bochum, Recklinghausen, Gelsenkirchen, and Herne). In cases of requisition of troops, soldiers had to be mobilised from the neighbouring district of Düsseldorf. In contrast, the important Münster garrison was located in a small provincial town in the rural part of Westphalia. This was very different from Nord-Pas-de-Calais, where several garrisons established in the years between 1890 and 1914 were located in industrial areas with the explicit purpose of facilitating intervention with troops.[50]

Another important difference between French and Prussian practice concerned the use of soldiers and reservists in performing non-military functions. In France, reservists and even civilian members of semi-military organisations (i.e. members of the voluntary fire-brigade, customs officers, pupils in the military academies, and even members of a military orchestra) were occasionally requested to participate in the maintenance of public order or in undertaking strike-bound work. In Prussia, by contrast, formal military status could be used to justify refusal of assistance to the civilian administration. A particularly pertinent illustration is the request made in December 1910 by the District Governor in Düsseldorf to the local Automobile Association (*Das freiwilligen Automobilkorps*) to borrow their cars for the transportation of policemen during major policing operations. The request referred to the Automobile Association's obligation to transport military troops in case of a general mobilisation. Interestingly the president of the association refused on the grounds that the Automobile Association was a military corps: because of its military status, he argued, the use of the Association's cars was only possible as part of a requisition of military troops. Furthermore, he pointed out that the vehicles had to be driven by the members of the Association and these would be in military uniform and covered by military legislation.[51] The case of the Automobile Association was rather thin since legally they would only obtain military status in case of a general mobilisation. However, it seems to have been sufficient to avoid further approaches from the provincial administration. The District Governor immediately drew the conclusion that it would not be worthwhile to address the request to the War Ministry, and instead suggested to his colleague in Münster that they hired the cars they needed from private companies.[52]

A similarly strict distinction between military and civilian society can be discerned behind the demand from the War Ministry in 1911 not to use soldiers for crowd management on the occasion of an air display.[53] Despite the fact that aviation associations were semi-military corps – like the automobile associations – and that aerodromes were usually located on military fields, soldiers were not allowed to participate in the management of the crowd. As with the Automobile Association, military status could be – and indeed was – used to justify non-assistance to the civilian authorities.

Given the unwillingness of the military authorities to meet the needs of the civilian authorities in crowd management within military territory, it is hardly surprising that there was even greater reluctance towards allowing soldiers to perform strictly non-military functions. Although sanctioned by law,[54] the use of military troops for non-military purposes appears to have been a very rare event. Throughout the entire German Empire, only two cases have been identified. One of these was in 1896, on the occasion of a strike among roof workers in Königsberg. Eleven soldiers from the engineers were sent to finish the roofing of a number of buildings. When Bebel asked in the *Reichstag* how soldiers could be used to undertake strikebound work, the War Minister, Walter Bronsart von Schellendorf, made clear that, in principle, the use of soldiers for such purposes was not allowed.[55] His justification for this exceptional use was that, in this particular case, the strikers were actually working on military barracks, and that the use of troops was not an attempt to favour the employer against the employees, but rather the need for the army to have the work done immediately. Bronsart von Schellendorf stressed that soldiers could be ordered to perform strike-bound work only if military interests or the financial interests of the State were at stake.

Similarly, in 1904, Prussian military authorities accepted that, in the case of a strike among rail personnel, soldiers could be sent to protect public and private railway lines.[56] This was justified, as in France, by referring to the strategic importance of the railway system. However the soldiers were only to be used to prevent sabotage against the rails. The fact that rail strikes paralysed the transport of persons and goods and affected industrial production and foreign trade was of no concern to the army.

Only at one occasion were troops mobilised to defend the interests of wider society. In October 1905, a strike broke out among electricians of the AEG company. Confronted with the possibility of Berlin's electricity being cut off, soldiers from the engineers were sent to ensure basic services.[57]

Despite these isolated cases where military personnel were involved directly in labour disputes, the military authorities generally refused any commitment or assistance to the provincial administration. Given this unwillingness to provide them with even minor practical assistance, it is hardly surprising that, when confronted with problems of policing popular protest, the province and district governors preferred to cooperate with local police authorities and chose to spend significant resources on developing sufficient policing forces rather than depending on military assistance. In contrast to Nord-Pas-de-Calais, where the regional administration was preoccupied with intensifying and improving cooperation with the army, the provincial administration in Westphalia sought to improve the organisation and efficiency of the civil forces, in order to avoid depending on the army. Whilst strategies developed in France that increasingly depended on military assistance, the strategies developed by the Prussian state authorities, in cooperation with local authorities, did not rely upon the army, either to provide manpower or material.

Entrenchment of the institutional compartmentalism

In the light of such strong military opposition to any form of preparation or commitment to assisting the provincial administration in handling popular unrest, it is striking that, after each military intervention in Westphalia, both civil and military authorities praised their excellent mutual relationship. After the intervention in Herne of June 1899, the civilian administrators from Province Governor Konrad Studt down to local governors, mayors and police authorities praised their excellent relationship with the military commanders throughout the crisis.[58] Similarly after the military intervention in March 1912, the civil-military cooperation was described as a success by both civilian and military authorities.[59]

However, in most of the documents 'excellent cooperation' appears to mean no more than lack of open conflict or perceived violation of the institutional integrity of either authority. Quite obviously both civilian and military authorities expected cooperation to be extremely difficult, conflictual and highly unpredictable. The low frequency of military intervention, limited communication and lack of coordination of plans, led to any practical cooperation between civil and military authorities being characterised by lack of mutual trust. Neither the civil nor the military authorities were entirely certain about each other's intentions, and both seemed to fear being trapped in actions and commitments that they would rather avoid.

During the Imperial era, military intervention in Westphalia was never sufficiently frequent for standard operating procedures to develop around the civil-military cooperation, as they did in Nord-Pas-de-Calais. Most commanders and civil servants would only experience military involvement in protest policing once during their time in service. In consequence, there was widespread uncertainty and confusion about the details of the legal framework for civil-military cooperation. After the 1912 intervention, General von Einem complained of widespread ignorance among civil servants about the legal definitions of authority during military intervention in peacetime.[60] Similarly many commanding officers did not know the law, particularly when it came to the clauses detailing the rights of strikers and civilians in general.[61] Yet even if the commanding officers had been acquainted with the details of the legislation, this still left many questions open concerning how to operate in practice. Moreover, since transfer of all civilian powers to the military authorities was a highly sensitive issue, the provincial administration and the military authorities had never reached a final agreement on the exact definition of this point. The practical relationship between civilian and military authorities therefore had to be re-negotiated at all levels each time the military troops were mobilised.

Together with the absence of standard operating procedures, important issues were left open to potential conflict, so that the civilian authorities, when calling on the army, had to operate with a high number of unknown factors. In the French system, the insistence on consensus between civil and military authorities, and the requirement of joint decision making, provided a certain degree of mutual confidence. In Nord-Pas-de-Calais the civilian administration could influence measures implemented by the military; conversely, when occasionally a sensitive situation went badly wrong, the

French military commander would be much less exposed to criticism because he implemented measures that had been agreed with the prefect. In Westphalia, by contrast, the uncertainty and lack of consensus about the procedures to be followed and the strategies to be implemented only exacerbated the potential for and expectation of conflict between civilian and military authorities.

Another significant element of uncertainty was the question of financial responsibility. The law stated that it was the requesting authority who was financially responsible. In 1889 when the military intervention in the great miners' strike was extended over many administrative units, the troops were solicited partly by local authorities and local governors, and partly by private companies, even if the formal requisition was issued by the district and province governors. The total costs of the 1889 intervention were 366,345 *Marks* and seventy-five *Pfennig* for the military troops and *gendarmes* in four military regions. However the financial responsibility was almost impossible to locate. The Prussian State eventually assumed financial responsibility after the 1889 strike, but this was an isolated and exceptional case; the question remained open and general confusion continued to exist amongst Prussian civil servants as to who was to carry the responsibility for the costs of a military intervention.

In 1903, during the row over who should pay the bill from the local rail company that had kept a train on steam for one month on the request of a garrison commander,[62] the War Minister declared that the bill should be paid by the municipality of Welten. Refusing to penalise the citizens of Welten for behaving in such an orderly manner that there had been no reason for mobilising the troops, the Interior Ministry finally agreed to pay the bill. Similarly in all the cases of intervention in Westphalia, the Interior Ministry eventually covered the costs, but only after months of discussion. After the intervention in June 1899, the issue was only settled in December, and following the 1912 intervention, the debate went on from March to November. It was only settled when the state again agreed to foot the bill.

This uncertainty made province and district governors seriously hesitate about calling upon the army. Factors in dispute, such as the lack of military preparedness, confusion about the details of the rules defining the distribution of powers, financial responsibility, and the strategies to be implemented, were exacerbated as military interventions became rare. With very few reference points to previous interventions and no standard procedures, it is hardly surprising that civilian authorities, from the province governors to local mayors, expected cooperation with the military to be cumbersome, frustrating and potentially very expensive.

The lack of mutual trust

The extent to which civilian authorities were allowed any influence on essential aspects of policing operation once the army was involved entirely depended on the individual army corps commander. Praise by civilian authorities of their 'excellent' relationship with the military authorities should be viewed in this light. Any level of cooperation where the military commander turned out to be attentive to the recommendation of the civilian authorities was therefore regarded as a success.

Prussian officers and general commanders were known for their arrogant attitude towards civilians and for their lack of respect for legal boundaries. Accordingly the civil servants in the provincial administration could never be sure which actions the military authorities might decide to go ahead with. Some senior commanders seemed to have no hesitation in intervening against civilians, with or without a formal requisition from the civil authorities. Similarly, von Albedyll, von Waldersee, or von Bissing had no qualms about implementing military measures without regard to the wishes of the civil administration.[63] In 1909 Hindenburg firmly insisted on making all decisions himself, down to the smallest detail, independent of the civilian authorities.[64] Similarly, neither the General Staff Study of 1907, nor the Instructions from General von Bissing, took the civilian authorities into consideration: both studies operate out of the assumption that a military state of siege would be declared so that all powers and responsibilities were transferred from the civilian to the military authorities.[65]

It appears from the correspondence in 1903–1904 between the District Governor in Potsdam and the Interior Minister, concerning the independent military initiative in Welten,[66] that the civil servants perceived the military authorities as a difficult, unreliable and often irresponsible partner for cooperation.[67] The incident in Welten was only one of many showing how difficult it was to hold military commanders accountable for their decisions and actions, or make the War Ministry assume financial responsibility for errors committed by any military officer. Even under the best of circumstances, province and district governors were unlikely to feel confident about handing over all powers to senior generals whose respect for civilian institutions and laws was known to be limited. The unsolicited military intervention against civilians in the Alsacian town of Zabern in 1913 showed all too clearly that anything might be expected from military commanders. It is therefore hardly surprising that the state administration considered any practical cooperation with the military authorities as a potential source of trouble.

Military compliance to the recommendations of the civilian authorities

Despite the lack of trust in the military commanders as reliable partners of cooperation, it appears that during the military interventions in 1899 and 1912 the military authorities generally followed the recommendations of the civilian administration.[68]

The military authorities carefully maintained the image of an army entirely in charge of legitimate violence, ready to intervene – if necessary – against civilian institutions and wider society. In practice, however, the civil-military cooperation in Westphalia slightly differed from this image. During the military interventions of 1889, 1899 and 1912, the army corps commander had both legal authority as well as orders directly from Wilhelm II to implement whatever measures he considered appropriate, without any regard for the wishes of the civilian administration.

Yet, by the intervention in Herne in 1899, General von Mikusch did not make much use of his right to independent decision-making. Although Wilhelm II had made him personally responsible for restoring order,[69] General von Mikusch implied in all his telegrams to Berlin that for all the important decisions concerning when to mobilise, where to intervene, and when to send back the troops, he closely followed the wishes of the Province Governor.[70] He thus detached himself from the responsibility which Wilhelm II had placed upon him.

Similarly in 1912, when General von Einem sent troops into the Westphalian mining areas, he emphasised that he mobilised troops at the explicit request of the civilian authorities.[71] Many years later, General von Einem claimed that he alone had been in charge of the handling of the measures implemented.[72] However the reports from the civilian authorities after the end of the strike provide a slightly different picture: that it was the civilian authorities who guided the military troops.[73] One local governor even claimed that there had been no proper command of the few conscript soldiers sent to his area, so that the military units had in fact been under police command.[74]

Part of the explanation for the military compliance may be that, despite the extended powers and freedom of action enjoyed by the army corps commander, he needed to cover his back. While mass strikes became increasingly politically sensitive, it was not always obvious what Wilhelm II would regard as a successful military intervention. Both a heavy handed or a smoother intervention might go badly wrong and if people were killed and the army were vilified in the press, the responsible commander might be reprimanded by the *Kaiser*.

Confronted with these sensitive situations General von Mikusch, and later General von Einem, repeatedly referred to the consensus with the provincial administration.[75] Similarly throughout the Zabern Affair, General von Deimling attempted to put the blame on the provincial administration for having verbally agreed to the illegal military intervention; this was a difficult case to argue and General von Deimling's difficulties can be discerned in some significant inconsistencies between the printed version of his memoirs and the unprinted manuscript.[76]

The most compelling reason for the military commanders to accommodate to the wishes of the civilian authorities seems to be that they had themselves no serious alternatives. In 1899 and in 1912, the military authorities were just as unprepared as they had been during the 1889 strike for intervention in a major labour conflict. They did not possess the experience and knowledge required for handling major policing operations and decisions had to be taken *ad hoc* at a moment when the conflict had already developed into a serious crisis. In both 1899 and 1912, this left the army corps commander with two options: he could, as Albedyll did in 1889, insist on his right of command and restore order with coercive military measures without regard to the wishes of the civil administration; the other option was to closely follow the recommendations of the civilian authorities.

It was the province and district governors who had both the detailed knowledge and the experience of dealing with labour conflicts. They provided the necessary detailed information about the number of policemen available in the area, the number of workers employed in the industries and mines concerned, the geographical position of the mine shafts, as well as the locations most exposed to sabotage and attacks on strike-breakers. It is therefore hardly surprising if military commanders ended up carefully following the indications from the province and district governors of how many soldiers were needed and where to send them.[77]

Bureaucratic procedures and demilitarisation of protest policing

The difficult and uncertain relationship between civilian and military authorities in Westphalia, the absence of standard procedures for military participation in large-scale policing operations, the lack of coordination of plans or exchange of knowledge, these were all significant factors in shaping the decisions by successive province and district governors as it made the military solution highly unattractive. It was merely coincidental that the increasing preference for non-military solutions was also in line with the recommendations issued by the Prussian Interior Ministry. The non-military solution was easy to justify in political terms, yet the driving force behind the demilitarisation lay as much in the dynamics between the civilian authorities and the military commanders as in any political considerations.

The high levels of compartmentalism in Westphalia sharply contrasts with the intensive exchange of information between prefects and army corps commanders in Nord-Pas-de-Calais and their close practical cooperation on planning for major strikes. Within the Prussian system, the exchange of knowledge and the process of settling practical issues concerning civil-military cooperation were both slower and far more cumbersome than in Nord-Pas-de-Calais. Issues were first discussed at different levels within the provincial administration, and only then, at a late stage, presented to the army corps commander.

There was also considerable uncertainty among Prussian authorities as to the political implications of military intervention. As it became an increasingly rare event in Westphalia, the political significance of calling upon military assistance increased. In Nord-Pas-de-Calais, the presence of troops had become almost trivial. The prefects who repeatedly called for military assistance had experienced these situations many times before, they had a good sense of what public reactions were likely to be, and how to limit the potential damage of a contentious military intervention. Westphalian authorities, by contrast, could not form a clear idea of how protesters were likely to react. Nor could they foresee the extent of public outcry in case of violent confrontations between civilians and the army: taking the unusual step of involving the army might spark the kind popular revolt that Prussian authorities most feared. Rather than taking a route that was full of uncertainties and unpredictable consequences, the leaders of the provincial administration in Westphalia tended to prefer handling mass protest much the same way they handled small-scale gatherings – and keep the military option as distant as possible.

Notes

[1] Henning (1987) pp. 140–145.
[2] Cabinet Orders of 29 October 1819 and of 17 October 1820. Similarly a confidential instruction of November 1846 from Interior Minister Bodelschwingh to the Province Governors. (cit. Lüdtke, 1982, p. 161.)
[3] CA, Potsdam III, R 43, film signature 12425–12426 (Documents 2–4): Instructions of 20 March 1890.
[4] The military Service Regulations, 1899, Article II,1.

[5] HSA, Münster, OP 6095 (document 103): Circular of 24 May 1910 from War Minister von Heeringen to the Army Corps Commanders.

[6] Decree from the War Ministry of 19 March 1891 'Allgemeine Gesichtspunkte für die Gestellung von militärischen Kommandos zur Hülfeleistung bei etwa eintretender Wassernoth'; Cabinet Order of 6 January 1899 'Bestimmungen über militärische Hülfs-Kommandos bei öffentlichen Nothständen'.

[7] French decree of 4 October 1891on civilian and military authorities in garrison towns, Article 63.

[8] See Chapter 8.

[9] MA, Freiburg, PH2 /466 or CA, Potsdam III, R 43, film signature 12425–12426: Instructions of 22 March 1890 from War Minister Verdy du Vernois to the army corps commanders.

[10] Deist (1991, 1) p. 25; Höhn (1969) p. 67.

[11] Höhn (1969) pp. 395–396.

[12] MA, Freiburg, PH2 /467–470, 'Bekämpfung socialdemokratischer und pazifistischer Bestrebungen, 1900–1912'.

[13] MA, Freiburg, PH2 /468 : Letter of 3 May 1911 from War Minister von Heeringen to the army corps commanders; Idem. (document 259–264): Confidential report (c. March 1911) established on behalf of War Minister von Heeringen on the increase of social democratic influence among reservists.

[14] MA, Freiburg, PH2 /466 (document 175–178): Letter of August 7 1891 from General von Waldersee, commander of the ninth army corps, to the War Ministry.

[15] Demeter (1965) pp. 171–172.

[16] MA, Freiburg, PH2 /466 (document 134): Report of February 1891 from General von Haenish, army corps commander in Magdeburg, to the War Ministry.

[17] Demeter (1965) p. 172; Messerschmidt (1980) p. 70; Deist (1991) p. 36.

[18] MA, Freiburg, PH2 /468: Letter of 5 April 1907 from War Minister von Einem to the army corps commanders.

[19] MA, Freiburg, PH2 /466 or CA, Potsdam III, R 43, film signature 12425–12426: Instructions of 22 March 1890 from War Minister Verdy du Vernois to the army corps commanders.

[20] HSA, Münster, OP 6095 (document 190): Letter of 27 November 1912 from Interior Minister Dallwitz to Province Governor von Ratibor of Westphalia.

[21] HSA, Münster, OP 6095 (document 186): Letter of 10 January 1913 from General Einem, army corps commander in Münster, to Province Governor von Ratibor.

[22] HSA, Münster, OP 6095 (document 187): Letter of 18 January 1913 from the Province Governor of Westphalia to the Army Corps Commander in Frankfurt. HSA, Münster, OP 6095 (document 192): Letter of 25 January 1913 from the Army Corps Commander in Frankfurt to Province Governor von Ratibor of Westphalia. HSA, Münster, Regierung Münster, VII–52 Vol.2/ 39-2 (document 78): Letter of 5 February 1913 from Province Governor von Ratibor of Westphalia to Province Governor von Rheinbaben of the Rhine Province.

[23] CA, Potsdam III, R 43, film signature 12425–12426, 'Militärische massnahmen im Falle von Unruhen. Belagerungszustand 1890–1918'.

272   *Soldiers as Police*

[24] HSA, Münster, OP 6095: (document 206–213): Decree of 8 February 1912 from War Minister von Heeringen to the army corps commanders entitled 'Verwendung von Truppen zur Unterdrückung innere Unruhen'; idem. (document 204): Letter of 28 June 1913 from Interior Minister von Dallwitz to the province governors.

[25] Henning (1987) p.160.

[26] GSA, Berlin, H.A.1, Rep. 77, Title 2513 /1, Beiheft 5 (documents 90–104). Correspondence January–February 1890 between the Interior Ministry, the Province Governor of Westphalia and the District Governor of Arnsberg concerning measures and preparations in case of requisition of troops.

[27] HSA, Münster, Regierung Münster, VII–57 Vol. 1 (document 197): Letter of 31 August 1904 from the Interior Minister to Province Governor von der Recke of Westphalia.

[28] HSA, Münster, OP 6095 (document 37): Letter of 6 September 1904 from Province Governor von Nasse of the Rhine Province to Province Governor von der Recke of Westphalia.

[29] HSA, Münster, OP 6095 (documents 69–70): Letter of 28 March 1906 from Province Governor von der Recke of Westphalia to the Army Corps Commander, General von Bissing. HSA, Münster, OP 6095: Letter of 7 March 1906 from Province Governor von Schorlemer-Lieser of the Rhine Province to Province Governor von der Recke of Westphalia.

[30] HSA, Münster, OP 6095 (document 71): Letter of 6 April 1906 from General von Bissing, army corps commander in Münster, to Province Governor von der Recke of Westphalia.

[31] HSA, Münster, OP 6095 (document 80): Letter of 16 October 1906 from Army Corps Commander von Bissing to Province Governor von der Recke.

[32] GSA, Berlin, HA1, Rep. 77, Titel 2513 /1, Beiheft 9 (documents 63–73).

[33] GSA, Berlin, HA1, Rep. 77, Titel 2513 /1 Beiheft 9 (document 103) Letter of 24 May 1904 from the Interior Ministry to all District Governors.

[34] HSA, Münster, OP 6095 (documents 206–213): Decree of 8 February 1912 entitled 'Verwendung von Truppen zur Unterdrückung innere Unruhen'.

[35] HSA, Münster, OP 6095 (document 204): Letter of 28 June 1913 from Interior Minister Dallwitz to the province governors.

[36] See Chapter 4.

[37] HSA, Münster, OP 6095 (document 157): Letter of 7 March 1912 from General von Einem, army corps commander in Münster, to the Province Governor von Ratibor of Westphalia.

[38] HSA, Münster, Regierung Münster, VII–14 Vol. 5/ 37–3 (document 22).

[39] Einem (1933) p. 168.

[40] CA, Potsdam III, R 43, film signature 11971–11972 (documents 71–90) or HSA, Münster, OP 14317, (documents 53–73): Minutes of the meeting in Dortmund, 10 May 1889.

[41] CA, Potsdam III, R 43, film signature 11971–11972 (documents 91–92) or HSA, Münster, OP 14317 (documents 74–75): Instructions from General von Albedyll, May 1889.

[42] GSA, HA1, Rep. 77, Titel 2513 /1, Beiheft 9 (documents 124–130): Minutes from meeting Düsseldorf, 7 July 1904; GSA, HA1, Rep. 77, Titel 2523 /1, Adh. 1, Vol. 20 or HSA Münster, Regierung Münster, VII–14, Vol. 1 /32–1: Minutes from meeting in Essen 1 June 1912.

[43] During the miners' strike of 1905, General von Albedyll's orders were still the only existing plans for Westphalia.

[44] HSA, Münster, OP 6095, (documents 206–215): Instructions from the War Ministry to the army corps commanders of 8 February 1912. "Neben den auf Seite 26 der 'Vorschrift über den Waffengebrauch des Militärs' vorgesehenen Vorbereitungen sind von den meisten Kommandostellen weitgehende Anforderungen getroffen".

[45] Lüdtke (1982) p. 238.

[46] Demeter (1965) pp. 171–172; Höhn (1969) pp. 395–396.

[47] Waldersee (1927) pp. 367–368.

[48] GSA, Berlin, HA1, Rep.77, Titel 2513/1, Beiheft 4, (document 221): Letter of 4 July 1889.

[49] GSA, Berlin, HA1, Rep.77, Titel 2513/1, Beiheft 5 (documents 19–20): Letter of 9 January 1890 from the War Minister to the Interior Ministry.

[50] See Chapter 9.

[51] HSA, Münster, Münster Regierung, VII–52 a. (document 22): Letter of 15 January 1911 from the District Governor in Düsseldorf to the District Governor in Münster.

[52] HSA, Münster, Münster Regierung, VII–52 a. (document 22): Letter of 15 January 1911 from the District Governor in Düsseldorf to the District Governor in Münster.

[53] HSA, Münster, OP 6095, (document 122): Letter of 16 April 1911 from the Interior Minister to the Prussian District Governors.

[54] Decree from the War Ministry of 19 March 1891 'Allgemeine Gesichtspunkte für die Gestellung von militärischen Kommandos zur Hülfeleistung bei etwa eintretender Wassernoth'; Cabinet Order of 6 January 1899 'Bestimmungen über militärische Hülfs-Kommandos bei öffentlichen Nothständen'.

[55] Minutes from the *Reichstag* of 19 February 1896.

[56] HSA, Münster, OP 6095 (documents 34–37): Regulations of 7 July 1904 'Gestellung militärischer Hilfe im Falle von Arbeitseinstellung der Eisenbahnbediensten einschließlich des Personals des amtlichen Bahnspediteure.'

[57] MA, Freiburg, PH2/14, (documents 216–221).

[58] HSA, Münster, Regierung Arnsberg, 14321: Correspondence between the commander, Colonel Taubert, and the senior administrators in Arnsberg and Bochum, 10–13 July 1899; idem.: Report of 17 July 1899 from the district governor of Arnsberg 'Zusammenfassender Bericht der Ereignisse im Herner Bergarbeiterausstande'.

[59] Einem (1933) p. 168. HSA, Münster, Regierung Münster, VII–14, vol. 1 /32–1, (documents 5–10): Report of 20 May 1912 from the District Governor in Münster to Interior Minister Dallwitz. HSA, Münster, Regierung Münster, VII–14, vol. 5

274   *Soldiers as Police*

/37–3 (documents 41–42): Daily report of 18 March 1912 from the Local Governor of Lüdinghausen to the District Governor in Münster.

[60] HSA, Münster, OP 6095 (document 177): Letter of 28 August 1912 from General von Einem to Province Governor von Ratibor of Westphalia.

[61] HSA, Münster, Regierung Münster, VII–14, vol. 1/ 32–1 or GSA, Berlin, HA1, Rep. 77, Titel 2523/1 (adh.1), vol. 20: Minutes from a meeting 1 June 1912 at the Local Governor in Essen.

[62] See above p. 258

[63] Waldersee (1922) vol. 2 p. 200. Diary entry of 15 March 1891.

[64] MA, Freiburg, PH2/14, (documents 246–248; 250–252): General Hindenburg's reports to Wilhelm II of 23 and 28 October 1909.

[65] CA, Potsdam III, R 43, film signature 12425–12426, (documents 47–50).

[66] GSA, Berlin, HA1, Rep. 77, Titel 2513 /1, Beiheft 9 (documents 63–73).

[67] GSA, Berlin, HA1, Rep.77, Titel 2513/1, Beiheft 9, (documents 63–66): Letter of 15 January 1904 from the District Governor in Potsdam to Interior Minister von Hammerstein.

[68] HSA, Münster, Regierung Münster, VII–14, vol.1 /32–1 (documents 5–10): Report of 20 May 1912 from the District Governor in Münster to Interior Minister von Dallwitz.

[69] MA, Freiburg, PH2 /14 (document 187): Telegram of 28 June 1899 from Wilhelm II to the Military Cabinet.

[70] MA, Freiburg, PH2 /14 (documents 188–189): Telegram of 28 June 1899 from General von Mikusch to Wilhelm II; MA, Freiburg, PH2 /14 (documents 204–206). Telegrams of 5–10 July 1899 from General von Mikusch to Wilhelm II.

[71] MA, Freiburg, PH2/14: Telegrams of 14 March 1912 from General von Einem to the King.

[72] Einem (1933) p. 168.

[73] HSA, Münster, Regierung Münster, VII–14, vol. 1 /32–1, (documents 5–10): Report of 20 May 1912 from the District Governor in Münster to Interior Minister von Dallwitz.

[74] HSA, Münster, Regierung Münster, VII–14, vol. 1 /32–1, or GSA, Berlin, Rep. 77, Titel 2523 /1 Adh. 1, vol. 20: Minutes from a meeting 1 June 1912 at the Local Governor in Essen.

[75] MA, Freiburg, PH2 /14 (documents 191–192): Telegram of 29 June 1899 from General von Mikusch to Wilhelm II; idem. (documents 205–206): Telegrams of 7 and 10 July 1899 from General von Mikusch to Wilhelm II; idem. (documents 209–211); Report of 2 July 1899 from General von Mikusch to Wilhelm II; idem. (documents 258, 260, 265): Telegrams of 13–21 March 1912 from General von Einem, army corps commander in Münster, to Wilhelm II.

[76] Deimling (1930) pp. 146–148; MA, Freiburg, N 559: Private papers of General von Deimling.

[77] HSA, Münster, Regierung Münster, VII–14, vol. 3 /37–1 (documents 102–105): Letters of 14 March 1912 from the District Governor in Münster to General von Einem, army corps commander in Münster.

Chapter 11

Conclusions:
Demilitarisation and 'Modern' Policing

The political and institutional context of dissimilar policing policies

When the Prussian Interior Ministry embarked on its policy of demilitarising protest policing the ministerial authorities justified it by pointing out the serious disadvantages connected with the use of conscript soldiers: that infantry and cavalry units could only operate in inflexible military formations; that the mere presence of military troops at a scene of conflict contributed to the escalation of violent confrontations; and that young conscript soldiers were unfit for the policing of sensitive conflicts because they lacked personal authority, were inexperienced, and might easily begin to shoot in panic. Historians have therefore tended to explain the gradual demilitarisation of protest policing during the Wilhelmine era in terms of this political rationale. Yet in order to fully understand the demilitarisation process we need to consider the dynamics that shaped the bureaucratic decision-making at the regional level.

In the first place, the difficult relationship with the military authorities was a major incentive for the Prussian Interior Ministry to recommend military involvement being kept to a strict minimum. Compared to their Prussian counterparts, the authorities of the French Third Republic had more urgent reasons to be deeply concerned about the potentially damaging effects of involving the army in the policing of protest because bloody confrontations could easily undermine the political legitimacy of the Republican regime. French authorities were equally aware that frequent military intervention might alienate important sectors of the French population; it might also affect soldiers' loyalty and increase the likelihood of soldiers joining the protesters. This was all the more serious since popular support for the regime was a precondition for maintaining the fragile political compromise upon which the Republic was established. At the same time, the regime desperately needed the support from those officers who were increasingly unhappy about their role in the policing of public disorder.

From this perspective, the policy of the French Interior Ministry to rely heavily on the army for the policing of protest appears extremely reckless and counter-productive. The frequent use of troops only makes sense if we accept that successive French Interior Ministers, as well as the senior civil servants and military commanders who were in charge of preparing and implementing large-scale policing operations, actually believed that this was the most effective way of preventing, or at least containing, violent clashes with protesters. As Paris Police Prefect Lépine began to experiment with new approaches to protest policing and crowd management, some of the features of his 'prevention and containment' strategy were used even when military troops were involved. In areas outside Paris, military participation was in fact a precondition for implementing strategies of prevention and containment because this approach required the mobilisation of extensive numbers of men.

Military involvement was politically controversial; however a protest that got out of hand and required unrestricted military actions – similar to the repression of the Paris *Commune* – might very well spell the end of the Republican regime. Confronted with this dilemma, the French Interior Ministry gave priority to the safe – although politically controversial – solution of involving the army in the policing of any situation with some potential for violence and disorder.

The dynamics of bureaucratic procedures: plans and preparations

From the 1890s, while the Prussian Interior Ministry began to urge provincial administrations to refrain from using soldiers for policing, the recommendations issued by the French Interior Ministry called for ever closer civil-military cooperation. In both Westphalia and Nord-Pas-de-Calais the ministerial recommendations were implemented with increasing consistency up to the outbreak of the First World War. The level of consistency is remarkable, since both senior civil administrators and army corps commanders enjoyed significant levels of discretion to implement the policing measures they thought most appropriate.

When comparing civil-military cooperation in Nord-Pas-de-Calais and Westphalia, it appears that the relationship between the civilian administration and the senior military commanders was a highly significant factor in shaping the priorities of the authorities at the regional level. Within the French and Prussian systems, the levels of military preparations as well as the existence of detailed plans and procedures for large-scale policing operations strongly shaped decisions towards re-implementing measures which had been followed previously.

In the French case, the bureaucratic mechanisms helped to sustain close civil-military cooperation, while the dynamics within the Prussian system exacerbated already existing tendencies towards institutional compartmentalism. In Westphalia, the leaders of the provincial administration and military commanders were first and foremost concerned with their institutional independence. Province and district governors became increasingly disinclined to cooperate with military commanders whose actions could neither be controlled nor constrained. For their part, Prussian commanding generals were increasingly reluctant to become involved in the messy and disagreeable task of policing strikes and demonstrations.

In both countries the establishment of plans for the handling of large-scale protest had major implications for the likelihood of involving the army or refraining from doing so. In France the ministerial plans for large-scale protest policing involved the army from the outset. Civilian and military authorities were both involved in the development of these plans, they shared all relevant knowledge, and were equally aware of the aims, strategies and procedures in case of military mobilisation.

In Prussia by contrast the plans developed by the civilian authorities only covered situations up to the moment when the military became involved; beyond this point the Prussian civilian authorities had no influence on the strategies followed by the commanding general. The military authorities, for their part, had little knowledge of the areas they were moving into: all relevant information had to be provided by the civilian authorities while the conflict was unfolding.

As the plans and strategies for large-scale policing operations became entrenched in the bureaucratic practice in Nord-Pas-de-Calais, the French authorities became increasingly likely to call for military assistance. Conversely, the civilian authorities in Westphalia did their best to postpone the requisition of troops in order to remain in control as long as possible. Long before reaching considerations of the wider political implications of involving the Prussian army in protest policing, the provincial administration would have to overcome numerous uncertainties, not least the possibility of outright obstruction from the military commanders. This made any cooperation with the military authorities, even on minor practical issues, cumbersome, unpredictable and highly unattractive.

At the same time, any deviation from the standard measures was a complicated undertaking because all logistics and preparations for large-scale policing operations were geared towards one particular type of approach. It is therefore not surprising that the strategies for handling large-scale protest were characterised by long-term continuity, just like other complex policy areas. Changes in the overall approach came slowly and there were strong tendencies to continue implementing strategies that had worked before. Occasionally bureaucrats and government ministers deviated from the main approach, but this required re-thinking of all aspects of strategies and procedures, and held significant potential for unpredictability and loss of control.

Patterns of elite cooperation in Westphalia and Nord-Pas-de-Calais

Studies of the German-Prussian State of the Wilhelmine era have observed numerous aspects of non-cooperation and mutual exclusion between the civilian sections of the German-Prussian state and the military establishment. Yet it is often assumed that civilian and military authorities would be strongly inclined to cooperate at least in defending the existing social and political order against popular protest and labour disputes. Officially there were attempts to unite major institutions (the civil service, the army, the Lutheran Church) with conservative and liberal forces in order to stop the rise of the Social Democratic Party. Yet the reality was all too often that civilian and military authorities worked in opposite directions. As this study shows, the fragmentation and compartimentalism characterised the functioning of the system not only in Berlin but also at the provincial level. Even when it came to policing mass protest in one of the largest industrial areas in Europe there was a lack of exchange of information and coordination between civilian and military authorities. Although this was hardly to be regretted by the protesters, it speaks volumes about the extent of the polycracy and fragmentation that characterised the Wilhelmine reign.

The extent of the compartimentalism within the German-Prussian system becomes particularly noticeable when compared to the close civil-military cooperation in France. The French Republic had to reckon with numerous latent conflicts in relation to its army: deep social, cultural and political fractures divided the military elite and the representatives of the Republican institutions: the Dreyfus Affair; the secret military files of War Minister André; the government's attempt to break the institutional independence of the French army; and the use of troops to implement highly controversial anti-Catholic legislation. All this fuelled widespread alienation and bitterness within the French officer corps. Nevertheless, when it came to the practical issue of policing popular protest, civilian and military authorities managed to establish a working relationship based on shared knowledge and negotiated plans. Thus, strategies and procedures were understood, agreed to and scrupulously followed by the majority of the military commanders involved.

In both countries, industrial pressure groups were largely marginalised from any influence on whether and how to use troops during labour disputes. The policies of protest policing in Westphalia and Nord-Pas-de-Calais were driven by government authorities and the senior civil servants in the provincial or *départemental* administration. Although support for trade and industry was a major concern for the French and German governments and administrations, industrial pressure groups and individuals were kept well away from influence on decisions concerning military involvement in policing. It was the perceived interest of the State that was the driving factor behind government policies and bureaucratic practices; that French employers benefited from the choice of strategy was a side effect rather than the actual cause. The Prussian State was generally as willing as was that of France to support the interests of great industry. However, when it came to involving the army in the policing of labour disputes, it was the military reluctance to become involved that prevailed over any consideration of benefit for great industry.

The nature of military involvement as violent and repressive

The comparison of the use of troops in Nord-Pas-de-Calais with Westphalia has implications for the interpretation of French and German policing of the late 19th and early 20th centuries. Whilst the marginalisation of the Prussian army from policing was most certainly an important step in the process of modernising Prussian policing, the approach to protesters (attitudes, strategies and aims of policing) remained fundamentally unchanged. The police and *gendarmerie* who took over the responsibility for policing mass-protest were highly influenced by military strategies and the aggressive and confrontational approach to protesters remained at the heart of Prussian thinking about policing. At the same time, policing mass-protest with very limited numbers of policemen and *gendarmes* left very little room for experimenting with strategies of crowd management or for adopting a more permissive attitude towards protesters. By contrast, the policing strategies developed by French authorities were aimed at preventing – or at least containing – violence, even when the army became involved. Moreover, military participation ceased to be reactive and *post-hoc*: decisions to request troops gradually became unrelated to the course of the individual protest movement, and the involvement of troops did not require that a situation had already deteriorated into violence or riots. Soldiers were mobilised simply on the basis of expectations of the number of protesters involved and the potential for violence.

The way in which troops were used in Nord-Pas-de-Calais as well as the strategies developed in the ministerial Plans for Protections carefully followed Police Prefect Lépine's principles for large-scale protest policing. The primary aim of military involvement was to ensure that protest remained under control because it would create more confrontation to force protesters away, than to prevent them from coming close to sensitive locations in the first place. The military backing was also intended to create more space for policemen and *gendarmes* to discriminate between protesters who committed acts of violence and peaceful demonstrators and bystanders with no connection to the ongoing dispute.

Military participation in the policing of protest was a politically controversial solution; yet the political consequences of bloody clashes with protesters were potentially far more devastating for any French governments – and for the Republican regime – than accusations from the opposition of imposing repressive policing measures. This helps to explain why successive French interior ministers proved so resistant to any suggestion of replacing massive military presence with a small specialised riot unit within the *gendarmerie*.

If we accept that military involvement was a precondition for introducing Lépinean policing strategies in areas outside Paris, that involvement must be seen as part of the modernisation process, rather than the persistence of traditional forms of policing. Accordingly, the participation of soldiers was not simply a matter of 'repression' in the sense of physically preventing protesters from gathering in public places. To be sure, Lépine's strategies were far from liberal and placed many restrictions around any form of organised gathering in public. Similarly successive Interior Ministers showed an obsession with control of popular protest and consciously sought to undermine the effectiveness of protest actions. Yet, the prevention and containment of violence was the key defining concern that shaped French policing measures.

In their approach to protest policing, French and Prussian authorities operated within two completely different paradigms: the discourse of violence both on the part of the protesters and on the part of the public authorities run along different lines. Accordingly, the presence of troops had dissimilar connotations and political implications in Republican France and in Imperial Germany. The violent encounters that occurred in France need to be understood against the background of strategies and instructions that were specifically designed to prevent violent encounters; this also included rewards to *gendarmes* and soldiers who managed to avert potential confrontations without the use of force. In Prussia, the idea of rewarding policemen, *gendarmes* or soldiers for refraining from the use of force seemed alien to the policing culture. There was little room for permissiveness or flexibility towards protesters. At the same time, any mediation was discouraged as indicating weakness, and Prussian policemen and *gendarmes* were encouraged to proceed to armed attacks against protesters at a much earlier stage in the process of escalating violence.

These differences had implications for the dynamics of violence between protesters and the troops involved in policing. In Westphalia, the intervention of the Prussian army was and remained a clear indication of 'Zero Tolerance' towards protest at any level. In Nord-Pas-de-Calais by contrast, the nature of military involvement changed between 1889 and 1914; it became more than the simple repression of protest actions. French protesters, for their part, were keenly aware of the demands on the recruits and officers to show restraint. This had implications for the ways in which French protesters challenged soldiers and officers, and engaged in violent confrontations.

Demilitarisation and modernisation of protest policing

How should the military aspect of policing be interpreted and how do the forms of policing reflect on the French Republican regime and the German Empire? The demilitarisation of protest policing neither confirms nor rejects the idea of a special German path towards modernity. At one level, Germany was in line with the general trend towards disengagement of military troops from civilian policing. Conversely in Republican France – a country which in the *Sonderweg* interpretation of German history often serves as positive model for a more politically 'modern' regime – the practice of involving the army continued right up until after the end of the First World War.

The French Third Republic, despite its high number of police officers and *gendarmes* per inhabitant, and despite the frequent military involvement in the policing of civilian society, could hardly be described as a 'police state' or a 'military state'. This was not simply because of the subjection of the French army to civilian authorities; nor was it simply due to the fact that the French Republican governments who made frequent use of troops were accountable to a democratically elected Parliament, whilst the Prussian-German ministers were not. The main difference lay in the concerns among ministers, bureaucrats and military commanders alike for the forms of intervention against civilians. It lay in the preventive strategies and in the instructions to policemen, *gendarmes* and soldiers to show moderation, followed by the rewarding of non-confrontational handling of conflicts with protesters.

It was the increasing concerns for public opinion that pushed French authorities to change their strategic approach to policing. The new strategies, however, required the presence of large numbers of men which only the army could provide. This led to the paradoxical situation that concern for public opinion and attempts to use preventive rather than confrontational policing strategies increased the reliance on military assistance. Thus, while France did not abandon military involvement, it radically transformed the role and purpose of military presence.

At the same time, the detachment of the Prussian army from its traditional involvement in protest policing does not seriously modify the image of the German Empire as a state where the policing of protest in public places was primarily a matter of brute force. If Prussian civilian authorities sought to avoid military involvement, it was due to the impossibility of establishing any form of working relationship with the army. Paradoxically, the demilitarisation of protest policing in Prussia and Germany was to a great extent conditioned by the particularly strong and independent position of the Prussian army. On their side, military commanders actively sought to avoid getting involved in the policing of civilians. While senior members of the Prussian military establishment boasted about their intensions to intervene against the *Reichstag* and the Social Democratic opposition, they increasingly saw disengagement from involvement in protest policing as being in the best interest of the army.

Although the Prussian army was only marginally involved in the policing of protest, the approach to the handling of popular discontent remained very traditional. Policemen and *gendarmes* remained fundamentally shaped by their own military training and attitudes. Despite the demilitarisation, the Prussian strategic approaches to strikers and demonstrators could not in any way be described as more forward looking or 'modern' than the measures and strategies implemented in France.

Many questions still remain about the dynamics between civilian and military authorities in Republican France and Wilhelmine Germany. Similarly, more comparative research is needed into the bureaucratic priorities that eventually led most European countries towards demilitarising the policing of civilian society. The different trajectories followed by the French Republic and the German Empire highlight the conflicting interests at stake, and show that the continued involvement of the army was not necessarily closely related to the nature of the political regime in place.

Appendix 1

Military Involvement in the Policing of Protest in the German Empire

1889 5–31 May	Westphalia	90,000 miners on strike	6,000–8,000 infantry 1,250 cavalry
1889 16 May–4 June	Waldenburg, Silesia	Miners' strike	1,500–3,750 infantry 200–500 cavalry
1889 19 May–4 June	Saarland	Miners' strike	800–1,000 infantry 1,600–2,000 cavalry
1889 24 Oct.–6 Nov.	Saarland	Miners' strike	3,600–4,000 infantry 300 cavalry
1890 January	Westphalia	Miners' strike	6,400–8,000 infantry 900 cavalry ready for intervention but not mobilised
1890 March	Waldenburg, Silesia	Miners' strike	800–1,000 infantry ready for intervention but not mobilised
1890 21–22 March	Köpenick, Brandenburg	Popular unrest	200–250 infantry 800–1,000 infantry ready for intervention but not mobilised
1890 18–23 April	Petrzniowitz close to the Austrian border	Fear of strikers crossing over from the Austrian side	150 cavalry
1890 20 April–6 May	Mülhausen, Saarland	Strike among 8,000 workers	200–250 infantry 300 cavalry

1890 1 May	Danzig	May Day demonstrations	400–500 infantry
1890 1 May	All Germany	May Day demonstrations	Soldiers kept ready for intervention but not mobilised
1890 August	Berlin	Riots	1,600–2,000 infantry ready for intervention but not mobilised
1891 April	Westphalia	12,000 miners on strike	All troops in the province kept ready for intervention but not mobilised
1893 10–23 Jan.	Westphalia	Miners' strike	6,400–8,000 infantry 1,200 cavalry ready for intervention but not mobilised
1893 12 June	Clausthal	Social democratic demonstrations	200–250 infantry ready for intervention but not mobilised
1899 28 June–10 July	Herne Westphalia	Strike amongst Polish miners	3,000 infantry 140 cavalry
1903 Oct–Nov.	Wilms Brandenburg	Strike amongst factory workers	A train kept ready to transport troops but no troops mobilised
1905, 1 February	Schopponitz near the Russian border	Fear of strikers crossing over from the Russian side	Unknown number of troops guarding the border
1905 October	Berlin	Strike amongst electricians	700 infantry ready for intervention but not mobilised
1906 January	Berlin	Social democratic demonstrations	4,450 infantry ready for intervention but not mobilised

Appendix 1

1908 19 Sept.	Berlin	Social democratic demonstrations	Troops kept ready for intervention but not mobilised
1909 18 June	Worms	Strike amongst construction workers	800–1,000 infantry
1909 13–16 Aug.	Karlsruhe, Baden	Strike amongst factory workers, followed by social democratic demonstrations	200–250 infantry armed with two machine guns
1909 22 Oct.–16 Nov.	Mansfeld near Magdeburg	16,000 miners on strike	1,600 infantry 900 cavalry
1910 February	Neumünster	Social democratic demonstrations	200–250 infantry
1910 March	All Germany	Social democratic demonstrations	Troops kept ready For intervention but not mobilised
1912 26 Jan.	Schwertz and Mariewerder	Electoral unrest	200–250 infantry
1912 14–22 March	Westphalia	190,000 miners on strike	5,000 soldiers
1913 November	Zabern, Alsace-Lorraine	Popular protest	Troops intervening without requisition from a civil authority

Appendix 2

Military Involvement in the Policing of Protest in Nord-Pas-de-Calais

1889 10 March–April	Lille and Armentières	7,000 miners on strike	Unknown number of troops
1889 9–30 Oct.	Entire Nord- Pas-de-Calais	13,000 miners on strike	At least 1665 soldiers
1891 1 May	Fourmies	May Day demonstrations	400–500 soldiers mobilised to Fourmies
1891 17 May	Roubaix and Lille	Strike amongst textile workers	200 cavalry
1891 15 June	Fourmies	Riots	100 cavalry
1891 November	Lens, Liévin, Billy-Montigny, and Courrières	15,000 miners on strike	1,987 soldiers
1893 18 Sept.–9 Nov.	Entire Nord- Pas-de-Calais	Strike wave with c. 42,000 strikers	At least 4,160 soldiers
1898 13–17 October	All France	Rail workers' strike	Troops kept ready for intervention but not mobilised
1900 Aug.– Sept.	Dunkirk	2,000 dockers on strike	Unknown number of troops
1901 February	Dunkirk	Dockers on strike	Unknown number of troops
1901 1 May	Dunkirk	Dockers on strike	Troops mobilised to the port

Appendix 2

Date	Location	Event	Troops
1901 1 May	Entire Nord-Pas-de-Calais	May Day Demonstrations	Troops from the entire region kept ready for intervention
1901 21–29 July	Roubaix	Election unrest	80 cavalry
1901 21–29 July	Lille	Election unrest	All troops in the Lille Garrison kept ready for intervention
1901 15–25 Sept.	Dunkirk	The Tzarina of Russia passing through the area	Troops mobilised to Ensure security
1901 Oct.–Dec.	Entire Nord-Pas-de-Calais	Nationwide strikes with max 14,700 strikers N-PdC	5,900 infantry 2,100 cavalry
1902 March	Entire Nord-Pas-de-Calais	Rumours of a miners' strike	All troops in the region ready for intervention but not mobilised
1902 July–Aug.	Vieux-Condé	Strike	80 cavalry mobilised and other troops kept ready for intervention
1902 8–11 Aug.	Anzin	1,529 miners on strike	156 infantry 130 cavalry
1902 1 Oct.–19 Dec.	Entire Nord-Pas-de-Calais	Nationwide strikes with 71000 miners and 5000 dockers on strike in N-PdC	16,715 infantry and cavalry mobilised according to the Plans for Protection
1903 9 Jan.	Lille	Crowd management during a public execution	200 infantry and an unknown number of cavalry
1903 28 April–24 July	La Gorgue-Estaire	Strike amongst textile workers	An unknown number of troops
1903 May	Entire Nord-Pas-de-Calais	Implementation of Anti-Catholic legislation	Unknown number of troops

1903 1 June	Dunkirk	Maintenance of order for religious processions	160–200 cavalry
1903 27 June	Dunkirk	Maintenance of order for religious processions	Unknown number of cavalry
1903 14–15 Aug.	Dunkirk	Maintenance of order for religious processions	Unknown number of cavalry
1903 15 Aug.	Saint-Pol-sur-Mer	Maintenance of order for religious processions	Unknown number of infantry
1903 6 Sept.	Baroeul	Strike amongst spinners	Cavalry kept ready for intervention but not mobilised
1903 10 Sept.	Boulogne-sur-Mer	Implementation of Anti-Catholic legislation	Unknown number of infantry
1903 27 Sept.– 14 Nov.	Lille, Roubaix, Tourcoing, Armentières Hallouin and Quesnay.	50,000 textile workers on strike	10,000 infantry 2,600 cavalry
1903 22 Oct.–Nov.	Entire Nord-Pas-de-Calais	Implementation of Anti-Catholic legislation	Unknown number of infantry
1904 31 Jan–14 April	Lille, Roubaix and Tourcoing	15,000 textile workers on strike	Troops kept ready from 31 January. 4,875 infantry and 880–1100 cavalry mobilised 18 March.
1904 29–31 July	Dunkirk	Election unrest	80 infantry and 160 cavalry kept ready for intervention but not mobilised.

Appendix 2

Date	Location	Reason	Troops
1904 (28 July) 29 Oct.–12 Dec.	Dunkirk	Dockers and sailors on strike	Troops kept ready for intervention from 28 July but were only mobilised 29 October
1905 6 Feb.	Entire Nord-Pas-de-Calais	Electrician strike	Soldiers called upon to stand in for strikers
1905 4 March	Calais	The Tzarina of Russia visiting	80 infantry
1905 March	Dunkirk	4,000 dockers on strike	375 infantry 400 cavalry
1905 10 June	Calais	The King of Spain visiting the region	310 infantry and 600 cavalry
1905 25–26 June	Lille	A public festival	60 infantry
1905 5 Aug.	Dunkirk	Public execution of two criminals	75 artillery soldiers 500 infantry
1905 3–6 Sept.	Boulogne-sur-Mer	Dock workers on strike	375 infantry
1906 Feb.–14 March	Entire Nord-Pas-de-Calais	Establishment of Inventories of the possession of the Catholic Church	Unknown number of troops mobilised in the entire region
1906 10 March–May	Entire Nord-Pas-de-Calais	Strike wave involving at most 92,000 strikers	35–38,000 troops
1906 8 Sept.	Valenciennes	(reason unknown)	100 infantry and 25 cavalry kept ready for intervention
1906 23 Sept.	Béthune	(reason unknown)	Unknown number of troops kept ready for intervention
1906 15 Oct.	Entire Nord-Pas-de-Calais	Major strikes in Many professions	Unknown number of soldiers

Date	Location	Reason	Forces
1906 19–23 Nov.	Entire Nord-Pas-de-Calais	Implementation of anti-Catholic legislation	Troops from the entire region mobilised to support the officials
1907 9 Feb.	Calais	King Edward VII passing through the region	100 infantry
1907 March	Dunkirk	Strike amongst shipyard workers	Unknown number of troops kept ready for intervention
1907 May	Valenciennes	Maintenance of order for religious processions	Unknown number of troops requested
1907 31 May–7 June	Dunkirk	Strike amongst 625 sailors	Unknown number of infantry mobilised to protect port installation
1907 5–12 June	La Vallée d'Aa	Unknown number of strikers	104 infantry and cavalry mobilised
1907 18 Aug.	Cambrai	Unauthorised procession for a historical commemoration	150 infantry and cavalry mobilised
1907 26 Sept.	Gravelines	Closing of a religious order	One military detachment
1908 17 April	Calais	King Edward VII passing through the region	50 infantry
1908 18 April	Dunkirk	The Tzarina of Russia passing through the region	50 infantry
1908 4 May	Calais	King Edward VII passing through the region	125 infantry mobilised to ensure security.
1908 4 May	Entire Nord-Pas-de-Calais	General elections	Troops from the entire region kept ready for intervention

Appendix 2

Date	Location	Event	Troops
1909 13–25 March	Entire Nord-Pas-de-Calais	Nationwide strikes amongst postal workers	Troops kept ready for intervention in the entire region
1909 May	Entire Nord-Pas-de-Calais	Nationwide strikes amongst postal workers	Troops kept ready for intervention in the entire region
1909 11–28 Oct.	Lille	2,400 textile workers on strike	320–400 infantry 100 cavalry
1909–1910 15 Dec–12 May	Ruyoulcourt	Strike amongst tile workers	Unknown number of infantry mobilised
1910 12 Feb.	Dunkirk	Strike amongst Icelandic sailors	100 infantry mobilised to protect the port installations
1910 1–5 March	Hallouin	Riots	893 infantry 37 officers
1910 24 March–26 May	Dunkirk	Strike amongst construction workers and 4,000 dockers	260–300 infantry to prevent sabotage, and 1000 soldiers for the maintenance of order
1910 8–9 May	Entire Nord-Pas-de-Calais	General elections	Troops from the entire region kept ready for intervention
1910 27 July–3 Aug.	Liévin	3–5000 workers on strike	110 infantry
1910 24 Aug.	Maubeuge	Political demonstration	Unknown number of troops
1910 Oct.–Nov.	All France	Nationwide strikes amongst rail workers	Troops mobilised to maintain order and stand in for strikers
1910 15–20 Oct.	Billy-Montigny	1600 miners on strike	Unknown number of troops mobilised
1910 5 Dec.	Dunkirk	Rumours about a 24 hours strike	500 infantry and 400 cavalry kept ready for intervention

Date	Location	Event	Military Response
1910 24–26 Dec.	Dunkirk	1,500 dockers on strike	Unknown number of troops mobilised
1911 9–14 Feb.	Hallouin	Strike amongst textile workers	Unknown number of cavalry mobilised
1911 Aug.– Sept.	Entire Nord-Pas-de-Calais	Bread riots	Troops mobilised from all garrisons in the region and from seven other military regions
1911 24–25 Oct.	Calais	Strike amongst dockers	200 cavalry mobilised
1911 October	Lille	Strike amongst dustmen	Soldiers called out to take away the rubbish
1911 8–29 Dec.	Tourcoing	Strike amongst gas workers	72 infantry mobilised to maintain order and to ensure basic service
1912 11–25 March	Calais	41,800 miners on strike	Troops kept ready for intervention, but never mobilised
1912 26 April	Dunkirk	Official visit by the Tzarina of Russia	Unknown number of troops
1912 9–20 July	Dunkirk	4,000 dockers on strike	2,000–2,300 infantry and cavalry mobilised to Dunkirk
1913 November	Entire Nord-Pas-de-Calais	73,000 miners on strike	All troops designated in the Protection Plans kept ready to intervene
1914 31 July	Dunkirk	Visit by the President of the Republic	2,525 infantry and cavalry called to Dunkirk

Bibliography

Manuscript sources

Military Archive, Vincennes

Papers from the French War Ministry

5 N 2	*Cabinet du Ministre, documents et réglementation, 1890–1895*
5 N 5	*Cabinet du Ministre, correspondance générale, 1878–1914*
5 N 6	*Cabinet du Ministre, correspondance générale, 1905–1906*
5 N 7	*Cabinet du Ministre, 1905–1911, section militaire*
5 N 8	*Réquisition des gendarmes*
6 N 146	*Maintien de l'ordre 1907–1917*

Papers from the French General Staff

7 N 12	*EMA: Circulaires, grèves, 1871–1914. Gendarmerie. Garnisons*
7 N 25	*EMA: Réquisitions*
7 N 100	*EMA: Au sujet des mesures à prendre en cas de grève, 1901*
7 N 104	*EMA: Projet d'instruction relatif à l'emploi des troupes réquisitionnées pour le maintien de l'ordre public, 1904*
7 N 105	*EMA: Instruction du 18 octobre 1907 relative à l'emploi des troupes réquisitionnées pour le maintien de l'ordre public, mise à jour à la date du 15 avril 1914*
7 N 107	*Instruction du 18 octobre 1907 l'emploi des troupes réquisitionnées pour le maintien de l'ordre public, mise à jours à la date du 30 janvier 1911*
7 N 114	*Troupes réquisitionnées pour le maintien de l'ordre public, 15 avril 1914*
7 N 115	*EMA: Mesures à prendre en vue d'assurer le maintien de l'ordre public notamment en cas de grève, 1893–1918*
7 N 127	*Grèves des chemins de fer. Mesures à prendre, avril–juin, 1898*
MR 2172	*Application des lois des congrégations*
MR 2224	*Décret du 24 messidor an XII sur les Honneurs et Préséances*
MR 2226	*Cérémonies publiques et religieuses, préséances*
MR 2366	*Comparaison des dépenses militaires et des effectifs en France et en Allemagne (EMA, août 1911)*

Documents from the garrison in Lille (1st A.C.)

2 I 286	*Elections, maintien de l'ordre public*
2 I 325	*Grèves, dispositions à prendre, 1902–1909*
2 I 326	*Grèves, dockers de Dunkerque, mars–avril 1910*
2 I 326	*Renseignements sur les troupes détachées aux grèves, 1901–1902*
2 I 327	*Grèves, 1903, 1904, 1906*
2 I 327	*Grèves, bassin houiller du Pas-de-Calais, mars–avril 1906*
2 I 327	*Inventaires des biens des églises*
2 I 328	*Grèves, rassemblement de la troupe, 1906–1909*
2 I 329	*Grèves diverses, 1904–1907*
2 I 330	*Grèves diverses, 1908–1913*
2 I 331	*Grèves. Intervention des militaires suite à des grèves*
2 I 332	*Grèves. Réquisitions préfectorales, rapports de gendarmerie, situation des troupes, 1901–1902*
2 I 333	*Grèves. Industrie textile, ouvriers détacheurs, éléctriciens, papetiers, chemins de fer, 1903–1910*
2 I 334	*Grèves. Bassin houillers, briquetiers, dockers, charretiers, gagiers, 1910–1912*
2 I 335	*Inventaires des églises, 1906*
2 I 224	*Honneurs militaires rendues à différentes personalités*
2 I 224	*Cérémonies publiques, préséances, ordres des autorités, 1907*
2 I 224	*Cérémonies publiques: obsèque des victimes du pluviôse, 1910*
2 I 224	*Fêtes publiques, 14 juillet, 1905–1913*
2 I 225	*Cérémonies publiques, 1905–1913*
2 I 225	*Voyages en France de personnalités étrangères et cérémonies publiques, 1889–1914*
2 I 226	*Entrées et visites officielles dans le 1ère Région 1898–1901*
2 I 1	*Lettres au cabinet du general, 1877–1882; 1882–1890*
2 I 15	*Correspondance recue par le commandant du C.A., 1904–1908*
2 I 2	*Correspondance générale confidentielle (Régistre), 1880–1888*
2 I 21	*Observations du général commandant du 1er C.A., 1911–1912*
2 I 21	*Correspondance confidentielle expédiée par la section chancellerie de l'état-major du 1er C.A., 1912–1914*
2 I 210	*Correspondance administrative, 1889*
2 I 211	*Correspondance du 1er C.A., 1891–1920*
2 I 212	*Correspondance générale, Gal. Jeannerod, 1898–1900*
2 I 215	*Correspondance générale 1904–1908*
2 I 217	*Correspondance avec les préfets et les maires 1905–1912*
2 I 218	*Gouverneur de Lille, correspondance, 1909*
2 I 218	*Correspondances diverses recues par le ACC, 1909–1911*
2 I 220	*Correspondance générale, 1910–1913*
2 I 221	*Gouveneur de Dunkerque, correspondance expédiée, 1912*
2 I 82	*Correspondance relative aux grèves expédiée par le 1er bureau de l'état-major du 1er C.A., 1900–1902*

2 I 83	*Correspondance expédiée par 1er C.A., 1900–1903*
2 I 103	*Correspondance relative aux grèves expédiée par le 1er bureau de l'état-major du 1er C.A., 1902–1903*
2 I 114	*Correspondance relative aux grève expédiée par le 1er bureau de l'état-major du 1er C.A., 1903*
2 I 149	*Correspondance relative aux grèves expédiée par le 1er bureau de la section active de l'état major du 1er C.A., 1906–1907*
2 I 227	*Ordres généraux, 1885–1893; 1893–1904; 1909–1914*
2 I 228	*Rapports de place 1910*
2 I 228	*Rapports de place 1912–1914*
2 I 229	*Rapports de place 1911–1912–1914*
2 I 229	*Rapports de place 1913–1914*
2 I 230	*Rapports de la 1ère division d'infanterie du 1er C.A., 1885–1914*
2 I 282	*Soldes et indemnités, 1889–1899; 1904–1912*
2 I 283	*Soldes, indemnités et frais de route, 1898–1906*

Personal Papers

1 K 16	Henri Brugière, *Mes Memoires, 1841-1914*, (unpublished manuscript, c. 1911)
392/GD/3	Emile Jourdy, *Memoires* (unpublished manuscript, c. 1913)
1 K mi 9	Charles Millet, *Souvenirs* (unpublished manuscript, c. 1913)

National Archive, Paris

F 7: Documents from the French Interior Ministry, Police Générale:

13321	*Anniversaire de Draveil, 1909–1912*
12399–12404	*Culte Catholique: Inventaires, 1905–1907*
12526	*Evénements de Montceau-les-Mines, 1882–1883*
12527	*Evénements de Fourmies, 1891*
12528–13271	*Premier mai, 1898–1911*
12722	*Police générale, pouvoirs des préfets. Emploi de la troupe pour le maintien de l'ordre, 1902–1916*
12773	*Instructions ministérielles; plan de protection, emploi des troupes, usage des armes; état chronologique des grèves*
12774	*Grèves: Mesures à prendre en cas de grève des chemins de fer*
12775–12776	*Plans de protection par département*
12777	*Protection des ports en cas de grève des dockers ou mineurs*
12778–12780	*Mesures à prendre en cas de grève générale des mineurs*
12781–12791	*Grèves*
12792	*Grèves: P.T.T., 1909*
12794	*Révolte des vignerons du Midi, 1907*

12912	*Rapports divers de la sûrété générale. Statistiques. Projets de lois. Mesures de protection, 1884–1907*
12913	*Commissions et sous-commissions instituées d'examiner les mesures à prendre en cas de grèves, 1908*
12914–12917	*Grève de Draveil-Vigneux, 1908*
12918	*Grève des employés des P.T.T., mars–mai, 1909*
12920	*Émeutes provoquées dans le Midi par la crise viticole, 1907*

Série AP: Personal papers

AP 270	Personal papers of General Antoine Chanzy
AP 475	Personal papers of Marshall Hubert Lyautey

Departmental Archive, Lille

Personal papers from prefects

M 6 /7	Paul Cambon (1877–1881)
M 6 /7	Jules Cambon (1882–1887)
M 6 /19	Henri Vel-Durand (1890–1897)
M 6 /13	André Laurenceau (1897–1898)
M 6 /19	Paul Vatin (1898–1899)
M 6 /20	Louis Vincent (1899–1911)
M 6 /18	Jean-Baptiste Trépont (1911–1916)

General Administration

M 109 /8	*Réquisition de la force armée, 1847–1900*
M 109 /12	*Correspondance chiffré, 1862–1904*
M 109 /14	*Circulaires, 1889–1912*

Political Police

M 145 /8	*Voyages présidentiels en France. Mesures de sûreté, 1907–1910*
M 146 /33	*Projet de voyage à Lille de M. Briand, ministre de l'instruction publique à l'occasion des fêtes universitaires – Danger d'une manifestation hostile, 1907*
M 146 /37	*Voyages ministériels divers, 1907–1909*
M 149 /1	*Instructions ministérielles, 1905*
M 149 /2	*Rapports généraux, 1880–1881*
M 149 /3	*Rapports mensuels des sous-préfets, 1887–1910*
M 150 /1/29–34	*Correspondance du cabinet du Préfet, 1906*
M 151/ 1–38	*Rapports des Commissaires*

Bibliography

M 153 /51	*Exécution de Ferrer – Manifestation, 1909*
M 154-161	*Partis politiques; sociétés politiques; détenus politiques; dossiers individuels; réunions publiques; manifestations 1 mai; fête du 14 juillet; fêtes diverses*
M 159 /1–20	*Manifestations du 1er mai, instructions et circulaires; rapports par année, 1889–1904*

Commerce and Industry: Dossiers for various professional categories

M 622 /1–4	Strikes amongst rail workers, 1898–1907
M 623 /1–2	Strikes amongst postal workers, 1906–1909
M 624 /7–13	Strikes amongst dock workers, 1901–1908
M 625 /4–31	Strikes amongst textile workers, 1903–1909
M 626 /18–61	Strikes amongst miners, 1889–1906
M 627 /1–20	Strikes amongst metal workers, 1880–1907
M 628 /1–5	Strikes amongst glass workers, Strike in Fourmies, 1903
M 629 /1–9	Strikes amongst construction workers

Departmental Archive, Arras

M 2440	*Agitations diverses dans les mines. Grèves, 1840–1902*
M 2488	*Agitation ouvrière et syndicale. Grèves diverses 1900–1901*
M 4859–4861	*Grève générale dans le bassin houiller, 1893. Télégrammes*
M 4862	*Grève générale dans le bassin houiller, 1893. Renseignements, instructions, correspondence*
M 4864	*Grève dans le bassin houiller, 1893. Correspondance avec les autorités administrative et militaries*
M 1231	*Grève générale dans le bassin houiller, 1889. Documents divers*
M 4865	*Grève générale dans le bassin houiller, 1891. Documents divers*
M 4868	*Grève générale dans le bassin houiller, 1893. Réquisitions*
M 4863	*Grèves diverses, 1887–1896*
M 1793	*Tentative de grève générale et partielle des mineurs, 1900*
M 1794	*Grève générale des mineurs, 1900–1901*
M 1795	*Grève générale des mineurs, 1902*
M 2439	*Grève générale des mineurs, 1902*
M 1799	*Grève générale des mineurs, 1900–1903*
M 1810	*Grève générale des mineurs, 1906*
M 1796–1797	*Grève générale des mineurs, 1906*
M 1800	*Grève générale des mineurs, 1908*
M 2284	*Grèves, émeutes, manifestations, 1885–1914*
M 1187	*Grèves, émeutes et manifestations, Béthune, 1901*
M 1185	*Grèves des bassins houillers, 1893–1906*
M 1785	*Calais: Grèves ouvrières, 1890–1907*
M 2111	*Calais: Grèves tuiliers, 1898*

298   *Soldiers as Police*

M 1733	*Calais: Grèves tuiliers, 1890–1898*
M 1735–1736	*Calais: Grèves tuiliers, 1900*
M 1783	*Calais: Grèves tuiliers, 1909*
M 1798	*Calais: Grèves des dockers, 1911*
M 1787	*Calais: Grèves des dockers, 1900–1908*
M 1788	*Calais: Grèves des dockers, 1911–1913*
M 2465	*Grèves des ouvriers du port, 1904; Grève des marins, 1912*
M 1801	*Grèves des employés des chemins de fer, 1910*
M 2291	*Grèves des employés des chemins de fer, octobre 1898*
M 1791	*Grèves des employés des P.T.T., 1909*
S 1476	*Mines de Courrières, Catastrophe de Courrières, 10 mars 1906: Envoi de la troupe, effectifs, télégrammes; mesures de police*

Série Z : Documents from the sub-prefects

1 Z 12 224	*Grèves, 1887–1893*
4 Z 659	*Saint Omer: Réquisitions militaires en temps de grève. Instructions 1907*
4 Z 660	*Grèves: Saint Omer. Emploi de troupes réquisitionnées pour le maintien de l'ordre public, 1904–1921*

Military Archive, Freiburg

PH2: Documents from the Prussian War Ministry

14	*Eingriff der bewaffneten Macht bei Unterdrückung von Unruhen, 1889–1914*
15	*Die sozialdemokratischen Bestrebungen 1905–1907*
16	*Deutschfeindliche Bestrebungen, Januar-September 1913*
361–368	*Bekämpfung sozialdemokratischer Bestrebungen, 1877–1911*
466–470	*Bekämpfung sozialdemokratischer Bestrebungen, 1890–1912*
455	*Gesammelten AKO, Gesetze, Urkunden, Ordnungen*
639	*Verhalten gegenüber der Sozialdemokratie, 1878–1912*

Private Papers of Prussian Army Corps Commanders

N 80	General Bruno von Mudra
N 80–81	General Colmar von der Goltz
N 87	General Otto von Below
N 188	General August von Goeben
N 274	General Herman von François

N 313	General von Schlichting
N 324	General Karl von Einem
N 429	General Paul von Hindenburg
N 513	General von Eichhorn
N 550	General Alexander von Kluck
N 559	General Berthold von Deimling
MSg 109	Ottomar von Krug, biographies of Prussian generals (1875–1918)

Geheime Staatsarchive, Berlin-Dahlem

HA1, Rep. 77, Titel 500: *Volksaufstände und Tumulte. Generalia*

1/5	*Maßnahmen gegen Volksaufstände und Tumulte, 1856–1900*
1/6	*Maßnahmen gegen Volksaufstände und Tumulte, 1901–1916*
20/12	*Maßnahmen gegen Unruhen und Aufstände unter den Fabrikarbeitern und Handwerkern, 1871–1892*
20/13	*Maßnahmen gegen Unruhen und Aufstände unter den Fabrikarbeitern und Handwerkern, 1871–1892*
27	*Anordnung über die Verhängung und Wiederaufhebung des Belagerungszustandes, 1848–1916*
42/10	*Maßnahmen gegen die sozialdemokratische Bewegung in Deutschland, 1870–1895*
51	*Volksunruhen aus Anlass der Wahlen 1912*
52	*Unruhen und Arbeitseinstellungen, 1916–1917*

HA1, Rep. 77, Titel 508: *Volkaufstände und Tumulte in Westfalen*

2/3	*Volksaufstände und Tumulte in Münsterschen Regierungsbezirk: Sicherheitsmaßregeln, 1857–1885*
3/5	*Volksaufstände und Tumulte in Mindenschen Regierungsbezirk: Sicherheitsmaßregeln, 1851–1892*
4/4	*Volksaufstände und Tumulte in Arnsbergschen Regierungsbezirk: Sicherheitsmaßregeln, 1851–1916*
4 Beiheft 2	*Die Unruhen in Westfalen, 1903–1905*

HA1, Rep. 77, Titel 2513: *Arbeitseinstellungen*

1/III	*Maßnahmen gegen Arbeitseinstellungen, 1890–1892*
1/IV	*Maßnahmen gegen Arbeitseinstellungen, 1892–1895*
1/V	*Maßnahmen gegen Arbeitseinstellungen, 1896–1898*
1 Beiheft 1	*Die Stellung der kgl. Staatsregierung gegenüber Streiks und Ausschreitungen, 1906*
1 Beiheft 2–3	*Die auf die Arbeitseinstellungen eingegangenen Telegramme, 1889–1890*

300   *Soldiers as Police*

1 Beiheft 4–13	*Die Entsendung von Gendarmen und Militärs in die Ausstandsbezirke, 1889–1912*
1 Beiheft 15	*Nachweisungen der für den Fall des Ausbruchs größerer Arbeiterbewegungen zur Verwendung in den einzelnen Provinzen bestimmten königlichen Schutzleute und Gendarmen*
1 Beiheft 16-17	*Zusammenstellungen für die Provinzen, und denen Gendarmen für das Streikgebiet gestellt werden*
1 Beiheft 18	*Die von Privatpersonen gemachten Vorschläge zum Vorbeugung von Arbeitseinstellungen, 1889–1912*
1 Beiheft 20–29	*Maßnahmen gegen Missbrauch der Koalitionsfreiheit: Schutz Arbeitswilliger bei Arbeitseinstellung, 1886–1914*
4	*Die Errichtung von Sicherheits-Korps gegen Unruhen der Arbeiter in den Bergwerken desgleichen die Anstellung von Hilfs-Polizeibeamten bei größeren Arbeiterbewegungen, 1872–1914*

HA1, Rep. 77, Titel 2523: *Arbeitseinstellung, Westfalen-Rheinprovinz*

1 /1–18	*Die Arbeitseinstellung in den Bergwerksbezirken der Provinz Westfalen und die daraus hervor-gegangenen Arbeiterunruhen in den Jahren, 1889–1912*
1 /20	*Erfahrungen aus dem Bergarbeiterstreik, Ruhrgebiet März 1912*
1 /21–22	*Die Verurtheilungen wegen Vergehen aus Anlass des Bergarbeiterstreiks im Ruhrgebiet 1912*
1 /23	*Anzeigen über die Heranziehung von Gendarmen anlässlich der Bergarbeiterbewegung 1912, ihre Zurücksendung nach beendigtem Streik und ihr Wiedereintreffen in ihren Standorten*
1 / 24	*Arbeiterbewegung im Rheinisch-Westfälischen Bergwerk, 1905*

HA1, Rep. 77, Titel 2524: *Arbeitseinstellungen in den Bergwerksbezirken der Provinz Westfalen*

1 /1–2	*Arbeitseinstellungen in den Bergwerken, Westfalen, 1893–1904*
3 /1–2	*Arbeitseinstellungen, Westfalen, 1899–1915*
3 Anhang 1	*Streik und Aussperrungen der Metallarbeiter in Minden, Kreis Iserlohn, August 1912– März 1913*

HA1, Rep. 90: *Preußische Staatsministerium: Sicherheitspolizei – Schutz der öffentlichen Ordnung*

1	*Maßregeln zur Aufrechterhaltung der Sicherheit und öffentlichen Ordnung gegen Aufruhr, Ruhestörungen ff., 1798–1848*
2 / 1	*Bestimmungen über die Verhängung des Kriegs- und Belagerungszustandes, 1848–1914*
3 / 1–2	*Verfügung des Ausnahmezustandes, 1848–1919*

7 / 1   *Verpflichtung der Gemeinden zum Ersatz des bei öffentlichen Aufläufen verursachten Schadens, 1848–1920*

HA1, Rep. 92: Personal papers

    Emil von Albedyll (1824–1897)
    Friedrich von Kühlwetter (1809–1882)
    Konrad von Studt (1838–1921)
    Alfred von Waldersee (1832–1904)

Central Archive, Potsdam III

R 43:   *Alte Reichskanzlei: Militärsachen*

12425–12426   *Militärische Maßnahmen im Fälle von Unruhen. Belagerungszustand, 1890–1918*
12429–12430   *Angelegenheiten höhere Militärpersonen, 1879–1900*
12449–12450   *Kommandierende Generale, 1901–1917*

R 43:   *Alte Reichskanzlei: Polizei*

12543–12544   *Polizei, Öffentliche Ruhestörungen, 1906–1908*

R 43:   *Alte Reichskanzlei: Handel und Gewerbe*

11971–11972   *Arbeitseinstellung, Westfalen, Rheinland, Schlesien, 1889–1896*

Hauptstaatsarchiv, Münster

OP: Documents from the Province Governor of Westphalia: *Police, Military*

688   *Politische Unruhen, Beschwerden, Einsatz von Militär, 1849–1850, 1874*
653   *Einsatz von Militär zur Wiederherstellung von Ruhe und Ordnung, 1822–1848*
685   *Einsatz von Militär zur Unterdrückung bzw. Verhinderung von Unruhen, enthält 1848–1852, 1880–1881*
6095   *Notstandsmaßnahmen 1822, 1840–1851, 1876–1929*
6681   *Verstärkung der Polizei im Ruhrgebiet, Arbeiterunruhen 1906–1911*
6889   *Verstärkung der Polizei im Ruhrgebiet, Arbeiterunruhen, 1912–1919*

Soldiers as Police

OP: Documents from the province governor of Westphalia: *Strikes*

2847b	*Berichte des Generalkommandos des VII Armeekorps betreffs den Bergarbeiterstreik, 1889, 1897*
2849, 7	*Bergarbeiterstreik 1905: Polizeiliche Maßnahmen in den Regierungsbezirken Arnsberg und Münster, 1904–1905*
2832, 1–5	*Verstärkung der Gendarmerie und Polizei bei Arbeiterunruhen im Ruhrgebiet, 1889–1906*
2832a	*Zusammenstellung der Bestimmungen betreffs Verstärkung der Gendarmerie bei Arbeiterbewegungen im Ruhrgebiet*
2832b	*Plan zur Verstärkung der Gendarmerie bei Arbeiterunruhen in den Regierungsbezirken Arnsberg und Münster, 1899–1900*
2832c	*Plan zur Verstärkung der Gendarmerie bei Arbeiterunruhen in den Regierungsbezirken Arnsberg und Münster, 1905*
2832d	*Plan zur Verstärkung der Gendarmerie bei Arbeiterunruhen in den Regierungsbezirken Arnsberg, 1899–1900*
2832e	*Plan zur Verstärkung der Gendarmerie bei Arbeiterunruhen in den Regierungsbezirken Münster, 1899–1900*

OP: Reports from local governors in Westphalia to the province governor

2934	*Zeitungs- und Verwaltungsberichte, 1860–1891; 1903–1918*
1406	*Zeitungs- und Verwaltungsberichte, Reg. Münster, 1873–1893*
1407	*Zeitungs- und Verwaltungsberichte, Reg. Arnsberg, 1903–1913*
7029	*Instruktion für den Oberpräsidenten, 1825–1888; 1900–1913*

Regierung Arnsberg I Pr: Documents from the district governor of Arnsberg

298	*Militärangelegenheiten, 1876–1895*
299	*Militärangelegenheiten, 1896–1913*

Regierung Arnsberg, I Pa: Documents from the district governor of Arnsberg

232	*Einsatz von Militär bei Unruhen: Instruktion über Waffengebrauch des Militärs, 1840–1851*
233	*Zusammenarbeit von Polizei und Militär, 1845–1860*
249	*Zusammenziehung und Verstärkung der Gendarmerie bei größeren Arbeiterunruhen, 1889–1899*
14296	*Arbeitseinstellung, Bergarbeitern, Ruhrkohlenbezirk, 1889–1892*
14300	*Arbeitseinstellung, Bergarbeitern, Ruhrkohlenbezirk, 1889–1892*
14315	*Arbeitseinstellung, Bergarbeitern, Ruhrkohlenbezirk, 1889–1892*
14316–14317	*Bergarbeiterstreik im Ruhrkohlengebiet 1889*
14319–14320	*Bergarbeiterstreik im Ruhrkohlengebiet 1893*
14321–14323	*Bergarbeiterstreik im Ruhrkohlengebiet 1899*
14325	*Bergarbeiterausstand im Ruhrkohlenrevier 1912*

Bibliography 303

Regierung Münster, I Pr: Documents from the district governor of Münster

2904	*Verschiedene Militärangelegenheiten, 1889–1911*
V–11–22	*Verwaltungs- und Zeitungsberichte, 1887–1902*
V–11–23	*Verwaltungs- und Zeitungsberichte, 1887–1902*

Regierung Münster, VII, 14: Documents from the district governor of Münster

1 / 32–1	*Der Bergarbeiterausstand von 1912*
3 / 37–1	*Der Bergarbeiterausstand von 1912*
4 / 37–1	*Der Bergarbeiterausstand von 1912*
5 / 37–3	*Der Bergarbeiterausstand von 1912*

Regierung Münster, VII, 52: Documents from the district governor of Münster

1 / 39–2	*Arbeitseinstellung und Streiks, 1904–1911*
2 / 39–2	*Arbeitseinstellung und Streiks, 1899–1916*
3 / 39–2	*Arbeitseinstellung und Streiks, 1912–1913*
a / 31–1	*Maßnahmen beim Bergarbeiterstreik, 1910–1918*

Regierung Münster, VII, 57: Documents from the district governor of Münster

1 / 40–1	*Das Verfahren bei Bekämpfung von Arbeiterunruhen, insbesondere Heranziehung von Gendarmen, 1890–1905*
2 / 40–2	*Bekämpfung von Arbeiterunruhen, 1904–1911*
3 / 40–2	*Bekämpfung von Arbeiterunruhen, 1912–1916*
4 / 40–1	*Bekämpfung von Arbeiterunruhen, 1906–1914*
5 / 37–5	*Nachweisung der für den Fall des Ausbruchs größerer Arbeiterbewegungen zur Verwendung in der Provinz Westfalen bestimmten Gendarmeriemannschaften, 1913*

Documents from the local governors of Münster District

Kreis Arnsberg, 301	*Die Erstattung der Zeitungsberichte, 1898–1913*
Kreis Gelsenkirchen, 53	*Bergarbeiterausstand Juli 1899*
Kreis Recklinghausen, 7–9	*Zeitungsberichte, 1875–1888*

Documents from the local governors of Arnsberg District

Kreis Lüdinghausen, 389	*Aufläufe, Aufruhr, Belagerungszustand, 1848–1905*
Kreis Lüdinghausen, 696	*Aufläufe, Aufruhr, Belagerungszustand, 1905–1908*
Kreis Lüdinghausen, 840	*Streiks, Aussperrungen, 1907–1920*
Kreis Lüdinghausen, 253	*Bergarbeiterunruhen, 1910–1914*
Kreis Lüdinghausen, 841	*Bergarbeiterbewegung 1912*

Kreis Schwelm, 214	*Unruhen, Bergarbeiterausstände, Heranziehung fremder Gendarmen, 1903–1913*
Kreis Steinfurt, 15	*Volksversammlungen, Vereine, Umtriebe, politische Stimmung der Bewohner, 1848–1878*
Kreis Steinfurt, 822	*Politische Verbrecher, Sozialdemokraten, Versammlungen und Vorträge, 1888–1921*
Kreis Steinfurt, 970	*Übertretungen der Vorschriften gegen Tumult und Aufruhr, 1843–1924*

Printed sources

Laws and Decrees

French legislation on civilian and military institutions
Decree of 28 February 1790 on the organisation of the French army.
Constitutional law of 3 September 1791 restricting the king's right to mobilise the army.
Constitutional law of 24 June 1793 subordinating the army to the civilian authorities.
Decree of 19 Vendémiaire Year IV (1795) on municipal police.
Law of 28 Germinal Year VI (1798) on the organisation of the *gendarmerie*.
Law of 28 Pluviôse Year VIII (1800) on municipal police.
Conscription law of 27 July 1872.
Constitutional law of 24 July–6 August 1873 on the organisation of the army.
Constitutional law of 25 February 1875 subordinating the army to the President of the Republic.
Law of 5 April 1884 on municipal powers and their policing powers.
Conscription law of 15–17 July 1889 introducing three years compulsory military service.
Conscription law of 21 March 1905 introducing two years military service
Conscription law of 7 August 1913 reintroducing three years military service

German and Prussian legislation on civilian and military institutions
Law of 5 February 1794: The Prussian General Code.
Decree of 11 November 1808 on policing powers of Prussian towns.
Edict of 30 July 1812 on the Prussian *gendarmerie*.
Decree of 30 April 1815 on the organisation of the provincial administration.

Decree of 17 August 1835 on the maintenance of public order.
Prussian Constitution of 31 January–6 February 1850.
Decree of 11–27 March 1850 on the organisation of the provincial administration in Prussia.
The Imperial Constitution of 16 April 1871.
Decree of 31 December 1872 on municipal powers.
Law of 2 May 1874 on the organisation of the military forces of the German Empire.
Decree of 31 July 1886 on municipal powers.

French legislation on maintenance of public order and the role of the army
Law of 6–12 December 1790 on the organisation of forces for the maintenance of public order.
Law of 8–10 July 1791 on civilian and military authorities in garrisons.
Law of 27 July–3 August 1791 on the requisition of soldiers for the maintenance of public order.
Law of 7 June 1848 on gatherings in public.
Law of 9 August 1849 on military states of siege.
Law of 3 July 1877 on military requisitions.
Law of 3 April 1878 on military states of siege.
Decree of 4 October 1891 on civilian and military authorities in garrison towns.
Decree of 20 May 1903 on the requisition of the *gendarmerie*.
Instructions of 24 June 1903 on military participation in the maintenance of public order.
Instructions of 20 August 1907 on military participation in the maintenance of public order.

Prussian legislation on maintenance of order and the role of the army
Decree of 30 December 1798 on military intervention in riots and gatherings at the request of the civilian authorities.
Cabinet Order of 17 October 1820 on the participation of a military authority in the restoration of order.
Instructions of 31 December 1825 on civilian and military authorities in Prussian provinces.
Decree of 17 August 1835 on the maintenance of public order.
Law of 20 March 1837 on the military use of weapons.
Law of 4 June 1851 on military siege.
Military Service Regulations of 23 March 1899 on the use of weapons and the military participation in the repression of popular unrest.
Military Service Regulation of 19 March 1914 on the use of weapons.

French legislation on workers' organisation and labour action
Law of 14–17 June banning professional associations.
Law of 22 Germinal of Year XI (12 April 1803) making coalitions illegal.
Decree of 25–29 February 1848 on freedom of association.
Law of 27 November 1849 legalising concerted action by workers.
Decree of 25 March 1852 banning associations.
Law of 25 May 1864 legalising strikes and labour organisations.
Law of 25 March 1868 legalising non-political assemblies.
Law of 30 June 1881 recognising political organisations and assemblies.
Law of 21 March 1884 legalising trade unions.

Prussian-German legislation on workers' organisation and labour action
Law of 1869 abolishing the prohibition of strikes and labour organisations.
Laws of 19 October 1878 outlawing the Social Democratic Party.
Decree of 11 April 1886 'The Puttkamer Decree' on strikes and labour organisations.

French Legislation on Honours and Rank
Decree of 24 Messidor Year II (1793) on civilian and military honours at public ceremonies.
Law of 15–20 June 1907 on Honours and Rank.

Memoirs and Biographies

André, Louis (1906) *Cinq ans de ministère*, Paris: Louis Michaud.
Barail, François du (1913) *Mes Souvenirs*, Paris: Henri Charles-Lavauzelle.
Berlepsch, Hans von (1925) *Sozialpolitische Erfahrungen und Erinnerungen*, Mönchen-Gladbach: Volksvereinsverlag.
Berlepsch, Hans-Jörg von (1987) *"Neue Kurs im Kaiserreich"? Die Arbeiterpolitik des Freiherrn von Berlepsch, 1890 bis 1896*, Bonn: Neue Gesellschaft.
Bernhardi, Friedrich von (1927) *Denkwürdigkeiten aus meinem Leben*, Berlin: Mittler.
Bernin, Gerhard (1903) *August von Goeben in seinen Briefen*, Berlin: Mittler.
Brabrant, Arthur (1924) *Generaloberst Max Freiherr von Hausen. Ein deutscher Soldat – Nach seinen Tagebüchern, Aufzeichnungen und Briefe*, Dresden.

Bremen, Walther von (1901) *Denkwürdigkeiten des Preußischen Generals der Infanterie Eduard von Fransecky*, Bielefeld and Leipzig: Velhagen & Klassig.

Bülow, Bernhard von (1930) *Denkwürdigkeiten*, Berlin: Ullstein.

Clemenz, Bruno (1919) *General-Feldmarschall von Woyrsch und seine Schlesier. Eigenhändige Auszüge aus seinem Kriegstagebuch*, Berlin: Carl Flemming.

Combes, Émile (1956) *Mon ministère. Mémoires 1902–1905*, Paris: Plon.

Conrady, C. von (1889) *Graf August von Werder. Kgl. preußischer General der Infanterie*, Berlin: Mittler.

Cuny, Léon (1911) *Quarante-trois ans de vie militaire*, Paris: Henri Charles-Lavauzelle.

Deimling, Bethold von (1930) *Aus der alten in die neue Zeit*, Berlin: Verlag Ullstein.

Dürckheim-Montmartin, Eckbrecht von (1910) *Erinnerungen alter und neuer Zeit*, Stuttgart: Metzlerschen.

Duroselle, Jean-Baptiste (1988) *Clemenceau*, Paris: Fayard.

Einem, Karl von (1933) *Erinnerungen eines Soldaten 1853–1933*, Leipzig: Koehler.

Erlanger, Philippe (1968) *Clemenceau*, Paris: Grasset.

Foerster, Wolfgang (1938) *Mackensen, Briefe und Aufzeichnungen*, Leipzig: Koehler.

Freycinet, Charles de (1913) *Souvenirs* (vols. 2, 1878–1893), Paris: Charles Delagrave.

Gallifet, Gaston (1902) 'Souvenirs', *Le Journal des Débats*, August 1902.

Gerog, Wilhelm (1915) *Unser Emmich. Ein Lebensbild*, Berlin: August Scherl.

Goltz, Colmar von der (1929) *Denkwürdigkeiten*, Berlin: Mittler.

Guiral, Pierre (1994) *Clemenceau en son temps*, Paris: Grasset.

Hindenburg, Paul von (1920) *Aus meinem Leben*, Leipzig: S.Hierzel.

Kluck, Alexander von (1929) *Wanderjahre – Kriege – Gestalten*, Berlin: Eisenschmidt.

Krieg, Thilo (1903) *Constantin von Alvensleben. Ein militärisches Lebenbild*, Berlin: Mittler.

Krieg, Thilo (1911) *Hermann von Tresckow, General der Infanterie. Ein Lebensbild*, Berlin: Mittler.

Landmann, K. (1908) *Konrad von Studt, ein preußischer Kultusminister*, Berlin.

Lépine, Louis (1929) *Mes souvenirs*, Paris: Payot.

Loë, Walther von (1906) *Erinnerungen von meinem Berufsleben 1849–1867*, Berlin: Mittler.

Lyautey, Hubert (1924) *Choix de lettres 1882–1919*, Paris: Armand Colin.
Merle, Gabriel (1995) *Émile Combes*, Paris: Fayard.
Miquel, Pierre (1996) *Clemenceau: la guerre et la paix*, Paris: Tallandier.
Monerville, Gaston (1968) *Clemenceau*, Paris: Fayard.
Risse, Jacques (1994) *Le petit Père Combes*, Paris: Harmattan.
Seeckt, Hans von (1938) *Aus meinem Leben, 1866–1917*, Leipzig: Hase & Koehler.
Sorlin, Pierre (1966) *Waldeck-Rousseau*, Paris: Armand Colin.
Waldersee, Alfred von (1922) *Denkwürdigkeiten des General-Feldmarschalls Alfred von Waldersee*, Berlin: Mittler.
Waldersee, Alfred von (1927) *Aus dem Briefwechsel des General-Feldmarschalls Graf von Waldersee*, Berlin, Mittler.
Wartensleben, Elisabeth von (1923) *Herman Graf von Wartensleben-Carow, ein Lebensbild 1826–1921*, Berlin: Mittler.
Witzleben, E. von (1913) *Adolf von Deines. Lebensbild, 1845–1911*, Berlin: Verlag der Liebelschen Buchhandlung.
Wolbe, Eugen (1917) *Alexander von Kluck*, Leipzig: Otto Spamer.
Wormser, Georges (1961) *La République de Clemenceau*, Paris: Presses Universitaires de France.
Zurlinden, Émile (1913) *Mes Souvenirs depuis la guerre, 1871–1901*, Paris: Henri Charles-Lavauzelle.

Biographical Manuals

Anonymous (1875–1913) *L'année militaire*, (Annual publication from the French War Ministry).
Anonymous (1908–1910) *Qui êtes-vous? Annuaire des contemporains*, Paris.
Curinier, B. (1898) *Dictionnaire National des Contemporains*, Paris.
Gothaisches genealogisches Taschenbuch.
Handbuch über den kgl. Preußischen Hof und Staat.
Priisdorf, Kurt von (1942) *Soldatisches Führertum*, Hamburg.
Rang- und Quartier-Liste der königlich preußischen Armee und des XIII (königlich Württembergischen) Armeekorps (1875–1913).
Vapereau, Louis Gustave (1893) *Dictionnaire universel des Contemporains*, Paris.

Contemporary published studies and pamphlets

Alapetite, Gabriel (1993) 'Grève des mineurs et convention d'Arras', (extracts from Alapetite's memoirs) *Le Mouvement Social*, Vol. 164, pp. 17–23.
Anonymous (1891) *L'Armée et l'ordre public*, Paris: Henri Charles-Lavauzelle.
Anonymous (1894) *L'Armée sous le régime civil et les questions militaires pendantes*, Paris: Henri Charles-Lavauzelle.
Bebel, August (1972) *Nicht stehendes Heer sondern Volkswehr!*, New York, London: Garland, (first published 1898).
Bonnerain, Paul (1885) *Autour de la caserne*, Paris.
Charmes, Francis (1907) 'Chronique de la quinzaine', *Revue des deux mondes* of 1 July 1907.
Darrien, Georges (1890) *Biribi*, Paris.
Descaves, Lucien (1889) *Les Sous-Offs, roman militaire*, Paris: Tresse & Stock.
Desveaux, Ludovic (1899) *Les grèves de chemins de fer en France et à l'étranger*, Paris: Marchal & Billard.
Donop, Raoul Marie (1908) *Le rôle social de l'officier*, Paris.
Dumont, A. (1891) *Les Offs, roman de moeurs militaries*, Paris.
Fèvre, Henry (1887) *Au Port d'armes*, Paris.
Fosdick, Raymond (1969) *European Police Systems*, Montclair NJ: Patterson Smith, (first published 1915).
Francfort, Commandant (1895) *Le corps d'officiers des principales armées européennes*, Paris: Henri Charles-Lavauzelle.
Gohier, Urbain (1898) *L'armée contre la nation*, Paris: Revue Blanche.
Goltz, Colmar von der (1890) *Das Volk in Waffen. Ein Buch über das Heerwesen*, Berlin: Mittler, (first published 1883).
Guyot, Yves (1911) *Les chemins de fer et la grève*, Paris: Félix Alcan.
Hermant, Abel (1887) *Le Cavalier Miserey, 21e Chasseurs. Moeurs militaires contemporaines*, Paris: Charpentier.
Jaurès, Jean (1932) *L'Armée nouvelle: Œuvres de Jean Jaurès, tome IV*, Paris: Rieder, (first published 1911).
Lamy, Ernest (1885) 'L'armée et la démocratie', *Revue des deux mondes*, Vol. 69.
Laurent, E. (1904) *Impressions de grève*, Paris: Henri Charles-Lavauzelle.
Lémétayer, Capitaine (1912) *Aide-Mémoire de l'officier aux grèves*, Paris: Henri Charles-Lavauzelle.
Lewal, Jules (1894) *Les troupes coloniales*, Paris: Baudoin.

Liebknecht, Karl (1973) *Militarism and Antimilitarism*, Cambridge: River Press, (first published 1907).
Luxemburg, Rosa (1899) 'Miliz und Militarismus', *Leipziger Volkszeitung*, 25 February 1899.
Luxemburg, Rosa (1913) *Die Akkumulation des Kapitals*, Berlin.
Lyautey, Hubert (1891) 'Le rôle social de l'officier', *La Revue des Deux Mondes*, March 1891.
Messimy, Adolphe (1913) *Le problème militaire,* Paris: Henri Charles-Lavauzelle.
Quidde, Ludwig (1893) *Der Militarismus im heutigen deutschen Reich*, Stuttgart.
Quidde, Ludwig (1977) *Caligula: Schriften über Militarismus und Pazifismus*, Frankfurt: Campus, (first published 1894).
Sila, Commandant (1907) *Une Vie infernale. Mémoires d'un officier de cavalerie*, Paris: Henri Charles-Lavauzelle.
Stein, Lorenz von (1872) *Die Lehre vom Heerwesen*, Stuttgart: Cotta.
Thile, Lucien (1914) *Pouvoir civil et pouvoir militaire*, Paris: Rousseau.
Thoumas, General (1887) *Les transformations de l'armée francaise*, Paris: Henri Charles-Lavauzelle.
Verfeuil, Raoul (1913) *Pourquoi nous sommes anti-militaristes*, Villeneuve-Saint-Georges.
Yvetot, Georges (1902) *Nouveau mauel du soldat. Patrie, l'Armée, la Guerre*, Paris.
Z., Le Lieutenant (1904) *L'armée aux grèves. Grève générale des mineurs octobre–novembre 1902*, Paris: Société nouvelle de librairie et d'édition.

Secondary literature

Agulhon, Maurice (1993) *The French Republic*, Oxford: Blackwell.
Agulhon, Maurice (1997) *Coup d'État et République*, Paris: Presses de Sciences Po, 1997.
Alary, Eric (2000) *L'histoire de la gendarmerie de la renaissance au troisième millenaire*, Paris: Calman-Lévy.
Arnold, Edward J. (1999) 'Counter-revolutionary themes and the working class in France of the Belle Epoque: The case of the *syndicats jaunes* 1899–1912', *French History*, vol. 13 /2, pp. 99–133.
Augustine, Dolores (1984) *Patricians and Parvenus: Wealth and High Society in Wilhelmine Germany*, Oxford: Berg.

Augustine, Dolores (1993) 'Arriving in the upper class: the wealthy business elite of Wilhelmine Germany', in David Blackbourn and Richard J. Evans (eds.), *The German Bourgeoisie*, London: Routledge.

Azéma, Jean-Pierre and Michel Winock (1970) *La Troisième République: 1870–1914*, Paris: Calman-Lévy.

Babington, Anthony (1990) *Military intervention in Britain: from the Gordon riots to the Gibraltar incident*, London: Routledge.

Barge, Walther S. (1982) *The Generals of the Republic: the corporate personality of high military rank in France 1889–1914*, (unpublished Ph.D. thesis) University of North Carolina.

Bargeton, René (1994) *Dictionnaire Biographique des Préfets, 1870–1982*, Paris: Archives Nationales.

Becker, Jean-Jacques (1973) *Le carnet B: les pouvoirs publics et l'antimilitarisme avant la guerre de 1914*, Paris: Klincksieck.

Bédarida, François (1964) 'L'armée et la République, les opinions politiques des officiers français 1876–1878', *Révue Historique*, July–September, pp.119–164.

Berghahn, Volker R. (1981) *Militarism. The History of an International Debate, 1861–1979*, Leamington Spa: Berg.

Berghahn, Volker R. (1993) *Germany and the Approach of War in 1914*, Basingstoke: Macmillan.

Berghahn, Volker R. (1994) *Imperial Germany 1871–1914: Economy, Society, Culture and Politics*, Oxford: Berghahn.

Berlière, Jean-Marc (1991) *L'Institution policière en France sous la Troisième République, 1875–1914*, (unpublished these d'État) University of Bourgogne, Dijon.

Berlière, Jean-Marc (1993, 1) *Le Préfet Lepine: Vers la naissance de la police moderne*, Paris: Denoël.

Berlière, Jean-Marc (1993, 2) 'Du maintien de l'ordre républicain au maintien républicain de l'ordre?', *Génèses*, vol. 12, May, pp. 6–29.

Berlière, Jean-Marc (1994) 'Aux origines d'un conception "moderne" du maintien de l'ordre', in Madeleine Rebérioux (ed.), *Fourmies et les Premier Mai*, Paris: Les Éditions de l'Atelier.

Berlière, Jean-Marc (1996) *Le monde des polices en France*, Paris: Éditions Complexe.

Bernstein, Serge and Pierre Milza (1990) *Histoire de la France au XXe siècle, 1900–1930*, Paris: Éditions Complexe.

Blackbourn, David and Geoff Eley (1984) *The peculiarities of German history: Bourgeois society and politics in 19th century Germany*, Oxford: Oxford University Press.

Blackbourn, David (1993) *The Marpingen Vision: Rationalism, Religion and the Rise of Modern Germany*, London: HarperCollins.

Blackbourn, David (1997) *The Fontana History of Germany, 1780–1918: The Long Nineteenth Century*, London: Fontana.

Böll, Friedhelm (1989) 'Changing forms of labor conflict: secular development or strike waves?', in Leopold Haimson and Charles Tilly (eds.), *Strike, Wars, and Revolutions in an international Perspective*, Cambridge: Cambridge University Press.

Böll, Friedhelm (1992) *Arbeitskämpfe und Gewerkschaften in Deutschland, England und Frankreich*, Bonn: Dietz.

Born, Karl Erich (1957) *Staat und Sozialpolitik seit Bismarcks Sturtz: Ein Beitrag zur Geschichte der innenpolitischen Entwicklung des deutschen Reiches, 1890–1914*, Wiesbaden: Franz Steiner.

Born, Karl Erich (1985) *Wirtschafts- und Sozialgeschichte des Deutschen Kariserreich 1867/71–1914*, Stuttgart: Deutsche Verlag.

Brocke, Berhard vom (1981) 'Die preußischen Oberpräsidenten 1815 bis 1945. Sozialprofil einer Verwaltungselite', in Klaus Schwabe (ed.), *Die preußischen Oberpräsidenten, 1815–1945*, Boppard am Rhein: Boldt.

Brunetaux, Patrick (1993) 'Le désordre de la répression en France, 1871–1912: des conscrits aux gendarmes mobiles', *Genèses*, vol. 12, May, pp. 30–46.

Bruneteaux, Patrick (1996) *Maintenir l'ordre*, Paris: Presses de Sciences Po.

Bushnell, John (1985) *Mutiny amid Repression: Russian Soldiers in the Revolution of 1905–1906*, Bloomington: Indiana University Press.

Carrot, Georges (1984) *Maintien de l'ordre, depuis la fin de l'Ancien Régime jusqu'à 1968*, (unpublished these d'État) University of Nice.

Carrot, Georges (1990) *Le maintien de l'ordre en France au XXe siècle*, Paris: Veyrier.

Challener, Richard (1955) *The French Theory of the Nation in Arms 1866–1939*, New York: Columbia University Press.

Chapman, Brian (1955) *The Prefects and Provincial France*, London: Allen & Unwin.

Charle, Christoph (1980) *Les Hauts Fonctionaires en France au 19e siècle*, Paris: Gallimard.

Charle, Christoph (1987) *Les élites de la République (1880–1900)*, Paris: Gallimard.

Chaussinand-Nogaret, Guy (1991) *Histoire des élites en France du XVIe au XXe siècle*, Paris: Hachette.

Chickering, Roger (1975) *Imperial Germany and a World without War*, Princeton: Princeton University Press.

Christian, David (1997) *Imperial and Soviet Russia: Power, Privilege and the Challenge of Modernity*, London: Macmillan.
Clark, Christopher (2000) *Kaiser Wilhelm II*, London: Longman.
Cooper-Richet, Diane (1987) 'Le Plan général de protection à l'épreuve de la grève des mineurs du Nord-Pas-de-Calais (Septembre–Novembre 1902)', in Philippe Vigier (ed.), *Maintien de l'ordre et polices en France et en Europe au XIXe siècle*, Paris: Créaphis.
Craig, Gordon Alexander (1955) *The Politics of the Prussian Army, 1640-1945*, Oxford: Oxford University Press.
Craig, Gordon Alexander (1978) *Germany 1866–1945*, Oxford: Oxford University Press.
Crew, David F. (1982) 'Steel, Sabotage and Socialism: the strike at the Dortmund "Union" steel work in 1911', in Richard J. Evans (ed.), *The German Working Class 1888–1933*, London: Croom Helm.
Critchley, Tom A. (1967) *A History of Police in England and Wales, 1900–1966*, London: Constable.
Davis, John A. (1988) *Conflict and Control: Law and Order in Nineteenth Century Italy*, London: Macmillan.
Deák, István (1992) *Beyond Nationalism: a Social and Political History of the Habsburg Officer Corps, 1848–1918*, Oxford: Oxford University Press.
Deist, Wilhelm (1991, 1) 'Die Armee in Staat und Gesellschaft 1890–1914', (first published 1977), in Wilhelm Deist (ed.), *Militär, Staat und Gesellschaft 1890–1945*, Freiburg: Militärgeschichtliches Forschungsamt, pp. 19–41.
Deist, Wilhelm (1991, 2) 'Zur Geschichte des preußischen Offizierkorps 1888–1918', (first published 1980), in Wilhelm Deist (ed.), *Militär, Staat und Gesellschaft 1890–1945*, Freiburg: Militärgeschichtliches Forschungsamt, pp. 43–56.
Deist, Wilhelm (1991, 3) 'Kaiser Wilhelm II als Oberster Kriegsherr', in Wilhelm Deist (ed.), *Militär, Staat und Gesellschaft 1890–1945*, Freiburg: Militärgeschichtliches Forschungsamt, pp. 1–18.
Delaperrière, Eugène (1898) *L'armée française, organisation*, vols. 1–2, Paris: Henri Charles-Lavauzelle.
Delaperrière, Eugène (1902) *L'armée française, administration*, vols. 1–2, Paris: Henri Charles-Lavauzelle.
Delmare, Danielle (1994) 'Entre Socialisme et Catholicisme: Le Nord', in Pierre Birnbaum (ed.), *La France de l'Affaire Dreyfus*, Paris: Gallimard.
Demeter, Karl (1965) *The German Officer Corps 1650–1945*, London: Weidenfeld & Nicolson (first published 1930).

Dissaux, Jean-Marc (1996) *Les préfet du Pas-de-Calais*, Arras: Publication du Conseil Général du Pas-de-Calais.
Dreyfus, Michel (1995) *Histoire de la C.G.T.*, Paris: Éditions complexe.
Dunnage, Jonathan (1995), 'Law and Order in Giolittian Italy: A case Study of the Province of Bologna', *European History Quarterly*, vol. 25, pp. 381–408.
Dupâquier, Jacques (1988) *Histoire de la population française de 1789 à 1914*, Paris: Presses Universitaires de France.
Eley, Geoff (1986) *From Unification to Nazism*, London: Allen & Unwin.
Emsley, Clive (1983) *Policing in its context, 1750–1870*, London: Macmillan.
Emsley, Clive (1996) *The English Police: a political and social history*, Harlow: Longman.
Emsley, Clive (1999) *Gendarmes and the State in Nineteenth-Century Europe*, Oxford: Oxford University Press.
Estèbe, Jean (1994) 'Un théâtre politique renouvelé', in Pierre Birnbaum (ed.), *La France de l'affaire Dreyfus*, Paris: Gallimard.
Euler, Friedrich Wilhelm (1980) 'Die deutsche Generalität und Admiralität bis 1918', in Hanns Hubert Hofmann (ed.), *Das deutsche Offizierkorps 1860–1960*, Boppard am Rhein: Boldt.
Evans, Peter, Dietrich Rueschmeyer and Theda Skocpol (1989) 'On the road towards a more adequate understanding of the State', in Peter Evans, Dietrich Rueschmeyer and Theda Skocpol (eds.), *Bringing the State back in*, Cambridge: Cambridge University Press.
Evans, Richard J. (1987) *Rethinking German History: Nineteenth Century Germany and the Origins of the Third Reich*, London: HarperCollins.
Evans, Richard J. (1997) *Rereading German History 1800–1996: From Unification to Reunification*, London: Routledge.
Förster, Stig (1985) *Der doppelte Militarismus: die deutsche Heeresrüstungspolitik zwischen Status-quo-Sicherung und Aggression, 1890–1913*, Stuttgart: Franz Steiner.
Fuller, William C. (1985) *Civil-Military Conflicts in Imperial Russia, 1881–1914*, Princeton: Princeton University Press.
Funk, Albrecht (1986) *Polizei und Rechtsstaat: Die Entstehung des staatsrechtlichen Gewaltmonopols in Preußen, 1848–1918*, Frankfurt: Campus.
Gall, Lothar (2000) *Krupp: Der Aufstieg eines Industrieimperiums*, Munich: Siedler.
Geary, Dick (1980) *European labour protest, 1848–1939*, London: Croom Helm.

Geary, Dick (1993) 'The industrial bourgeoisie and labour relations in Germany 1871–1933', in David Blackbourn and Richard J. Evans (eds.), *The German Bourgeoisie*, London: Routledge.

Geary, Roger (1985) *Policing Industrial Disputes: 1893 to 1985*, Cambridge: Cambridge University Press.

Gildea, Robert (1994) *The Past in French History*, New Haven: Yale University Press.

Girardet, Raoul (1953) *La société miliaire dans la France contemporaine 1815–1939*, Paris: Plon.

Girardet, Raoul (1962) 'Civil and Military Power in the Fourth Republic', in Samuel Huntington (ed.), *Changing Patterns of Military Politics*, Glencoe: Free Press.

Goguel, François (1970) *Géographie des élections françaises sous la Troisième et la Quatrième République*, Paris: Armand Colin.

Gooch, John (1989) *Army, State and Society in Italy, 1870–1915*, London: Macmillan.

Gorce, Paul-Marie de la (1963) *The French Army: a military-political history*, London: Weidenfeld & Nicolson.

Gordon, David (1898) 'Liberalism and Socialism in the Nord', *French History*, vol. 3 /3, 1989, pp. 312–341.

Groh, Dieter (1978) 'Intensification of Work and Industrial Conflict in Germany, 1896–1914', *Politics and Society*, vol. 8, pp. 349–397.

Haupt, Heinz-Gerhard (1986) 'Staatliche Bürokratie und Arbeiterbewegung: Zum Einfluss der Polizei auf die Konstituierung von Arbeiterbewegung und Arbeiterklasse in Deutschland und Frankreich zwischen 1848 und 1880', in Heinz-Gerhard Haupt (ed.), *Arbeiter und Bürger im 19. Jahrhundert. Varianten ihres Verhältnisses im europäischen Vergleich*, Munich: Beck.

Hélie, Jerôme (1994) 'L'Arche Sainte fracturée', in Pierre Birnbaum (ed.), *La France de l'Affaire Dreyfus*, Paris: Gallimard.

Henning, Hansjoachim (1984) *Die deutsche Beamtenschaft im 19. Jarhundert: Zwischen Stand und Beruf*, Stuttgart: Franz Steiner.

Henning, Hansjoachim (1987) 'Staatsmacht und Arbeitskampf: Die Haltung der preußischen Innenverwaltung zum Militäreinsatz während der Bergausstände 1889–1912', in Hansjoachim Henning (ed.), *Wirtschafts- und sozialgeschichtliche Forschung und Probleme – Festschrift für Karl Erich Born*, Frankfurt: Campus Verlag.

Heywood, Colin (1998) 'Mobilising the Workers in fin-de-siècle France', *French History*, vol. 12 /2, pp. 172–194.

Hickney, Stephen (1978) 'The shaping of the German Labour movement: miners in the Ruhr', in Richard Evans (ed.), *Society and Politics in Wilhelmine Germany*, London: Croom Helm.

Hickney, Stephen (1985) *Workers in Imperial Germany: Miners of the Ruhr*, Oxford: Clarendon.

Hobsbawm, Eric (1997) *The Age of Empire, 1875–1914*, London: Abacus (first published 1987).

Höhn, Reinhard (1956–1969) *Sozialismus und Heer*, (vols. 1–3), Bad Homburg: Max Gehlen.

Huber, Ernst R. (1963) *Deutsche Verfassungsgeschichte seit 1789*, (vol. III), Stuttgart: Kohlhammer.

Huber, Ernst R. (1969) *Deutsche Verfassungsgeschichte seit 1789*, (vol. IV), Stuttgart: Kohlhammer.

Hughes, Daniel (1980) 'Occupational Origins of Prussian Generals, 1871–1914', *Central European History* XIII, vol.1, pp. 3–33.

Hughes, Daniel (1987) *The King's Finest: a Social and Bureaucratic Profile of Prussia's General Officers 1871–1914*, New York: Atheneum.

Hughes, Steven C. (1994) *Crime and Disorder and the Risorgimento: the politics of policing Bologna*, Cambridge: Cambridge University Press.

Huntington, Samuel (1957) *The Soldier and the State*, Cambridge, MA: Harvard University Press.

Ingenlath, Markus (1994) *Mentale Aufrüstung: Militarisierungstendenzen in Frankreich und Deutschland vor dem Ersten Weltkrieg*, Frankfurt am Main: Campus.

Jauffret, Jean-Charles (1983) 'Armée et Pouvoir Politique: la question des troupes spécialisées chargées du maintien de l'ordre en France de 1871 à 1914', *Revue Historique*, vol. 270, pp. 97–144.

Jauffret, Jean-Charles (1987) *Parlement, Gouvernement, Commandement. L'armée de métier sous la IIIe République 1871–1914*, (vols. 1–2), Vincennes: Société Historique de l'Armée de Terre.

Jeserich, Kurt, Hans Pohl and Georg-Christoph Unruh (1984) *Deutsche Verwaltungsgeschichte: Das deutsche Reich bis zum Ende der Monarchie*, Stuttgart: Deutsche Verlags-Anstalt.

Jensen, Ralph Bach (1991) *Liberty and Order: The Theory and Practice of Italian Public Security Police, 1848 to the Crisis of the 1890s*, New York: Garland.

Jessen, Ralph (1991) *Polizei im Industrierevier: Modernisierung und Herrschaftspraxis im Westfälischen Ruhrgebiet 1848–1914*, Göttingen: Vandenhoeck & Ruprecht.

Jessen, Ralph (1992) 'Unternehmerherrschaft und staatliches Gewaltmonopol. Hüttenpolizisten und Zechenwehren im Ruhrgebiet 1870–1914', in Alf Lüdtke (ed.), *Sicherheit und Wohlfart: Polizei, Gesellschaft und Herrschaft im 19. und 20. Jahrhundert*, Frankfurt am Main: Suhrkamp.

Johnson, Eric A. (1995) *Urbanisation and Crime: Germany 1871–1914*, Cambridge: Cambridge University Press.

Julliard, Jacques (1965) *Clemenceau, briseur de grève: l'affaire de Draveil-Villeneuve-Saint-George*, Paris: Julliard.

Kaeble, Hartmut (1980) 'Long-term changes in the recruitment of the business elite: Germany compared to the U.S., Great Britain and France since the Industrial Revolution', *Journal of Social History*, vol. 13, pp. 404–423.

Kaudelka-Hanisch, Karin (1993) 'The Titled Businessman: Prussian Commercial Councillors in the Rhineland and Westphalia during the nineteenth century', in David Blackbourn and Richard J. Evans (eds.), *The German Bourgeoisie*, London: Routledge, pp. 87–114.

Kehr, Eckart (1977, 1) 'The Genesis of the Prussian Reserve Officer', in Gordon Alexander Craig (ed.), *Economic Interest, Militarism and Foreign Policy*, Berkeley: University of California Press.

Kehr, Eckart (1977, 2) 'The Genesis of the Prussian Bureaucracy and the *Rechtsstaat*', in Gordon Alexander Craig (ed.), *Economic Interest, Militarism and Foreign Policy*, Berkeley: University of California Press.

Kitchen, Martin (1968) *The German Officer Corps, 1890–1914*, Oxford: Clarendon.

Klückmann, Harald (1978) 'Requisition und Einsatz bewaffneter Macht in der deutschen Verfassungs- und Militärgeschichte', *Militärgeschichtliche Mitteilungen*, vol. 1, pp. 7–43.

Knöbl, Wolfgang (1998) *Polizei und Herrschaft im Modernisierungsprozeß: Staatsbildung und innere Sicherheit in Preußen, England und Amerika 1700–1914*, Frankfurt am Main: Campus.

Knopp, Gerhard (1974) *Die preußische Verwaltung des Regierungsbezirks Düsseldorf 1899–1919*, Cologne: Grote.

Kocka, Jürgen (1999) *Industrial culture and bourgeois society: business, labor and bureaucracy in modern Germany*, Oxford: Berghahn Books.

Krumeich, Gerd (1980) 'Zur Problematik des Konzepts der "nation armée" in Frankreich', *Militärgeschichtliche Mitteilungen*, vol. 2, pp. 35–43.

Krumeich, Gerd (1994) 'Zur Entwicklung der "nation armée" in Frankreich bis zum Ersten Weltkrieg', in R. G. Foerster (ed.), *Die Wehrpflicht: Entstehung, Erscheinungsformen und politisch-militärische Wirkung*, Munich: Oldenburg.

Le Clère, Bernard and Vincent Wright (1973) *Les Préfets du Second Empire*, Paris: Armand Colin.
Le Clère, Marcel (1947) *Histoire de la police*, Paris: Presses Universitaires de France.
Leesch, Wolfgang (1992) *Verwaltung in Westfalen 1815–1945. Organisation und Zuständigkeit*, Münster: Aschendorff.
Léquin, Yves (1988) *La Mosaïque France*, Paris: Larousse.
Liang, Hsi-Huey (1992) *The Rise of Modern Police and the European State System from Metternich to the Second World War*, Cambridge: Cambridge University Press.
Lieven, Dominic (1992), *The Aristocracy in Europe, 1815–1914*, London: Macmillan.
Linden, Marcel van der and Wayne Thorpe (1992) 'Essor et decline du syndicalisme révolutionnaire', *Le Mouvement Social*, vol. 159.
Lindenberger, Thomas (1993) 'Politique de rue et action de classe à Berlin avant la première guerre mondiale', *Génèses*, vol. 12, pp. 47–68.
Lindenberger, Thomas (1995) *Straßenpolitik. Zur Sozialgeschichte der öffentlishen Ordnung in Berlin*, Bonn: Dietz.
Loth, Wilfried (1996) *Das Kaiserreich: Obrigkeitstaat und politische Mobilisierung*, Munich: Deutscher Taschenbuch Verlag.
Luc, Jean-Noël (ed.) (2002) *Gendarmerie, État et société au XIXe siècle*, Paris: Publications de la Sorbonne.
Lucas, Erhard, James Wickham and Karl-Heinz Roth (1977) *Arbeiter-Radikalismus und die 'andere' Arbeiterbewegung*, Bochum: Edition Egalite.
Lüdtke, Alf (1977) 'Praxis und Funktion staatlicher Repression: Preußen 1815–1850', *Geschichte und Gesellschaft*, vol. 3, 1977, pp. 190–211.
Lüdtke, Alf (1979) 'The Role of State Violence in the Period of Transition to Industrial Capitalism: the Example of Prussia from 1815 to 1848', *Social History*, No. 4, pp. 175–221.
Lüdtke, Alf (1982) *"Gemeinwohl", Polizei und "Festungspraxis". Staatliche Gewaltsamkeit und innere Verwaltung in Preußen, 1815–1850*, Göttingen: Vandenhoeck & Ruprecht.
Lüdtke, Alf (1991) *Herrschaft als soziale Praxis: historische und sozialanthropologische Studien*, Göttingen: Vandenhoeck & Ruprecht.
Lüdtke, Alf (ed.) (1992) *Sicherheit und Wohlfart: Polizei, Gesellschaft und Herrschaft im 19. und 20. Jahrhundert*, Frankfurt: Suhrkamp.
Machelon, Jean-Pierre (1976) *La République contre les libertés*, Paris: Fondation Nationale des Sciences Politiques.
Magraw, Roger (1992) *Workers and the Bourgeois Republic*, Oxford: Blackwell.

Magraw, Roger (1996) 'Management, Labour and the State in France, 1871–1939: Industrial relations in the Third Republic', in Peter Mathias and John A. Davis (eds.), *The Nature of Industrialisaiton*, Oxford: Blackwell.
Magraw, Roger (2002) *France 1800–1914: A Social History*, London: Longman.
March, James and Johan Olsen (1989) *Rediscovering Institutions: The Organisational Basis of Politics*, New York: The Free Press.
Mayeur, Jean-Marie (1984) *La vie politique sous la Troisième République*, Paris: Seuil.
Messerschmidt, Manfred (1970) 'Die Armee in Staat und Gesellschaft. Die Bismarckzeit', in Michael Stürmer (ed.), *Das kaiserliche Deutschland*, Düsseldorf: Droste.
Messerschmidt, Manfred (1975) *Militär und Politik in der Bimarckzeit und im wilhelminischen Deutschland*, Darmstadt: Wissenschaftliche Buchgesellschaft.
Messerschmidt, Manfred (with E. von Matuschka and Wolfgang Petters) (1979) Militärgeschichte im 19. Jahrhundert, 1814–1890, (Part IV-2 of Hans Meier-Welcker (ed.), *Handbuch zur deutschen Militärgeschichte 1648–1939*), Munich: Beck.
Messerschmidt, Manfred (1980) 'Preußens Militär in seinem gesellschaftlichen Umfeld', in Hans-Jürgen Puhle (ed.), *Preußen im Rückblick*, Göttingen: Vandenheock & Ruprecht.
Messerschmidt, Manfred (1994) 'Militär, Politik, Gesellschaft. Ein Vergleich', in Manfred Messerschmidt and William Serman (eds.), *Eliten in Deutschland und Frankreich im 19. und 20. Jahrhundert*, Munich: Oldenburg.
Miller, Paul (2002) *From Revolutionaries to Citizens: Antimilitarism in France 1870–1914*, Durham, NJ: Duke University Press.
Miller, Wilbur R. (1973) *Cops and Bobbies: Police Authority in New York and London, 1830–1870*, Chicago: University of Chicago Press.
Mitchell, Allan (1981) 'A Situation of Inferiority: French Military Reorganization after the defeat of 1870', *American Historical Review*, vol. 86, pp. 49–62.
Mitchell, Allan (1984) *Victors and Vanquished*, Chapel Hill: University of North Carolina.
Moeller, R. G. (1984) 'The Kaiserreich Recast?', *Journal of Social History*, vol. 17.
Mommsen, Wolfgang J. (1995) *Imperial Germany, 1867–1918: Politics, Culture and Society in an Authoritarian State*, London: Arnold.

Mommsen, Wolfgang J. and Gerhard Hirschfeld (eds.) (1982) *Social Protest, Violence and Terror in 19th and 20th Century Europe*, New York: St. Martin's Press.
Monkkonnen, Eric (1981) *Police in Urban America, 1860–1920*, Cambridge: Cambridge University Press.
Monteilhet, J. (1926) *Les institutions militaires de la France (1814–1932)*, Paris: Felix Alcan.
Morgan, Jane (1987) *Conflict and Order: the Police and labour disputes in England and Wales, 1900–1939*, Oxford: Clarendon.
Nipperdey, Thomas (1992) *Deutsche Geschichte 1866-1918: Machtstaat vor der Demokratie*, Munich: Beck.
Pedroncini, Guy (ed.) (1992) *Histoire Militaire de la France de 1871 à 1940*, (vol. 3) Paris: Presses Universitaires de France.
Perrot, Michelle (1974) *Les ouvriers en grève, France 1870–1890*, Paris: Mouton.
Pierenkemper, Toni (1979) *Die Westfälischen Schwerindustriellen 1852–1913. Soziale Struktur und unternehmerischer Erfolg*, Göttingen: Vandenhoeck & Ruprecht.
Preradovich, Nikolaus von (1955) *Die Führungsschichten in Österreich und Preußen (1808–1918)*, Wiesbaden: Franz Steiner.
Puhle, Hans-Jürgen (1980) 'Preußen: Entwicklung und Fehlentwicklung', in Hans-Jürgen Puhle and Hans-Ulrich Wehler (eds.), *Preußen im Rückblick*, Göttingen: Vandenhoeck & Ruprecht.
Ralston, David B. (1967) *The army of the Republic: The place of the military in the political evolution of France, 1871–1914*, Cambridge: Cambridge University Press.
Rebérioux, Madeleine and Jean-Marie Mayeur (1989) *The Third Republic from its Origins to the Great War, 1871–1914*, Cambridge: Cambridge University Press.
Rebérioux, Madeleine, 'Introduction', in Madeleine Rebérioux (ed.), *Fourmies et les Premier Mai*, Paris: Les Éditions de l'Atelier.
Reif, Heinz (1979) *Westfälischer Adel 1770–1860*, Göttingen: Vandenhoeck & Ruprecht.
Reif, Heinz (1999) *Adel im 19. und 20. Jahrhundert*, Munich: Oldenburg.
Reinke, Herbert (ed.) (1993) *"Nur für die Sicherheit da?..." Zur Geschichte der Polizei im 19. und 20. Jahrhundert*, Frankfurt am Main: Suhrkamp.
Rémond, René (2002) *La République souveraine: La vie politique en France 1879–1939*, Paris: Fayard.
Repp, Kevin (2000) *Reformers, Critics and the Path of German Modernity*, Cambridge, MA: Harvard University Press.

Ritter, Gerhard (1972) *The Sword and the Sceptre: The problem of Militarism in Germany*, vols. 1–2, London: Penguin, (originally published in 1954).

Ritter, Gerhard A. and Klaus Tenfelde (1992) *Arbeiter im deutschen Kaiserreich, 1871/1875 bis 1914*, Bonn: Verlag Dietz.

Rohkrämer, Thomas (1990) *Der Militarismus der "kleinen Leute": Die Kriegervereine in deutschen Kaiserreich, 1871–1914*, Munich: Oldenburg.

Röhl, John (1996) *The Kaiser and his Court: Wilhelm II and the Government of Germany*, Cambridge: Cambridge University Press.

Rothenberg, Gunther E. (1998) *The Army of Francis Joseph*, West Lafayette: Purdue University Press.

Roynette-Gland, Odile (1997) 'L'armée dans la bataille sociale: maintien de l'ordre et grèves ouvrières dans le Nord de la France (1871–1906)', *Le Mouvement Social*, vol. 179, April–June.

Sauer, Wolfgang (1966) 'Das Problem des deutschen Nationalsataates', in Hans-Ulrich Wehler (ed.), *Moderne deutsche Sozialgeschichte* Berlin: Kiepenheuer & Witsch.

Saul, Klaus (1974) *Staat, Industrie, Arbeiterbewegung im Kaiserreich. Zur Innen- und Sozialpolitik des wilhelminischen Deutschland 1903–1914*, Düsseldorf: Droste.

Saul, Klaus (1981) 'Zwischen Repression und Integration: Staat, Gewerkschaften und Arbeitskampf im kaiserlichen Deutschland 1884 bis 1914', in Klaus Tenfelde, Heinrich Volkmann and Gerd Hohorst (eds.), *Zur Geschichte des Arbeitskampfes in Deutschland während der Industrialisierung*, Munich: Beck.

Schmidt-Richberg, Wiegand and Edgar von Matuschka (1979) 'Von der Entlassung Bismarcks bis zum Ende des Ersten Weltkrieges, 1890-1918', in Hans Meier-Welcker (ed.), *Handbuch zur deutschen Militärgeschichte 1648-1939*, part V, Munich: Beck.

Schoenbaum, David (1982) *Zabern 1913: Consensus Politics in Imperial Germany*, London: Allen & Unwin.

Schwabe, Klaus (1981) 'Einführung', in Klaus Schwabe (ed.), *Die preußischen Oberpräsidenten, 1815–1945*, Boppard am Rhein: Boldt.

Skocpol, Theda and Paul Pierson (2002) 'Historical Institutionalism in Contemporary Political Science', in Ira Katznelson and Helen Milner (eds.) *Political Science: the State of the Discipline*, New York: Norton.

Serman, William (1970) 'Les Généraux français de 1870', *Revue de Défense Nationale*, August–September, pp. 1319–1330.

Serman, William (1982) *Les officiers français dans la nation, 1848–1914*, Paris: Aubier.

Serman, William (1994) 'Les élites militaires françaises et la politique, 1871–1914', in Manfred Messerschmidt and William Serman (eds.), *Eliten in Deutschland und Frankreich im 19. und 20. Jahrhundert*, Munich: Oldenburg.

Sieman, Wolfram (1985) *Deutschlands Ruhe Sicherheit und Ordnung: Anfänge der politischen Polizei, 1806–1866*, Tübingen: Niemeyer.

Siwek-Pouydesseau, Jeanne (1969) *Le corps préfectoral sous la Troisième et la Quatrième République*, Paris: Armand Colin.

Sorlin, Pierre (1969) *La société francaise, 1840–1914*, Paris: Arthaud.

Spencer, Elaine Glovka (1974) 'Businessmen, Bureaucrats and Social control in the Ruhr, 1914', in Hans-Ulrich Wehler (ed.), *Sozialgeschichte heute*, Göttingen: Vandenhoeck & Ruprecht.

Spencer, Elaine Glovka (1984) *Management and Labor in Imperial Germany. Ruhr Industrialists as Employers, 1896–1914*, New Braunswick, NJ: Rutgers University Press.

Spencer, Elaine Glovka (1985) 'Police-Military Relations in Prussia 1848–1914', *Journal of Social History*, vol. 19, pp. 305–317.

Spencer, Elaine Glovka (1992) *Police and the Social Order in German Cities: the Düsseldorf District, 1848–1914*, DeKalb: Northern Illinois University Press.

Spenkuch, Hartwin (2003) 'Vergleichsweise besonders? Politische System und Strukturen Preußens als Kern des "deutschen Sonderwegs"', *Geschichte und Gesellschaft*, vol. 29 /2, 2003, pp. 262–293.

Stargardt, Nicholas (1994) *The German Idea of Militarism: Radical and Socialist Critics, 1866–1914*, Cambridge: Cambridge Univeristy Press.

Storch, Robert D. (1975) 'The Plague of the Blue Locust. Police Reform and Popular Resistance in Northern England, 1840–1857', *International Review of Social History*, vol. 20, pp. 61–90.

Storch Rober D. (1975–1976) 'The Policeman as Domestic Missionary: Urban Discipline and Popular Culture in Northern England, 1850–1880', *Journal of Social History*, vol. 9, pp. 482–509.

Stürmer, Michel (1983) *Das ruhelose Reich, Deutschland 1866–1918*, Berlin: Severin & Siedler.

Tenfelde, Klaus (1979) 'Die "Krawalle von Herne" im Jahre 1899', *Internationale wissenschaftliche Korrespondenz zur Geschichte der deutschen Arbeiterbewegung*, vol. 15, pp. 71–104.

Tenfelde, Klaus, Heinrich Volkmann and Gerd Hohorst (eds.) (1981) *Streik. zur Geschichte des Arbeitskampfes in Deutschland während der Industrialisierung*, Munich: Beck.

Teuteberg, Hans-Jürgen (1980) *Westfälische Textilunternehmer in der Industrialisierung. Sozialer Status und betriebliches Verhalten im 19.*

Jahrhundert, Dortmund: Gsellschaft für Westfälische Wirtschaftsgeschichte.
Thompson, Alastar P. (2000) *Left Liberals, the State and Popular Politics in Wilhelmine Germany*, Oxford University Press.
Tilly, Charles and Edward Shorter (1971) 'Déclin de la grève violente en France, 1890–1935', *Le Mouvement Social*, vol. 7.
Tilly, Charles and Edward Shorter (1974) *Strikes in France 1830–1968*, Cambridge: Cambridge University Press.
Tilly, Charles, Louise Tilly and Richard Tilly (1975) *The Rebellious Century 1830–1930*, Cambridge, MA: Harvard University Press.
Tilly, Charles (1986) *The Contentious French*, Cambridge MA: Harvard University Press.
Tilly, Richard (1970) 'Popular disorders in nineteenth-century Germany: a preliminary survey', *Journal of Social History*, vol. 4, pp. 1–40.
Tilly, Richard and Gerd Hohorst (1976) 'Sozialer Protest in Deutschland in 19. Jahrhundert: Skizze eines Forschungsansatzes', in Konrad Jarausch (ed.), *Quantifizierung in der Geschichtswissenschaft. Probleme und Möglichkeiten*, Düsseldorf: Droste.
Tombs, Robert (1996) *France 1814–1914*, London: Longman.
Trempé, Rolande (1995) *La France ouvrière*, Part II: 1871–1914, Paris: Les Éditions de l'Atelier.
Trumpener, Ulrich (1979) 'Junkers and others: the rise of commoners in the Prussian army, 1871–1914', *Canadian Journal of History*, vol. 14, April, pp. 29–47.
Ullmann, Hans-Peter (1976) *Der Bund der Industriellen*, Göttingen: Vandenhoeck & Ruprecht.
Ullmann, Hans-Peter (1995) *Das deutsche Kaiserreich*, Frankfurt: Suhrkamp.
Vagts, Alfred (1959) *A History of Militarism: Civilian and Military*, London: Hollis & Carter.
Verhey, Jeffrey (2000) *The Spirit of 1914: militarism, myth and mobilisation in Germany*, Cambridge: Cambridge University Press.
Vogel, Jakob (1997) *Nationen im Gleichschnitt: der Kult der "Nation im Waffen" in Deutschland und Frankreich, 1871–1914*, Göttingen: Vandenhoeck & Ruprecht.
Vogel, Jakob (1999) '"Folklorenmilitarismus" in Deutschland und Frankreich', in Wolfram Wette (ed.), *Militarismus in Deutschland 1871 bis 1945*, Hamburg: LIT.
Wal, Ronald van der (2003) *Of geweld zal worden gebruikt! Militaire bijstand bij de handhaving en het herstel van de openbare orde 1840–1920*, Hilversum: Verloren.

Weber, Eugen (1976) *Peasants into Frenchmen*, Stanford: Stanford University Press.
Wegmann, Dietrich (1969) *Die leitenden staatlichen Verwaltungsbeamten der Provinz Westphalen, 1815–1918*, Münster: Aschendorff.
Wegner, Günter (1990) *Stellenbesetzung der deutschen Heere, 1815–1933*, Osnabrück: Institut zur Erforschung historischer Führungsschichten.
Wehler, Hans-Ulrich (1970) 'Symbol des halb-absolutistischen Herrschaftssystems: Der Fall Zabern von 1913/1914 als Verfassungskrise des wilhelminischen Kaiserreichs', in Hans-Ulrich Wehler (ed.), *Krisenherde des Kaiserreichs, 1871–1918,* Göttingen: Vandenhoeck & Ruprecht.
Wehler, Hans-Ulrich (1985) *The German Empire 1871–1918*, Oxford: Berg.
Wehler, Hans-Ulrich (1995) *Deutsche Gesellschaftsgeschichte, 1849–1914*, Munich: Beck.
Wesseling, Hendrick L. (2000) *Soldiers and Warriors: French attitudes towards the army at the era of the First World War*, Westpoint, Conn.: Greenwood Press.
Westwood, N. J. (1993) *Endurance and Endeavour*, Oxford: Oxford University Press.
Whittam, John (1977) *The Politics of the Italian Army, 1861–1918*, London: Macmillan.
Winkler, Heinrich August (2000) *Der lange Weg nach Westen*, Munich: Beck.
Winock, Michel (1973) 'Socialisme et Patriotisme en France (1891–1894)', *Revue d'histoire moderne et contemporaine*, vol. 20.
Winock, Michel (1999) *La France Politique, XIXe-XXe siècle*, Paris: Seuil.
Winock, Michel (2002) *La Belle Époque: La France de 1900 à 1914*, Paris: Perrin.
Wright, Vincent (1990) 'The History of French Mayors: Lessons and Problems', *Jahrbuch Europäischer Verwaltung*, vol. 2, 1990, pp. 268–280.
Wright, Vincent (1994) 'La réserve du corps préfectoral', in Pierre Birnbaum (ed.), *La France de l'affaire Dreyfus*, Paris: Gallimard.
Zunkel, Friedrich (1962) *Der Rheinisch-Westfälische Unternehmer, 1834–1879*, Cologne, Opladen: Westdeutscher Verlag.

Index

Administration, France
    Civil-military cooperation, 15–16, 18–21, 45, 220–43, 275–9
    Municipal authorities, 183–89
    Organisation, 44–5
Administration, Prussia
    Civil-military cooperation, 15–16, 18–21, 49–51, 68–70, 249–70, 275–79
    Municipal authorities, 50, 68–70, 175–83
    Organisation, 49–50
Affaire des Fiches, 210–11, 227, 278
Alapetite, Gabriel (Prefect of 'Pas-de-Calais') 92, 104, 188
Albedyll, General Emil von, 74, 76–8, 164, 180, 203, 205, 207, 255, 258–60, 267, 269
André, General Louis, 210, 223, 228, 239, 278
Anti-Catholic Legislation (France)
    The closing of religious congregations (1880s), 116, 215, 236
    The separation of Church and State (1902–1906), 116, 129, 163–64, 215, 226, 235–6, 278
    Inventories of the possessions of the Catholic Church (1906), 97, 163–4, 192, 214–15, 234, 235–6, 243
Anti-Catholic Legislation (Germany) see *Kulturkampf*
Anzin, 87, 93–4, 156
Army, French
    Attitudes of senior commanders, 34, 210–16
    Authority of command, 34, 54
    Constitutional position, 43–4, 48–9
    Desertions, 42
    Officer corps, 43–5
    Pernicious effect on soldiers, 3, 34–7, 54
    Prestige, 37, 40–43
    Universal conscription, 34–6, 223, 232, 241
    Use for non-military functions, 223, 240–1
Army, Prussian
    Attitude of senior commanders, 34, 72–6, 180
    Authority of Command, 34, 37, 48–9, 51–4
    Brutality against soldiers, 39
    Constitutional position, 12–13, 47–9
    Declaration of state of siege, 48, 52, 63–4, 67–9
    Involvement in the fight against the Social Democratic Party, 12, 60, 62–7, 251–3, 278, 282
    Officer corps, 12, 38–9, 48
    Pernicious effect on soldiers, 3, 34–7, 54
    Prestige, 38–40
    Reorganisation 1807–1815, 37, 49
    Universal conscription, 34–7
    Use for non-military functions, 262–4
Arnsberg, 255, 260, 262
Arras, 45

Basly, Émile, 97, 191
Bebel, August, 39, 73, 263
Berlepsch, Hans von, 67–8, 178

Bernhardi, General Friedrich von, 202, 206
Bismarck, Otto von, 52, 63, 119, 199
Bissing, General Moritz von, 65, 73, 76, 180, 257, 258, 260, 267
Bochum, 115, 260, 262
Boulanger movement, 116, 129, 156–7
Briand, Aristide, 85, 113,
Bronsart von Schellendorf, General Walther (Prussian War Minister), 73–74, 263

Calais, 114, 122, 228, 231
Casualties among protesters
　France, 8, 89, 101–102, 130, 132–5
　Germany, 130, 132–5
　Italy, 102
　Russia, 102
Clemenceau, Georges, 41, 86, 91, 95–8, 103–105, 113, 189, 234
Combes, Émile, 41, 86, 91, 95–6, 103, 189
Commune, the Paris, 1–2, 36, 42, 105, 156, 276
Confédération générale du travail (C.G.T.) See Trade Unions
Constans, Jean Antoine (French Interior Minister), 92,
Courrière, the Catastrophe of (1906), 96, 163

Dallwitz, Hans von (Prussian Interior Minister), 253
Decazeville, 87, 156
Deimling, General Berthold von, 182, 207, 269
Desoille, General Emile, 225–6
Dortmund, 115, 259–60, 262
Dreyfus Affair, the, 40, 41, 44, 116, 129, 208–209, 211, 224, 227, 278
Dunkirk, 114, 122, 160–1, 221, 226, 228, 231

Düsseldorf, 257, 260, 262
Einem, Karl von (Prussian War Minister; Army Corps Commander in Westphalia, 75–8, 155, 202, 206, 253, 258–9, 265, 268–9
Elites, 12, 19–21, 175–93, 198–216
Essen, 115, 145, 260, 262

Fourmies, 42, 84, 89, 92–3, 96, 102–103, 105, 133, 185, 190, 212, 235
France, General Camille Louis de, 228
Franco-Prussian War 1870–1871, 36, 40, 45,
Freyciner, Charles de, 85, 86–7, 92–3, 95, 103–104

Galliffet, General Gaston, 208, 236
Gelsenkirchen, 115, 145, 177, 260, 262
Gendarmerie, French, 3
　Establishment, 142
　Number of gendarmes, 19–21, 85–86, 140–41, 144–51
Gendarmerie, Prussian
　Establishment, 143
　Number of gendarmes, 19–21, 60–62, 140–41, 144–51
　Under military command, 52, 261
Gendarmerie Mobile, France
　Debates on the establishment of, 9, 85, 103–104, 280
　The establishment of (1921), 1
Guesde, Jules, 42, 117
Guyot, Yves, 241

Hagenmeister, Robert (Province Governor in Westphalia), 67–68, 204, 260
Hamburg, 66, 75, 78, 159
Hamborn, 127
Hammerstein-Loxten, Hans von

(Prussian Interior Minister), 256
Heeringen, Josias von (Prussian War Minister), 65, 72–3, 251, 258, 261
Hennion, Célestin, 225
Herrfurth, Ernst Ludwig von (Prussian Interior Minister), 201–202, 260
Herne, 77, 134, 159–60, 165–6, 251, 262, 264, 268
Hindenburg, General Paul von, 65, 75, 267
Historical institutionalism, 15–17, 220

Industrial Pressure groups, France, 175, 189–91
Industrial Pressure groups, Prussia, 68, 175–83

Jaurès, Jean, 36–7, 42
Jourdy, General Emile, 211, 213

Kluck, General Alexander (von), 203
Koeller, Ernst von (Prussian Interior Minister), 68–9,
Krupp Company, the 148, 181–2
Kühlwetter, Friedrich (von), 201, 204
Kulturkampf, 60, 117, 158, 204–205

Lafargue, Paul, 117
Lebon, General Félix, 225–7, 229, 232
Legislation, France
  On the maintenance of public order, 46–7, 54, 117, 227–31, 238
  On the organisation of civilian and military authorities, 44–5, 54
  On municipal policing, 88–9, 142, 184–5
  On workers' organisation, 87, 116–17
Legislation, Germany and Prussia
  Constitution (Prussia) of 1850, 47, 50, 64
  Constitution (Imperial) of 1871, 12, 37, 48
  Prussian Civil Code (*Allgemeines Landrecht*), 50, 118, 143
  On the maintenance of public order, 50–51, 54
  On the organisation of civilian and military authorities, 49–51, 54
  On municipal policing, 143
  On social security, 63, 66–7
  On workers' organisation, 118–19
Lens, 96–7, 163, 184, 191
Lépine, Louis (Paris Police Prefect), 86, 95, 98–102, 104–105, 156, 167, 225, 276, 280
Lewal, General Jules, 212
Liebknecht, Karl, 5, 39
Lille, 17, 45, 115, 117, 144, 187
Loë, General Walther von, 74, 76, 207, 262
Loizillon, General Julien, 93, 235
Luxemburg, Rosa, 39

Macmahon, Patrice (French Marshal and President of the French Republic), 44
Messimy, Adolphe, 42
Mikusch-Buckberg, General Victor von, 77–8, 202, 268–9
Militarism/ Antimilitarism
  France, 14, 41–3
  Germany, 14, 38–40
Millet, General, Charles, 213

Nasse, Bertold von (Province Governor of the Rhine Province) 256–7
Nation-in-Arms, 36–7
National Guard, the French, 36, 156

Picquart, General Georges (French War Minister), 100, 211, 227
Plans for Protection, France, 86, 93–5, 98, 100–101, 105, 123, 149, 167, 192, 221–6, 276–7, 279
Plans for Protection, Germany, 277–8
   Civilian plans, 256, 259–61
   Instructions from War Minister Verdy du Vernois (1890), 63–5, 251
   General Staff Study of 'Fighting in Insurgent Towns' (1907), 65, 75, 267
   Instructions from General von Bissing (1907), 65, 73, 255, 258, 260, 267
   Instructions from General von Hindenburg (1908), 65, 75, 267
Poles in Westphalia, 60, 119, 127, 164
Police, France, 19–21, 140, 148–51
   Municipal police, 140–42, 144–5
   Paris police, 142, 144
Police, Prussia, 19–21, 61–2, 140, 148–51
   Municipal police, 143–5
   Private security corps, 147–8
   Royal Guards (*königliche Schutzmänner*), 143–6
   See also *Gendarmerie*
Puttkamer, Robert von (Prussian Interior Minister), 201–202

Quidde, Ludwig, 39

Ratibor und Corvey, Karl Egon zu (Province governor of Westphalia), 202, 253, 258–9
Recklinghausen, 115, 260, 262
Recke von der Horst, Eberh. von der 68–9, 202, 256
Regime

French Third Republic, 2–3, 5, 8–10, 19, 21, 33
German Empire, 2–3, 5, 10, 12–14, 19, 21, 33
Richter, Eugen, 39
Roubaix, 115, 117, 144, 156, 163, 184, 221

Social Democratic Party, the German, 12
   Anti-socialist legislation 1878–1890, 60, 119
   Attitudes towards violent protest, 117, 125, 134
   Attitudes towards the army, 38–40, 60
Strikes (Nord-Pas-de-Calais)
   Dockers' strikes, 121–2, 162, 228, 231
   Miners' strike of 1889, 160, 162, 165–6
   Miners' strike of 1891, 160, 162, 166, 239
   Miners' strike of October 1901, 94–5, 160, 162, 166, 225, 239
   Miners' strike of March 1902, 95–6, 121, 160, 166, 223, 232
   Strike wave of March–May 1906, 96–7, 121, 160, 162–4, 166, 223, 232, 241
   Miners' strikes of 1912–1913, 65, 121
   Postal strikes, 98, 122, 160, 242
   Rail workers' strike, 98, 121–2, 160, 222–3, 240–41
   Textile strikes, 122–3
Strikes (Westphalia)
   Miners' strike of 1889, 60–61, 63, 67–8, 74, 77–8, 120, 158–9, 164–6, 249, 258, 266, 268–9
   Miners' strike in Herne 1899, 77, 158–9, 164–6, 249, 264, 266, 268–9

Index 329

Miners' strike of Jan. 1905, 50, 70–71, 120, 159, 164–6
Miners' strike of March 1912, 65, 70, 75, 77–8, 120, 150, 158–9, 165–6, 249, 259, 265–6, 268–9
Textile strikes, 122–3
Stolberg-Wernigerode, Wilhelm zu, 204
Studt, Konrad (Province Governor in Westphalia), 181, 201, 204–205, 264

Thiers, Aldophe, 36
Tourcoing, 115, 156, 184
Trade Unions, 119–21
 La Confédération générale du travail (C.G.T.), 41, 91, 120–21, 124–5, 134, 190–91
 Social Democratic Free Unions, 119–21
Trépont, Jean-Baptiste (Prefect of 'Pas-de-Calais' and 'Nord'), 188, 225

Vel-Durand, Henri (Prefect of 'Pas-de-Calais' and 'Nord'), 93, 185, 188, 190

Verdy du Vernois, Julius von (Prussian War Minister) 63–5, 73, 251, 253
Vincent, Louis (Prefect of 'Nord'), 100–102, 188, 225–6, 233

Waldeck-Rousseau, René (French Interior Minister), 41, 86–7, 93–5, 100, 113, 117, 189, 223–5, 234
Waldersee, General Field Marshal Alfred von, 66, 74–6, 78, 203, 207, 252, 267
Wilhelm I, 48
Wilhelm II
 Attitude towards workers, 62–3, 66, 76, 78, 119, 253
 Influence on the use of troops, 48–9, 74–8, 268
 Interactions with bourgeois e elites, 184
 Personal Rule, 48, 62, 200, 202
 Personnel policy 201–203

Yvetot, Georges, 42

Zabern Affair, The (1913), 51, 53, 207, 267, 269